Crossing and Controlling Borders

Mechthild Baumann
Astrid Lorenz
Kerstin Rosenow (eds.)

Crossing and Controlling Borders

Immigration Policies and their Impact on Migrants' Journeys

Budrich UniPress Ltd.
Opladen & Farmington Hills, MI 2011

A CIP catalogue record for this book is available from
Die Deutsche Bibliothek (The German Library)

www.budrich-unipress.eu

ISBN 978-3-940755-76-6

Die Deutsche Bibliothek – CIP-Einheitsaufnahme
Ein Titeldatensatz für die Publikation ist bei Der Deutschen Bibliothek erhältlich.

Budrich UniPress Ltd.
Stauffenbergstr. 7. D-51379 Leverkusen Opladen, Germany

28347 Ridgebrook. Farmington Hills, MI 48334. USA
www.budrich-unipress.eu

Typeset editing: R+S Beate Glaubitz, Leverkusen, Germany

Jacket illustration by disegno, Wuppertal, Germany – www.disenjo.de
Printed in Europe on acid-free paper by

Table of Contents

List of Tables and Figures

Linking Immigration Policies and Migrants' Journeys: An Interdisciplinary Endeavor

Mechthild Baumann, Astrid Lorenz, Kerstin Rosenow

Migration and the Political Will for Control

Both the interests of nation states to manage migration and the behavior of migrants during their individual journeys have mutually reinforcing effects on the design and functioning of contemporary migration regimes. This assumption has motivated the interdisciplinary approach of this volume. The aim is to understand how immigration policies affect migrants' journeys and vice versa. We want to find out whether or not the assumptions that lead to the design of immigration policies reflect reality. Does border control prevent irregular immigration? And what is the role of the various actors, including the countries of origin, transit, and arrival, and the migrants themselves?

In order to answer these questions, we bring together insights from political science and ethnographic field work—two disciplines which have so far debated their insights mainly within separate research frameworks. The articles take into account the interests of the migrants' countries of origin, transit and arrival, as well as the motives and strategies of the migrants themselves. The resulting findings are relevant to both policy makers and scientific experts, but also to anyone interested in governing migration.

Our joint efforts started from the observation that migration has increasingly been perceived as a challenge to modern nation states since the end of the Cold War. The globalization of entrepreneurial activities, evolving common markets, and the fall of the Iron Curtain have led to greatly increased border-crossing movements. Worldwide, the media present images of places where peace, education, welfare, and happiness seem to be easier to access, and modern traffic infrastructure has further facilitated the migration process.

Politicians and citizens in the countries of arrival such as the U.S. and the member states of the European Union feared that migration flows would blur territorial borders, challenge stable political environments, disturb systems of values, and flood the welfare systems. Migration has provoked heated debates about 'good' and 'bad' immigrants, their rights to acquire full citizenship and their rights to vote, about the proliferation of low-wage employment and crimes committed by immigrants, about the politics of cultural and religious diversity, and about possibilities and limitations of inclusion. In short, increasing global migration has often been perceived as questioning the traditional social, political, economic, and cultural policies of nation states.

Ever since migration was identified as a risk, European and North American democracies have developed risk avoidance strategies and tightened their migration regimes—often with the support of the majority of their citizens. Both the U.S. and the EU have developed a self-centered and defensive approach with the objective of channeling migration. For this purpose, the governments have sharpened the distinction between legal and illegal immigration. Regular migration within common markets was facilitated, but severely limited at the external frontiers through various and "increasingly confusing restrictions on entry, stay, and participation" (Bade 2004: 351). People who do not meet these conditions but still attempt to cross the borders are regarded as criminals. Countries of arrival consider such 'irregular' migration a problem that must be minimized. To do this, both the U.S. and the EU have tried to optimize their instruments for managing immigration.

Generally speaking, the decision as to which migrants are welcome and which are authorized to cross the border is a purely political one—not just because it is made by politicians, but also because there is no 'objective', value-free basis for designing a best possible migration policy. It is often based on economic and national security considerations, as well as on human security considerations regarding refugee and asylum status, among other things (Graham/Poku 2000).

Labor immigration policies are intended to benefit the national labor markets through 'quality selection', classifying potential immigrants according to their qualifications into highly skilled, low-skilled and unskilled migrants. Depending on their qualification level, immigrants can be employed in different economic sectors. In order to attract highly skilled migrants, the U.S. adopted the United States Permanent Resident Card, known informally as the green card, after the end of the Second World War, which allows immigrants to work and live permanently in the U.S. The European Union copied the idea and in 2009 adopted a directive introducing the so-called Blue Card. However, it has not been as effective as the green card (Council of the EU 2009) and is being debated controversially (Angenendt/Parkes 2010). 'Mobility partnerships' are another recent attempt of the EU to channel labor migration. In return for the limited access to EU member states, the eligible countries must support the EU in preventing irregular migration (European Commission 2007).

The other dimension of considerations underlying the migration policies mentioned above are security concerns. Migrants who are not welcome but come to Europe or the U.S. anyway are portrayed by policy makers as a "threat"[1]. European and American political decision makers argue that the protection of the borders and the territorial integrity of the nation states is a natural necessity because ignorance of these principles undermines a state's sovereignty and causes present and future threats to the domestic society. In this context of an increasing securitization[2] of migration movements, migration control has become a popular mechanism to protect societies against the perceived external 'threat' of immigration (Ibrahim, 2005). This control finds expression in various forms, including internal control in U.S. and EU member state territory, external control such as control and surveillance by border guards at borders with third countries, control exercised by airline staff and other non-state actors, and control exercised by neighboring countries such as Morocco and Mexico.[3]

Research on border control techniques and on the underlying "speech act" of securitization (Wæver et al. 1993) has increased in the last decades, mainly in the discipline of political science (cf. Bigo 2001; Buzan et al. 1998; Huysmans 2000; Weiner 1995). Even so, political scientists often fail to recognize how these policies influence the migrants themselves, their decisions, and their journeys. The authors of this volume contribute to filling this research gap by focusing on the impact of immigration policies on migrants, taking into account the political dimension of the ongoing negotiation of migration policies.

While it is unquestioned that states have readjusted their migration and border management policies, it remains controversial whether or not these readjustments have been adequate to reach the political objectives. Recent estimates put the number of undocumented migrants staying within the EU-27 in 2008 at 1.9 to 3.8 million (HWWI 2009: 4), with millions of people believed to be waiting in countries neighboring the EU for a chance to enter the European Union irregularly (Bade 2004: 353 ff.). For the U.S., official statistics estimate that the number of irregular immigrants increased by 515,000 during the period 2000 to 2006 (Hoefer et al. 2007: 3). At the beginning of 2009, the Department of Homeland Security, which is in charge of immigration matters, estimated the total number of undocumented migrants to be between 10.8 and 12 million. This signifies a slight decrease over the previous

1 The following quote is an example of this official rhetoric: "Europol supports law enforcement activities by producing reports and assessments of the threat from organized illegal immigration" (Europol 2008: 6).

2 Huysmans defined the securitization of migration as the "political construction of migration [that] increasingly refers to the destabilizing effects of migration on domestic integration and to the dangers for public order it implied" (Huysmans 2000).

3 Concerning the industry of migration management, see the interdisciplinary research network on Migration Industry and Markets for managing migration (The MIM Network). [online] Available at: http://www.diis.dk/sw101546.asp [Accessed December 4, 2010].

years due to the economic downturn in the U.S. in 2007 and 2008 that caused Mexican-born U.S. residents to lose their jobs and reduced undocumented immigration numbers (*Associated Press*, February 9, 2010; see Bloch/Rocha Silva and Staudt/Garcia-Rios in this volume).

Are the Policies Suitable for Controlling Migration?

As we mentioned earlier, the central objective of this book is to scrutinize the migration control measures. Are these institutions and policies up to the challenges that present themselves? How are they implemented? How do migrants—the target group of these measures – act and react? And what are possible unintended effects of migration policies?

With regard to rationalist theories, we see one possible source of error in the fact that political and administrative decision makers tend to perceive migration as something abstract, as a movement of a large and homogenous group of people. Human rights and refugee organizations seem to be the only ones interested in calling public attention to the fact that immigrants are actually individuals, whereas nation states often do not anticipate the individual strategies of migrants. This abstraction from individuals to masses and from specific events to phenomena or threats makes it easier to justify border control (hardly anyone would dare speak of "combating" or "fighting" illegal immigrants). However, this generalization also largely ignores how and why migrants decide to migrate in the first place. It is therefore unclear whether the policy measures are suitable to sway people's individual decisions about entering the European Union or the U.S.

In order to create a more systematic basis to answer our question regarding the appropriateness of border management policies, we first operationalized "migration" at the level of individual migrants. We examined, with reference to ethnographic research or, where this was not available, to quantitative statistics, what happened when North American and European migration control policies were implemented or altered. In addition, to investigate intended and unintended consequences of migration control policies, we closely examined how individual migrants reacted and whether or not the different measures influenced their behavior.

However, the depersonalization of migration policies may not be the only factor that causes inefficiency. Rationalist theories, including theories on international relations, contend that the disregard of the political strategies of negotiation partners may be a second source of error. This implies that both the EU and the U.S. wrongly consider themselves to be the most powerful actor in the game, able to dictate decisions top-down and to solve problems technically without being forced to adapt their political programs to the demands and perceptions of others. While this may be true in general, actors who seem to be marginal at first glance may also derive significant power from various sources, such as from coalition capacity or blackmailing capacity. Strategic actors have to consider the interests and strategies of such "significant actors" to avoid undesired effects (Sartori 2005: 108 f.). Therefore, we were also interested in the interests and roles of the various nation states involved in the political negotiations on current and future migration policies.

The book focuses primarily on the impact of border control in two major areas of immigration, the European Union and the United States of America. The EU and the U.S. face similar challenges resulting from irregular migration, ranging from border control technologies to legalization processes to civil rights movements. The majority of articles in this book deal with the European Union, for two reasons. First, the EU has more neighbors than the U.S. and thus there are more potential countries of origin and transit. Second, assuming that the political, social, economic, and cultural contexts may affect the functioning of EU border control, it was necessary to cover countries with varying contexts to avoid misinterpretation.

Interdisciplinarity as a Distinguishing Feature of the Book

Research on migration and migration policies is usually strictly separated along different disciplines. However, we were interested in overcoming this separateness, so we decided to bring together scholars from various academic backgrounds, ranging from political science to sociology to anthropology. All of these disciplines have extensive expertise in the study of individual behavior, social interactions, and the effects of institutions.

Ethnographers generally focus more on human behavior—in our case the questions of how individuals select their routes and modes of migration and how this is connected with other people and the overall social and political context. Migration control is a way used by a state to effect a certain behavior in a specific group of human beings. In other words, the controlling states seek to physically prevent and deter migrants from crossing their borders. This is coupled with the expectation that irregular migrants give up their plan to emigrate when they perceive the borders to be insurmountable. However, ethnographic studies have shown that in many cases migrants do not act as expected. Our preliminary studies on Morocco, Spain, and the U.S. indicated that migrants often continue their border-crossing attempts despite extensive control measures. Another phenomenon is that migrants accept control measures as given and organize their lives around them in interim settlements along borders and through new forms of self-organization in camps within the transit zones, which affects the lives of many people, including non-migrants. The articles presented in this book investigate whether there is empirical evidence for this in various transit countries.

Generally speaking, the world of 2011 is characterized by a fragmented world order and a diffuse perception of threats to security. This leads to changes in the ways in which societies conceive of themselves, particularly with regard to the definition of 'the other'[4]. The role of migrants within national identity constructions[5] and their possible marginalization are another potential effect of border management. The preliminary studies observed the emergence of a hostile, xenophobic environment for migrants in the country of arrival, which includes aspects of criminalization of immigrants and the linking of the topic to security discourses, which is critically discussed as the "securitization" of migration (e.g., Huysmans 2000; Ibrahim 2005). At the same time, certain portions of the host society, particularly individuals living in the border area, seem to show solidarity with undocumented immigrants. The analyses in this book are intended to clarify these observations by taking into consideration the general perception of migration, which differs considerably across national contexts.

While political scientists are also interested in the topic of 'irregular' migration, their main interest lies in the overarching research questions of strategic action, the legitimacy and the efficiency of public institutions and public policies, and policy change. They want to understand how institutions, regulations, and policies (such as border regimes) are developed and negotiated, whether they show the intended effects, how this functioning is affected by different context variables, and how institutions change over time. Analyses by political scientists usually pay much more attention to the level of nation states, to their interests, and to the power relationship between countries of origin, transit, and arrival than ethnographic studies do. Such aspects should not be ignored when examining the effects of border regimes. One of the challenging observations regarding the changing migration regime is that the U.S. and the EU member states delegate the task of migration control to states of origin and transit. Our preliminary studies indicated that the behavior of undocumented migrants is not just affected by the policies of (reluctantly) 'receiving' countries or state unions such as the U.S. and the EU, respectively, but also by the policies of countries of origin and transit. We assumed that their measures can "reinforce" or "soften" the original objective of immigration control of the EU and the U.S., depending on their own interests.

Given the explorative character of the research on the topic, the lack of theory and the small number of countries whose border regime effects are to

---

4 Cf. Barker (1981), who coined the term "new racism", as well as Huntington's (2002) much-discussed assumption of a "clash of civilizations".

5 See, for example, the discussions on "societal security", according to which a "survival of society is a question of identity" (Wæver et al. 1993: 24).

be determined, we decided to collect qualitative, in-depth country studies to determine the complex causal relationships between actors. We invited ethnographers and political scientists who are experts in the field of migration research to contribute to a common book project. The interdisciplinary nature of this volume is its most distinguishing feature in methodological terms.

This book is based on two workshops. The first workshop, with six of the authors, was held at the 13th International Metropolis Conference in Bonn in October 2008. Preliminary versions of the papers were discussed and a joint study group was initiated. The second workshop, with additional authors, took place at the European Academy in Berlin in 2010. Based on the discussions at these workshops, the articles were finalized following a similar structure, which is outlined below.

Structure of the Book and the Articles

Based on the assumption that both the interests of nation states and the behavior of migrants have mutually reinforcing effects on the design and functioning of contemporary migration regimes, and using the theoretical considerations outlined above, we derived the following research questions for the authors of the articles[6]: From an ethnographic point of view it is important to learn more about two questions: How do migrants react to the policies during their journey? How do these policies influence their settlement in the countries of transit or arrival? Along with this, the authors were also invited to include answers to the following questions which are especially relevant for political scientists: In what way do the different national interests of countries of origin, transit, and arrival influence the implementation of migration control policies initiated by the EU and the U.S.? How do the policies of the countries of origin and transit affect the initial objectives of the EU and the U.S.?

The country studies are based either on the evidence of the empirical field work conducted by the authors or on empirical secondary data. To ensure consistency, all papers start by describing the general situation of their national case study regarding migration patterns and the institutional setting. Following this, they discuss the linkages between the policies of the countries of arrival, transit, and origin, and the behavior of migrants. The focus is on the migration process itself—that is, the journey—rather than on the migrants' behavior after arriving in the receiving state.

---

6 For summaries of the findings and their interpretation, see our Conclusion in the end of the volume.

Overall, the book is structured in the following way: The first part is concerned with the impact of national and European migration policies on migrants' journeys. It starts with an article by Sandra Gil Araújo (Granada), which provides an introduction to the EU border regime with a strong focus on political interests and institutional outcomes. She identifies delocalization and externalization to third countries as the main characteristics of EU migration control. The harmonization of immigration, asylum, and refugee policies originally intended by the Treaty of Amsterdam (1997/1999) did not result in a consistent European approach to migration. The most popular countries of arrival, such as Italy and Spain, usually use bilateral agreements and individual implementation policies. Axel Kreienbrink (Nuremberg) analyzes the interest-based use and the effects of regularization as an instrument of migration management in Spain, the EU member country with the highest number of 'irregular' workers.

This introduction is followed by articles which focus on specific countries of origin and transit of undocumented migration to the EU. We chose countries with a high proportion of irregular emigration. Gerda Heck (Cologne) explores migration management and migrants' strategies in Morocco where she conducted intense field work. Florence Tsagué Assopgoum (Siegen) gives an overview of migration policies and their implementation on the route from Senegal to Europe. Marianne Haase (Nuremberg) investigates the Europeanization of Ukraine's migration policy and its impact on migrants. Finally, Basak Bilecen-Süoglu (Bielefeld) analyzes the case of Turkey as a bridge for people smuggling at the border between the Middle East and the EU.

The second part of the book deals with experiences migrants have had with the U.S. migration regime. As mentioned before, border management is less diverse in the U.S. than in the EU and it is concentrated along the border to Mexico. However, the U.S. migration regime has also changed over the course of time (see Tichenor, 2009, among others), which provides the opportunity to examine the short- and long-term effects of policy changes. Avital Bloch and Ma. Alejandra Rocha Silva (Colima, Mexico) have taken this approach, focusing on the society's response to policy changes. Their study includes an investigation of how undocumented Mexicans enter the U.S. and how they live in the country, as well as the emergence of migrant communities in California, their contacts, and their possible return to Mexico. Wayne Cornelius (San Diego) provides an evaluation of recent U.S. immigration control policies based on 4,000 interviews with Mexican migrants conducted in Mexico and in the United States between 2005 and 2008. Kathleen Staudt and Sergio Garcia-Rios (El Paso, Seattle) complement the portrait by describing the effects of migratory management with a special focus on the intervening effect of economy, public policies, and institutions in the countries of origin and arrival.

The last part of the volume traces recent efforts in empirically-based theory building regarding the effects of border management and summarizes the findings of the articles. Sabine Hess (Göttingen) was invited to contribute her reflections on the social construction of risks and fears through processes of the labeling of migration phenomena and migrant categories such as the emerging "transit migrant". Assuming that categorizations may transport, disseminate, and perpetuate distinct perceptions of reality, we wanted to know whether and, if so, how such processes affect migration policies. Heidrun Friese (Bochum) was invited to present the concept of "hospitality", which she applies to the events on the Italian island of Lampedusa, where Italian inhabitants and migrants spontaneously united against the politics of the Italian government. The last article of the volume draws conclusions regarding the effectiveness of the current border management policies based on the empirical analyses presented in this volume. The editors investigate how policies designed to control 'irregular' migration affect the behavior of (would-be) migrants and whether these policies produce unintended effects rather than achieving the objectives of the policy designers.

On thc whole, we observed that interdisciplinary work is always a challenging process. We have learned that ethnographers and political scientists see the issue under investigation through completely different analytical lenses, interpret their own role as scientists in different ways, and each use their own specific concepts and terminology. The results of our joint work, however, convinced us that this interdisciplinary approach is very effective. We would like to thank the authors for contributing to this volume and for their patience in discussing their articles. Special thanks goes to the Foundation for German-American Academic Relations for generously sponsoring this project.

References

Angenendt, S./Parkes, R. (2010): The Blue Card Impasse, SWP Comments 2010/C 14; June 2010.

Associated Press (2010): DHA: The Number of Illegal Immigrants in U.S. Fell. In: New York Times, February 9.

Bade, K. J. (2004): Legal and Illegal Immigration into Europe: Experiences and Challenges in: European Review, 12, 3, pp. 339-375.

Barker, M. (1981): The New Racism. Conservatives and the Ideology of the Tribe. London: Junction Books.

Bigo, D. (2001): Migration and Security. In: Guiraudon, Virginie; Joppke, Christian (Ed.): Controlling a New Migration World. London: Routledge, pp. 121-149.

Buzan, B./Wæver, O./Wilde, J. de (1998): Security. A New Framework for Analysis. Boulder, Colo.: Lynne Rienner.

Council of the European Union (2009): Directive on the conditions of entry and residence of third-country nationals for the purposes of highly qualified employment, No. 2009/50/EC, 25 May 2009.
European Commission (2007): Communication on circular migration and mobility partnerships between the European Union and third countries, No. KOM(2007) 248 final, May 16, 2007.
Europol (2008): Facilitated Illegal Immigration into the European Union, March 2008.
[online] Available at: http://www.europol.europa.eu/publications/Serious_Crime _Overviews/Facilitated _illegal_immigration_2008.pdf [Accessed February 14, 2011].
Graham, D. T./Poku, N. K., Eds. (2000): Migration, Globalisation and Human Security. London: Routledge.
Hoefer, M./Nancy R./Ch. Campbell (2007): Estimates of the Unauthorized Immigrant Population Residing in the United States: January 2006. Washington, DC: U.S. Department of Homeland Security, Office of Immigration Statistics.
Huntington, S. P. (2002): The clash of civilizations and the remaking of world order. London: free press.
Huysmans, J. (2000): The European Union and the Securitization of Migration. In: Journal of Common Market Studies 38, 5, pp. 751-777.
HWWI [Hamburger Weltwirtschaftsinstitut] (2009): Comparative Policy Brief -Size of Irregular Migration, October 2009 [online] Available at: http://irregular-migration.hwwi.de/typo3_upload/groups/31/4.Background_Information/4.2.Policy_ Briefs_EN/ComparativePolicyBrief_SizeOfIrregularMigration_Clandestino_Nov 09_2.pdf [Accessed February 14, 2011].
Ibrahim, M. (2005): The Securitization of Migration: A Racial Discourse. In: International Migration 43, 5, pp. 163-186.
Sartori, G. (2005, 1976): Parties and Party Systems: A Framework for Analysis. Colchester: ECPR Press.
Tichenor, D. J. (2009): Navigating an American Minefield: The Politics of Illegal Immigration, in: The Forum 7, 3, Article 1.
Wæver, O./Buzan, B./Kelstrup, Morten et al. (eds.) (1993): Identity, Migration and the New Security Agenda in Europe. London: Pinter.
Weiner, M. (1995): The Global Migration Crisis. Challenge to States and to Human Rights. New York: HarperCollins College Publ.

Part One: Linkages between national and European migration policies and their impact on migrants' journeys

Reinventing Europe's Borders: Delocalization and Externalization of EU Migration Control through the Involvement of Third Countries

Sandra Gil Araújo[1]

Introduction

EU cooperation on migration policy has undergone three substantial transformations which offer some clues for understanding its current direction: First, changes in the form of labor organization began in the 1970s, and the consequent weakening in the labor statutes affected all workers, including immigrant workers. Second, the end of the Cold War coincided with the emergence of drug trafficking, terrorism, immigration, and organized crime as new sources of conflict. Third, the measures taken after the September 11 attacks, have strengthened the link between migration and terrorism.[2] In the meantime, there has been very little progress in the harmonization of policies directed at the immigrant population that has been settling in the territory of the European Community for more than four decades.

Malcolm Anderson (2000: 15) defines "frontier regimes" as bilateral or multilateral border agreements with neighboring states, the practices around them, the administration and management of controls, policing systems, cross-border cooperation agreements, and the institutions involved in their implementation. Implicit in these regimes are distinct conceptions of the functions that borders should have, along with the significance and meaning that are attached to them. One of the clearest indicators of the gradual formation of an EU frontier regime is the increasing externalization of migration control. The extension of visas, the development of an immigration liaison officers network, the imposition of the Schengen regulations upon those who, until recently, were candidates for accession to the EU, the readmission agreements with migrants' countries of origin or transit, and the pressure on transportation companies to implement inspections in ports of embarkation are just some of the forms that the "government at a distance" (Miller and Rose, 1990) has taken in recent years. At the same time, an increasing number of new actors—employees, local social services, mayors, multinational

1 The author is very grateful to the editors for their invaluable comments and suggestions regarding previous versions of this article.

2 For a more detailed analysis, see Bigo 2005; d'Appollonia 2008; Gil Araujo 2002, 2010a.

policy groups, companies, NGOs, and third countries—continue to support the body of the state like artificial tentacles (Guiraudon 2001).

"It is probably fair to say that remote control has become an intrinsic feature of the way in which states and other international agencies imagine and pursue border control. It is written in to the conceptual architecture of the Europe's Schengen Agreement and, in different ways, the American idea of homeland security" (Walters 2006: 194). This article focuses on this very process: that of integrating the migrants' countries of origin and transit into EU migration control. In the first section, several analytical tools from the field of governmentality studies will be defined. The second section summarizes a series of documents, instruments, and practices which have been progressively promote the delocalization of migration control. This is followed by a review of recent migration-related initiatives in EU territory, which forcibly shift powers and responsibilities related to the management of immigration and asylum from the EU to third countries. The final section of the article explores the implications of this regime of migration control, being considered as an example of the political rationalities and technologies of government that are characteristic of advanced liberalism.[3]

Governmentality, Political Rationalities, and Technologies of Government: A Brief Conceptual Outline

Governmentality studies attempt to understand how thinking influences the ways things are done, as well as the systems of practice, their ambitions, and their effects. "Government" and "governmentality" are terms which appear relatively late in Foucault's work, dating back to the end of the 1970s (Foucault 2009). One meaning of the term *governmentality*—a portmanteau which combines the meanings of "government" and "mentality"—refers to how government is thought of, and makes reference to the different mentalities and modalities of government. When we talk of how one thinks of the government, we begin from the supposition that thinking is a social activity, that the way in which we think is related to a body of knowledge, beliefs, and opinions in which thinking is immersed. The idea of government mentalities emphasizes the fact that the thinking involved in governing practices is collective and relatively naturalized. But saying that these mentalities are collective does not mean maintaining that they are linked to specific groups or

[3] For a description of advanced liberalism as a way of government from the perspective of governmentality studies, see Rose (1999) and Dean (1999), among others. On the convenience of using this approach to exploring the European integration process, see Walters and Haahr (2005b).

classes. Rather, it is supposed that the way in which one thinks about the exercise of authority is constituted of ideas, philosophies, and forms of knowledge that constitute social and cultural products.

The semantic link between governing and mentalities or models of thinking indicates that the study of the technologies of power is not possible without an analysis of the political rationalities that support them (Lemke 2001). The Foucauldian concept of government revolves around three distinct yet interconnected notions: "*conduire des conduites*" ("the conduct of conduct"), political rationalities, and technologies of government.[4] Governing sets forth a real possibility of influencing others and itself, producing effects of reality. Keeping in mind this primary dimension of government as "the conduct of conduct", the analysis of governmentality should focus on two instances: political rationalities and technologies of government. The concept of rationality refers to any type of thought that attempts to be relatively clear, systematic, and explicit about the aspects of existence, about how things are or should be (Dean 1999). This concept of rationality does not have a great normative value associated with reason, but a meaning relative to certain historical practices: it has to do with a form of concordance of rules, modes of thinking, tactical procedures, and a set of other conditions under which, at a certain moment, it becomes possible to perceive and describe something as a *problem* and to develop practical alternatives to resolve this problem. The current dominant political rationality is *advanced liberalism*.[5]

In this conceptual framework liberalism, welfarism, and neoliberalism or advanced liberalism, are understood not as policy doctrines but as problematicizations, as government programs which have arisen in specific historical and geographical contexts. The relation between political rationalities and government programs is articulated and develops through technologies of government. A technology of government is an ensemble or mechanism of forms of practical knowledge, with modes of perception and inculcation of habits; techniques of annotation, ordering, and calculation; forms of presen-

---

4 Foucault uses the concept of government in a broad sense, strongly connected to its former meaning and highlighting the proximity between power relations and subjectivization processes (Lemke 2001). In the Foucauldian sense, government refers to the conduct of other's as well as one's own conduct. Through this lens, governing assumes every intention of molding, with some degree of deliberation, aspects of human behavior in accordance with a series of norms and a variety of goals. In contrast to domination, which ignores the capacity for action of those upon whom it is exercised, government recognizes this ability and acts through it; unlike discipline, it does not target the body's actions, but rather one's own actions and the actions of others. To govern is not to restrict the ability to act, but to recognize it and utilize it for one's own ends.

5 The term "advanced liberalism", introduced into the literature on governmentality by Nikolas Rose (1993), designates a broad domain of diverse ensembles of rationalities, technologies, and agencies that constitute the characteristic forms of governing in contemporary liberal democracies.

tation such as tables; processes of examination and evaluation; the inauguration of specialties and vocabularies; legal, professional, and administrative norms, architectonic forms; human abilities and non-human means through which authorities of different kinds seek to form, normalize, and instrumentalize the behavior of others, with the goal of achieving objectives that they consider desirable (Miller and Rose 1991; Rose and Miller 1992; Rose 1999). There is no governmentality perceived in an abstract and general manner, only governmentalities, different modes of joining both analytical instances, with the government's own "*conduire des conduites*" dimension always present. The key is to focus on concrete historical functioning, to the variable combinations of political rationalities and technologies of government in specific spatial and temporal contexts. To explore immigration policies from this perspective begs the following questions: How have they been elaborated, and in relation to which problems, defined in what way, and under what kind of justification? What are the objectives they hope to achieve and through which techniques? Starting with an analysis of the process of constructing an EU migration policy, I propose to illuminate the (old and new) forms of conceiving of the EU's migration control, to identify some of the actors which have been involved in this control, and the technologies that those policies intend to activate in order to avoid the *problems* that present themselves as by-products of immigration.

Constructing the EU Migration Policy: The Path toward the Externalization of Migration Control

After the Second World War, the process of European economic reconstruction and the dynamics of the Fordist production system increased the need for foreign workers. During the 1950s and 1960s, Central and Northern European countries actively encouraged immigration. However, in the beginning of the 1970s, the oil crisis, the development of technology, industrial delocalization, and changes in the form of organization of salaried work eliminated many jobs. Working conditions deteriorated and long-term unemployment became a structural element of European societies (Castel 1997). The transformations in the form of organized salaried work caused profound changes in the modes in which immigration was perceived, defined, and managed. In the beginning of the 1970s, the policy of recruiting immigrants was discontinued and borders were closed. Migration came to be perceived as a security issue (Doty 2003; Freedman 2004; Huysmans 2000). Increasingly, in most of the European immigrant receiving countries, policy makers—irrespective of their political affiliations—began to theorize citizenship in terms of cultural and moral demands upon new members as proof of their identification with the nation (Favell 2006).[6] This rhetoric was followed by practices and these discourses were translated into specific policies which accompanied the closing of the borders: the system of quotas, the programs of return, and the *integration* policies regarding the population classified as immigrants or minorities. But the migrants did not return to their countries of origin. On the contrary, they have settled in the countries of immigration and reunited their family members.[7] Since then, in European receiving countries, *non-EU immigrants* have been perceived as a threat to national unity and political identity because their presence necessitates a rethinking of the bases of citizenship and the relationship between state and nation (Sayad 2002; Schnapper 1994).

Cooperation on immigration in the communitarian space began with the creation of TREVI (terrorism, radicalism, extremism, international violence)[8]. In this framework, in 1986 the Ministers of Justice and the Interior authorized the Ad Hoc Group on Immigration. Among the "products" of this group is the Dublin Convention on the management of asylum, which was ratified by all member states in 1997.[9] The agreement and subsequent Schengen Convention[10] and the treaties of Maastricht and Amsterdam, have

---

6 This process is evidenced in most EU countries: the (dominant) way to problematize the immigrant presence under the umbrella concept of integration. The notion of integration is interwoven with the paradigm of nation building utilized in the 19th and 20th centuries to create unified national territories out of a patchwork of religions and groups of diverse nature, as was characteristic in Europe (Favell 2006). The theoretical concept of social integration, which has as its premise the notion of a territorially delimited, historically rooted, and culturally homogenous society, underlies integration policy. On France and the UK, see Favell (2000); on the Netherlands, Vermeulen and Penninx (2000); on Germany, Ha (2010); on Spain, Gil Araujo (2010a). Some of the current positions on the integration of immigrants recall the technologies of moral training once applied to the working classes and their families as a key instrument of government. As a sign of radicalization of these ways of thinking non-EU immigrants: the civic integration courses, contracts, and exams in the UK, Germany, the Netherlands, Austria, France, and Denmark.

7 Since the 1980s, family migration has become the first source of regular migration to the EU member states in Central and Northern Europe. In the name of better integration, during the last ten years some of these countries (the Netherlands, the UK, France, Denmark, Germany, and Austria) have been tightening control over family migration (see Kraler 2010).

8 TREVI was created by an initiative of the Netherlands on November 1, 1975 in a meeting of the heads of state of the then European Economic Community (EEC) in Rome.

9 In this framework, the EURODAC Convention is preparing a system for comparing fingerprints of asylum seekers or clandestine immigrants to facilitate the implementation of the Dublin Convention. On the Schengen Information System, the Eurodac database, and the Visa Information System and their significance for the internal control of irregular migrants, see Broeders 2007.

10 On June 14, 1985, France, Germany, Belgium, the Netherlands, and Luxembourg signed the Schengen Agreement to abolish border controls, which was

defined the foundations and contents of the process of harmonization of EU migratory policies. But there also are a number of reports, resolutions, recommendations, conclusions, directives, and agreements which, if they may not be binding in many cases, have nonetheless consolidated a certain type of practice designed to control the population of non-EU countries to be displaced to other spaces and externalized to other actors.[11]

Two of these means are contained in the London Resolutions of November 30, 1992. The first corresponds to the so-called *safe third countries* and permits any asylum seeker to be returned to the first country considered safe which was crossed en route to the EU. This type of practice has been fairly frequently used in Germany and Austria, which used to return asylum seekers to the countries of Eastern Europe through which they had immigrated. The second resolution refers to the designated *safe country of origin* and implies that applications for asylum from people originating from countries classified as safe will not be considered for being *manifestly groundless*. This concept gives a collective dimension to a right that used to be individual. Each country develops its own list of safe countries and until now no common list has been agreed on. By using these two mechanisms, the member states have reduced the number of applications for asylum that can be formally accepted.

In mid-1998, the Austrian Presidency of the European Council developed the Document on Migration and Asylum Policy Strategy (Documento de estrategia sobre la política migratoria y de asilo), which expresses the ways of thinking about population movements (political rationalities) and proposes (new and old) instruments (technologies of government) in order to stimulate its control. In certain ways it anticipated many of the means that were implemented in the last few years. (Presidencia de la Unión Europea 1998). The Document on Strategy for Migration and Asylum Policy recommended the development of a new concept of control, to be practiced in the distinct times and geographies that compose south-north/east-west displacements, from the country of origin to countries of destination. A set of measures was specified, intended to involve the different migrants' countries of origin and transit in population control. The document stressed the urgent need to develop a *comprehensive approach* to dealing with international migrations, linking economic aid with visa issues, the reduction of border controls with guarantees of readmission, the availability of economic cooperation with means effective for reducing factors of attraction (Presidencia de la Unión Europea 1998). The text describes trafficking, crime, and immigration

---

supplemented by the Convention implementing the Schengen Agreement (Schengen II) in June 1990. For a genealogy of the Schengen area from a governmentality perspective, see Walters 2006 and Walter and Haahr 2005b.

11 For a clarifying analysis of this processes from a governmentality perspective, see van Munster 2009.

network, highlighting the importance of involving countries of origin or transit in the fight against *illegal immigration*, thus showing its value for the political and economic power that the EU possesses in international relations and in relation to those countries:

> "The agreements of expulsion with states of origin acquire particular relevance. In this respect, the phenomenon of states of origin which, increasingly, refuse to readmit their own nationals, ought to be counteracted. In the face of this situation, only two solutions are possible: either the EU as an ensemble obtains, in virtue of its international political and economic weight, that those states sign said conventions, or an international juridical instrument is fashioned that will make it possible for another institution also to determine the nationality of a person in accordance with objective criteria, and that this determination follows the juridical effect of obliging the state considered 'of origin' to effect a readmission." (Presidencia de la Unión Europea 1998: 112)

An effective concept of controlling entry should cover all the steps taken by immigrants, from the beginning of their travels to their arrival at their destination. For this reason, according to the document, the EU needs a form of control that can be exercised in specific geographical and temporal contexts: in the country of departure, through visas and liaison officers; during the trip, through the transportation companies; in countries of transit, by implementing the Schengen Convention; and upon arrival, by means of border control at airports; and in the country of destination, through asylum and immigration regulations and checks by the police. The most suitable model, however, is the model of center and periphery:

> "A model of concentric circles of migration policy can be established as a base for a differentiated exterior strategy. For obvious reasons, the most rigorous means of control are currently those of the Schengen states. Their neighboring states (especially associates and perhaps Mediterranean countries) should be gradually included in an analogue system, which will be continually approximated according to the norms of those, above all with regard to visa policy, border control, and readmission. (...) The states of the third circle (such as the space of the CEI, some Baltic states, Turkey, and North Africa) will concentrate their efforts above all on the transit control and the struggle against networks of illegal immigration and a fourth group (Middle East, China, and Black Africa) in the elimination of those factors that make emigration attractive." (Presidencia de la Unión Europea 1998: 112)

The document recommends that for the second circle states conforming with the Schengen conventions should be a criterion for admittance to the EU. In effect, along with drug policy and the fight against organized crime, migration policy and legislation were some of the variables which are used to evaluate eligibility of accession candidates. In the last five years, the EU-15 exported its practices and technologies of border control to the east, which generated tensions in the zone, since these measures such as the imposition of visas break the economic, social, and political ties between the states that were candidates and those that were not. The new members of the EU, mere followers of the policies they had no ability to influence, found themselves faced with the dilemma of maintaining cordial relations with their neighbors to the east while at the same time implementing the Schengen border rules

(Grabbe 2000). Although they were officially EC countries, they continued to tolerate limitations on free movement several years after the enlargement. The restrictions were based on a transition agreement according to which the old members could limit access to their labor markets and systems of social welfare for citizens of Estonia, Lithuania, Hungary, Poland, the Czech Republic, Slovenia, and Slovakia. In the case of third countries, the Austrian Presidency proposed to exert pressure through commercial relations and economic cooperation, with fourth circle countries facing the loss of development aid. All of these recommendations were taken up again in subsequent initiatives. Since then the *immigration problem* has been a topic of debate in various European Council meetings.

In October 1999, the Tampere European Council stressed the need for a global vision that would approach the causes of migratory movements from the beginning, recommending the inclusion of readmission clauses in the agreements with immigrants' countries of origin or transit.[12] The first initiative in this direction was taken two years later. In February 2000, following a suggestion by the Netherlands, a readmission clause was introduced into the Cotonú Cooperation Agreement (a revision of the Lomé Convention put into force in 1975) with the African, Caribbean, and Pacific Group of States (ACP); a clause that this group of countries, the most impoverished on the planet, had to accept in order to receive €13.5 million in development aid for their cooperation in the period 2000-2005.[13] At the end of 2001, the Conclusions of the Laeken European Council again emphasized the need to include a policy regarding immigration flows in the EU external policy, stressing the importance of concluding readmission agreements with interested countries. Several months later, during an informal meeting of the ministers of justice and home affairs in Santiago de Compostela on February 14, 2002, the Global Plan to Combat Illegal Immigration was presented, proposed by the Spanish Presidency. One of the main points of the Plan was "Support for Countries of Origin and Transit," which proposed the development of measures to be taken prior to border-crossing and to be implemented in cooperation with

---

12 The clauses and agreements of readmission aim to oblige the signing countries to accept the deportation of their citizens and of any person who may have entered the EU in an irregular manner by crossing their territory.

13 The Cotonú Convention, signed in 2000, was revised in 2005 and 2010. All sub-Saharan African countries are ACP countries. More information on this is available online at:
http://ec.europa.eu/development/geographical/regionscountriesa_en.cfm
[Accessed February 14, 2011]. In recent years, the EU has implemented other association and agreements with the African countries, including the Euro-African Partnership for Migration and Development (2006) and the Africa-EU Strategic Partnership (2007). In April 2009, the Spanish government approved the Plan Africa 2009-2012. For more information, see http://www.casafrica.es/casafrica/Inicio/PlanAfrica2009-2012.pdf [Accessed February 14, 2011].

countries of origin, including the coordination of European civil servants as liaison officers in the concerned countries, technical and financial cooperation in combating human trafficking and honoring readmission obligations. In the Seville Council of June 2002, the heads of state of Spain and the UK attempted to reduce development aid for countries of origin which refuse to implement immigration control strategies. France, Sweden, and Finland eventually opposed this initiative, but the Presidency Conclusions include other possible sanctions:

"The European Council considers it necessary to carry out a systematic assessment of relations with third countries which do not cooperate in combating illegal immigration. That assessment will be taken into account in relations between the European Union and its Member States and the countries concerned, in all relevant areas. Insufficient cooperation by a country could hamper the establishment of closer relations between that country and the Union (...) the Council may unanimously find that a third country has shown an unjustified lack of cooperation in the joint management of migration flows. In that event the Council may, in accordance with the rules laid down in the treaties, adopt measures or positions under the Common Foreign and Security Policy and other European Union policies, while honouring the Union's contractual commitments but not jeopardising development cooperation." (Seville European Council 2002: 11)

In summary, despite having been rejected at the time, the policy of using aid and commerce to guarantee readmission agreements is beginning to spread. Since the end of 2002, the Commission has signed readmission agreements with Hong Kong, Macao, Sri Lanka, Albania, Russia, Ukraine, Bosnia and Herzegovina, Montenegro, Serbia, and Moldova. Agreements with Pakistan, Georgia, Morocco, Turkey, Cape Verde, China, and Algeria are currently under negotiation or pending ratification (Statewatch 2010).[14] During the negotiations some countries established a connection between the signing of the agreements and systems for facilitating visas. By means of an agreement signed in February 2004 and in effect since September of the same year, China for the first time accepted the inclusion of a readmission

---

14 Recently, Today's Zaman, a Turkish newspaper, reported that Turkey and the EU have reached an agreement on 19 articles of a draft readmission agreement. They have been unable to agree on five articles. "The disagreement on the negotiations focuses on sharing the financial burden which stems from screening, hosting and eventually repatriating illegal immigrants, as well as on Ankara's insistence on placing a so-called Turkey clause in EU agreements with third countries such as Iran, Iraq, and Pakistan. Without having EU agreements on countries of origin, Turkey fears it will be left alone in dealing with the massive cost of hosting and repatriating immigrants and is asking for inclusion in third party negotiations." ("Hurdles Remain on Readmission Agreement Between Turkey and EU", Today Zaman, June 1, 2010.)

clause in what is, basically, an agreement to facilitate visas for groups of Chinese tourists visiting the EU.[15]

In like manner, the liaison officers stationed in non-member states have achieved a legal base through Council Regulation 377/2004 of February 19, 2004, which defines *immigration liaison officer* (ILO) as a representative of one of the member states, stationed abroad in the service of immigration or other appropriate authorities, with the objective of establishing and maintaining contacts with authorities from destination countries, with an eye on contributing to the prevention of and struggle against illegal immigration, the return of illegal immigrants, and the management of legal migration. The Directive serves as a basis for harmonizing the tasks of the different ILOs as constituents of a network attentive to the collection and exchange of information. The ILOs can offer support in establishing the identities of nationals from third countries and facilitate in their deportation to their countries of origin.

This section focused on the analysis of a series of documents, instruments, and practices which have been promoting the process of delocalized migration control. In opposition to the *comprehensive approach* recommended by the European Commission, the focus was limited to immigration control. The involvement of safe third countries and recent accession candidates in this control has established a pan-European migration regime in which migration control is also the responsibility of countries which were or are not EU members (Lavenex 2007).

In the next section I will review a number of recent migration-related initiatives which try to reinforce the transfer of responsibilities in the management of immigration and asylum from the EU to third countries. The analysis will focus on the European Neighborhood Policy (ENP) and the off-shore camps or reception centers. As other scholars such as Lavenex (2007) and van Munster (2009) have argued, these practices are the most recent and clear examples of the externalization process through the involvement of third countries in EU migration control.

Advances in Delocalized and Transnational Migration Control

It has been noted that, although the Hague Programme—a tool of political planning on immigration and asylum from 2005 through 2010—talks about strengthening freedom, security and justice, "a closer reading or the document reveals that freedom and justice are overdetermined by the meaning of

15 The so-called Authorized Destination Status Agreement.

security" (van Munster 2009: 142). Four years later, in the evaluation document of the Hague Programme and its Action Plans, the Commission indicates that migration is now much more integrated in the EU's foreign and development policies. This, in the opinion of the Commission, reflects the shift from a perspective on migration centered on security to a global and integrated perspective (Commission of European Communities 2009a: 8).

Some of the activities envisaged by the Hague Programme had the objective of deepening the process of including countries of origin and transit in the immigration control sponsored by the EU. One of the tools implemented with this aim is the European Neighbourhood Policy.[16] *Off-Shore* camps are clear examples of these "new" ways of governing migrations. Both are discussed below.

The European Neighbourhood Policy as a New Technology of Government

One of the latest initiatives regarding EC foreign relations is the design and implementation of a new, recently extended package of measures for countries to the south and east of the EU: the European Neighbourhood Policy (ENP).[17] In the words of the Commission, the ENP was developed in response to the changes resulting from the enlargement of the EU, whose objective is to share the benefits of enlargement with neighboring countries and to reinforce stability, security, and well-being for all involved. It is designed to prevent the emergence of a new dividing line between the enlarged EU and its neighbors and to offer opportunities to participate in various activities through political, economic, cultural, and security cooperation.

"The ENP should reinforce the EU's contribution to promoting the settlement of regional conflicts. The ENP can also help the Union's objectives in the area of Justice and Home Affairs, in particular in the fight against organised crime and corruption, money laundering and all forms of trafficking, as well as with regard to issues related to migration. It is im-

16 Lavenex notes that the ENP is the result of the difficulties associated with the readmission agreements. "The second and partly related source of reorientation lies in the broader reconfiguration of the EU's approach towards its close neighbours and more generally its external relations" (Lavenex 2007: 144).

17 In March 2003, the Commission presented a communication that defined illegal immigration as one of the threats to common security, such that the EU should aid neighboring countries in stepping up their efforts to combat it. Readmission agreements are an essential element, beginning with Morocco, Russian, Algeria, Ukraine, Belarus, and Moldova (Commission of the European Communities 2003: 11). In July of the same year, the Commission presented another communication developing a new instrument of financial cooperation. The document indicates that it will be of crucial importance to facilitate commerce and transit, while EU borders are being secured against contraband, trafficking, organized crime (including terrorist threats), and illegal immigration (including migratory transit) (Commission of the European Communities 2003a: 5).

portant for the EU and its partners to aim for the highest degree of complementarity and synergy in the different areas of their cooperation." (Commission of the European Communities 2004: 6)

The ENP addresses some old neighbors and a number of new ones, which are now closer as a result of the EU enlargement. It currently applies to Armenia, Azerbaijan, Ukraine, Belarus, Georgia, Moldavia, Algeria, Egypt, Israel, Jordan, Lebanon, Libya, Morocco, Syria, Tunisia, and the Palestinian territories[18], and is implemented through Action Plans, initiated by the Commission and agreed upon with its counterparts. "Border management is likely to be a priority in most Action Plans as it is only by working together that the EU and its neighbours can manage common borders more efficiently in order to facilitate legitimate movements." (Commission of the European Communities 2004: 16)

The Action Plans include measures to improve the efficiency of border management, such as the support of the creation and training of professional, non-military border security forces, and the means to make travel documents more secure. The priorities of the Action Plans may include cooperation on migration, asylum, visa policies, and the means to combat terrorism, organized crime, drug and arms trafficking, money laundering, and economic and financial crimes. "Action Plans should also reflect the Union's interest in concluding readmission agreements with the partner countries." (Commission of the European Communities 2004: 17)

Moving toward the realization of this initiative, the Commission presented the proposal for a draft regulation establishing a *European Neighbourhood and Partnership Instrument* in September 2004 as a new tool to provide EC economic assistance to ENP countries during the financial period of 2007–2013. Its second article specifically mentions the issue of immigration among its aid objectives. Some months later, in December 2004, the Commission published a communication on its Action Plans, which was focused on the priority areas of the ENP (Commission of the European Communities, 2004c), presenting the results of the queries carried out from reports on Israel, Jordan, Moldavia, Morocco, the Palestinian territories, Tunisia, and Ukraine. In the case of Morocco, for example, the national visa poli-

[18] There are other policies and agreements involving other countries, which also link migration policies with foreign relations and development cooperation. One of them is the MEDA Programme, designed to implement the cooperation measures to help Mediterranean non-member countries. MEDA is the principal tool of cooperation under the Euro-Mediterranean partnership. Launched in 1996 (MEDA I) and amended in 2000 (MEDA II), it is directed at Algeria, Cyprus, Egypt, Israel, Jordan, Lebanon, Malta, Morocco, the Palestinian territories, Syria, Tunisia, and Turkey. Another example is the Migration, Asylum and Refugees Regional Initiative (MARRI), which involves Albania, Bosnia and Herzegovina, Croatia, Macedonia, Montenegro, and Serbia. For more information, see http://www.marri-rc.org [Accessed February 14, 2011].

cy and the conclusion of bilateral readmission agreements with EU countries are reviewed. The Communication states that, if Morocco has good relations with sub-Saharan countries, this has not been reflected in the readmission agreements signed with them. “Recently, however, the authorities managed to repatriate nationals of sub-Saharan countries in a series of ad hoc operations.” (Commission of the European Communities 2004a: 11). According to a researcher of Colectivo Al Jaima, deportations are carried out in two ways in Morocco: (1) through raids in the medina quarters or in the woods where sub-Saharan migrants hide. The new immigration law establishes that they should be heard before a judge within 24 hours, but there is no place to keep them, they are on the ground floor of the commissariat, they are not given food or water, and in some cases they are not even allowed to take the medication they need. Judges usually speak Arabic, with no interpreter present. They are then handcuffed and sent in military trucks or inter-city buses to the Algerian border, which has been closed since 1994. (2) Many migrants who enter El Auin, a zone that was militarized during the conflict with the Polisario Front, are returned to the desert without food, drink, and other supplies.[19]

The report on Tunisia specifies that Italo-Tunisian maritime patrols are operating throughout the Strait of Messina to combat illegal immigration into the EU (Commission of the European Communities 2004b).[20] As in the case of Morocco, a working group on social and immigration issues was established under the provisions of the Association Agreement of 1998. In the last ENP assessment of 2009, immigration policy is again present in the relationship with Morocco: “The dialogue with the EU in certain sensitive sectors has further intensified, notably on the fight against organized crime and co-operation on border management issues. Negotiations on a readmission agreement have not progressed as much as expected.” (Council of European Communities 2009b: 6)

Although in recent years the Commission, the Parliament, and the Council have produced a series of documents in which each in its own way has defended the need for a global and integrated perspective—emphasizing the link between development, commerce, and cooperation as tools to reduce or eliminate the causes of the expulsion of populations (Commission of the European Communities 2008)—the instrumental and unilateral perspective has prevailed. For now, in practice, the emphasis continues to be placed upon signing readmission agreements, providing third countries with technical and

---

19 Interview with an Al Jaima Collective researcher in “Territories of Forgetting,” Chapter III of the program “Immigrate at Any Cost”, produced for Radio Netherlands Worldwide by Blanca Diego and Leire Otegi 2004. See also Heck in this volume.

20 Between the end of 1998 and the beginning of 2003, Tunisian authorities detained more than 37,000 people, 20,000 of Tunisian nationality, and the rest repatriated to their countries of origin (Commission of the European Communities 2004b).

financial support needed to improve border controls with the objective of halting immigration toward Europe and to combat irregular immigration, reaffirmed once more in the European Pact on Immigration of 2008 (Council of the European Union 2008). The general strategy aims at ensuring the co-operation of these countries on issues of immigration control and the return of such migrants arriving in the EU by crossing these countries.

The External Dimension of Asylum and Migration

The launch of the ENP coincided with another strategic initiative: the proposal of the British government to create so-called *safe havens* in neighboring countries and regions of origin in order to return the asylum seekers to the countries or zones from which they have fled. The first step would be the immediate transference of all asylum seekers arriving in EU territory to transit centers located in one or two member states, where asylum appeals can be dealt with in summary proceedings within less than one month. Immigrants whose need for protection is recognized would be distributed among the countries of the EU, whereas those classified as economic migrants would be immediately deported back to their countries of origin under the readmission agreements or sent to detention centers in their regions of origin. One of the points of discussion was where these centers should be located. The UNHCR, which supported the project, insisted that the camps be located in EC territory, but the UK and Denmark suggested Albania and Ukraine instead.[21] As for the *safe havens* in the regions of origin, Kenya and Tanzania were mentioned as possible locations for camps for people fleeing from Somalia (Statewatch 2004).

In October 2004, after the British proposal had been rejected by the 2003 Thessaloniki European Council, the EU opened the door for another controversial reform: the establishment of pilot reception centers for asylum seekers in North African countries. This reform is different from the British initiative in that these centers are only for migrants who are intercepted in international waters or who arrive in the North African countries without having entered the EU. According to the then European Commissioner of Justice and Home Affairs, António Vitorino, this system does not result in a shifting of the burden, but rather in the sharing of the burden, because some of the asylum seekers who achieve refugee status will be able to enter EC territory. In reference to the asylum seekers who are rejected, Dominique de Villepin, the then Minister of the Interior of France, explained: "From there, it will always

[21] The United Nations High Commissioner for Refugees, Ruud Lubbers, had a similar idea for an exile camp when he was Prime Minister of the Netherlands in the first half of the 1990s (Statewatch 2004).

be easier to return them home as they came, by bus or other mode of transport." (Cañas 2004a: 11)

In late September 2004, in continuing this process of delocalizing immigration control to the periphery of the EU, Italy and Germany proposed the creation of what they termed "off-shore camps"[22]—immigrant detention camps located in non-EU countries such as Libya and Morocco, both cosignatories of the ENP. However, rather than building new camps, existing ones were used where possible. Some sources confirm that such refugee and migrant camps have existed in Libya since at least the mid-1990s.[23] The deportation of African migrants from Italy beginning in October 2004 can be considered as another indicator that the system is already in motion. Libya has become the first non-European country to allow its camps to be integrated into the EU's deportation policies (Dietrich 2005)[24]. It does not seem to be a coincidence that the First Ministerial Conference on Migration and Development (Nov. 22-23, 2006) was held in Tripoli.

Even though Morocco rejected the German-Italian proposition at the time, there are many ad hoc encampments in the country, principally in Tangiers and the nearby Spanish exclaves of Ceuta and Melilla, some of which have been operational for four to five years. According to Colectivo

---

22 The proposal was presented at The Hague, in the European Council of Justice and Home Affairs that brings together ministers of the interior from the 25 member states. Germany, Austria, Italy, the UK, and, in a veiled way, the Netherlands, supported the proposal, whereas France and Spain expressed resistance to the initiative, and the government of Morocco rejected it (Cañas 2004).

23 "After nearly a decade of negotiation, Italy and Libya signed The Treaty of Friendship, Partnership and Cooperation between the Italian Republic and Great Socialist People's Libyan Arab Jamahiriya (the 'Friendship Pact') on August 30, 2008. The real trade-off for Libya's cooperation in stopping irregular migration appears to be Italian investments in Libya: The Friendship Pact provides for $5 billion in compensation for abuses committed during Italy's rule in Libya (from 1911 to 1943). The money will be invested by Italy over a 25-year period at the rate of $200 million per year in infrastructure projects in Libya. (...) The Friendship Pact calls for 'intensifying' cooperation in 'fighting terrorism, organized crime, drug trafficking and illegal immigration.' The two parties agree to strengthen the border control system for Libyan land borders (50 percent funded by Italy and 50 percent to be sought from the EU), and to use Italian companies in this endeavor." [online] Available at: http://www.hrw.org/en/node/85582/section/7 [Accessed February 14, 2011].

24 For Helmut Dietrich (2005), the second component of the German-Italian proposal regarding Libya was of an economic nature. Since the mid-1990s, the Libyan government has slowly opened its economy, and with it access to its gas and oil reserves, to foreign investment. Libya is the most important non-European supplier of oil for Germany, while Italy and Germany are the most important suppliers of goods to Libya. The third reason is of a military nature. Like Pakistan and Turkey, Libya may soon be able to become a privileged partner of the west in the fight against Islamic fundamentalism in the fragile African states.

Al Jaima, Morocco already acts as a buffer zone, with an estimated 15,000 to 20,000 sub-Saharans from Sierra Leone, Liberia, Mali, and Cameroon living in the country. "In Tangiers there are non-places where non-citizens have no rights yet exist. These non-places are easily created and easily destroyed. (…) I would speak of encampments, real refugee camps, don't call them political refugee camps, call them economic refugee camps."[25] Various civil organization have criticized the legal and social vulnerability of these migrants and the violations of their humans rights by Moroccan police and other authorities (APDH 2010). Some female migrants have become victims of sexual violence on their way to Europe (Médicos sin Fronteras 2010). Some of these people are expelled from Morocco and brought to the Algerian frontier or to the desert.

During the last decade, the involvement of sending and transit countries in EU migration control has notably increased. Step by step, these technologies of government are shaping a new frontier regime, which is located outside the communitarian space. In doing so, competencies and responsibilities regarding the rights of migrants and asylum seekers are transferred to third counties with no democratic governments. This provides considerable advantage for the EU countries by reducing the need for controls at their immediate borders and providing the opportunity to prevent unwanted immigrants from entering the communitarian space. At the same time the EU countries avoid any kind of social or political control over the effects of their measures. Both the ENP and the off-shore camps achieve the practice of a "new" concept of control, as recommended by the Austrian Presidency in 1998, which could be carried out in specific spaces and times, and by various kinds of actors.

The changes in border regulations also reflect transformations in the international system. The disappearance of the confrontation between the East and the west profoundly changed the notions of security that had been dominant, leading to the emergence of a new discourse which defines crime as the principal threat to the common space of freedom, security, and justice. Mafia activities, drug trafficking, illegal immigration, human trafficking, black market trade in arms and diamonds, organized crime, and terrorism are some of the dangers the EU is now confronted with and which have replaced confrontations with powers or foreign militarized blocs. The official reports concerning the September 11 attacks prepared and distributed by the United States and the European Union and the measures taken since the incidents, have only radicalized the image and security treatment of south-north and

---

[25] Interview with a Colectivo Al Jaima researcher in "Territories of Forgetting," Chapter III of the program "Immigrate at Any Cost", produced for Radio Netherlands Worldwide by Blanca Diego and Leire Otegi 2004. See the map of the Externalisation of European Borders Control in *Le Monde diplomatique*, June 2010.

east-west migration (Bigo 2006; van Munster 2009; d'Appollonia and Reich 2008). The implications of this regime of migration control are explored next, considered as an example of the *political rationalities* and *technologies of government* that are characteristic of advanced liberalism.

New Actors and New Spaces of Control: Instruments of Government at a Distance

One of the clearest tendencies in the formation process of an EU frontier regime is the gradual externalization of control: externalization through prevention, such as economic transfers and assistance, early warning systems, humanitarian aid, and the creation of safe zones in the vicinity of conflicts, or through determent—such as the concepts of safe third country or safe country of origin. Visas, the development of liaison officers networks, the imposition of the Schengen convention upon candidates for enlargement, the readmission agreements with migrant's countries of origin or transit, and the pressure on transportation companies to implement controls in ports of embarkation[26] are some of the forms this practice of remote control has taken, a practice that is no longer used directly at the edges of territories, nor involves only central state administrations.

As a consequence, the setting of actors has become much more complex, including different venues and levels of action (EU, national, local, and transnational levels). During the last twenty years private actors, businesses, and international and supranational companies have emerged onto the scene. Local and regional administrations also find themselves involved in control duties, such the city councils which grant housing certificates for family reunification transactions and take control over social services with regard to the administrative situation of their *users*, or the mayors who can refuse to officiate at a marriage if they consider it fraudulent.

This paradigm of post-1970s displacement and externalization has reinforced old instruments, such as development cooperation, that makes use of

26 In April 2004, the Council approved a directive regarding the obligation of transportation companies to communicate information about passengers (Council Directive 2004/82/EC, 6/8/2004), as the regulation indicates, with the goal of improving control of foreign borders and reinforcing the means to combat illegal immigration. The new regulation stipulates that in the case that they are requested to do so, the companies are obliged to transmit relevant information about the passengers they are transporting into EC territory. For an analysis of the implications of the sanctions upon the transport companies in the externalization of migration control from a Foucauldian perspective, see Walters (2006).

third actors (third countries, private companies, local authorities) for the government of migration. Its incorporation has taken three forms: vertical displacement upward and downward in state administration; geographic displacement toward other points of border control; and an externalization of responsibilities to the private sector and the governments of third countries. These initiatives can be understood as the application of neoliberal technologies of government, which make possible the practice of *government at a distance*. Miller and Rose (1990) elaborate on this concept of government, inspired by the perspective developed by social scientists Bruno Latour and Michel Callon, who in their analysis of scientific generalizations and technological innovations have examined the complex mechanism through which it is possible to link calculations that are carried out in one place with actions taken in another, not through the imposition of forms of conduct by force, but through a delicate affiliation of ensembles of agents and agencies within networks of operation. The interdependence between one agent and another can be based on the existence of funding, legitimacy, power, or some other resource, but it can also be the result of persuasion, the process by which an actor convinces another that their problems and objectives are intrinsically linked, and that each can solve his difficulties or achieve his goals jointly with the other and by working along the same lines. This is the hope that is clear from the documents that delineate the European Neighborhood Policy: migrants' countries of origin and transit must think and act about immigration in the same manner as the European Council.

From the perspective of *governmentality studies*, governing in an advanced liberal mode involves creating distance between the decisions of formal political institutions and other social actors, conceiving of those actors as subjects with responsibility and choice, and to attempt to act upon them through their freedom. It is important not to interpret this transference of the practice of certain functions on the part of the state as neglecting activities in other periods under its jurisdiction. But delegation does not mean loss of control. On the contrary, the change in the structure of state functions and a greater public or private complexity are signs of an advanced liberal government. What is revealed is not a withdrawal of the state, but a deployment of the art of government throughout a network constituted by diverse actors and spaces, which links objects, loyalties, and responsibilities[27]. In this way, the management of immigration is practiced through multiple actors and agencies in diverse spheres and on various levels, rather than from a centralized state apparatus, which allows for the optimization, rationalization, and efficient use of resources and the overcoming of certain tensions.[28]

---

27 Concerning the involvement of the International Organization for Migration (IOM) and other international organizations, see Hess in this volume.

28 Pat O'Malley (1999) defines liberal government as economic government in a double sense, as a cheap government and a government adapted to protecting the

These forms of governing at a distance are less subject to scrutiny, because not all actors have the same capacity for deterritorialized action. "Apart from increasing the number of states participating in exercise of control, this strategy of extraterritorialization is especially attractive to liberal democratic states. (…) [O]nce an (irregular) immigrant reaches the territory of their jurisdiction, his or her removal faces significant juridical and societal constrain." (Lavenex 2007: 137–138) These areas of *no man's land* intended to be international detention zones in airports (where legal assistance become almost unattainable) make sense. In this way one of the greatest dilemmas of the European governments seems to be solved: the tension between humanitarian obligations and the constraints of *realpolitik* (Brochmant 1999).

But there is another fundamental, generally overlooked, fact which is helpful in understanding these developments: the international hierarchy that makes these practices possible and is in turn reinforced by them. From a decolonizing perspective, north-south migrations are among the structural components of colonial power relations still in force, which support the migration of peripheral workers to provide cheap labor for metropolitan centers (Grosfoguel 2007; Gutiérrez Rodríguez 2010).[29] Each and every migrant carries the weight of historical relations of domination, material as well as symbolic, between the country of origin (dominated) and that of destination (dominant), a legacy of past encounters between the metropolis and its for-

---

conditions for an optimum economic performance. This liberal rationality is thus necessarily linked to an optimum economic return and minimal social and political cost.

29 The idea of the coloniality of power expresses one of the constitutive elements of contemporary patterns of power: "the imposition of an ethnic/racial classification on the world's population as a cornerstone for said pattern of power [which] operates on material and subjective planes, realms, and dimensions of social existence and on a societal scale" (Quijano 2000: 342). The coloniality of power lies in the intersection of multiple and heterogeneous global hierarchies of sexual, political, epistemological, economic, linguistic, and racial domination, and it reconfigures the remaining structures of power in the world system. From a de-colonizing perspective, the international division of labor into center and periphery and the hierarchical ranking of ethnic/racial populations devised over centuries of European colonial expansion were not transformed with the actual end of colonial administration. "Rather we are experiencing a transition from modern colonialism to global colonialism, a process which has certainly modified the forms of domination unleashed by modernity, but not the structure of the center-periphery relationship on a global scale" (Castro Gómez and Grosfoguel 2007: 13). Kitty Calavita (2005) invites us to think about the importation of workers from the periphery to the metropolis, the reconstruction of these workers into different 'others', and the material utility derived from this otherness as an inverse colonialism, a colonialism toward within. Although the outsider status of (im)migrant workers in part results from permanent inequalities inherited from the colonial era, their peripheral condition is reproduced through migration policies, business strategies, gender relations, stigmatization, racialization, and other dominant visions and divisions. (Gil Araujo 2010b)

mer colonies. The history of colonization has shaped the history of immigration between Europe and its periphery (Sayad 1996; Gil Araujo 2010b). The current EU migration policy confirms the persistent existence of the link between colonial order and migration order.

Conclusion

This article has focused on the process of involving the migrants' countries of origin and transit into EU migration control. In the first section, I specified some methodological and analytical points of departure. The second section summarized a set of documents, instruments, and practices, which facilitated the processes of delocalized migration control. I then focused the attention on the latest EU initiatives, which aim to transfer responsibilities in the management of immigration and asylum from the EU to third countries. Finally, I analyzed these trends from the perspective of governmentality studies, arguing that these discourses and practices can be seen as an example of the *political rationalities* and *technologies of government* that are characteristic of advanced liberalism.

The north-south migrations are a structural component of colonial power relations still in force. The history of colonization has shaped the history of immigration between Europe and its periphery. The welcome removal of borders does not affect all populations equally. Borders do not disappear, but are displaced, mutate, and multiply. We are witnessing the installation of border controls and a redefinition of their functions. The controls, similar to capital, seem to have exceeded the limitations of the nation-state's territorial boundaries. The freedom of movement attained by one class of people is accompanied by the proliferation of instruments to achieve the immobility of others. The current EU migration policy confirms the persistent existence of the link between colonial order and migratory order. While the national borders are being abolished for EU citizens, the walls of migration control, immigration law, readmission agreements, detention camps, internment centers, security policies, and integration exams and contracts against postcolonial migrants are on the rise and are multiplying.

References

Anderson, M. (2000): The Transformation of Border Controls: A European Precedent? In: Andreas, P./Snider, T. (eds.): The Wall around the West. State Border

and Immigration Controls in North America and Europe. Lanham: Rowman and Littlefiel Publishers, pp. 15-29.
APDH (2010): Derechos humanos en la frontera sur, Sevilla, APDH. [online] Available at: http://www.apdha.org/media/informeFS2009.pdf [Accessed February 14, 2011].
Bigo, D. (2005): From Foreigner to 'Abnormal Aliens'. How the Faces of the Enemy Have Changed Following September 11th. In: Guild, Elspeth/van Selm, Joanne (eds.): International Migration and Security. Opportunities and Challenges. Oxon: Routledge, pp. 63-171.
Brochmann, G. (1999): The Mechanisms of Control. In: Brochmann, G./Hammar,T. (eds.): Mechanism of Immigration Control. A Comparative Analysis of European Regulation Policies. Oxford: Berg.
Broeder, D. (2007): The New Digital Borders of Europe. EU Database and the Surveillance of Irregular Migrants. In: International Sociology 22, 1, pp. 71-92.
Calavita, K. (2005): Immigrants at the Margins. Law, Race, and Exclusion in Southern Europe. New York: Cambridge University Press.
Cañas, G. (2004): España y Marruecos rechazan los centros de acogida de inmigrantes. In: El País, October 1st. [online] Available at: http://www.elpais.com/articulo/internacional/Espana/Marruecos/rechazan/centros/acogida/inmigrantes/elpepiint/20041001elpepiint_18/Tes/ [Accessed February 14, 2011].
Cañas, G. (2004a): La Comisión pondrá en marcha con la ONU centros de inmigrantes en el Magreb. In : El País, October 2nd, p. 11.
Castel, R. (1997): La metamorfosis de la cuestión social. Una crónica del salariado. Buenos Aires: Eudeba. (English edition: Castel, Robert (2003): From manual workers to wage laborers. Transformation of the Social Question. New Jersey: Transaction Publishers.)
Castro-Gómez, S./Grosfoguel, R. (2007): El giro decolonial. Reflexiones para una diversidad epistémica más allá del capitalismo global. Bogotá: Siglo del Hombre Editores.
Commission of the European Communities (2003): Communication from the Commission to the Council and the European Parliament. Wider Europe-Neighbourhood: A New Framework for Relations with our Eastern and Southern Neighbours. March 11, Brussels. COM (2003) 104 final.
Commission of the European Communities (2003a): Communication from the Commission. Paving the Way for a New Neighbourhood Instrument. July 1, Brussels. COM (2003) 393 final.
Commission of the European Communities (2004): Communication from the Commission. European Neighbourhood Policy. Strategy Paper. May 12, Brussels. COM (2004) 373 final.
Commission of the European Communities (2004a): Commission Staff Working Paper, European Neighbourhood Policy. Country Report. Morocco, May 12, Brussels, COM(2004)373 Final.
Commission of the European Communities (2004b): Commission Staff Working Paper, European Neighbourhood Policy. Country Report. Tunisia, May 12, Brussels. COM(2004)373 Final.
Commission of the European Communities (2004c): Communication from the Commission to the Council on the Commission proposal for Action Plans Under the

European Neighbourhood Policy (ENP). December 9, Brussels. COM (2004)795 final.
Commission of the European Communities (2004d): Commission Staff Working Paper Annual report on the development of a common policy on illegal immigration, smuggling and trafficking of human beings, external borders, and the return of illegal residents, Commission of the European Communities, October 25, Brussels.
Commission of the European Communities (2008): Communication from the Commission to the European Parliament, the Council, the European Economic and Social Committee and The Committee of the Regions Strengthening the Global Approach to Migration: Increasing Coordination, Coherence and Synergies, COM(2008) 611 final, October 8, Brussels.
Council (2005): Council and Commission Action Plan implementing the Hague Programme on strengthening freedom, security and justice in the European Union (2005/C 198/01). In: Official Journal of the European Union C 198/1, 12/08/2005.
Commission of the European Communities (2009a): Communication From the Commission to the Council, the European Parliament, the European Economic and Social Committee and the Committee of the Regions Justices Freedom and Security In Europe Since 2005: An Evaluation Of The Hague Programme And Action Plan, Brussels, June 2. COM (2009) 263 Final.
Commission of the European Communities (2009b): Communication room the Commission to the European Parliament and the Council. Implementation of the European Neighbourhood Policy in 2008, Brussels, April 23, 2009, COM (2009) 188/3
Council of European Union (2004): Council Regulation (EC) N 377/2004 of 19 February 2004 on the creation of an immigration liason officers network," Official Journal of the European Union, 2/03/2004, L. 64/1 a L. 64/4.
Council of the European Union (2008): European Pact on Immigration and Asylum. No 13440/08, ASIM 72, September 24, Brussels.
Dean, M. (1999): Governmentality. Power and Rule in Modern Society. London: Sage.
Dietrich, H. (2005): The desert front - EU refugee camps in North Africa? In: Statewatch on-line, March. [online] Available at: http://www.statewatch.org/news/2005/mar/12eu-refugee-camps.htm [Accessed February 14, 2011]
Doty, R. L. (2003): Anti-Immigrantism in Western Democracies. Statecraft, desires and the politics of exclusion. London: Routledge.
Favell, A. (2000): Philosophies of Integration: Immigration and the Idea of Citizenship in France and Britain. Houndmills Basingstoke: Macmillan.
Favell, A. (2006): The nation-centered perspective. In: Giugni, Marco/Passy, Florence (eds.): Dialogues on Migration Policy. Lanham, MD: Lexington, pp. 45-56.
Foucault M. (2009): Security, Territory, Population. Lectures at the Collège de France 1977-1978. New York: Picador.
Freedman, J. (2004): Immigration and Security in France. Hants: Ashgate.
Gil Araujo, S. (2010a): Las argucias de la integración. Políticas migratorias, construcción nacional y cuestión social. Madrid: IEPALA.
Gil Araujo, S. (2010b): The Coloniality of Power and Ethnic Affinity in Migration Policy: The Spanish Case. In: Gutiérrez Rodríguez, Encarnación/Boatca, Ma-

nuela/Costa, Sérgio (eds.): Decolonizing European Sociology. Transdisciplinary Approaches. Surrey: Ashgate, pp. 179-194.
Gil Araujo, S. (2005): Muros alrededor de El Muro. Prácticas y discursos en torno a la inmigración en el proceso de construcción de la política migratoria comunitaria. In: Miranda, M. J./Martín, M. T. (coords.): Delitos y Fronteras. Mujeres Extranjeras en prisión. Madrid: Instituto de Investigaciones Feministas, Universidad Complutense de Madrid, pp. 113-137.
Gil Araujo, S. (2003): Las migraciones en las políticas de la Fortaleza. Sobre las múltiples fronteras de la Europa comunitaria. In: Gil Araújo, Sandra/Dahiri, Mohamed (eds.): Movimientos migratorios en el Mediterráneo occidental. ¿Un fenómeno o un problema? Córdoba: Ayuntamiento de Córdoba, pp.31-58.
Gil Araujo, S. (2002): Extranjeros bajo sospecha. Lucha contra el terrorismo y política migratoria en Estados Unidos y la Unión Europea. In: Aguirre, Mariano/González, Mabel (eds.): De Nueva York a Kabul. Anuario. CIP 2002. Barcelona: ICARIA, pp. 127-144.
Guiraudon, V. (2001): De-Nationalizing Control: Analyzing State Responses to Constraints on Migration Control. In: Guiraudon, Virginie/Joppke, Christian (eds.): Controlling a New Migration World. London: Routledge, pp. 31-64.
Gutiérrez-Rodríguez, E. (2010): Migration, Domestic Work and Affect. A Decolonial Approach on Value and the Feminization of Labor. Oxon: Routledge.
Grabbe, H. (2000): The Sharp Edges of Europe: Extending Schengen Eastwards. In: International Affairs 76, 3, pp. 519-536.
Grosfoguel, R. (2007): Migrantes coloniales caribeños en los centros metropolitanos del sistema-mundo. Los casos de Estados Unidos, Francia, Los países Bajos y el Reino Unido. Documento CIDOB Migraciones, nº 13, Barcelona, CIDOB.
Ha, Kien N. (2010): Integration as Colonial Pedagogy of Postcolonial Immigrants and People of Colour: A German Case Study. In: Gutiérrez Rodríguez, Encarnación/Boatca, Manuela/Costa, Sérgio (eds.) Decolonizing European Sociology. Transdisciplinary Approaches. Surrey: Ashgate, pp. 161-178.
Huysmans, J. (2000): The Euroepan Union and de Securitization of Migration. In: Journal of Common Market Studies 38, 5, pp. 751-77.
Kraler, A. (2010): Civic Stratification, Gender and Family Migration Policies in Europe. Final Report. Revised and updated public version. Vienna: BMWF/ICMPD.
Laeken European Council (2001): Presidency Conclusions, 14-15 December.
Lemke, Th. (2001): 'The birth of bio-politics': Michel Foucault's lecture at the Collége de France on neo-liberal governmentality. In: Economy and Society 30, 2, pp. 190- 207.
Lavenex, S. (2007): Shifting UP and Out: The Foreign Policy of European Immigration Control. In: Lahav, Gallya/Guiraudon, Virginie (eds.): Immigration Policy in Europe. The Politics of Control. Oxon: Routledge, pp.129-150.
Médicos sin Fronteras (2010): Violencia sexual y migración. La realidad oculta de las mujeres subsaharianas atrapadas en Marruecos de camino a Europa. Barcelona: MSF.
Miller, P./Rose, N. (1990): Governing Economic Life. In: Economy and Society 19, 1, pp. 1-31.

O'Malley, P. (1999): Consuming Risks: Harm Minimization and the Government of 'Drug-users' In: Smandych, R. (ed.): Governable Places. Readings on Governmentality and Crime Control. Ashgate/Datmouth: Hants, pp. 191-214.
Presidencia de la Unión Europea (1998): Documento de Estrategia sobre la Política migratoria y de asilo. Brussels.
Quijano, A. (2000): Colonialidad del poder y clasificación social. Journal of World-System Research VI, 2, pp. 342-386.
Rose, N. (1999): Powers of Freedom. Reframing Political Thought. Cambridge: Cambridge University Press.
Rose, N. (1997): El gobierno en las democracias liberales 'avanzadas': del liberalismo al neoliberalismo. In: Archipiélago 29, pp. 25-40.
Rose, N. (1996): The Death of the Social? Re-Figuring the Territory of Government. In: Economy and Society 25, 3, pp. 327-356.
Rose, N./Miller, P. (1992): Political Power beyond the State. Problematic of Government. In: British Journal of Sociology 43, 2, pp. 173-205.
Salónica European Council (2003): Presidency Conclusions, 19-20 June.
Sayad, A. (2002): La doppia assenza. Dalle illosioni dell'emigrato alle sofferenze dell'immigrato, Milán, Rafaello Cortina Editore.
Sayad, A. (1996): Entrevista colonialismo e migraçoes. In: Mana. Estudos de Antropologia Social 2, 1, pp. 155-170.
Schnapper, D. (1994): The Debate on Immigration and the Crisis of National Identity. In: Baldwin-Edwards, Martin/Schain, Martin A. (ed.): The Politics of Immigration in Western Europe. Essex: Frank Cass, pp. 127-139.
Seville European Council (2002): Presidency Conclusions, 21-22 June. [online] Available at: http://www.consilium.europa.eu/ueDocs/cms_Data/docs/pressData/en/ec/72638.pdf [Accessed February 14, 2011].
Statewatch (2010): EU: Readmission Agreements: Overview. In: Statewatch News Online, 28 January.
Statewatch (2004): EU Buffer States and UNCHR 'processing' centres and 'safe havens'. In: Statewatch News Online.
Tampere European Council (1999): Presidency Conclusions, 15-16 October.
Van Munster, R. (2009): Securitizing Immigration. The Politics of Risk in the EU. Hampshire: Palgrave.
Verrmeulen, H./Penninx, R. (2000): Immigrant Integration. The Dutch Case, Amsterdam, Het Spinuis.
Walters, W. (2002): Mapping Schengenland: Denaturalizing the border. In: Environment and Planning D: Society and Space 20, pp. 561-580.
Walters, W. (2006): Border/Control. In: European Journal of Social Theory 9, 2, pp. 187–203.
Walter, W./Haahr, J. H. (2005a): In/secure community. Governing Schengenland. In: Walter, W./Haahr, J.H. (eds.): Governing Europe. Discourse, Governmentality and European Integration. Oxon: Routledge, pp. 91-113.
Walters, W./Haahr, J. H. (2005b): Governing Europe. In: Walter, W./Haahr, J.H. (eds.): Governing Europe. Discourse, Governmentality and European Integration. Oxon: Routledge, pp. 1-20.

Success at Second Glance: Regularizations of Irregular Migrants in Spain

Axel Kreienbrink

The Spanish government has implemented a whole array of policies to stop irregular immigration, which has turned into an endemic problem since Spain became an immigration country.[1] Most instruments of migration control and migration management have at least one component aimed at preventing or reducing irregular migration. However, since none of these instruments has produced the expected or desired results, Spain, along with a number of other countries along the southern border of the European Union, has adopted an additional instrument to correct the situation: regularization. Since 1985, several regularization programs have been implemented, under varying preconditions and with different outcomes. The aim has been to legalize irregular migrants to allow them, among other things, to enter the legal labor market. In many cases, however, the mid- and long-term results do not seem to have met expectations, given that the estimated number of irregular migrants has continued to rise.

This essay challenges this perception. First, it will contextualize the instrument of regularization within the Spanish system as an example of an EU border state that has to reconcile national interests with EU interests concerning the prevention of irregular migration. It then discusses the development of the consecutive regularization campaigns with respect to their formal arrangements and preconditions. Finally, the outcomes for the migrants themselves will be assessed on the basis of statistics and qualitative research literature, especially in regard to long-term effects.

---

1 Opinions expresssed in this article are exclusively those of the author.

The Pressure of Irregular Migration as a Structural Characteristic in Spain

As González-Enríquez and Triandafyllidou (2009) have recently noted, the migratory situation in Spain is characterized by certain aspects that are comparable to situations in countries like Portugal and Italy. Some of these aspects are of interest with respect to irregular migration:

- The country belongs to the southern frontier of the Mediterranean, a line that divides Europe and Africa both economically and demographically and induces immigration—a division that becomes even more obvious between the two neighbors Spain and Morocco.
- The labor market is highly segmented, with a considerable share of informal economy and the need for cheap, unskilled (irregular) work, which attracts migrants.
- At least in the beginning of the immigration experience, Spain suffered from a lack of appropriate laws and administrative experience.
- Insufficient regulations for the management of migration to restrain legal entry do not lead to a reduction in immigration. Rather, due to the attractiveness of the shadow economy, irregular migration and shadow economy mutually reinforce one another, a phenomenon referred to as "rebound effect" (Solanes Corella, 2008: 203).
- However, migration management and control policies implemented in the past have shown a high degree of continuity, irrespective of the ideological background of the political parties in power.
- The combination of a rather weak and/or mistrusted state with ineffective bureaucracies has created a political culture in which irregularities have been widely accepted, and not just with regard to immigration, but in several other areas as well. If situations arise in which the outcomes of such irregular situations become intolerable and have to be remedied, amnesties are the common solution.

But even if one can say that these factors motivate irregular migration, there are different forms of this type of migration, with different causes and consequences. The ways of becoming an irregular migrant include illegal entry, expiration of residence permits, expiration or official refusal to renew residence permits, irregular work, ignoring deportation orders, denial of asylum, and loss of refugee status.

In most of the cases in Spain, undocumented stays are the result of "overstaying", that is, staying in the country beyond the permissible duration after entering the country legally. Individual migrants, as well as those financed through organized networks or mafias, utilize the tourist route to gain entry. In a survey among immigrant residents conducted in 2000, nearly one third of interviewees stated that they had entered the country with a tourist visa (Díez Nicolás/Ramírez Lafita 2001: 24f.). Many of those involved in this form of migration are citizens of non-EU countries in Eastern Europe, Africa, Latin America or Asia. According to the aforementioned survey, half of the interviewed Latin Americans had come this way. Actual illegal entry is significantly less common than overstaying. Even so, landings attempted from Northern Africa across the Strait of Gibraltar and to the Canary Islands in small boats—commonly known as *pateras* and *cayucos*—result in dramatic humanitarian situations which attract considerable media attention. Consequently, this kind of undocumented migration often comes across as being the central problem. To shed some light on this, the National Immigrant Survey of 2007 asked which means of transportation the immigrants used to come to Spain. The use of *pateras* or similar boats was minimal: only 1% of interviewees indicated to have used such means. However, broken down by regions of origin, it turned out that 9% of Sub-Saharans and 4.9% of Maghrebians had arrived at the Spanish coast in this manner. So, at least for these groups, such a share cannot be considered minimal (Instituto Nacional de Estadística 2009a: 26, 145).

Table 1: Evolution of irregularity in Spain

Year	TCN in the padrón municipal	TCN with residence permit[a]	TCN with students permit	TCN with expired permits in renovation (positive silence)	TCN irregularly staying	% of irregularity
	A	B	C	D	I=A-B-C-D	I/A
2001	927,978	589,517	28,816	59,000	260,645	27%
2002	1,457,661	777,708	29,402	78,000	572,551	39%
2003	2,042,083	971,446	23,756	97,000	949,881	46%
2004	2,358,040	1,208,755	30,254	121,000	998,031	42%
2005	2,894,712	1,478,416	36,545	148,000	1,231,751	43%
2006	2,164,302	2,169,648	30,640	217,000	747,014	23%
2007[b]	2,769,664	2,089,305	33,267	209,000	438,092	16%
2008	3,070,484	2,432,705	42,852	241,000	353,927	12%

Source: González-Enríquez 2009b: 24 (Asylum seekers excluded from calculation due to small numbers). [a] Numbers as of 31 December of the previous year. [b] Romanians and Bulgarians excluded due to EU accession.

But what is the scope of irregular migration in Spain? Because migration flow is generally difficult to measure (González-Enríquez 2009b: 29), this essay will focus on irregular residence. In the absence of official statistics, one has to rely on estimations. While in earlier years estimates were little more than "informed guesstimates," estimation techniques have improved considerably in recent years (Cebolla Boado/González Ferrer 2008: 55-59). The method used most often today is a subtraction method based on the *padrón municipal*, the municipal registries.[2] The estimate is calculated by taking the number of third country nationals (TCN) provided in the *padrón* and subtracting the number of valid residence authorizations for TCN, the number of authorizations for students from third countries, and the (approximate) number of TCN with expired residence authorizations pending renewal. Based on this calculation, the numbers and quotas of irregular staying immigrants have been considerable during the last decade, as can be seen in Table 1. The percentage of irregular staying TCN varied between 27% in 2001, 46% at the beginning of 2003 and 43% in 2005, in spite of the huge regularization campaigns that took place in these years (see below). The numbers decreased only after 2005 and especially after the EU enlargement of 2007 (Romania, Bulgaria). The latest estimation for January 2009 confirms the decreasing trend first seen in 2008, suggesting that there are 300,000 to 390,000 irregular immigrants currently living in Spain (González-Enríquez 2009c).

The Constant Search for Effective Measures Against Irregular Migration

From a state perspective irregular migration cannot be accepted, so the state has to find ways to reduce or even prevent this form of migration. There are several ways to reduce the influx and the total number of irregular migrants: a) external enforcement, mainly through tightening the border (policy measures include visa policy, the fortification of border installations and intensification of border patrols, and a strict policy of detention and deportation); b) the management of legal migration by trying to organize the incoming flows; and c) internal enforcement against the foreign population already irregularly residing and/or working (e.g., through workplace raids and employer sanctions).

2 To register with the municipality, a person must provide their name, gender, city of residence, date of birth, passport number (or the number of a similar document) and, when applicable, educational certificates. The authorities are not permitted to ask for proof of legal residency status.

External Enforcement

Most people would associate the term “border” with land borders. In the case of Spain, however, the country’s land borders are of minor concern because it is not so much the Spanish mainland on the Iberian Peninsula that is directly affected but rather the autonomous cities of Ceuta and Melilla on the north coast North Africa. Until the end of the 1980s, the borders were relatively easy to cross. The Ministry of the Interior has intensified upgrades to the enclosures since the mid-1990s, until the cities were surrounded with multiple walls. Although the number of persons apprehended is decreasing, there is still a sizable number of migrants who succeed in scaling the walls. In September and October 2005, the problem received widespread media attention, when hundreds of people made a collective effort to climb the border fences simultaneously. Almost one thousand of them succeeded, hundreds were injured and 14 died (cf. Heck in this volume).

The most visible part of enforcement measures is the defense of the sea borders. This is due to the media attention to the often dramatic crossings of the Strait of Gibraltar or the Atlantic Ocean towards the Canary Islands in small boats. As a result of the public debate on this undisputable humanitarian problem, sealing the external sea borders physically has become a top priority of the agenda. By the end of the 1990s, the Spanish government started to develop the surveillance system SIVE (*Sistema Integral de Vigilancia Exterior*), which combines long-range radar, thermal cameras, night vision equipment, infrared illuminators, helicopters, and other means to close off access from the sea. However, the intensified border control caused shifts in migration routes, with the Canary Islands in particular becoming a migration destination after the Strait of Gibraltar had been sealed off. Thus, the departure points for crossings moved further south as a consequence of Spanish and equally intensified Moroccan controls. Boats now cast off from Mauritania or even Senegal. In response to this development, Spain extended the SIVE to the Canary Islands (Carling 2007a). The system was later further extended along the east coast of the Iberian Peninsula. More and more, SIVE constitutes an integral part of the increasingly intense surveillance mechanisms of the borders of the entire European Union (cf. Jeandesboz 2008).

The largest number of illegal immigrants arriving sea was recorded in 2006, with approx. 31,700 seizures on the Canary Islands and 7,500 on the Andalusian coast. In response to this, Spain requested assistance from the European Union agency for external border security, Frontex. This Spanish request of the relatively newly created European agency to become operational in its waters can be judged as crucial for the further development and increase of Frontex (Hernández i Sagrera 2008). The agency set up a regional coordination center on the Canary Islands and carried out several operations during 2006/2007 (Operations HERA I–III). In addition, supplementary bilateral patrols were organized in Morocco, Mauritania and Cape Verde. As a result, growing numbers of irregular immigrants could be intercepted right after, or even before, their departure. However, migrants did not stop their attempts to cross the sea, but faced increased risks and costs and relied more on the services of organized smugglers. The longer the crossings, the more hazardous they are. It is not known how many never reach their destination and die during the crossing. The number of people dying every year is believed to be significantly higher than the 800-odd bodies that were salvaged by the authorities on the Canary Islands and along the Moroccan coast in 2006. According to some NGOs, the estimated number of casualties ranges between 6,000 and 7,000 (Carling 2007b).

Facing these situations at its land and sea borders, Spain intensified its diplomatic efforts to bring this issue onto the European agenda, on the grounds that these were problems which affected the European Union as a whole and which were best solved through cooperative efforts. This strategy proved successful. The European Commission encouraged immigration initiatives to intensify their external action efforts, and at the European Council meeting in Seville in 2002, the Spanish Aznar administration successfully brought its irregular migration concerns onto the Council's agenda for the first time. However, the other EU Member States rejected Aznar's "negative conditionality" approach, which was aimed at reducing development aid for countries that failed to comply with the terms of agreements on readmission and flow control. The succeeding socialist Zapatero administration then changed the approach towards a "positive conditionality", offering more aid and benefits to those countries showing greater willingness to cooperate in managing migration (Pinyol 2008). This positive conditionality has been translated into the *Global Approach to Migration: Priority actions focusing on Africa and the Mediterranean*, adopted by the Council in December 2005 (European Commission 2006). Since then, this orientation can also be found within the European Neighborhood Policy and the policy dialogue with ACP countries (Alberdi Bidaguren/Bidaurratzaga Aurre 2008: 210f.).

This renewed external action approach induced Spain to establish national-level "migration diplomacy" (Pinyol 2008) with sub-Saharan countries which were previously neglected. This was achieved by the adoption of "Plan Africa" (2006-2008). While on the face of it this plan included several different goals, it was rather obvious from the very beginning that its central objective would be the nexus between development cooperation and migration control (despite the government repeatedly denying this) (Guerrero 2008). To achieve the planned effects, agreements with the relevant countries were concluded. These "agreements of cooperation in migration matters" (also referred to as "second generation" agreements) provided strategies to control irregular migration and recruit workers in countries of origin with certain guarantees, such as integration and development measures. Even so, the quotas for legal workers were small, unspecific and bound to the commitment to act against irregular emigration and accept nationals and migrants from third countries who have passed through the respective countries in transit to be repatriated (Asín Cabrera 2008). Along with this agreement-based "migration initiative", increased efforts have been undertaken to expand diplomatic presence, including the establishment of new embassies and consulates, the creation of new technical offices for cooperation, economics and trade, and the assignment of attachés for defense in the region. The new "Plan Africa" (2009–2012) follows along the same basic lines in the fight against irregular migration.

When it comes to immigration from Africa, Spain's air borders are the most important gateway for irregular migrants who enter the country as tourists. The Spanish government implemented a number of strategies to reduce the influx of these immigrants, including stricter border controls and the introduction of visa obligations, particularly for migrants from South American countries, which used to have visa waiver agreements with Spain. As early as in the first half of the 1990s, Spain imposed visa obligations on the Dominican Republic and Peru.[3] Later, already bound to the common "visa regime" of the European Union, Colombia (2002), Ecuador (2003) and Bolivia (2007) followed. However, because of the special historical relations between Spain and Latin America, the Spanish government took great care not to hurt its external relations—even though the introduction of the visa obligations within the common European visa policy was clearly in the interest of Spain, especially with regard to irregular immigrants from Colombia[4] (Kreienbrink 2004: 198-205).

Generally speaking, the control measures seem to have been successful. The number of apprehended irregular immigrants arriving by sea has decreased dramatically, by more than 50% in 2007 and by 26% and 46% in 2008 and 2009, respectively. Between 2006 and 2009, their number decreased by 81%[5] (Ministerio del Interior 2010), reaching the levels of 2000, with several months without any seizures on the Canary Islands and with reportedly not a single *cayuco* from Senegal. Along this same line, there was a decrease in the number of refusals of entry at Spanish airports and harbors

---

3 In 1991 Spain had already imposed the visa obligation on Morocco and the other Maghreb countries, but this measure has to be seen as a necessity in the course of Spain's Schengen accession.

4 The intention was to curb irregular migration. The regularization program of 2000 revealed almost 13,000 irregular Colombian immigrants residing in Spain, approximately the number of regular Colombian residents in 1999 (i.e., an increase of 100%). In addition, the problems of drug smuggling and permanent civil strife contributed to the Spanish position.

5 Numbers of seizures 39,180 (2006); 18,057 (2007) (a decrease by 54% over the previous year); 13,425 (2008); 7,285 (2009) (Ministerio de Trabajo y Asuntos Sociales, 2006; Ministerio del Interior, 2010).

(which are favorite gateways for Latin Americans and irregular Maghrebi immigrants, respectively), by 44.6% at Madrid-Barajas Airport, 72.7% at Barcelona El Prat Airport, 75.1% at the harbor of Algeciras and 83.6% at the harbor of Tarifa in the first four months of 2009 alone (*El País*, April 28, 2009). Even so, the responsible officials, such as the Spanish minister of the interior, admitted that these effects were not the result of intense controls alone—although they certainly have a deterring effect—but also were a consequence of the global and especially the Spanish economic crisis that hit the country's labor market extremely hard[6] (Kreienbrink 2009: 276f., 286).

Management of Regular Migration

Because of the close relation between the opportunities of the Spanish labor market and (irregular) migration, Spain employs various additional strategies to channel migration flows, including annual quotas for foreign workers. Although these quotas were introduced as early as 1993, during the 1990s they served primarily as a means to legalize persons already residing in Spain. The effect was that no more than 20% to 30% of all new entries to the country were admitted as foreign workers under this quota. From 2002 onward, the quota system became more associated with the control system: the contracts had to be established in the country of origin. The size of the quota was defined by the Spanish government, which signed agreements with several states, granting them privileged access to the quota (see below). However, the system did not work properly. Firstly, the size of the quota was not defined based on the actual requirements of the Spanish labor market. In addition, job offers were generic and not specified to existing demands, so there was no guarantee that applicants would actually find employment. In 2004, the new government modified the procedure by creating a list of vacancies in each of the provinces that are difficult to fill (*Catálogo de ocupaciones de difícil cobertura*). The list is revised every three months, but the system is not particularly effective, partly because recruiting staff through the quota system is a protracted affair for employers. Furthermore, the annual quotas (e.g., 16,900 (2006)) were not in line with the real demand for labor, which was several times greater than the quotas. Given this, the whole system has been called utopian and extremely rigid for the regulation of labor immigration (Cebolla Boado/González Ferrer 2008: 40-45, cit. p. 45; cf. also Aparicio Wilhelmi/Roig Molés 2006: 151-165). In view of the current economic cri-

6 In early 2008, unemployment already increased considerably compared to the end of 2007, by 13.56% among foreigners and 6.22% among Spaniards. While the unemployment rate during the first quarter of 2008 was 9.63% (8.73% among Spaniards and 14.65% among foreigners), it exploded within one year to 17.36% (15.24% among Spaniards and 28.39% among foreigners) (Instituto Nacional de Estadística, 2008, 2009b).

sis, the annual quota for 2009 was fixed at only 911, and the ministry of labor reduced the list of vacancies to one third, eliminating professions which had previously generated most of the contracts, including bricklayers, cleaners, unskilled agricultural laborers and waiting staff.

As already stated, in recent years Spain concluded agreements with various countries of origin to control migration movements in general and labor migration in particular, including return options. Such agreements have been concluded with Colombia, Ecuador, Morocco and the Dominican Republic (all in 2001), with Romania and Poland (both in 2002) and with Bulgaria (2003). Generally speaking, such agreements give nationals of these countries privileged access to the above-mentioned quota system and regulate labor conditions and returns. However, it seems doubtful whether these agreements will meet the expectations. Critics have observed that the selection of workers in these countries is not based on their professional skills but rather on local clientele relations of the applicants. The governments of these countries also face public criticism because agreements such as these are often considered to be little more than trade-offs for repatriation measures. However, due to the recent economic downturn and the current recruitment stop, the agreements are now virtually inactive (Ferrero Turrión/López Sala 2009: 129f.).

Internal Controls

As previously stated, irregular employment is the real magnet for irregular immigration to Spain. Consequently, the logical reaction of the state should be to combat this irregular employment. The responsible authority for this task is the National Labor and Social Security Inspectorate. However, the effectiveness of the Inspectorate's work depends on its acting in the field and the means it receives (both financially and in terms of personnel) (Aparicio et al. 2008: 284). Concerning its action, the Inspectorate sees its main focus on promoting voluntary compliance with labor and social security obligations, emphasizing prevention instead of sanctioning. With regard to their personnel, the Inspectorate is chronically understaffed. Also, some of the controls do not seem to be particularly effective, such as in the rural areas, where local administrations must be notified of inspections in advance, with the result that employers are warned, thanks to their close friendships and family ties with authorities. Another factor is the social acceptance of irregular employment in small (rural) enterprises (Aparicio et al. 2008: 287). It is therefore not surprising that recent analyses of governmental action in this field have concluded that the Spanish government has so far failed to implement effective measures, either out of negligence or deliberately, in view of the competitive advantages for the national economy (Eigmüller 2007: 213-214).

Regularization of Irregular Immigrants as a Solution

Since the different instruments have not had the expected nor the desired results, the Spanish government, along with the governments of several other countries on the southern border of the EU, made an ad hoc decision to introduce an additional instrument to resolve the situation: regularization. The main motivation for these actions was to legalize irregular migrants, mainly to allow them to enter the legal labor market. However, in the mid and long term these government efforts to curb irregular residence did not yield the expected results. After the regularization, the number of irregular migrants continued to increase. Since 1985, several other regularization campaigns have taken place under varying preconditions and with different outcomes. Although they were never meant to be repeated, they have become a structural element of Spanish migration policy – at least until 2005.

Types of Regularization

What characterizes regularization? Generally, regularization gives "migrants who are in a country irregularly the opportunity to legalize their resident status, whether it is on a temporary or permanent basis" (Levinson 2005: 4; similar Baldwin-Edwards/Kraler 2009: 7). The way this is organized can be quite diverse. Cachón Rodríguez (2009: 194-198) identifies three main types: the first and most important type is extraordinary processes (i.e., one-off processes). The second category comprises "other processes" which, in most cases, took place only once but were not usually defined as regularizations. Thus, the quota system during the 1990s (see above), the EU enlargements of 2004 and 2007, and the special regulations in 2001 (see below) would fit into this category. The third category is the individualized and permanent regularization possibility on the basis of rootedness (*arraigo*). Currently there are three types for regularization by rootedness: *arraigo laboral* (two years of residence and having worked for one year), *arraigo familiar* (three years of residence and having provided an employment contract and proof of family bonds in Spain), and *arraigo social* or *local* (three years of residence and having provided an employment contract and a report from the city council on social integration[7]).

7 In addition to other information, this report must contain (following the form prescribed by the Ministry) information on time of residence in the municipality, income, level of language knowledge, level of social integration, participation in educational or labor formation programs and an expressed approval or (founded) disapproval of the city council.

Extraordinary Processes

Spain has implemented five regularization processes (in the narrower sense of the term) and several sub-processes and extra processes; the latter are italicized in the following table (see Table 2).

Table 2: Regularization processes in Spain

Year	Party in Government	Name	Applications submitted	Applications accepted
1985/86	PSOE	Regularization	43,815[8]	ca. 23,000
1991	PSOE	Regularization	135,393	108,321
1991/92	*PSOE*	*Regularization of family members*	*6,777*	*5,889*
1996	PP	Redocumentation	25,128	21,294
2000	PP	Regularization	247,598	178,436
2001	*PP*	*Re-exam of denied applications*		*61,365*
2001	*PP*	*Rootedness*	*351,269*	*239,174*
2001	*PP*	*Voluntary return of Ecuadorians*	*24,884*	*24,352*
2005	PSOE	Normalization	691,655	576,506

Source: Author's own calculation using data provided in Cebolla Boado/González Ferrer 2008: 52f.

The regularization of 1985/86 was a consequence of the first Spanish Foreigner Act adopted in mid-1985. The Act defines regularization as a *tabula rasa* solution to start the new era of the law without irregular immigrants. However, the intention was not fulfilled because the government was mistaken in supposing that the procedure could be executed without clear criteria and preparation. Of the total number of almost 44,000 applications, approx. 23,000 were denied. The estimated number of irregular migrants being between 300,000 and 400,000, the responsible ministries of labor and interior assessed the process as a failure (Colectivo Ioé 1987: 97; Kreienbrink 2004: 167f.).

The next regularization process of 1991 was part of the government's newly-started "active immigration policy". In contrast to 1985 and due to the official concept of migration as temporary labor migration, this process was limited to the foreign labor force. Family members only had a chance to be regularized if the worker had already been granted regular status. This time,

8 Other publications put the number at 38,181. However, according to Izquierdo Escribano (1992: 182f.), this is the number of applications processed by the authorities.

procedures were to be transparent and required documents easy to procure. The procedure took half a year and was accompanied by a broad information campaign, supported by trade unions and NGOs, under the slogan "*Sal a la luz"* (Come out to the light). As a result, more than 135,000 applications for a a one-year residence permit (a title beyond the regular permit system) were counted, more than 108,000 of which were approved. The additional regularization for family members, which took place until March 1992, covered only 6,500 persons. Beyond political appraisals of this altogether successful process, the question was raised as to whether it were possible for the recently regularized to maintain legality. The special renewal of permits in 1992 was considered as a success, since 84% out of 100,000 permit holders[9] applied for renewal instead of the expected 65%. Eventually, 81,000 received it (Kreienbrink 2004: 248-254).

In 1996, the new process, implemented under the newly elected conservative People's Party (PP) administration but already resolved from the former government led by the Spanish Socialist Workers' Party (PSOE), was called "redocumentation". It was again part of a legal reform, but this time it was the reform of the regulation of the foreigner law (Real Decreto 155/1996). The rationale behind the regularization was that expectations regarding social integration were to be frustrated if the authorities were unable to provide documents to all irregular residing migrants whose irregular status was (partly) a result of the prior regulation. Thus, the former government conceded that its policy failed to a certain extent because, obviously, maintaining it was diffcult to maintain legal status. This time, the only persons able to apply were those who had possessed a residence or work permit at some point since the prior regulation came into force in 1986. Contrary to high expectations, the result of the four-month process was that only about 25,000 rather than the expected 65,000 applications were lodged (Kreienbrink 2004: 255f.).

In contrast to this experience, the regularization of 2000, a result of the new foreigner law (Organic Law 4/2000), adopted by the parliamentary majority in December 1999 against the will of the minority government led by the conservative PP, exceeded all expectations, with more than 247,000 persons rather than the expected 80,000 applying during the process, a sign that irregular migration was a bigger problem than the government had perceived. In the end, more than 178,000 persons received legal status. This number was used by the conservative government to alert the public that Spain would be flooded by irregular migrants due to the alleged "pull effect" (*efecto llamada*) of the new law and the existing regularization opportunities. Hav-

9 Of 108,000 accepted applications 2,000 to 3,000 had not been picked up and 5,000 pertained to EC citizens who fell out of the process in 1992 due to the internal freedom of movement (Aragón Bombín 1994: 14).

ing won an absolute majority in March 2000, the PP had the power to reform the law again in December (Organic Law 8/2000).

Although for the first time this major reform of the Foreigner Act caused no immediate regularization process, the year 2001 saw three sub- and extra processes. Firstly, there was the "re-exam". During the drafting of the Organic Law (LO) 8/2000 all opposition parties had pleaded for a revision "ex officio" of all the applications denied in the first round (some 60,000), without the necessity to present the original documents again. Although the government initially opposed this proposal, it eventually gave in. At the same time, another special regularization took place as a reaction to groups of irregularly staying migrants who had sought refuge in churches in Barcelona, Valencia, Murcia, Almería and several other Spanish cities, putting pressure on the government to grant them legal status, most of them having failed in the regularization of 2000 and/or during the re-exam (see Suárez-Navaz et al. 2007; Laubenthal 2005). Once again, the government first tried to uphold its tough policies, but eventually conceded, on a regional level, by resolutions of the delegates of the government.[10] The prerequisite to qualify for regularization was that the person concerned had resided in the country before January 23, 2001 and displayed some form of rootedness (i.e., participation in the labor market, earlier legal residence in Spain or family bonds in the country) (Trinidad García 2002). This form of regularization was an anticipation of the provision for the individual regularization by rootedness that was implemented by the new regulation of the LO 8/2000 (Aja 2006: 33; see also above). Of the more than 351,000 applicants, 239,000 received a residence permit via this procedure. Last but not least, there was the special regularization process for Ecuadorians for humanitarian reasons. An accident with 12 deaths involving irregularly staying Ecuadorians in Lorca (Murcia) received extensive media coverage which shed light on the situation in the southern agricultural sectors and the inefficacy of Spanish migration control measures. As a result of an unexpected wave of public sympathy for the fate of the Ecuadorians and considerable pressure from 4,000 regional farmers, the government conceded a restricted regularization for some 25,000 Ecuadorians (González-Enríquez 2009a: 146).

In spite of its negative stance toward regularization, the PP-led government regularized nearly 325,000 immigrants. In a way, one could say that if regularization really worked as an incentive for further immigration, as the government never tired to maintain, it was the government itself that gave this impression. In any case, with the years 2000/2001 the exponential

---

10 Delegates of the Government belong to the so-called peripheral organization of the State. They have a political function and represent the central government in the autonomous communities. In addition, they are in charge of the state administration within the autonomous communities and coordinate its work with the autonomic administrations.

growth of immigration into Spain began, which led to a six-fold increase of the foreign population by 2009 and a somewhat higher rise if we look only at the evolution of third country nationals.[11]

Against this steady rise in immigration and concurrent rise in irregularity, the most recent campaign in 2005 took place under the newly-elected socialist government. As often before, it accompanied a major reform of the Foreigner Act. This time it was the reform of the regulations governing the implementation of the Act, rather than again reforming the Act itself. In contrast to previous years, applicants in this so-called normalization (*normalización*) process were required to prove that they already had an (informal) employment contract as well as a guarantee from the employer that the work contract would be continued. Generally speaking, it was the employer who had to file the application. Moreover, the work permit became valid only if the employment was subsequently registered in the social security system and initial contributions had been paid into it. Only domestic workers with more than one employer could apply on their own. It was hoped that the introduction of these requirements would reduce clandestine employment and boost social security funds. As a result, 578,375 out of 691,655 applications for legal residence status were approved, making it one of the most extensive regularizations to date in Spain and Europe.

The government considered the result of the 2005 regularization a great success because a considerable part of the underground economy had been revealed. But in addition to criticism from the conservative opposition regarding the "pull effect" that was to be expected, the government had to face harsh criticism from several other EU member states and the European Commission, criticizing Spain for not having acted in a coordinated manner. At the informal Council meeting at Tampere in early 2006 Germany in particular criticized Spain for requesting European funds for the fortification of the external borders while not asking, or at least informing, the partners before such a large-scale regularization (even though Spain was not required to do so). France claimed that regularization was not a solution to the problem of irregular migration, but could even have the opposite effect of increasing the number of irregular migrants in other Schengen countries. As a consequence of the criticism and to appease the members, the Luxemburg presidency and the Commission proposed a mutual information and early warning mechanism which was established by the Council on October 5, 2006 as the Mutual Information Mechanism (MIM)[12] (García Martínez 2006: 41; Pinyol 2008).

---

11 In 2000 (as of January 1) the padrón accounted for 923,879 foreign residents, in 2003 for 2,664,168, in 2006 for 4,144,166, and in 2009 for 5,648,671. The figures for third country nationals are: 514,443 (2000), 2,042,083 (2003), 3,164,302 (2006) and 3,294,676 (2009).

12 Decision 2006/688/EC.

However, it can be concluded that the MIM did not perform to the expected standard (European Commission 2009: 9).[13]

Meanwhile, in 2008, during its presidency, France tried to obtain a general veto against further mass regularizations. At least the draft formulation of the European Pact of Immigration and Asylum proposed by President Sarkozy reflected this position, seconded by the Commission (European Commission 2008). However, this was too obviously a critique of the Spanish regularization of 2005. The Zapatero administration opposed this position successfully and reached a compromise: the final formulation of the adopted Pact now favors "case-by-case regularization, rather than generalized regularization, under national law, for humanitarian or economic reasons". Under this formulation, regularizations were not disapproved of in general, nor was the Spanish regularization condemned, since, for the Spanish government, the measure had clearly had economic reasons. Furthermore, this (non-binding) clause left sufficient room for maneuver for member states to employ regularization measures when they seemed politically appropriate. This took place, for instance, when France undertook regularizations in 2006 and 2008, but unlike in Spain, both cases were only small-scale regularizations based on either humanitarian or selective economic reasons. Other countries, such as Italy (2006), Greece (2007), and Belgium (2009), applied regularizations with similar rationales (Sohler 2009: 19-23, 29-31; Ruspini 2009: 74f.; Baldwin-Edwards 2009: 59f.).

When assessing the sequence of regularizations Spain has implemented, it is inappropriate to assume a *circulus vitiosus* of regularization and reillegalization of migrants, as was feared during the 1990s. This cannot hold true, at least for the vast majority, due to the continued and partly spectacular increase of immigration into Spain. That is to say that most of the migrants regularized had newly arrived after the last regularization. Concomitantly, the sequence has to be seen as more of a perpendicular movement, in which the increase of the stock of irregular migrants forced the administration to react and to deter irregularity. Although it cannot be denied that the regularization processes were partly responsible for the continuing growth of immigration, it is more than probable that it was actually the opportunities in the labor market that played the crucial role. From the perspective of the European partners, such a policy could be seen as potentially worrisome, putting into question the sincerity of Spain (and others, like Italy) in controlling and restricting immigration into the European Union. But this strategy, considered by Baldwin-Edwards (1999: 12) as a specific treatment of immigration

13 As a reaction to the imperfect flow of information within the MIM system, in the future the Commission will rely on its annual report on the implementation of the European Pact on Immigration and Asylum (adopted 2008), which is based on the reports of governments and the respective National Contact Points of the European Migration Network.

by Southern European countries, was perhaps a confrontation much closer to reality than other countries were willing to accept, although it did not solve the underlying structural problems. But policy aside, what were the outcomes for the migrants themselves?

Impact on Migrants

While in most cases the impact of regularizations is measured in the number of migrants who have been brought out of irregularity, this chapter will discuss the outcome of regularization processes for migrants, both in the short and the long term. There are no specialized studies on this particular subject, but a review of studies dealing with different aspects of the rapidly changing situation of immigration in Spain provides some insights.

The meaning of Being an Irregular Migrant

In the narrowest sense, regularization is a way for migrants to regularize their irregular status. A research project conducted in the late 1990s in which several irregularly staying persons were interviewed sheds light on the situation of irregular immigrants. Most migrants perceive an irregular situation as a given when they start their migration projects, especially those who tried to enter the country illegally in *pateras* or in similar ways. Thus, though the irregular situation does not always come unexpectedly, it must be stressed that it is not sought after either. Anticipated and expected as a price to be paid for a better future, it is tolerated solely as a transitory status (Ruiz Olabuénaga et al. 1999: 97, 100). This is not surprising, because the living conditions for a irregularly staying person can prove to be rather difficult. Migrants live in conditions of social reclusion, which prevents them from living a relatively normal life, meeting other people, finding proper work, renting or buying a flat, getting legal advice, participating in social services, and so on. Constant fear of being identified by the police leads to social isolation and, consequently, to a loss of resources and personal talents (Ruiz Olabuénaga et al. 1999: 115). Altogether, the (prolonged) irregular status leads to a situation that has been called "civil death" or "absence of freedom" (Ruiz Olabuénaga et al. 1999: 135-137; Wagner 2010: 156f.)[14], and the data from studies and regularizations show that most of the immigrants in Spain indeed stay in a phase of irregularity. Studies on Andalusia and Catalonia

[14] This situation with all its hardships is vividly described in the form of a diary by Nini (2002).

conducted in 2003 show that about 50% of migrants were staying irregularly at the time of study (González-Enríquez 2009: 151, citing Pérez Yruela/Rinken 2005 and Pajares 2004).

Since immigrants expect that their irregular status should eventually become a legal one, obtaining "papers" is a primary concern for them. A study based on several polls from the years 2000 to 2004 shows that aside from finding employment this point is perceived as the primary concern for migrants after entering Spain. Both aspects are mentioned with comparable frequency but over time getting regularized seems to become more important, perhaps because of stricter controls and repatriation policy and easier access to work during the boom years of the Spanish economy (Díez Nicolás 2005: 67). The sheer extent of irregularity is shown by further results of the cited studies. About half of the immigrants who stated that regularization had been their primary concern after arriving had obtained their "papers" at the time of questioning, but about 40% were still in the process of regularizing, which shows that despite the existing problems the majority of migrants achieve regularization (Díez Nicolás 2005: 69).

Maintaining Legal Status

Once having achieved a legal status, how does one maintain it? All regularization campaigns—especially the campaign of 1996—showed that some of the migrants who gained legal status lost it later because of difficulties in renewing it. One reason is that the requirements for renewing work and residency permits had become stricter than those at the time when the immigrants applied for regularization. In addition, given the volatility in the economic sectors in which most immigrants work, many were simply unable to produce an employment contract when the time came to have their permits renewed. However, the requirements have become less strict over time, with the result that unemployment at the time of renewal did not automatically lead to a refusal of the permit. To obtain more information on the stability of legal residence status, Arango and Finotelli (2009: 87) compared the aggregated number of regularized immigrants since 1985 (1,176,300) with the number of third country nationals in 2006 (2,361,000) and assumed that, in the long term, regularization was responsible for the inclusion of almost half of the immigrant population. While this is a very rough approximation, the analysis of the relation between the number of initial residence permits and the number of permits of first and second renewal after the regularization of 2005 shows that most of the migrants were able have their residence permits renewed (Arango/Finotelli 2009: 87).

Labor and Upward Mobility

The other top priorities of recent immigrants beside obtaining legal residence status are getting work and a work permit, as already stated above. But starting to work often begins in an irregular situation.[15] Several polls from the first half of the decade show that only 14% to 20% of incoming immigrants were in possession of a working permit (Díez Nicolás 2005: 67), these results being confirmed by the National Immigrant Survey of 2006. The survey also shows that most of the migrants found it relatively easy to find employment. Almost 84% of the interviewed immigrants who were working at the time of the survey stated to have come to Spain with the intention of working but without a prior permit. Concomitantly, more than 35% of those who came without a working permit stated they had found work within two weeks. Only about 10% of those who were working at the time of the survey needed more than one year to find a job. In other words, (irregular) immigrants in Spain had the security of finding a job within a short time (Instituto Nacional de Estadística 2009a: 28), and although they possibly knew that they would earn less and live in poorer conditions than legally staying workers, at least they could be confident that they would be hired and paid (Solanes Corella 2008: 211).

As this data has already implicitly shown, a high percentage of regularized immigrants manage to remain in the labor market. The evaluation of data of the National Social Security Institute of Spain confirms this. The Institute has monitored the labor careers of all regularized migrants since the 2005 regularization. As Arango and Finotelli (2009: 89) explain, the regularized foreign workers increased the stock of foreign workers considerably. The year 2005 closed with a number of 1,404,449 foreign workers, 578,313 of whom had entered during that year. This means that one third of all registered foreigners were regularized in 2005. For 2006, the same database showed that almost 80% of regularization-related enrolments were still valid, meaning that the concerned foreign workers were still working legally at least one year after the regularization process. In 2007, there was a slight decrease in the quota of the regularized persons in the social security system.

But in comparing the different sectors of activity there were some interesting shifts within the group of registered foreign workers. Looking at the figures of January 2007, for the first time ever, the number of registered foreign women among the population of domestic workers (*Régimen especial de Empleados de Hogar*) decreased by about 60,000. Between January 2005

[15] There are different forms of working irregularly: without a working permit, working in another geographic region or activity than allowed with the restricted permit, not renewing the initial working permit, working with a temporary work permit and not returning home but working for another employer, and students working although they only have student visa (Aguilera Izquierdo 2006: 176).

and January 2006 there had been an increase from 70,000 to 221,000 (i.e., from 16.9% to 31.7%) registered foreign women in this category (mainly from Eastern Europe and Latin America), but these women did not fall into an irregular status again. Instead, they became part of the general social security system (*Régimen General*). This can be explained by the fact that regularization in the domestic work sector had been much easier, so obviously a large number of women used this way as a means to get their "papers", although they probably had another job and then changed jobs again during 2006 (Pajares Alonso, 2007: 221). When looking at other sectors (now for both sexes), one can see that the construction, commerce and hotel industries experienced increases, while agriculture and the domestic work industry lost workers. According to interviews conducted with a farmers' association by Arango and Finotelli (2009: 89), only 10% to 20% of regularized immigrants worked in this industry at the end of 2007. Similar studies (Ferri et al. 2006; Pumares Fernández 2006) corroborate the finding that shifts in the labor market have occurred (especially from the domestic and agricultural industries to the service and autonomous industries)

This indicates a certain level of upward mobility of the regularized immigrant workers. Since there has been a steady and increasing influx of new immigrants over a long period of time, at first glance the statistics seemed to suggest that immigrants remain at the same low level of the labor market. However, the large figures masked the fact that the relatively smaller group of longer staying migrants can receive a higher position in the social system (Pumares Fernández 2006: 623)—even though the data (for January 2007) shows that more than 40% of all foreigners in the social security system did unskilled work (Pajares Alonso 2007: 222). However, according to research conducted in the autonomous region of Navarre labor transitions of immigrants showed a positive effect: seven in ten immigrants staying irregularly in 2000 had a job by the year 2003, and irregular work within the group of legally staying immigrants decreased by 50%. Almost half of all unskilled day laborers left agriculture during this time, as did one in three domestic workers. Altogether, four in ten immigrant workers moved from these "unprotected" sectors into more desirable ones (Cachón Rodríguez 2009: 242, citing Laparra 2008 176f.). Cachón Rodríguez (2009: 244) calls this process "upward counter mobility" because, as the data of the National Immigrant Survey showed, the majority of newly-arrived immigrants had found their first jobs on a considerably lower level than the one they had in their countries of origin before migrating. Therefore, the observable upward mobility is a regaining of socioeconomic status, although there is some form of glass ceiling, given that immigrants rarely find white-collar jobs.[16] However, this

16 Of the interviewed immigrants in the National Immigrants Survey only 2.8% reached a technical profession and 2.3% an administrative one (Instituto Nacional de Estadística 2009a: 37).

upward mobility affects only a smaller amount of immigrants, the National Immigrant Survey showing that in total 61% of all workers remain on their level[17] and about 20% even show downward mobility.

Social Integration/Living Conditions

Once stability in the residence status and stability in working conditions are achieved, stability in living conditions is sought after. One of the aspects of this stability is a decent form of living and having access to proper housing. Being irregular implies considerable disadvantages in this respect because the official real estate market is virtually closed to irregular immigrants. Without "papers" it is impossible to get a mortgage or to rent a flat. Consequently, many persons have to rely on subletting by fellow countrymen, friends or relatives (Colectivo IOE 2005: 208). Studies have shown that in agricultural regions irregular migrants are forced to live in small barns, shelters, warehouses, half-demolished houses, hovels or even tents, shacks, and abandoned greenhouses. In cities, irregular migrants are often housed in the oldest and/or most degenerated districts (Fernández/Checa 2003; Requena 2003). But there are differences in time and between regions; the housing conditions for irregular immigrants on the Canary Islands were considered somewhat better than on the Iberian Peninsula (Parreño/Guerra 2006). Generally, it can be stated that regularization gives important momentum for stabilization. For example, after the regularization of 2005 it was reported that Ecuadorians started to buy flats right after the process. However, this development has to be seen in context with the general level of integration and the length of stay in the different communities. Other communities, like the Bolivians, who have a shorter immigration history in Spain and therefore are less established, did not follow this pattern to the same extent as the Ecuadorians (Pajares 2009: 67).

Generally speaking, the legal status of the immigrants is perceived as the decisive factor for social integration. Having "papers" not only signifies having legal residence status but also access to work, housing and society as a whole. Of course, aspects such as language proficiency, cultural proximity, the length of stay and the existence of social networks also have a certain influence, but the "papers" are the decisive factor (Díez Nicolás/Ramírez Lafita 2001: 139f.). Having mentioned social networks, Diéz Nicolás (2005: 70) points out that if irregular immigrants receive help in the regularization process such networks, especially those of family members and friends, offer much more help than any other source (authorities, NGOs, etc.). Only one in

---

17 Wagner (2010: 328) for Ecuadorian domestic workers.

five immigrants interviewed in the polls stated not to have received any help of this kind.

Family Reunification

Another mid-term effect of regularization and growing stability is family reunification, which in itself is another indicator of an intended longer stay in the country. There is no specific data on the nexus of regularization and the application for a family reunification visa, but embassies and consulates of the main countries of origin of regularized immigrants reported an increase in applications in the years after the 2000/2001 and 2005 regularizations (Arango/Finotelli 2009: 88). However, there is some reason to believe that processes of family reunification did not start until after the migrants had achieved legal status. The National Immigrant Survey of 2007 confirmed that about 84% of married foreigners lived together with their spouses. While research shows that the average time for family reunification (of the spouse) is two years in Spain, half of the interviewees stated that they were already living together with their spouse one year after arrival, while only 25% of them took more than three years. This is a strong indicator that such family reunifications take place despite legal regulations, because the shortest time possible for the proceeding is slightly above one and a half years, and this applies only in cases where the applicant stayed legally from the very beginning, because the prescribed waiting time is one year and furnishing proof of sufficient means for living and the normal delay in the issuance of a visa lead to even longer waiting time. Thus, the migration pattern that emerges here is that both spouses enter the country to find work, rather than one partner staying at home (González Ferrer 2008). Unlike in northern countries, family reunification is not yet one of the main immigration patterns. The most recent figures on residence permits as of 31 December 2009 show that only 229,200 persons hold a temporary residence permit for reasons of family reunification (Observatorio Permanente de la Inmigración 2010: 8).

The next step after successful family reunification is naturalization. Interviews with immigrant associations conducted by Arango and Finotelli (forthcoming) confirmed that naturalization was one of the foremost objectives of immigrants after they achieved the other steps discussed above. This objective is significantly easier to achieve for Latin Americans who need only two years of regular residence in Spain, compared to ten years for other foreigners. Indeed, in the aftermath of the regularization processes since 2000, there was a fivefold increase in the number of naturalized Latin Americans in comparison to that of migrants from other regions of the world, from a total of 16,743 naturalizations in 2001 to 84,170 in 2008. While 58% of all naturalizations were from Latin Americans in 2001, this group accounted for 81% in 2008.

Final Considerations

The example of Spain shows that over the years different approaches to regularization were employed to address the problem of irregular migration. Given the multifaceted character of (irregular) migration, regularization is only one of several specially-tailored approaches used to prevent and combat the phenomenon. The figures presented in this essay may lead one to believe that regularization is indeed the measure of choice, although many critics have argued that regularization has a strong "pull effect" that is conducive to more illegal immigration. All things considered, however, regularization is neither a universal remedy to nor a trigger of irregular migration. There are many reasons for irregular migration that are intertwined with a whole array of migration regulations (especially in Spain, with its relatively limited access to the legal labor market), so there can be no simple solution. Generally, regularizations have not impeded the reappearance of considerable stocks of irregular migrants in many years. But surely it was more the demand of the Spanish labor market and the widespread knowledge or anticipation that work was available in Spain, rather than the "pull effect" of regularizations (and possibly less the effect of one process itself than the expectation of regularly recurring processes. Regularizations were responsible for uncovering a good part of the underground economy and bringing the state considerable additional contributions in the form of social security benefits. In terms of foreign and European policy, such a strategy was not uncontested and on the European level there was the attempt to prohibit future mass regularizations. However, due to Spanish opposition, this attempt was unsuccessful.

As far as the migrants themselves are concerned, the conclusion derived from the National Immigrant Survey holds true, especially for irregular ones: In contrast to the hypothesis that people emigrate to find a better life but actually chase after an illusion without any real basis—an image perpetuated by the media with photos of shipwrecks and stranded or even dead migrants—the data presents a different picture. Notwithstanding existing difficulties, immigrants are able to adapt to their situation (Instituto Nacional de Estadística 2009a: 32), even more so if they are given the opportunity to regularize, with all the consequences: stabilization of work and life, family reunification, naturalization, and, at least since 2005, a reduction of the quota of irregularity (mainly as a result of the enlargement of the EU). But with the emerging economic crisis since 2008, the situation has begun to change. Rising unemployment has made it more difficult for recently regularized immigrants to have their temporary residence permits renewed. Irregular immigrants have also found it more difficult to find a job in the shadow economy a minimum requirement to be regularized on the basis of rootedness. The future will show if the Spanish government will impede strict access regulations to reduce the influx of needed foreign workers again—with the consequences that have been seen in the past—once the economy will recover and start growing.

References

Aguilera Izquierdo, R. (2006): El acceso de los inmigrantes irregulares al mercado de trabajo: Los procesos de regularización extraordinaria y el arraigo social y laboral. In: Revista del Ministerio de Trabajo y Asuntos Sociales N° 63, pp. 175-195.

Aja, E. (2006): La evolución de la normativa sobre inmigración. In: Aja, Eliseo/Arango, Joaquín (eds.): Veinte años de inmigración en España. Perspectivas jurídica y sociológica (1985-2004). Barcelona: CIDOB, pp. 17-44.

Alberdi Bidaguren, J./Bidaurratzaga Aurre, E. (2008): La nueva política exterior y de cooperación de España con el continente africano. El asociacionismo interesado del Plan África. In: Revista CIDOB d'Afers Internacionals, 84, pp. 201-220.

Aparicio, R./Tornos, A. et al. (2008): Combating illegal employment of foreigners in Spain: Scale and reasons behind the phenomenon; laws and policies against. In: Kupiszewski, M./Mattila, Heikki (eds.): Addressing the irregular employment of immigrants in the European Union: Between sanctions and rights. Budapest: IOM, pp. 251-296.

Aparicio Wilhelmi, M./Roig Molés, E. (2006): La entrada por razones laborales y el trabajo de los extranjeros. El progresivo desarrollo de un sistema ordenado de entrada laboral. In: Aja, Eliseo/Arango, Joaquín (eds.): Veinte años de inmigración en España. Perspectivas jurídica y sociológica (1985-2004). Barcelona: CIDOB, pp. 145–174.

Aragón Bombín, R. (1994): Balance del proceso de regularización y los nuevos proyectos para la integración de los inmigrantes. In: Aragón Bombín, R. et al. (eds.): Regularización de trabajadores y reagrupación familiar de inmigrantes extranjeros en España (Itinera Cuadernos nº 6). Barcelona: Fundación Paulino Torras Domènech, pp. 11-21.

Arango, J./Finotelli, C. (2009): Spain. In: Baldwin-Edwards, M./Kraler, A. (eds.): REGINE – Regularisation in Europe. Study on practices in the area of regularisation of illegally staying third-country nationals in the Member States of the EU. Appendix A Country Studies. Vienna: ICMPD, pp. 83-93.

Arango, J./Finotelli, C. (forthcoming): Evaluación del proceso extraordinario de normalización del año 2005. Madrid: Ministerio de Trabajo e Inmigración.

Asín Cabrera, A. (2008): Los acuerdos bilaterales suscritos por España en materia migratoria con países del continente africano: especial consideración de la readmisión de inmigrantes en situación irregular. Revista de Derecho Constitucional Europeo 5, n° 10. [online] Available at: www.ugr.es/~redce/REDCE10/articulos/04MAsuncionAsinCabrera.htm [Accessed February 14, 2011].

Baldwin-Edwards, M. (1999): Where free markets reign: Aliens in the twilight zone. In: Baldwin-Edwards, M./Arango, J. (eds.): Immigrants in the informal economy in Southern Europe. London/Portland: Frank Cass, pp. 1-15.

Baldwin-Edwards, M. (2009): Greece. In: Baldwin-Edwards, M./Kraler, A. (eds.): REGINE – Regularisation in Europe. Study on practices in the area of regularisation of illegally staying third-country nationals in the Member States of the EU. Appendix A Country Studies. Vienna: ICMPD, pp. 41-69.

Baldwin-Edwards, M./Kraler, A. (2009): REGINE – Regularisation in Europe. Study on practices in the area of regularisation of illegally staying third-country nationals in the Member States of the EU. Final Report. Vienna: ICMPD.

Cachón Rodríguez, L. (2009): La "España inmigrante": marco discriminatorio, mercado de trabajo y políticas de integración. Barcelona: Anthropos.

Carling, J. (2007a): Unauthorized migration from Africa to Spain. In: International Migration 45, 4, pp. 3-37.

Carling, J. (2007b): Migration control and migrant fatalities at the Spanish-African borders. In: International Migration Review 41, 3, pp. 316-343.

Cebolla Boado, H./González Ferrer, A. (2008): La inmigración en España (2000-2007). De la gestión den flujos a la integración de los inmigrantes. Madrid: Centro de Estudios Políticos y Constitucionales.

Colectivo Ioé (1987): Los inmigrantes en España. Documentación Social, Nr. 66. Madrid: Cáritas Española.

Colectivo Ioé (2005): Inmigración y vivienda en España. Documentos de Observatorio Permanente de Inmigración 7. Madrid: Ministerio de Trabajo y Asuntos Sociales.

Díez Nicolás, J. (2005): Las dos caras de la inmigración. Documentos de Observatorio Permanente de Inmigración 3. Madrid: Ministerio de Trabajo y Asuntos Sociales.

Díez Nicolás, J./Ramírez Lafita, M. J. (2001): La voz de los inmigrantes. Colección Inmigración y Refugio 4. Madrid: Ministerio de Trabajo y Asuntos Sociales.

Eigmüller, M. (2007): Grenzsicherungspolitik. Funktion und Wirkung der europäischen Außengrenze. Wiesbaden: VS-Verlag.

European Commission (2006): Communication from the Commisison to the Concil and the Parliament – The Global approach to migration one year on: Towards a comprehensive European migration policy. COM (2006) 735 final. Brussels.

European Commission (2008): Communication from the Commission to the European Parliament, the Council, the European Economic and Social Committee and the Committee of the Regions. A common immigration policy for Europe: Principles, actions, and tools. COM (2008) 394 final. Brussels.

European Commission (2009): Report from the Commission pursuant to Article 4 and Article 5 of the Council Decision of 5 October 2006 on the establishment of a mutual information mechanism concerning Member States' measures in the areas of asylum and immigration. COM (2009) 687 final. Brussels.

Fernández Gutierrez, F./Checa Olmos, J. C. (2003): Vivienda y segregación de los inmigrantes en Andalucía. Scripta Nova. Revista electrónica de geografía y ciencias sociales, VII, 146 (061). [online] Available at: www.ub.es/geocrit/sn/sn-146(061).htm [Accessed February 14, 2011].

Ferrero Turrión, R./López Sala, A. (2009): Nuevas dinámicas de gestión de las migraciones en España: el caso de los acuerdos bilaterales de trabajadores con países de origen. In: Revista del Ministerio de Trabajo y Asuntos Sociales N° 80, pp. 119-132.

Ferri, J./Gómez-Plana, A. G./Martín-Montaner, J. A. (2006): Illegal immigration booms and welfare in the host country. In: European Journal for Population 22, pp. 353-370.

García Martínez, J. (2006): Procesos de regularización y Unión Europea. In: Pinyol, G. (coord.): Inmigración y derechos de ciudadanía. Barcelona: CIDOB, pp. 37-44.

González-Enríquez, C. (2009a): Spain, the cheap model. Irregularity and regularisation as immigration management policies. In: European Journal of Migration and Law 11, pp. 139–157.

González-Enríquez, C. (2009b): Country report Spain. Report for the European research project CLANDESTINO. Undocumented migration – Counting the uncountable. Data and trends across Europe. Hamburg: HWWI. [online] Available at: irregular-migration.hwwi.net [Accessed February 14, 2011].

González-Enríquez, C. (2009c): Update report Spain: Estimate on irregular migration for Spain in 2009. Database on Irregular Migration. Update report November 2009. Hamburg: HWWI. [online] Available at: irregular-migration.hwwi.net [Accessed February 14, 2011].

González-Enríquez, C./Triandafyllidou, A. (2009): Introduction: Comparing the new hosts of Southern Europe. In: European Journal of Migration and Law 11, pp. 109-118.

González Ferrer, A. (2008): La reagrupación familiar en España: algunas cifras para el debate. In: Aja, E./Arango, J./Alonso, J. Oliver (eds.): La inmigración en la encrucijada. Anuario de la inmigración en España Edición 2008. Barcelona: CIDOB, pp. 120-137.

Guerrero, F. (2008): Las relaciones España- África subsahariana: ¿a remolque o en la vanguardia de la UE?. In: Barbé, E. (coord.): España en Europa 2004-2008. Monografías del Observatorio de Política Exterior Europea 4. Bellaterra (Barcelona): Institut Universitari d'Estudis Europeus.

Hernández i Sagrera, R. (2008): FRONTEX: Projection at the European level of the vision of Spain on border control? In: Barbé, Esther (ed.): Spain in Europe 2004-2008. Monograph of the Observatory of European Foreign Policy 4. Bellaterra (Barcelona): Institut Universitari d'Estudis Europeus.

Instituto Nacional de Estadística (2008): Encuesta de Población Activa (EPA). Primer semestre 2008. (Nota de prensa, 25 de abril de 2008). Madrid: INE.

Instituto Nacional de Estadística (2009a): Encuesta Nacional de Inmigrantes 2007: una monografía. Madrid: INE.

Instituto Nacional de Estadística (2009b): Encuesta de Población Activa (EPA). Primer semestre 2009. (Nota de prensa, 24 de abril de 2009). Madrid: INE.

Izquierdo Escribano, A. (1992): La inmigración en España 1980-1990. Madrid: Ministerio de Trabajo y Seguridad Social.

Jeandesboz, J. (2008): Reinforcing the surveillance of EU borders: The future development of FRONTEX and EUROSUR. Challenge Research Paper N° 11. Brussels: Centre for European Policy Studies.

Kreienbrink, A. (2004): Einwanderungsland Spanien – Migrationspolitik zwischen Europäisierung und nationalen Interessen. Frankfurt am Main/London: IKO – Verlag für Interkulturelle Kommunikation (also available in Spanish: España, país de inmigración. Evolución política entre europeización e intereses nacionales. Madrid: Ministerio de Trabajo e Inmigración 2008).

Kreienbrink, A. (2009): Las políticas migratorias en tiempos de crisis económica. In: Bernecker, W./Iñíguez Hernández, W./Maihold, G. (eds.): ¿Crisis? ¿Qué crisis? España en busca de su camino. Madrid/Frankfurt am Main: Iberoamericana/Vervuert, pp. 273-294.
Laubenthal, B. (2005): "Papiere für alle". Proteste illegaler Einwanderer in Murcia (Spanien). In: IMIS-Beiträge 27, pp. 109-129.
Laparra, M. (2008): La dinámica de la integración social de los inmigrantes y su impacto en la sociedad de acogida. La perspectiva desde Navarra. In: Política y Sociedad 45, pp. 167-186.
Levinson, A. (2005): The regularisation of unauthorized migrants: Literature survey and country case studies. Centre on Migration, Policy and Society. University of Oxford.
Ministerio del Interior (2010): Balance de la lucha contra la inmigración ilegal 2009. Madrid. [online] Available at: www.mir.es/DGRIS/Balances/Balance_2009/pdf/np011502_bal_lucha_inm_ilegal_2009.pdf [Accessed February 14, 2011].
Ministerio de Trabajo y Asuntos Sociales (2006): Balance de la Secretaría de Estado de Inmigración y Emigración de las embarcaciones interceptadas en 2005. In: Notas de prensa 5. January 2006. Madrid.
Nini, R. (2002): Diario de un ilegal. Guadarrama (Madrid): ediciones del oriente y del mediterráneo.
Observatorio Permanente de la Inmigración (2010):
Informe trimestral. Extranjeros con certificado de registro o tarjeta de residencia en vigor y extranjeros con autorización de estancia por estudios en vigor a 31 de diciembre Madrid: Ministerio de Trabajo e Inmigración. [online] Available at: extranjeros.mtin.es/es/InformacionEstadistica/Informes/Extranjeros31Diciembre 2009 /Archivos/Informe_Trimestral_31diciembre_2009.pdf [Accessed February 14, 2011].
Pajares, Miguel, ed. (2004): Inmigración irregular en Cataluña. Análisis y propuestas. Barcelona: CERES/CCOO.
Pajares Alonso, M. (2007): El proceso de regularización de 2005: sus efectos posteriores sobre la inserción laboral de la población inmigrada. In: Aja, E./Arango, J. (eds.): La inmigración en España en 2006. Anuario de inmigración y políticas de inmigración. Barcelona: CIDOB, pp. 212–225.
Pajares, M. (2009): Inmigración y mercado de trabajo. Informe 2009 (Documentos del Observatorio Permanente de Inmigración 21). Madrid: Ministerio de Trabajo e Inmigración.
Parreño, J. M./Guerra, R. (2006): La vivienda de los inmigrantes indocumentados residentes en Canarias (España). In: Scripta Nova. Revista electrónica de geografía y ciencias sociales X, 207. [online] Available at: www.ub.es/geocrit/sn/sn-207.htm [Accessed February 14, 2011].
Pérez Yruela, M./and Rinken, S. (2005): La integración de los inmigrantes en la sociedad andaluza. Córdoba: CSIC.
Pinyol, G. (2008): Spain's immigration policy as a new instrument of external action. In: Barbé, E. (ed.): Spain in Europe 2004-2008. Monograph of the Observatory of European Foreign Policy 4. Bellaterra (Barcelona): Institut Universitari d'Estudis Europeus.
Requena Hidalgo, J. (2003): "La peor casa en el peor barrio". Barrios de inmigración y marginalidad en la periferia urbana de Barcelona. El caso de Badalona. In

:Scripta Nova. Revista electrónica de geografía y ciencias sociales. Barcelona: Universidad de Barcelona, 1 vol. VII, núm. 146 (058). [online] Available at: www.ub.es/geocrit/sn/sn-146(058).htm [Accessed February 14, 2011].

Ruiz Olabuénaga, J. I. /Ruiz Vieytez, E. J./Vicente Torrado, T. L. (1999): Los inmigrantes irregulares en España. La vida por un sueño. Bilbao: Universidad de Deusto.

Santos Arnau, L. (1993): De nuevo sobre el trabajador extranjero y la regularización de 1991 (Itinera Cuadernos nº 5). Barcelona: Fundación Paulino Torras Domènech.

Sohler, K. (2009): France. In: Baldwin-Edwards, M./Kraler, A. (eds.): REGINE Regularisations in Europe. Study on practices in the area of regularisation of illegally staying third-country nationals in the Member States of the EU. Appendix A. Vienna: ICMPD, pp. 1-40.

Solanes Corella, A. (2008): Combatiendo la inmigración irregula: La insuficiencia de la regularizaciones y las sanciones. In: Alberdi Bidaguren, J./Goizueta Vértiz, J. (coords.): Algunos retos de la inmigración en el siglo XXI. Madrid: Marcial Pons, pp. 201-231.

Suárez-Navaz, L./Macià Pareja, R./Moreno García, Á. (2007): El Estado y las luchas de los sin papeles en España: ¿una extensión de la ciudadanía?. In: Suárez-Navaz, L./Macià Pareja, R./Moreno García, A. (eds.): Las luchas dc los sin papeles y la extensión de la ciudadanía. Perspectivas críticas desde Europa y Estados Unidos. Madrid: Movimiento, pp. 185–213.

Trinidad García, M. L. (2002): Los inmigrantes irregulares en la Ley 4/2000 y en su reforma: una regularización que no cesa. In: Revista de derecho migratorio y extranjería Nº 1, pp. 99-112.

Wagner, H. (2010): Dasein für Andere – Dasein als Andere in Europa. Ecuadorianische Hausarbeiterinnen in Privathaushalten und katholischen Gemeinden Madrids. Wiesbaden: VS-Verlag.

“It's Been the Best Journey of My Life”: Governing Migration and Strategies of Migrants at Europés Borders: Morocco

Gerda Heck

Introduction

In the evening of June 22, 2008, the Spanish national team was in a penalty shootout against the Italian team in the quarter-final of the European Football Championship. At the same time, a few dozens of sub-Saharan migrants tried to break through the border fence between Morocco and Melilla in an attempt to reach the Spanish exclave in mainland Africa. Apparently they had hoped that the Spanish security forces would be too distracted by the dramatic last minutes of the match to notice. However, they were stopped and pushed back by the Moroccan authorities while still on the Moroccan side.

This was the second incident of this kind within 24 hours. On the previous night, 70 Africans had managed to reach Melilla in much the same way. According to the Spanish newspaper *El País*, about 50 of them were later caught and deported back to Morocco (El Pais 2008).

In the fall of 2005, the border fences around the Spanish exclaves in North Africa, Ceuta and Melilla, were upgraded and fortified with financial support of the European Union, rendering these fences nearly impossible to scale and therefore making many migrants change their routes. The two incidents described above were the first attempts by migrants to break through the border fences around the exclaves since the installation of the new fence.

These attempts, although unsuccessful, illustrate various aspects of the realities and effects of European migration policies in the countries neighboring the EU: the inherent conflicts on the borders and in the so-called transit spaces in the periphery resulting from the reorganization of European migration policy (Balibar 1998: 216ff.) and the strategies the migrants develop in their hope to realize their dream of migrating to Europe. Borders cannot be sealed hermetically. The experience and knowledge that exclusionary border policies have had limited success has led to changes in the political strategies of European immigration policy over the last decade. At the turn of the millennium, the then EU Commissioner for Justice and Home Affairs, António Vitorino, had already acknowledged that Europe had lost its battle against clandestine migration. The so-called zero-immigration policies of the previous twenty years, he argued, had done nothing to halt the flow of clandestine migrants. It was suggested that an opening policy be introduced (Sassen 2000). The official use of the term "migration management" instead of "migration control" is indicative of this change in Europe's approach, which had already begun in the mid-1990s. The shift away from rigid and undifferentiated migration control to the regulation or, rather, management of migration movements has been generally welcomed by liberals as a form of "rational handling" in the face of ongoing and increasing migrant mobility. In this sense, dialogue and cooperation with third countries have become important instruments of European migration policy. Economic aid, the facilitation of allocation of visas, and legal immigration options for the citizens of EU neighbor states all depend on the willingness to cooperate in terms of border control and on the consent to the externalization of European migration policy on their territory (European Commission 2007). Actual practice, however, has nothing to do with what the term "migration management" suggests. There is no shift away from restrictive migration policy—what happens is the exact opposite.

In a communication of May 16, 2007, the EU Commission proposed the negotiation of so-called mobility partnerships between the EU and third countries to facilitate circular and temporary migration in response to the labor market needs within the EU, which would counteract undocumented immigration to European states through the implementation of legal migration options and migration control in third countries and implement enhanced possibilities of mobility between third countries and the EU in terms of legal migration opportunities and short-term movements (issuance of short-stay visas) particularly to combat irregular migration. The extent of the mobility partnerships depends on the commitment of the third countries regarding the struggle against so-called illegal migration.

This includes, among other things, commitment by the third countries to readmit its own deported nationals, third-country nationals, and stateless persons who enter the EU through the territory of these countries; efforts to improve border control and/or border management; specific measures and initiatives to combat migrant smuggling and human trafficking; and initiatives to discourage illegal migration through targeted information campaigns (European Commission 2007).

In the following, I will describe how the changes in European migration policy effect the situation of sub-Saharan migrants in Morocco and illustrate the strategies migrants develop to achieve their goal of reaching their intended destinations. In doing so, I will also consider different discourses and practices concerned with governing migration. This text is based on several ethnographic field research trips to Morocco which I undertook between 2006 and 2009.[1]

---

1 The places and cities I visited several times included Oujda, Nador, Tangier, Rabat, Casablanca, and the Spanish exclaves Ceuta and Melilla. During my stays, I conducted interviews with various actors in the field of migration: staff

Morocco as a Country of Emigration, Transit Migration and Immigration

Over the last fifteen years, Morocco, for many decades an emigration country, has become an important transit country for migrants from Sub-Saharan Africa on their way to Europe. This fact has received extensive public and media attention in Europe in recent years. However, with regard to migration flows within the Maghreb, one has to understand that cross-border movements between Sub-Saharan Africa and the Maghreb have existed for centuries (Lahlou 2008). According to Hein de Haas (2007), there are probably more sub-Saharan Africans living permanently in the Maghreb than in Europe. Therefore, common views which consider North African states to be just a transit zone to Europe are inaccurate (de Haas 2008). Nevertheless, each year several thousand sub-Saharan migrants from such countries as Sierra Leone, Liberia, and Ivory Coast cross Morocco on their way to Europe. Since the turn of the millennium, there have also been an increasing number of migrants from countries such as Nigeria, Ghana, Sudan, and Cameroon. Migrants heading to Europe from Asian countries such as India, Pakistan, and Bangladesh pass through Morocco as well (de Haas 2007). And although the image of the sub-Saharan migrant has been predominantly male for a long time, there are a growing number of women who travel through Morocco to Europe by land (Interview with Hicham Baraka, 9/15/2008, Association Beni Znassen pour la Culture Developpment et Solidarité [ABCDS], Oujda).[2]

According to estimates, there are currently between 10,000 and 15,000 sub-Saharan migrants living in Morocco (Lahlou 2008: 15). At the same time, there are about 2.5 million migrants of Moroccan descent living in Europe. The importance of the Moroccan emigrants becomes clear when considering the scale of remittance transfers. With an official annual total of

members of supranational organizations such as the United Nations High Commission for Refugees (UNHCR), the International Organization for Migration (IOM), NGOs, human rights activists, researchers, and migrants, mainly from sub-Saharan countries. Conducting longer interviews with sub-Saharan migrants, however, proved to be particularly difficult because they were too anxious not to attract public attention and risk being arrested by Moroccan police. In such cases, I just talked to them and took notes afterwards. During my stays, I only had a few opportunities to talk to female migrants. It is much more difficult to approach migrant women: aside from their precarious situation, many women rarely leave their homes or the places where they stay in Morocco. Also, many of the female migrants I met were traveling with male companions, such as family members, relatives, acquaintances, and friends, who "protected" them from public attention. The interviews were conducted in Spanish, French, or English. All names were anonymized.

2 In Mehdi Lahlou's empirical research on sub-Saharan migrants in Morocco, 36% of interviewees were women (Lahlou 2008: 19).

US$5.7 billion in remittances, Morocco stands prominent among the remittance-receiving countries. According to recent World Bank estimates, the country was among the developing world's top ten remittance recipients in 2007, behind India, China, Mexico, the Philippines, Romania, Bangladesh, Pakistan, Indonesia, and Egypt (Ratha/Xu 2008).

The majority of sub-Saharan migrants have already traveled for up to two years before they even enter Morocco, having crossed several African countries on foot, by bus or by share taxi. One of these migrants was Jeffrey George, a Nigerian whom I met twice during my research stays in Tangier. He had left Nigeria at the end of 2003 and traveled through the desert in share taxis, on buses, and on trucks. While in Algeria, he had thrown away his passport and crossed the border to Morocco near the border town of Oujda on secret paths. Since then, he has been trying his luck in Morocco, waiting for an opportunity to travel on to Europe. Many migrants have to interrupt their journey from time to time to earn some money or to wait for money to be transferred from relatives in their home country or in Europe.

"What you need during the passage is 'craftiness'. Craftiness, patience, flexibility and courage!" stressed the Cameroonian migrant Emile Bekolo in my interview with him. "On the journey you need to cross several borders: from Mali to Algeria and then from Algeria to Morocco, for example. There are many obstacles you have to overcome, you may have to dupe or bribe police or border officials if they stop you. You have to find someone to guide you over the border, you may have to change your route several times if you realize that you're stuck, or you have to change your tactics. And you need to be patient enough to try to cross the border again and again until you make it." (Interview with Emile Bekolo, 9/22/2008, Rabat). At the time of the interview, Emile had been living in Morocco for about three and a half years and had already unsuccessfully tried to cross the borders to Europe three times.

Even though the majority of these migrants regard Morocco as just a transit country on their way to Europe, a growing number of them find themselves stranded in Morocco when they are unable to continue their journey. According to de Hass (2007), about 10,000 transit migrants have become immigrants, many of them now living in Casablanca, Rabat, and Tangier.

Agreements on Combating "Illegal" Migration Between Morocco and the EU

Since the mid-1990s, the European Union and the Mediterranean buffer states have held regular consultations on how to combat "illegal" migration. The neighboring countries gradually became involved in the process and started to implement externalized border control mechanisms outside the EU's borders.

However, for many years this measure did not make a great impact in Morocco, despite the fact that, in accordance with an agreement signed in 2000, Moroccan nationals who had been intercepted in Europe without documents were readmitted to the country (Holert/ Terkessidis 2006). Even so, the transit migration issue was handled rather carelessly.

Ever since the European Union intensified cooperation with Morocco, the Moroccan police has toughened its stance against migrants.[3] In November 2003, the government passed a law concerning the entry and residence of foreigners on Moroccan territory[4], requiring non-citizens to provide evidence for "means of survival, the reasons for visiting Morocco, and the guarantees for the return" (Sadiqi 2004: 12) and for the first time defining undocumented entry as a criminal offense carrying harsh penalties, with increased penalties for repeat offenders. Undocumented border crossing can be punished by a fine of up to €360 and imprisonment for six months. Migrants who are discovered to be living in Morocco in undocumented status, including visa overstayers, can be punished by imprisonment, fines, and deportation (Sadiqui 2004: 10). The same law also provides for the prosecution of Moroccan citizens who host foreigners without a residence permit or assist them with their transit (Kimball 2007: 124). In 2004, the Moroccan authorities started to intensify their fight against networks specializing in human trafficking (Lahlou 2008: 17).[5] As of 2005, sub-Saharan migrants who are detected by the police are deported to the Algerian borderlands outside the Moroccan border town of Oujda.

In August 2006, government representatives of 30 European and 27 African countries introduced an action plan to combat illegal migration from Africa to Europe which guarantees Morocco additional financial support of €67 million. The Moroccan government used the money to tighten border control and strengthen the police and the judicial system (die tageszeitung, 2006). According to the European Commission, Morocco will receive funds totaling some €600 million between 2007 and 2013, of which €70 million will be allocated for border protection.

---

3 The EU support for the economic transition of North African states is implemented mainly through Mesures d'Accompagnement (MEDA), a program created to encourage and support reform of economic and social structures of Mediterranean partners in view of the establishment of a free trade area around the Mediterranean Sea by 2010. MEDA also targets the stated goal of immigration reduction through advancing (rural) development in countries of origin (de Haas 2008).

4 This law, known as Law No. 02-03, was adopted unanimously by the Moroccan Parliament on May 22, 2003, a few days after the terrorist attacks in Casablanca of May 16, 2003 which killed 45 people (Lahlou 2008: 13).

5 The Moroccan authorities claim to have disbanded 1,800 networks between 2004 and 2008 (Ibid.).

Currently, the EU is providing €24 million to support 18 projects addressing five key issues: 1) the promotion of legal immigration, 2) migrant protection, 3) the preparation of a legal framework, 4) combating illegal immigration, and 5) accompanying measures for repatriation and reintegration in the home countries (von Leipzig 2007).

The latter measures are implemented by IOM, which acts as a non-governmental actor in Morocco. In cooperation with the Moroccan authorities, IOM has been operating in the field of voluntary return of migrants to Sub-Saharan Africa as well as to Asia since the end of 2005 (Interview with Laura Lungarotti, 9/24/2008, IOM Rabat). However, most of the migrants I interviewed expressed serious doubts about the voluntary nature of these repatriations. "What do they mean by 'voluntary'? You don't believe that someone returns voluntarily to his home country after he already made it to Morocco, do you? The people return only if they are at the end of their tether, if there is no other way left for them. How can you call this 'voluntary'," Emile Bekolo emphasized (Interview with Emile Bekolo, 9/22/2008, Rabat). According to IOM, 1,200 migrants had been returned to their countries of origin by September 2008 (Interview with Laura Lungarotti, IOM Rabat, 9/23/2008, Rabat).

There are various reasons for the Moroccan government to be willing to cooperate in migration management and restrictive procedures against transit migrants. I would like to argue that, in addition to such factors as xenophobia, political and economic factors are the main driving force behind Morocco's anti-transit migration activities.

Specifically, Morocco's recent migration policy has been influenced by political pressure from the European Union in general (and Spain in particular) and the Moroccan king's desire to become more integrated with the EU through a free trade agreement, to receive development assistance, and to improve the status of Moroccan emigrants in Europe, thereby sustaining the continual flow of migrant remittances (Kimball 2007: 111). Currently, the EU is Morocco's most important trading partner and, as mentioned earlier, the main destination of Moroccan emigrants (Sadiqi 2004: 2).

There are also adjusted migration opportunities in the context of the mobility partnerships in several European Union countries of destination. Particularly in the south of Spain, there is a heavy demand for seasonal workers. As many as 80% of seasonal workers in Spain are Moroccans; of these, 80% work in the hotel and catering industry. As an example, Moroccan government agencies refer to an agreement with the southern Spanish municipality of Cartaya (Huelva), which hired 10,000 seasonal workers in 2007 (von Leipzig 2007). According to Nora El Qadim (2007), the Moroccan state benefits greatly from the increase in irregular migration. Being one of the strongest European partners in combating "illegal" migration, Morocco has considerably strengthened its position in negotiations with the EU and its member states.

The Effects of Restrictive Migration Policies

Up until 2005, most transit migrants went to cities and places on the north coast of Morocco, hoping either to cross the Strait of Gibraltar to Spain on small boats called *pateras* or to scale the border fences around the Spanish exclaves of Melilla and Ceuta. In the summer of 2002, the Spanish authorities installed the radar-supported Integrated System of Exterior Surveillance (SIVE) on the coast of Andalusia. In 2003, Spain and Morocco began to collaborate in joint naval patrol and implemented readmission agreements in return for aid (de Haas 2008: 5). After these measures were implemented, passage by sea not only became much more difficult and dangerous, but also much more expensive. In the fall of 2005, the fences around the two Spanish exclaves of Ceuta and Melilla were fortified. They are now six meters high, topped with razor wire and guarded by watchtowers about 40 meters apart. Between the fences there are directional microphones and search lights installed, as well as a tear gas deterrent system. These reinforcements were funded by the EU, which promised Morocco around €40 million to improve its border enforcement (EU 2005).

As mentioned above, since 2005 the Moroccan authorities have regularly been conducting raids in Moroccan cities and deporting undocumented sub-Saharan migrants to the Algerian borderlands outside the Moroccan border town of Oujda. The majority of the deported migrants subsequently make their way back to where they had stayed before, such as El Aaiún, and Rabat. Many of them have done this several times, among them interviewee Jeffrey George in Tangier. He has been arrested and deported to the Algerian borderland outside Oujda twice. Like many other immigrants, he covered the 600 kilometers back to Tangier on foot, mostly at night, along the railway tracks. Migrants cannot use public transportation for fear of being arrested by the police who have significantly increased controls on trains and buses, and truck drivers charge hefty amounts for a ride.

In reaction to these developments, many migrants have shifted their travel routes to the south, to the coasts of West Sahara, Mauritania, and Senegal, from which they to try reach the Canary Islands in *cayucos*, as they call unused fishing boats (Interview with Jean-Marie Kalla, 1/6/2007, Rabat). Since 2006, the European border control agency Frontex has been particularly instrumental in intercepting the boats of immigrants off the coast of the Canary Islands long before they reach the gates to Europe. In 2006, the agency prevented more than 5,000 migrants from crossing over to the Canaries (Frontex

Annual Report 2006: 12), and in 2008, 5,969 migrants were intercepted off the Canary Islands and returned to the African coasts (Pro Asyl 2009).

However, the migration route through Morocco was never given up. "To overcome the fences of Ceuta or Melilla has become nearly impossible", Paula Domingo, a Carmelites and human rights activist based in Ceuta points out." Still, about 15 to 20 immigrants per week manage to sneak into Ceuta. The majority of them are Asian migrants who cross the border either hidden in cars or with forged documents. Such a passage costs approximately €1,800" (Interview with Paula Domingo, 9/29/2006, Ceuta). A new method is to swim across the water into the exclave. Equipped with a neoprene suit and on the towline of a good swimmer, immigrants manage to get into the town. With the help of such a swimmer Jeffrey George managed to reach Ceuta after nearly four years in Morocco.

Places of Transit

The university town of Oujda is located near the border to Algeria. In 1999, Oujda became a transit station for migrants from Sub-Saharan Africa, who usually reach the town after having crossed the Algerian desert.

In Oujda itself most migrants went to the university campus and waited there until they had the opportunity to continue their journey. For many years, there were about 50 to 100 migrants staying there at any given time. The places for stopovers where migrants rest, gather together, and organize their daily lives are generally well-known among the travelers. Some get these addresses in their hometowns before setting off, others learn about them during the journey.

Since December 2006, the situation in the border town has changed dramatically. Large-scale nationwide raids take place regularly in cities such as Rabat, Casablanca, El Aaiún, and Nador. The Moroccan authorities arrest men, women, and children and deport them to the Algerian borderland. The deportees often go into hiding, waiting until nightfall and then walking along the shut-down railroad line back to Oujda.[6] Due to the intensified controls on buses and trains leaving Oujda, it has become extremely difficult for the migrants to return to where they had stayed before. From January to July 2007, the largest self-organized migrant camp in Morocco existed on the university campus of Oujda, with at times as many as 700 migrants living there. At the end of July 2007, the camp was raided and destroyed by police and military forces. Since then, most migrants in Oujda have been staying in smaller

6 The border between Morocco and Algeria was closed in 1994 after Morocco suspected Algerian involvement in an attack at a Marrakesh hotel.

groups in mini camps called *tranquilos*[7] in the outskirts of the city and in the woods close to the border. Some of these *tranquilos* are mobile, which means that they can be taken down within minutes and set up in another area. In this way the migrants can escape the continuous persecution by the authorities.[8] According to estimates, around 1,700 migrants are currently staying in Oujda (Interview with Hicham Baraka, 9/15/2008, ABCDS, Oujda). On an almost daily basis, the Moroccan authorities raid and destroy *tranquilos* in the region and deport all inhabitants to the Algerian borderland.

The deportation strategy of Moroccan police does not seem to make any sense at all, because after a few days the deported migrants show up in Oujda again. This was the case with Moses Janneh, whom I interviewed in Oujda in September 2007. At that time he had been living in Morocco for four years, waiting for an opportunity to move on. He had already tried to enter the Spanish exclave of Melilla three times, every time ending up in the borderland between Morocco and Algeria (Interview with Moses Janneh, 9/5/2007, Oujda).

In the summer of 2007, Moroccan authorities claimed to have intercepted more than 80,000 migrants without valid residence permits within the first half of the year (Koufen 2007). Compared to estimates on the number of transit migrants in the country, this figure hardly seems believable. Even human rights activists have expressed doubts about these data. Actually, on closer examination, it appears that the Moroccan government may be trying to prove its rigid stance against transit migration by deporting migrants three or four times. This is consistent with the results of Collyer (2006: 23), according to which transit migrants in Morocco are usually deported back to the border one to three times. Some of the migrants he interviewed had even been deported as many as seven times.

Living in Transit

It was evident from all of the talks and interviews that migrants usually have to struggle to satisfy their basic needs, such as food, clothing, housing, medical care, and so on, so they are constantly under pressure to solve basic problems. Medical assistance is provided by some NGOs such as Médecins Sans Frontières (MSF) and Médecins du Monde (MDM) and church organiza-

7 The term *tranquilo* is Spanish, meaning “rest” or “calm”. A *tranquilo* is usually a small camp with three or four tents in the forest, in the outskirts of Oujda, or in the borderland between Morocco and Algeria. Between 8 and 30 people live in a *tranquilo*.

8 Since the summer of 2008, however, 300 migrants have again been camping out on the university campus in the border town.

tions, though it is usually limited to emergency care and drugs. Most of the sub-Saharan migrants live in shantytowns and in the outskirts of cities or, as in the case of Oujda, in self-constructed camps in the forest or on the university campus. Earning opportunities for sub-Saharan migrants are meager. One of the interviewees told me: “You know, most Moroccans do not have a job. Given that, it's obviously even more difficult for sub-Saharans to find one.” (Interview with Jeffrey George, 9/24/2006, Tangier) Most migrants do casual jobs, working at the market or repairing shoes in the streets, some work in the construction industry, others simply beg (Interviews with Jean-Marie Kalla, 1/7/2007, Rabat, and Emile Bekolo 9/22/2008, Rabat). In the migrant neighborhoods of Rabat, such as Takadoum, so-called Afro barbershops and several other businesses have been established to cater specifically to sub-Saharan people. Women sometimes get jobs as housekeepers or they work as sex workers. Another way to earn money is to sell smuggled goods. Migrants who commute between the Algerian town of Maghnia and Oujda often buy MP3 players, mobile phones, and other gadgets in Algeria and try to sell them for a small profit in Oujda (Schapendonk 2008: 138).

In order to cope with life in transit, migrants organize themselves and establish structures and networks during their journey. They keep in touch with their families via mobile phones, fellow travelers, and other important contact persons; travelers learn about new opportunities to cross the border, addresses of friends and useful persons, contact points on their next stages, and so on. Having lived in cities such as Rabat, Tangier, and Casablanca for over four or five years, many migrants already have created a structure in their daily lives. Although they try new routes and different ways from time to time to reach Europe, they return to the cities, using them as a base to rest and earn money. Jean-Marie Kalla said in an interview that in a neighborhood in Rabat where many sub-Saharan migrants live, newcomers do not have to pay rent for the first four weeks. This gives them some time to settle into their new surroundings. After this initial period they have to get along on their own (Interview with Jean-Marie Kalla, 1/7/2007, Rabat).

At their stopovers migrants organize themselves in small communities, usually from 8 to 20 members. These communities are usually formed on the basis of a common language or common national or ethnic heritage and organized hierarchically. Every community elects or determines a so-called chairman as the head of the group. This is often a person with experience in migration or someone who has held a senior position in the home country. In crisis situations, the chairman must be able to quickly make decisions for the rest of the group. The various chairmen of larger areas meet regularly to discuss “issues of organization”, political considerations, and different problems or conflicts within the community. Emile Bekolo pointed out in the interview that to pass through the journey one has to join such communities at the various stops to find someone who can guide you across the border and so on.

What is more, a community offers protection against burglary and violence. But although this structure helps to share information, resolve conflicts, and provide some degree of protection, it does not always benefit the migrants, for it can also sometimes create conflicts and even lead to forms of abuse, corruption and patronage.

So what starts off as an individually considered migration project gradually turns into a collectively organized enterprise in the course of the journey (Alioua 2007). This "communitarization" of immigration, as Moroccan economist Mehdi Lahlou (2008: 22) describes it, also facilitates the flow of information within the group and leads to a strong sense of solidarity which can balance to a large extent—also in psychological terms—the effects of precarious situations and poverty of the migrants during their journey.

Conclusion

Even though there are no reliable figures on transit migrants, some studies (de Collyer 2006; de Haas 2007; Kimball 2007) have assumed that the numbers have not decreased, but rather that the origin of the migrants, the migration routes, and the strategies used to cross the border have changed. Migration control does not hinder migration, it just locates migrants in a special situation characterized by a form of social hierarchy, which Etienne Balibar (2003: 93) has called the "new system of Apartheid" with regard to Europe's migration regime. By implementing new immigration policies far away from the European borders, it prevents the migrants from making any claims against EU member states by reclassifying these migrants as "illegal" and disenfranchising them once again before they can even enter the European Union. This has significant effects on the situation of transit migrants, in that they have to take greater risks and use longer, increasingly expensive routes.

The externalization of European migration policy to Africa, outside the European borders, can be seen as a neo-colonial act (Düvell 2002). Yet at the same time it would be wrong to interpret this process as a sovereign act of the European Union alone, as a simple enlargement of competencies and power. It has become clear that various factors are important in this process. The Moroccan state itself benefits greatly from the increase in irregular migration. Being one of the strongest committed European partners in the "fight against illegal migration", Morocco has considerably strengthened its position in negotiations with the EU and its member states regarding financial support, economic integration, immigration quota for Moroccans, and the position of Moroccan immigrants living in Europe. The implementation of the policies of cooperation and dialogue between European and African states, the inclusion of various economic and social aspects in migration policy, and the use of self-regulation and self-governing capacities of countries and non-governmental actors have created a new migration regime that can be defined as "governmental" in the sense of Foucault (2004). What emerges is a heterogeneous and hierarchical space of circulation with graded zones of sovereignty (Hess/Tsianos 2006).

In the discourse on migration management migrants become "objects which have to be steered". However, migrants cannot be steered quite so easily. As this article shows, migrants create networks and communities on their journey. Through the creation of these networks and the establishment of a system of communities, the migration project gradually turns into a collectively organized enterprise during the journey. In addition, mutual solidarity such as by sharing information and forming collectives, is an important survival strategy along the passage, and to some extent it can also counteract the effects of precarious situations and poverty during migration, especially in psychological terms.

Strategies to deal with situations on borders are flexible and adaptable to constant change. The migrants do not give up trying to cross borders, despite extremely adversary conditions. Instead, they react to border reinforcement by either taking new routes or using new strategies to overcome the borders themselves. And by doing so, they also interfere with the border regime. New escape routes are discovered, new ways to adapt are found—sometimes even on behalf of one's own life.[9]

However, I would like to finish this contribution with the words of Cameroonian transit migrant Jean-Marie Kalla: "Do you know that game? The cat hunts the mouse and the mouse is always faster. And so are we, always. Migration has always existed, since the beginning of human existence and why should that end now? In Africa nothing is changing, actually. So we were sent by our families on the journey which changes us so much that we can't go back. I came here by accident. And it has been the best journey ever. The trek has been the best experience of my life."

References

Alioua, M. (2006): La migration transnationale des jeunes Africains subsahariens au Maghreb: émancipation individuelle, circulations collectives et transgression des frontières. Toulouse: Université de Toulouse le Mirail. [online] Available at: http://www.jeunes-et-societes.com/public/archives/2005/ALIOUA.pdf [Accessed February 14, 2011].

9 According to the human rights organization Pro Asyl, more than 1,500 dead migrants were counted outside the EU borders in 2008 (Pro Asyl 2009).

Balibar, E. (1998): The Borders of Europe. In: Peng, Chea/Robbins, Bruce (eds.): Cosmopolitics. Thinking and Feeling beyond the Nation. Minneapolis: University of Minnesota Press, pp. 216-229.

Commission of the European Communities (2007): Communication from the Commission to the European Parliament, the Council, the European Economic and Social Committee and the Committee of the Regions on circular migration and mobility partnerships between the European Union and third countries, COM(2007) 248 final. [online] Available at: http://eur-lex.europa. eu/LexUriServ/LexUriServ.do?uri=COM:2007:0248:FIN:EN:PDF [Accessed February 14, 2011].

Collyer, M. (2006): States of insecurity: Consequences of Saharan transit migration. COMPAS. Centre on Migration, Policy and Society. Working Paper No. 31, University of Oxford. [online] Available at: http://www.compas.ox.ac.uk/filead min/files/pdfs/WP0631-Collyer.pdf [Accessed February 14, 2011].

de Haas, H. (2007): The myth of the invasion. Irregular migration from West Africa to the Magreb and the European Union. IMI research report 2007. Oxford: University of Oxford.

Düvell, F. (2002): Die Globalisierung des Migrationsregimes. Berlin, Göttingen, Hamburg: Verlag Schwarze Risse.

El Qadim, N. (2007): Gérer les migrations: Renouveau d´un objet de négociations entre le Maroc et les pays Européens. Geneva: Graduate Institute of International and Development Studies.

EU (2005): Reaktionen auf das Flüchtlingsdrama in Ceuta/Melilla. Migration und Bevölkerung, Nr. 09/05, [online] Available at: www.migration-info.de [Accessed February 14, 2011].

Foucault, M. (2004): Geschichte der Gouvernmentalität 1. Sicherheit. Territorium, Bevölkerung. Frankfurt am Main: Suhrkamp.

FRONTEX (2006): Annual Report 2006. [online] Available at: http: www.frontex.europa.eu/gfx/frontex/files/justyna/microsoft word - frontex-2008-001-00-00-ende.pdf [Accessed February 14, 2011].

Geiger, M. (2007): Internationale Regierungsorganisationen und die Steuerung von Migration: die Ukraine im Vorfeld der Europäischen Union. IMIS Beiträge. Migration, Staat, Politik 32, pp. 63-88.

Hess, S./Tsianos, V. (2007): Europeanizing Transnationalism! Provinicializing Europe! Konturen eines neuen Grenzregimes. In: Transit Migration Forschungsgruppe (eds.): Turbulente Ränder. Neue Perspektiven auf Migration an den Grenzen Europas. Bielefeld: Transcript, pp. 23-38.

Holert, T./Terkessidis, M. (2006): Fliehkraft. Gesellschaft in Bewegung – von Migranten und Touristen. Köln: Kiepenheuer & Witsch.

Kimball, A. (2007): The Transit State: A Comparative Analysis of Mexican and Moroccan Immigration Policies. San Diego: University of California. [online] Available at: http://www.ccis-ucsd.org/PUBLICATIONS/wrkg150.pdf [Accessed February 14, 2011].

Koufen, K. (2007): Vor der Festung Europa. Afrikanische Flüchtlinge. In: die tageszeitung, 30 August 2007) [online] Available at: http://www.taz.de/1/politik /afrika/artikel/1/vor-der-festung-europa/ [Accessed March 24, 2009].

Lahlou, M. (2008): Undocumented migration. Counting the Uncountable. Country report – Morocco.
CLANDESTINO Research Project, 2007-2009. [online] Available at: http://clandestino.eliamep.gr/wp-content/uploads/2009/02/morocco.pdf [Accessed February 14, 2011].

Ratha, D./Xu, Y. (2008): Migrants and Remittances Factbook 2008. Washington, D.C.:
The World Bank. [online] Available at: http://siteresources.worldbank.org/INT PROSPECTS/Resources/334934-1199807908806/Developing.pdf [Accessed February 14, 2011].

Sadiqi, F. (2004): Migration-Related Institutions and Policies in Morocco. European University Institute: RSCAS. [online] Available at: https:www.carim.org/Publica tions/CARIM-AS04 05-Sadiqi.pdf.

Sassen, S. (2000): Migration und Staatssouveränität. Arbeit ohne Grenzen. In: Le Monde diplomatique, November 10, 2000.

Schapendonk, J. (2008): Stuck between the Desert and the Sea: the Immobility of Sub-Saharan African 'Transit Migrants` in Morocco. In: Erdemir et al. (eds.): Rethinking Global Migration: Practices, Policies and Discourses in the European Neighbourhood. Ankara: KORA, METU & Zeplin Iletisim Hizm, pp. 129-142.

El Pais (2008): Interior Refuerza Ceuta y Melilla tras las oleadas de inmigrantes. 24 June 2008.

Radio M. (2008: Kanarische Inseln – 60 Prozent weniger Immigranten als 2006. 11 January 2008. [online] Available at: http://www.megawelle.com/Nachrichten. 2907.Kanarische.Inseln.60.Prozent.weniger.Immigranten.als.2006.html [Accessed March 24, 2009].

von Leipzig, Wolf (2007): Unfreiwilliger Torwächter Europas. Luxemburger Word, 3 July 2007. [online] Available at: http://www.immigration.lu/pdf/Einwanderung ausAfrikawort030707.pdf [Accessed February 14, 2011].

The Senegalese Predicament: Migration from Senegal to Europe: Policies, Control, and Implementation

Florence Tsagué Assopgoum

Introduction

One of the fifty poorest countries in the world, Senegal has been classified as a least developed country (LDC) by the World Trade Organization since 2001. The country has a population of 12 million (World Bank 2008), 26.3% of whom live in extreme poverty, living on less than US$1 per day. Life expectancy at birth is 55.4 years (Human Development Report 2009: 173). Political, socioeconomic, and environmental problems, the lack of resources, and unemployment among young people are the strongest motivating factors for emigration from Senegal to Europe. The gap between the rich and the poor has visibly widened and the middle classes have been considerably affected by the economic crisis.

With an increasing number of unauthorized transit migrants traveling through Senegal and emigrants leaving the country, migration has become a major challenge and a central social, economic, and political issue. As a consequence of expectations raised by the European Union, Senegal now plays a major role in partnerships with the European states to provide global and tangible solutions to alleviate the pressure of migration from Africa to Europe. The Senegalese government has already initiated several programs to increase public awareness of the dangers of irregular migration and has developed projects and programs to create employment opportunities for young people to keep them in the country. In addition, the government plans to support farming, tourism, fishing, and crafts as the main potential development sectors in Senegal to encourage migrants to return home and start businesses as proposed in the Dakar Framework for Action to combat illegal migration.

Due to changes caused by globalization, it has become increasingly difficult for people from developing countries to travel legally to industrialized countries (Ndione/Broekhuis 2006: 5). In general, the immigration policies of the European Union have made access to the continent less achievable. The current policies include the First Action Plan 2008–2010, which is meant to promote peace and security, democratic governance and human rights, trade and regional integration, and other key development issues (European Commission 2007) Due to tightened border control measures such as the Spanish

SIVES[1] program, migrants have resorted to using highly dangerous alternative routes which have led to the deaths of a large number of migrants attempting to cross the sea between the West African coast and the Canary Islands, with some 3,200 deaths reported in 2006 alone (Gerdes 2007: 8). Between 1993 and April 2009 UNITED for Intercultural Action, a European network against nationalism, racism and fascism and in support of migrants and refugees, documented 13,250 casualties caused by the "Fortress Europe", with most of the dead having come from Africa (UNITED 2009). It is a humanitarian tragedy that calls upon the shared responsibility of the countries of origin, transit, and destination.

After reviewing European initiatives and agreements with Senegal to encourage legal migration, curb irregular migration, keep would-be migrants in the country, reinforce tighter border controls, improve police cooperation with the African states, and make the provision of development aid dependent on the readmission of expelled nationals, the following research questions arise: How can European countries influence the national migration policies of Senegal? How does Senegal reconcile the European pressure to prevent illegal emigration with its own interests?

This article addresses these questions. To this aim, a historical overview of migration from Senegal to Europe is provided which shows that in the last decade the traditional migratory flows from Senegal to France have shifted to other destination countries such as Italy and Spain. Senegal's migration programs and EU activities concerning combined policies of readmission, labor migration quotas, voluntary return programs, border control aspects, and development issues are discussed. The article then describes different categories of migrants and the factors which motivate them to migrate. Remittances from migrants now being a significant financial source for their countries of origin, the role of Senegalese migrants in Europe with regard to the development of their local communities in their country of origin is explored. For illustration purposes, the article includes passages from a migrant's account of his journey which was published in a newspaper and a narrative interview with a Senegalese migrant (Mansour) conducted in Austria[2] to understand what motivated them to migrate to Europe.

1 "Already at the end of the 1990s, the Spanish government started to create the surveillance system SIVE (*Sistema Integral de Vigilancia Exterior*), which combines long-range radar, thermal cameras, night vision equipment, infrared beams, helicopters, etc. in order to 'close off' the sea routes" (see Kreienbrink 2006: 6, as well as Kreienbrink in this volume).

2 All interviewee names were changed for the sake of anonymity.

Migration from Senegal to Europe

Historically, migration from Senegal to Europe began during the Second World War when many Senegalese[3] fought as soldiers on the side of the French army against Germany. After the war, many of them found employment at the Old Port of Marseille, so the city became an important center for Senegalese migrants. After the independence of Senegal from France in 1960, a large number of Senegalese—many of them Soninke, Serer, and Toucouleur people—migrated to France to settle in Paris and major industrial cities such as Marseille. Thus, Senegal became an emigration country. As of 2004, 76% of households in the Senegalese cities have a family member abroad (République du Sénégal 2004: 224), which shows that migration is an important social issue in Senegal.

The economic boom in Europe after the Second World War was a significant factor in attracting immigration from Senegal to France. However, when France introduced visa requirements for Senegal in 1985, migrants began seeking other destination countries, such as Italy in the 1990s.[4] Of the 168,953 Senegalese living abroad in 2004 (République du Sénégal 2004: 227) 53.5% were living in Europe, the U.S., and Canada, 30% in other African countries, 6.6% in Ivory Coast, 3.2% in Guinea-Bissau, and 2.4% in Mali (République du Sénégal, 2004: 232). Since the end of the 1990s, France, Spain, and Italy have been the most important countries of destination for Senegalese migrants (Some 2009: 33). In 1968, about 5,688 Senegalese were living in France, but by 1982 their number had increased to 32,350, and in 1999/2000 to 40,848 (Jettinger 2005: 4). In 2007, 148 Senegalese refugees were registered in France, with only 45 in 2000 (Some 2009: 131). In 2003, about 49,700 Senegalese were officially registered in Italy (although between 65,000 and 75,000 were estimated) and in 2004, about 10,200 Senegalese were living in Spain (Gerdes 2007: 6).

Senegal is facing emigration pressure from both highly qualified migrants and low-skilled migrants. Cheikh Omar Ba, a researcher on international migration, estimates that a large percentage of irregular migrants trying to cross the sea to Europe are Senegalese (Walfadjri, September 21, 2004). In 2006, 30,000 irregular African migrants were living in the Canary Islands. The Senegalese irregular migrants come from different social and professional backgrounds. Among them, there are football players, fishermen, traders, farmers, illiterates, and students as well as highly qualified people with

---

3 The so-called tirailleurs.

4 The United States also became an important destination for middle-class Senegalese migrants, with the help of traders importing electronic goods to Senegal and exporting African goods to the U.S.

no legal opportunity to migrate who have chosen to try dangerous route of migration instead.

Economic Migration

The majority of international migrants from Senegal are male (16% female in 2004), between 18 and 35 years old, low-skilled, and working in the informal sector (Fall 2010: 21). The increase in the number of Senegalese migrants coming to Europe in the last decade is due to the economic crisis, which began in the mid-1970s and further aggravated in the 1990s, the high population growth rate (2.5% per year) and related problems of unemployment. The economic crisis has had a significant impact on the fishing and agricultural sectors, which are the key sectors of the Senegalese economy, given the country's geographical location along the Atlantic Ocean. The economic crisis and the over-exploitation of waters by European fleets have affected the fishing sector. This explains why a large number of low-skilled migrants who worked in these sectors now take the considerable risk of irregular emigration on the sea route. Many fishermen have turned to people smuggling and earn their money by assisting irregular migrants in crossing the sea to the Canary Islands (Ndione/Broekhuis 2006: 5). The business of people smuggling is organized with the complicity of the fishermen, who were deprived of their livelihood by European fishing companies. In 1989, for example, about 70,000 tons of fish were fished in Senegalese waters, but in 2005, national fisheries production was less than 6,000 tons. Because fish stocks have reduced considerably, about 6,000 young professional fishermen have lost their employments and now face the risks of irregular migration. A study by ActionAid on the European Partnerships Agreements (EPAs) under negotiation between the EU and West African countries suggests that EPAs will have negative impacts on the Senegalese fishing companies, worsening the food crisis, aggravating the unemployment problem and causing women to lose revenues, which will have a direct impact on livelihoods, damage the national economy, and lessen government control over this strategic sector, thus fuelling irregular migration in the future (Lossa et al. 2008: 13). The EU has greatly contributed to the depletion of Senegal's marine resources (see 2.1).

According to a study of the International Organization for Migration (IOM) (World Migration Report, 2000: 157), pressure to emigrate from Africa will increase in the coming years because a) internal migrants will move to urban areas and subsequently participate in international migration; b) the Gulf States which have attracted African laborers are now themselves facing a need for economic restructuring; c) Europe, which includes the traditional countries of destination, have tightened entry requirements, immigration laws, and external border control; e) South Africa's capacity to absorb migrants from Sub-Saharan Africa is limited; and f) the number of sub-Saharan job seekers is increasing year by year and unemployment turns them into potential emigrants. Today, the pressure to move to Europe can be explained by the deteriorating socioeconomic situation and a general lack of job opportunities for young people. The key factors which have led to the local fishermen losing their main source of revenue include the crisis in the fishing and agricultural sectors, unequal trade exchanges between industrialized countries and developing countries, subsidies for European agricultural actors, and overfishing in West African waters by European fishing companies.

Babacar Niang, a 33-year-old trader from a large suburb of the city of Pikine in Senegal unsuccessfully attempted to cross the sea to reach the Canary Islands. In his account of the journey he explained the reasons for his adventure, which apparently is the same for all of those who attempt to reach Europe irregularly: he had to leave the misery in his country behind to build a better life in Europe. A matter of do or die! Having failed to cross the sea, he returned to Senegal and founded a trade organization with the help of other disappointed irregular migrants. He has given up the dream of living in Europe and is determined to start a new career in trade between Gambia and Senegal (Le Quotidien, May 30, 2006).

Refugees, Asylum, Irregular Migration

In the last decades, there have been increasing attempts by African migrants to reach Europe via Lampedusa, Ceuta and Melilla, Gibraltar, the Canary Islands, and Malta. In the period from January to October 2006 alone, 27,000 African migrants were counted on the Canary Islands and 17,000 on Lampedusa. In 2004, Libya announced the deportation of 54,000 Africans who had been trying to irregularly migrate to Europe (Jamfa 2007: 22). Most of these migrants, who were mainly from Mauritania and Senegal, lived under extremely poor conditions in their native countries and were therefore willing to accept any risk involved in traveling thousands of miles in small, unsafe, overcrowded boats to reach Europe. Spain's Canary Islands is a particularly attractive destination, where they hope to find better economic opportunities. Due to its geographical location, Senegal has not only become a source country of migrants fleeing to Europe, but also a transit country for migrants from Mali, Gambia, Guinea, and Guinea-Bissau (Ndione/Broekhuis 2006: 5). They continue their journey from there to either North Africa or straight to the Canary Islands.

Compared to many other African countries, Senegal is relatively stable politically. Nevertheless, there are reports of repression and abuse of press freedom. Due to conflicts between the government and rebel secessionists[5] in

5 The Movement of Democratic Forces of the Casamance (MFDC).

the extreme southwest, about 6,000 citizens have become internal refugees. Internationally, political refugees have not played an important role in the migration history of Senegal. Although German authorities classify Senegal as a safe country, 311 Senegalese were recognized as political refugees or have applied for asylum in Germany in 2005 (Gerdes 2007: 7).

Academic Migration

As in many African countries, the decision to migrate for academic purposes is very often more a collective matter than an individual one. The choice of the destination country and the sources of financing—including the decision to migrate in the first place—are made and supported by the family. Because families perceive their support as investments, their expectations are quite high. The fear of failure or of disappointing one's family puts enormous pressure on the migrants, sometimes so much so that they would actually rather die *en route* than be deported back home. For many Senegalese migrants, staying abroad is planned as a short-term experience. However, many of them cannot return home early because they have started a family abroad or have to continue sending money to their dependent families at home. In some cases, migrants are afraid they would lose their social status if they returned home.

Even though media coverage is focused primarily on irregular migrants from Africa, it should be noted that students and highly qualified persons represent a significant percentage of African migrants coming to Europe. Students use other migration routes than irregular migrants, have different reasons to migrate, and choose different destination countries. The following is an interview with a Senegalese migrant currently living in Austria, which was included in this article to illustrate the complexity of reasons to emigrate and the challenges that arise along the way. His case study provides information from the point of view of the migrants who are, after all, the main actors of the debate.

Mansour's Story

Many students in Senegal decide to immigrate to Europe because they hope to be admitted to a university where they can study subjects which are not taught at universities in their own country. Degrees from a European university are also considered to be more valuable by employers than degrees from a local university and the qualification and experience gained abroad gives migrants social prestige. Even after the end of colonization, many schools in

African countries still perpetuate the school system of the former colonial powers. Consequently, a certain discrepancy exists between the subjects learned at school, the reality in Africa, and employment prospects. As a result, scholars prefer to migrate to Europe rather than living and working in Africa. Intellectual and academic careers are still held in higher esteem in Senegal than technical and vocational training (Panizzon, 2008: 5). Mansour perceives himself as a victim of this system. While studying sociology at a university in Senegal, he read mainly French, American, and German authors. This Eurocentrism in the academic world in Africa made him believe that knowledge is in Europe. This was one of the reasons for Mansour to decide to go there. Mansour is a 33-year-old Senegalese with a Master's degree in sociology who lives in Austria. He left Senegal to go to Europe because he was disappointed in his former university, the lecturers, and the grim future employment prospects. In the interview he stated that since his departure from Senegal he had been aware "that migrants are not welcomed in Europe, particularly in Austria, due to the national socialist past of this country. I knew that I would have to face racism and discrimination. But the reality was harder than I had expected," he said. When Mansour came to Austria, he planned to work hard for two years to build a better life. But, he said, "After six years I'm still fighting and my future in this country is still uncertain."

According to the *Migration and Remittances Factbook*, the emigration rate of tertiary educated people from Senegal was 24.1% in 2000 (World Bank 2008). France is still the first-choice destination for Senegalese academics with 9,399 students in 2006 (Some 2009: 134).[6] There is intensive academic, cultural, and scientific exchange between Senegal and France, which is facilitated through linguistic ties and the shared education systems (Panizzon 2008: 5). The colonial relationships between France and Senegal and the French language spoken in both countries are among the factors which motivate Senegalese to decide to study in France. These were also the factors that motivated Mansour, but his application for a French visa was denied. After this disappointment, he then decided to go to Austria to study and obtained a student visa. Mansour's migration story is to some extent typical of many African students from French-speaking countries who would have liked to go to France for the reasons stated above but had to choose a different European country with less restrictive visa regulations.

When Mansour arrived in Austria, he was confronted with accommodation, language, and financial problems. In many African countries, Europe is perceived as a "paradise". This image is perpetuated not only by the media and the elite, but also by many Africans living in Europe and North America, who survive by doing odd jobs but present themselves as prosperous people

6 In 2006 80% of the Senegalese students abroad were living and studying in France (Some 2009: 56).

from Europe and North America when they return to Africa. During their holidays in Senegal, Senegalese migrants exhibit a luxurious lifestyle. Their cars, clothes and general well-being make young people believe that life in Europe is better than in Africa (Schapendonk & Van Moppes 2007: 10). They convey the image of wealth that also motivated Mansour to go to Europe. Aside from this one positive image, many people who decide to migrate from Senegal do not really have a clear idea of what their living conditions will be in Europe before they actually arrive there. They come to Europe with high expectations but are soon confronted with the bitter reality of racism, unemployment, poverty, and social vulnerability (Ibid.).

Migration Policies

Senegal is an important partner in matters of migration for the EU and its member states because of its position as both a source and a transit country. External control of the EU borders by Frontex with support of the ministries of defense and the interior of Senegal is implemented on the coast of Senegal to prevent irregular migrants from reaching the Canary Islands (Some 2009: 79).

Migration has become a significant instrument for cooperation between Senegal and Europe. Even so, the pressure from Europe, Senegal's own interests, and the interests of the migrants still pose a great challenge to Senegal, since the interests of the actors involved are as complex as the causes, effects, and categories of migration from Africa to Europe.

Interests and Policies of the EU and Its Member States

The issue of migration is addressed by the Cotonou Agreement, which was signed by the European Commission and the African, Caribbean and Pacific Group of States (ACP)[7] in 2000 and entered into force in 2003. It is aimed at reducing illegal migration and requires from all parties that they readmit their own illegal citizens present in the territory of another party.

In addition, Spain, Senegal, the European Commission, and IOM signed a memorandum of understanding related to a rapid reaction mechanism (RRM) to address the problem of the increasing number of irregular migrants in the Canary Islands in 2006. This memorandum has an experimental quality of emergency intervention in the face of a humanitarian crisis (which is defined as irregular migration and its risks). It demands readmission of illegal

7 Senegal is a member state.

migrants, frames legal interventions of Frontex, and supports IOM programs for reintegration. It is intended to pave the way for future migration agreements between Senegal and France or Spain.

Determined to curb irregular migration, Senegal has become internationally acclaimed for its high level of airport security. Dakar Airport, for example, has received an excellent score (AA) from the American Federal Aviation Authority (FAA) for many years, with Johannesburg, Addis Ababa, Nairobi, and Accra being the only other airports in to have received this honor (Ndiaye 2001). As a reward for its cooperation with Europe, development aid to Senegal has been increased. Spain agreed to increase development aid after Senegal facilitated the deportation of 3,000 irregular Senegalese migrants from Spain in compliance with the agreements of 2006 (Gerdes 2007: 4). One of the key results of the EU-African Conference in July 2006 was to provide funds to support the Senegalese authorities in tightening the control of irregular migration. In addition, the industrialized countries and the African Development Bank have agreed to finance a US$6 billion project in agricultural and rural development extending from 2007 to 2011 in eight West African countries, including Senegal (Ibid.).

Senegal's Own Interests

The Senegalese diaspora plays an important role in the development of their country through the transfer of funds, which constitute a significant source of foreign currency in Senegal (Panizzon 2008: 17). According to the World Bank, Senegalese abroad transferred US$1.288 million back home in 2008, representing 9.8% of the growth domestic product (GDP) (World Bank 2008). The domestic policy efforts are devoted to using the emigrant potential for development and to encourage Senegalese abroad to invest in the country. In Senegal emigration has long been considered to have a positive influence because of the transfer of funds from migrants. In 1980, Senegalese abroad transferred about US$74.8 million to Senegal, while in 2004, about US$500 million were transferred to Senegal through official banking channels such as Western Union. A large part was also transferred through informal und unrecorded channels. All of these remittances are a highly significant contribution to the national economy of Senegal.

Many home countries have benefited from the remittances from their migrants for a long time without regarding them as important actors in long-term development. The remittances from the migrants now constitute a significant financial source for the countries of origin and have important impacts upon their development (Chappell & Glennie, 2009). According to the World Bank's *Global Economic Prospects*, migrants worldwide transferred an estimated US$167 billion to developing countries in 2005 (Elvers-Guyot 2006). In 2004, remittances from migrants exceeded official development aid in several developing countries, totaling US$126 billion of worldwide remittances, according to the International Monetary Fund. In its issue of January 19, 2004, the American news magazine *Newsweek* described remittances as "effectively a new form of foreign aid".

Many surveys on migration and development show that the families of migrants tend to invest the resources they receive in household expenditure rather than in long-term projects (Dayton-Johnson et al. 2008: 8; Dander and Barro 2005: 11). A study on the Senegalese diaspora in Germany revealed that the main recipients of the remittances are family members and friends of the migrants, who spend the money on education, health care, and to raise living standards. In addition, religious communities and organizations receive aid from their members abroad to build schools and mosques or to organize religious or cultural festivities (Faye 2007: 6). One example is the significant financial support from the members of the Mouride brotherhood[8] in Germany for the construction of the hospital in the Senegalese city of Touba. In addition, many migrants also send electronic equipment such as computers and television sets, cars, and domestic appliances to families, friends, organizations, business partners, schools, and religious communities (Ibid.: 7). The construction sector benefits in particular from remittances and has consequently experienced high growth rates. Remittances are often used to build private houses for migrants or their families, thus providing employment and leading to more investments for construction companies.

In order to connect its diaspora to the development, Senegal has created a Ministry for Senegalese Abroad[9] to meet the capacities and needs of migrants, encouraging them to invest or return home with their experience gained abroad and to take responsibility for the development of their local communities. In 2000, the Investment Promotion and Major Works Agency (APIX)[10] was founded, which now plays an important role in attracting capital and investments from the Senegalese migrants (Panizzon 2008: 6). Even so, the migrants still encounter significant social and administrative hurdles when trying to return to Senegal or to invest their remittances profitably. Many African migrants have difficulties finding honest business partners at home and only trust their own family members, though in many cases these relatives spend the business funds to serve their own needs (Sieveking 2009: 24). Because of the high expectations generally set in migration in Senegal, many families do not welcome their relatives back with open arms, which makes returning and reintegration difficult for the return migrants, who are

---

8 Mouride is an Islamic Sufi order in Senegal, with headquarters in the holy city of Touba. Other religious communities in Senegal include Tijaniyyah, Qadiriyya, and Layene.

9 Ministère des Sénégalais de l'Extérieur.

10 http://www.investinsenegal.com, accessed December 10, 2009.

confronted with the prospect of unemployment[11] and the hostility of their families.

Emigration management constitutes a new challenge. In response to the migration flows to Europe, the Senegalese government has initiated a number of programs to reintegrate return migrants, attract investments from Senegalese abroad, create small and medium enterprises, and develop Senegal's infrastructure using the diaspora networks to stimulate investments from companies in the host countries. In cooperation with national and international partners such as IOM, PNUD[12], and Migration for Development in Africa (MIDA), three programs have been developed to draw upon the development expertise of migrants : MIDA Senegal, Transfer of Knowledge Through Expatriate Nationals (TOKTEN), and the Initiative Co-développement" (Some 2009: 23). The areas of tourism, agriculture, and information and communication technology benefit from these programs.

The promotion of employment for young people was a priority for Senegalese president Abdoulaye Wade during the political campaign in 2000. With the help of the National Agency for Employment, about 42,000 jobs for young people were created. The then Minister of Youth, Aliou Sow, announced that in three years 22,358 employment opportunities and 15,000 jobs in the public sector were created.[13] The government initiated several public infrastructure construction projects in Dakar in the hope of creating employment opportunities for a large number of unemployed young people.

Several programs and projects were initiated in the agricultural sector to reduce unemployment and encourage would-be emigrants to stay in the country. Returning Migrants to Agriculture (REVA), a program aimed at providing professional training to unemployed people and return migrants received financial support (République du Sénégal 2006) the agriculture ministry providing supplies, farms, and the expertise. This approach produced favorable results in some regions of Senegal in 2008. In the city of Nioro du Rip, agricultural projects implemented in cooperation with the Austrian NGO Horizon 3000 provided opportunities for young people to return to their regions, thus leading to the reduction of emigration (Fall 2008). It should be noted that the agricultural projects intended to curb unemployment in young people in Senegal do not seem to address the core of the problem, considering that fishermen are still not involved in these projects and thus are threatened with unemployment – a situation that turns them into would-be migrants. Therefore, one of the Senegalese government's primary objectives

---

11 In 2007, the unemployment rate in Senegal was 48% (http://www.statistiques-mondiales.com/senegal.htm [Accessed June 10, 2010]).

12 The United Nations Development Programme.

13 However, the *Sud Quotidien* of May 26, 2006 noted that the Wade government failed to fulfil its promise and that irregular emigration has increased considerably.

must be to define suitable measures which can help the fishermen to engage in agricultural activities.

Aside from the projects of the Senegalese government to curb irregular migration and keep young people in the country, there are also several bilateral agreements with the destination countries in the EU.

Senegal has taken part in several international migration conferences organized in cooperation with the European Union: the first Afro-European ministerial conference on migration and development held in Rabat in July 2006 aimed at raising awareness of the impact of migration on development, curbing irregular migration, and promoting legal migration. Being a country of origin and transit, Senegal has an interest in playing a major role in the negotiations with the European countries and acting as a mediator between the EU and other African countries of origin.

Implementation of Migration Policies by Senegal

While France has always been the primary traditional destination of Senegalese students and workers, Spain has become one of the main countries of destination in recent years, with migratory flows (of irregular migrants in particular) increasing significantly of late. In 2006, 16,224 irregular Senegalese were listed in Spain and 2,820 were deported back to Senegal (Some 2009: 135). France and Spain have signed several agreements on migration management with Senegal and "will certainly pave the way for a future EU-wide migration agreement, the so-called mobility partnerships" (Panizzon 2008: 1). Senegal, as the model West African country of origin of migrants coming to Europe, has been chosen by France and Spain to test a new generation of bilateral agreements aimed at combating irregular migration. The partnerships between France, Spain, and Senegal support immigrant associations, employers associations, local authorities, and non- governmental programs aimed at facilitating procedures of migrant recruitment, return, and reintegration.

France and Senegal have cooperated on issues of migration management since the 1980s. In 1983, a bilateral agreement between the two countries provided funding for a vocational training program for migrants who were willing to return to Senegal. In 1987, the Office for Reception, Orientation and Support for the Reintegration of Emigrants (BAOS) was founded to help Senegalese abroad to return to Senegal and find employment in the country. In October 2006, an agreement was signed between France and Senegal to facilitate faster deportation of irregular migrants and easier legal entry into France for students, professionals, and artists (Gerdes 2007: 4). In accordance with bilateral agreements, the best Senegalese professionals received capacity and talent visas which allowed them to work in France. An agreement with Spain provided 4,000 short-term work visas to Senegalese migrants for a period of two years (2007/2008) (Ibid.).

During Nicolas Sarkozy's presidency, the focus of French migration policy has been on *immigration choisie*, which means selected immigration. French political authorities explain this position as an attempt to achieve legal migration for students, workers, and professionals without encouraging irregular migration. Language, academic level, age, and professional skills are key aspects of this type of immigration. France's migration management strategy also aims at supporting the voluntary return by providing return aid. Spain combines an approach of linking recruitment of lower-skilled workers with readmission quotas for irregular migrants and Senegalese police cooperation in border control. This apparently pragmatic policy contributes to reducing unemployment and migration pressure. France promotes voluntary return and the "brain drain policy" (Panizzon 2008: 2), that is, the capacity and visa policy which is more targeted at the highly qualified migrants from Senegal.

Conclusion

This article examined some of the main factors of migration from Senegal to Europe: agricultural crisis, tourism, and overfishing - by European companies - have destroyed the livelihood of people in many regions, turning them into migrants or would-be migrants in the process.

As a departure point and a transit country for many migrants from Sub-Saharan Africa, Senegal plays an important role in Euro-African migration management. Agreements signed with France and Spain aim at combining migration and development, readmission of migrants, and quotas for labor migrants. However, political authorities in Senegal and Europe are confronted with the increasingly dramatic effects of irregular emigration and the anxiety of families mourning their children who have died or disappeared while crossing the sea to the Canary Islands.

It is important to note that Senegal's migration policy and the implementation of this policy are influenced by specific European policies concerning migration from Africa. In fact, some European countries such as France and Spain support Senegal in its efforts to curb irregular migration by linking readmission quotas for irregular migrants with visas for labor migrants, and development aid with cooperation efforts with police forces in border control.

The reasons for current migration from Africa to Europe include poverty, corruption, bad governance, and terms of trade in the world market. Rather than blaming the *clandestins* (irregulars), who are not only the main actors of migration, but also the victims of the underdeveloped systems of their countries, these migrants should be given the opportunity to start a better life in Senegal. The government of Senegal has initiated various programs and projects to create employment opportunities (mainly in agriculture) and keep young people in the country. The interviewees perceived the opportunities created for young people in the cities as positive but not effective enough, considering the enormous level of unemployment in their country. According to the president of the migrant association of Senegal, the program REVA, focusing primarily on the agricultural sector, fails to address the needs of fishermen, and the projects aimed at returned migrants are being implemented in other sectors (Fall 2010: 41). The main research question of this article is: How does Senegal reconcile the pressure from the EU to prevent unwanted emigration with its own interests?

Although the remittances from Senegalese abroad represent a large percentage of the country's GDP (see 3.2), it is believed that these remittances do not compensate for the negative impacts of the emigration of young and highly-qualified people on sustainable development. As a developing country, Senegal is facing a range of economic and social difficulties and needs the development cooperation of the European countries. The program REVA is largely financed by Spain, Senegal's key partner in combating irregular emigration to Europe (Fall 2010: 41). The European countries use development aid as a bargaining tool to negotiate migration issues with African countries of origin, so Senegal has to reconcile the pressure from the EU to curb irregular emigration with the pressure from Senegalese people who seek better lives and job opportunities as well as its own interests in forming partnerships with European countries. This became evident in 2006, when the deportation of Senegalese immigrants from France and Spain led to massive protests among the deported migrants in Senegal.[14] This article has shown that, although Senegal is in a predicament and its values and interests in migration are in opposition to the expectations of European countries, it remains a cooperative partner, supporting the EU in combating and preventing irregular migration from Africa to Europe.

References

Chappell, L./Glennie, A. (2009): Maximising the Development Outcomes of Migration: A Policy Perspective, United Development Programmes. In: Human Development Reports, Research Paper: 6.

14 Although the country officially suspended cooperation with the EU, irregular migrants were still secretly deported with the government's complicity. See: Wieland 2006: 6.

Dayton-Johnson, J./Pfeiffer, A./Schüttler, K./Schwinn, J. (2008): Migration and Employment. discussion paper. Deutsche Gesellschaft für Technische Zusammenarbeit-GTZ: Eschborn. [online] Available at: http://www.gtz.de/de/dokumente/en-migration-and-employment-2008.pdf [Accessed October 10, 2009].

Elvers-Guyot, J. (2006): Rücküberweisungen lindern die Armut, [online] Available at: http://www.dw-world.de/dw/article/0,2144,1845312,00.html [Accessed January 17, 2006].

European Commission (2007): First Action Plan 2008-2010 [online] Available at: http://ec.europa.eu/development/icenter/repository/EAS2007actionplan20082010 en.pdf.

Fall, A. (2008): Lutte contre l´émigration clandestine. Pourquoi Nioro fait exception. In: Sud Quotidien, 2 April 2008.

Fall Papa, D. (2003): Migration internationale et droits des travailleurs au Sénégal. Section de la migration internationale et des politiques multiculturelles/Série UNESCO: Rapports par pays sur la ratification de la Convention des Nations Unies sur les droits des migrants. [online] Available at: http://unesdoc.unesco.org/images/0013/001395/139532f.pdf [Accessed July 2, 2009].

Fall, Papa D. (2010): Sénégal, migration, marché du travail et développement, document dc travail. Organisation internationale du Travail (Institut international d´études sociales). [online] Available at: http://www.ilo.org/public/french/bureau/ inst/download/senegal.pdf [Accessed August 25, 2010].

Faye, M. (2007): Die senegalesische Diaspora in Deutschland. Ihr Beitrag zur Entwicklung Senegals. Deutsche Gesellschaft für Technische Zusammenarbeit GmbH: Eschborn. [online] Available at: http://www.gtz.de/de/dokumente/de-senegalesische-diaspora-2007.pdf [Accessed February 14, 2011].

Gerdes, F. (2007): Senegal, Country Profile, No. 10, focus Migration. Hamburg Institute of International Economics (HWWI). [online] Available at: http://www.focus-migration.de/uploads/tx_wilpubdb/CP_10_Senegal.pdf [Accessed February 14, 2011].

UNDP (2009): Human Development Report 2009. Overcoming barriers: Human mobility and development. UNDP: New York.

IOM & United Nations (2000): World Migration Report.

Jamfa, L. (2007): Europa gegenüber der Herausforderung massive Einwanderung von Afrikanern: Eine "Entwicklungssteuer" als Lösungsmöglichkeit? In: Afrika & Science (African Development Initiative) 1, 2, pp. 14-83.

Jettinger, B. (2005): Senegal Country Study. A part of the report on Informal Remittance Systems in Africa, Caribbean and Pacific (ACP) countries (Ref: RO2CS008), ESRC Centre on Migration, Policy and Society (COMPAS): University of Oxford.

Kreienbrink, A. (2006): Spain, Country Profile, No. 6, focus Migration. Hamburg Institute of International Economics (HWWI). [online] Available at: http://www.focus-migration.de/typo3_upload/groups/3/focus_Migration_Publikationen/Laenderprofile/CP_06_Spain.pdf [Accessed June 10, 2010].

Le Quotidien 30 May 2006.

Lossa, M./Niang, P. N./Polack, A. May (2008): Selfish Europe: How the Economic Partnership Agreements will further contribute to the decline of fish stocks and exacerbating the food crisis in Senegal. ActionAid. [online] Available at:

http://www.actionaid.org/docs/selfish20europe20brochure20en.pdf [Accessed August 25, 2010].
Marfaing, L./Hein, W. (2008): Das EU-Einwanderungsabkommen–kein Ende der illegalen Migration aus Afrika. Hamburg: in GIGA German Institute of Global and Area Studies (GiGA Focus Global), Nr. 8.
Ndiaye, A. R. (2001): Emigration Clandestine. Plus de 200 voyageurs refoulés en un mois. In: Le Soleil, 25 Juillet 2001.
Ndione, B./Broekhuis, A. (2006): International migration and development in Senegal, viewpoints and policy initiatives. Working papers and Development Series, Report No. 8, Research Group Migration and Development (Department of Human Geography).
Panizzon, M. (2008): Labour mobility: A win-win-win model for trade and development. The case of Senegal, Geneva Trade and Development Forum, Background study integrating report from theme group's workshop 2 of April 24–25, 2008. [online] Available at: http://www.gtdforum.org/download/080620%20Background%20study%20labour%20mobility%20-%20Senegal%20-%20final.pdf [Accessed October 10, 2009].
République du Sénégal, Ministère de l'Economie et des Finances. Direction de la Prévision et de la Statistique (2004):
Rapport de la Synthèse de la Deuxième Enquête Sénégalaise auprès des Ménages (ESAM-II), Juillet 2004. [online] Available at: http://www.ansd.sn/publications/rapports_enquetes_etudes/enquetes/ESAM_2.pdf [Accessed February 11, 2010].
République du Sénégal (2006): Plan REVA Retour Vers l'Agriculture. [online] Available at: http://www.bameinfopol.info/IMG/pdf/PlanREVA_150706_3_.pdf [Accessed February 14, 2011].
Ruhs, M.Y. (2009): United Development Programmes. In: Human Development Reports, Research Paper.
Schapendonk, J./Van Moppes, D. (2007): Migration and Information. Images of Europe, migration encouraging factors and en route information sharing. Working Papers Migration and Development Series Report 16. Nijmegen: Radboud University. [online] Available at: http://socgeo.ruhosting.nl/html/files/migration/migration16.pdf [Accessed October 10, 2009].
Sénégal (2010): Statistiques. [online] Available at: http://www.statistiques-mondiales.com/senegal.htm [Accessed June 10, 2010].
Sieveking, N. (2009): Das entwicklungspolitische Engagement von Migrantinnen afrikanischer Herkunft in NRW mit Fokus auf Ghana. Expertise für das Ministerium für Generationen, Familie, Frauen und Integration des Landes Nordrhein-Westfalen, COMCAD- working Papers, No 65. [online] Available at: http://www.uni-bielefeld.de/tdrc/ag_comcad/downloads/workingpaper_65_sieveking.pdf [Accessed October 21, 2009].
Some, AN (2009): Organisation Internationale pour les Migrations (OIM), Migration au Sénégal. Profil National 2009. Genève. [online] Available at: http://publications.iom.int/bookstore/free/Senegal_Profile_2009.pdf [Accessed February 11, 2010].
Walfadjri 21 September 2004.
Wieland, L. (2006): Ein belegtes Brot, ein Fahrschein und dann adiós. Afrikaner in Spanien. In: Frankfurter Allgemeine Zeitung, 24 August 2006, Nr. 196, p. 6.

World Bank (2008): Migration and Remittances Factbook 2008. [online] Available at: http://econ.worldbank.org/WBSITE/EXTERNAL/EXTDEC/EXTDECPROSPECTS/0,,contentMDK:21352016~pagePK:64165401~piPK:64165026~theSitePK:476883,00.html [Accessed March 3, 2010].

Dead End for Migrants? The Europeanization of Ukraine's Migration

Marianne Haase

Introduction

Being a major country of transit and origin for migration into the European Union (EU), Ukraine is an important partner for the EU in combating irregular migration, which explains the EU's efforts to shape Ukrainian migration policies.[1] The EU's aim is to build a *cordon sanitaire* through close cooperation on migration issues with neighboring third countries (Wolff 2008) and it is assumed that preventing and fighting illegal migration in Ukraine will lead to less migration pressure on the EU borders. For this reason, migration policies are transferred to neighboring countries. One effect of this transfer of policies is a (partial) Europeanization of Ukraine's migration policy. The aim of this article is to analyze this Europeanization from three points of view: the EU's interest in exporting their migration policies; Ukraine's willingness to cooperate in matters of migration and control policies; and the impact of these transfer processes on migrants in Ukraine.

It is argued that the transfer of migration policies from the EU to Ukraine and its Europeanization lead to ambiguous results for migrants in Ukraine. The EU introduces international standards such as the principle of non-refoulement and supports Ukraine in setting up an asylum system, but the EU's influence also results in tighter border controls and transforms Ukraine into a "buffer zone" (Zimmer 2008) for migrants whose initial destination had been the EU. Consequently, Ukraine has become an immigration country of second choice while lacking infrastructure and experience in dealing with immigrants. In particular, Ukraine still fails to protect vulnerable groups, such as asylum seekers, refugees, and other migrants who often face discrimination, xenophobia, inadequate infrastructure, and barriers in their everyday life resulting from non-existing or deficient asylum and integration policies. Furthermore, Europeanization and "Schengenization" are making this situation even worse because they are preventing more and more migrants from crossing the borders into the EU which exacerbates this already difficult situation for migrants.

Ukraine participates in the institutional framework of the European Neighbourhood Policy (ENP), which facilitates transfer of policies (here:

[1] Opinions and views expressed in this chapter are exclusively those of the author.

migratory) to the ENP partners (Wichmann 2007).[2] The transfer, however, is mostly one-sided, usually running from the EU to the ENP countries.[3] Conditionality is the main principle which allows for the successful export of migration policies by EU countries and the import of these policies by ENP countries (Schimmelfennig and Sedelmeier 2005). The prospect of increased integration in the EU and issue linkages stimulate the third countries' willingness to cooperate on migration-related questions. With Ukraine being a country still in transition, the conditions for policy import are assumed to be more favorable than in cases where the EU pursues this kind of external governance (cf. Heck and Bilecen-Süoglu in this volume): "In a transition society, the vast majority of policy inputs are exogenous in character as there are few valid sources for indigenous inputs." (Evans 2004: 109)

In order to analyze the transfer of EU policies to ENP countries, the governance modes of negotiation and network governance will be applied to the case of Ukraine (Lavenex 2008). "[Governance] can be considered both a process and a state whereby public and private actors engage in the intentional regulation of societal relationships and conflicts. Governance is thus different from government, the latter stressing hierarchical decision-making structures and the centrality of public actors, while the former denotes the participation of public and private actors, as well as non-hierarchical forms of decision-making." (Kohler-Koch and Rittberger 2006: 28) It will be shown in the following that network governance is a dominant mode applied in Ukraine's Europeanization accounting for the transfer of migration policies including border management, control policies, and protection standards for migrants and refugees. Thereby, non-state actors like NGOs, as well as intergovernmental organizations are important actors in Ukraine, compensating for deficiencies in Ukrainian governance when it comes to the treatment of migrants and refugees.

The first part of this article assesses Ukraine's migration profile, showing that Ukraine serves as a sending and transit country for migration to the EU and, more recently, as an immigration country (of second choice). The cooperation between Ukraine and the EU within the institutional framework of the ENP and their migration-related cooperation will then be briefly ex-

---

2 Applying a (neo)institutionalist approach, Simon Bulmer and Stephen Padgett (2005: 105) argue that "institutions matter, shaping actor preferences and structuring both the processes of policy making and substantive policy. Transfer processes and outcomes will thus be shaped by the institutional settings in which they take place." Following this assumption, this article assumes that the European Neighbourhood Policy accounts for special forms of transfer which are characterized less by hierarchical means than by softer governance modes.

3 Dolowitz and Marsh (2000: 5) define policy transfer as a "process in which knowledge about policies, administrative arrangements, institutions and ideas in one political setting (past or present) is used in the development of policies, administrative arrangements, institutions and ideas in another political setting".

plained in order to analyze the transfer of migration policies. The next part of this analysis will look at the actual transfer through two governance modes (negotiation and network governance), taking into account the interests of Ukraine and the EU as well. The final part discusses the impact of Ukraine's Europeanization on migrants, concluding that Europeanization has had ambiguous effects with regard to migrants.

Ukraine's Migration Profile

As an immigration, transit, and source country, Ukraine plays an important role for migration movements in the eastern European neighborhood. Because of its geographical location and its linking function between Europe and Asia, Ukraine is a highly frequented transit country for migrants heading for the EU.[4] Ukraine shares a border approximately 1380 km long with four EU member states (Poland, Hungary, Slovakia, and Romania) and borders three non-EU-countries (Belarus, Russia, and Moldova). Transit migrants usually enter Ukraine via the "green" and only partly demarcated Ukrainian-Russian border (see Söderköping Process (2009) for statistics of the Ukrainian State Border Guard Service). The most frequently used transit route runs via Transcarpathia to Slovakia (Zimmer 2008: 2). Thanks to visa-free travel agreements with many countries (in particular with post-Soviet republics), immigrating into Ukraine is not difficult for these nationals.[5] Even though Franck Düvell (2008) considers Ukraine to be one of the major sending countries of irregular migrants to the EU, he asserts that Ukraine's role as a transit country is much more important than its role as a sending country of illegal migration. In addition, trafficking of migrants from Southeast Asia, the Middle East, and North Africa is a widespread phenomenon in Ukraine.

The actual extent of illegal migration, which may include transit migration as well, is difficult to determine, but statistics give an idea of the dimension of illegal migration in Ukraine: The State Border Guard Service (SBGS) apprehended around 96,000 illegal migrants between 2005 and 2008 (Söderköping Process 2009), while the Clandestino Project (2009: 2) estimates that there is a stock of 100,000 migrants staying irregularly in Ukraine. Most of the apprehended illegal migrants are from Moldova and Uzbekistan. However, these data do not indicate where these migrants were apprehended, so it remains unclear whether these migrants entered for purposes of transit. It is likely that illegal immigration is detected mainly at the western border of

---

4 See Dietz (2007) and Pylynskyi (2008: 37f.) for determinants which drive migration movements to and from Ukraine.

5 A list of countries whose citizens can travel to Ukraine without a visa is available online at ukrconsul.org/visa/visa_drops.htm (accessed June 10, 2010).

Ukraine, since the Ukrainian-Russian border is still permeable and border controls in the west have been improved with EU and U.S. support (Gatev 2008: 101ff.).

As a result of these enhanced control measures, it has become difficult for transit migrants to pass the border from Ukrainian territory to an EU member state and the number of apprehensions of illegal migrants has increased significantly (Söderköping Process 2009; Zimmer 2008: 2). The Schengen accession of some new eastern member states in 2007 led to even less permeable borders to the EU (Pylynskyi 2008: 28).[6] For this reason, a growing number of transit migrants are forced to stay in Ukraine and may find themselves in a position where reaching the EU is impossible and returning to their country of origin may become increasingly difficult due to tighter border controls in the east. For many migrants returning home is not an option because of unfavorable living conditions in their home countries and the latest developments at the eastern border have made re-entry into Ukraine difficult. As Yaroslav Pylynskyi (2008: 40) points out, "a majority of immigrants in Ukraine (except Moldavians and Belarusians) are transit migrants. [...] Only few migrants want to stay and reside in Ukraine. However, some migrants are to stay in Ukraine by force of circumstances, they can neither leave for the West, nor return home as they have no required documents, money, etc." The EU's support in building up a migration policy such as through more effective border controls, tightened rules[7] for access into Ukrainian territory, and the Schengen accession of eastern EU member states in 2007 explain why Ukraine has become an immigration country of second choice for those originally intending to migrate to any EU member state.

The International Organization for Migration states that 6.8 million immigrants actually lived in Ukraine legally in 2005, which made up around 15% of the entire Ukrainian population (IOM 2008: 460) and Ukrainian statistics indicate a growing immigration flow[8], with Russians representing the largest group of foreigners. Apart from this rather large group of ethnic Russians, most immigrants legally living in Ukraine come from Moldova, Uzbekistan, Azerbaijan, Armenia, Georgia, and China (Söderköping Process 2009). Ethnic minorities in Ukraine can be distinguished into two groups: the

---

6 In December 2007, Poland, the Czech Republic, Slovakia, Slovenia, Hungary, Estonia, Latvia, Lithuania, and Malta dropped its border controls to the other Schengen member states due to their accession to the Schengen area.

7 See ECRE (2010) for recent changes in Ukrainian legislation on the rules of entry of foreigners.

8 Statistics on migration in Ukraine are available online at ukrstat.gov.ua/operativ/operativ2010/ds/mr/mr_e/arh_mr2010_e.html (accessed June 13, 2010). While being an immigration country, Ukraine is affected by constant emigration movements of Ukrainians, an overall decline in birth rates, and an ageing population, which contributes to an overall negative demographic development.

so-called "old minorities" composed of Jews, Roma, and ex-Soviet diaspora groups like Russians and Moldovans, and the "new minorities" in Ukraine which consist mostly of refugees, students, and irregular migrants from Africa, the Middle East, and Asia.

Whereas issues of refuge and asylum were unknown in Soviet times, at the beginning of the 1990s the first asylum and refuge seekers began to come to Ukraine because of the various ethnic conflicts in post-Soviet countries (Malynovska and Kubanova 2008: 318). The conflict in the Trans-Dniester region led to an estimated influx of 60,000 refugees into Ukraine (Ibid.: 327), but refugees from Afghanistan and Chechnya immigrated to Ukraine as well (Zimmer 2008: 2). However, Ukraine's asylum policy is characterized by low asylum recognition rates; of the 9,000 asylum applications submitted in Ukraine between 2003 and 2007, only 3% were eventually approved (Söderköping Process 2009). The number of people who received refugee status plummeted and remained low while the number of applications increased (Söderköping Process 2009). Due to a lack of fair and efficient refugee status determination procedures in Ukraine, asylum seekers are forced into irregularity. Explaining these low recognition rates, Franck Düvell (2010) considers Ukraine's asylum system to be "insufficient and corrupt". Institutional shortcomings such as the cumbersome and still inadequately developed State Migration Service contribute significantly to the malfunctioning of the Ukrainian asylum and migration system (European Commission 2010: 13; ECRE 2010).[9]

As well as being a transit and immigration country (of second choice), Ukraine is a source country for migration to the EU. Ukrainians represent one of the largest groups of immigrants in the EU. Recent data reveal that some 100,000 Ukrainians reside legally in the EU-27 (Eurostat 2008), the majority living in Italy (41,000), the Czech Republic, and Hungary. Shortly after independence, the successor states to the USSR became the main destination countries for Ukrainians (Dietz 2007: 6). Nowadays, the EU is one of the favorite destinations for Ukrainian emigration (Malynovska and Kubanova 2008: 320; IOM 2008: 23).

---

9 The setting-up of the State Migration Service was vetoed by the Ukrainian President in August 2009, which led to the suspension of a large number of asylum cases.

The Legal and Institutional Framework of EU-Ukraine Co-operation on Migration

Nearly all neighboring countries participate in some kind of EU regional policy through which cooperation in matters of migration takes place. Ukraine participates in the European Neighbourhood Policy, which addresses those third countries which, by definition, are not eligible to become members of the EU.[10] Thanks to the EU's role as a regional power, its economic strength, and the prospect of greater political and economic integration, ENP third countries are motivated to cooperate closely with the EU even without the prospect of a future accession to it (Dannreuther 2006; Barbé and Johannson-Nogués 2008; Magen 2006). Justice and Home Affairs (JHA) is an important policy area addressed within the ENP, since some issues, particularly those of international migration, mobility, and transnational crime, call for cooperation between the EU and its neighboring countries (see Gil Araújo in this volume on the external dimension of EU migration policy). This cooperation on migration is marked by two different, potentially conflicting interests: the EU aiming to lower migratory pressure on its external borders by shifting migration control policies to neighboring countries and setting up largely impenetrable borders, while also endeavoring to implement international standards of refugee protection in these countries. This export of international standards stems from the EU's self-perceived role as a "force for good" (Barbé and Johansson-Nogués 2008) and explains its transformative impact on third countries, while the third countries are interested in, among other things, a mobility regime through which migration of their nationals to the EU would be facilitated.

As a policy transfer arena or transfer platform with specific instruments and processes, the ENP enables the shift of policies from the EU to third countries which results in the approximation of the legislation and policies of third countries to the *acquis communautaire* (Petrov 2008). The ENP affords an opportunity to reach compromise on the various migration-related interests outlined above by offering a venue for negotiation which might be facilitated by issue linkages or other package deals (Kelley 2006). The EU is able to exert pressure on these partner countries to adapt policies by hierarchical—or, rather, partially hierarchical—governance modes. The EU princi-

---

10 See ec.europa.eu/world/enp/index_en.htm [accessed June 10, 2010]. Ukraine also participates in the Eastern Partnership which was launched in 2009 under the general framework of the ENP in order to intensify the cooperation with countries in the eastern neighbourhood. The Eastern Partnership envisions close relations with six countries (Armenia, Azerbaijan, Belarus, Georgia, Moldova, and Ukraine), through, *inter alia*, the conclusion of association agreements, free trade areas, visa liberalization, and close cooperation related to border management and irregular migration.

ple of conditionality is applied through action plans, monitoring through progress reports, and rewards for compliance.

Cooperation between Ukraine and the EU is based on the Partnership and Cooperation Agreement (PCA), which was signed in 1994 and came into force in 1998.[11] Article 27 of the PCA establishes a migration-related cooperation between the EU and Ukraine. Using the PCA as a basis, several action plans were negotiated[12], which contain political, economic, institutional, and administrative reforms to be made by the ENP country. The progress made on the basis of the action plans was assessed as part of a monitoring process and published in progress reports. Apart from these rather general action plans, Ukraine and the EU negotiated an additional thematic action plan on JHA which is unique when compared to the plans of other ENP countries, in that it highlights the very close relationship between Ukraine and the EU and shows how important Ukraine is considered to be in managing migration on the EU border. The first JHA action plan was adopted in 2001 and a revised version followed in 2007. According to these JHA action plans, a scoreboard was to be set up to monitor progress. This JHA-related monitoring process complements and refines the general monitoring process included in the general action plan.

Ukraine has been called upon to set up an efficient migration system. The 2009 Progress Report states that "[despite] multiple reforms, Ukraine still lacks a clear migration policy and a unified, efficient migration service." (Commission of the European Communities 2009: 12). A core aspect of the JHA Action Plan is the conclusion of a readmission agreement and of an agreement on visa facilitations with the European Community (EC). In addition, the accommodation of apprehended (illegal) migrants has been subject to criticism and improvements have been demanded. Generally, international standards of asylum and refugee protection are to be implemented in Ukraine. A special focus is put on the Geneva Convention and on the implementation of these principles of refuge. Specifically, the 2010 Progress Report mentions violations of the principle of non-refoulement, the suspension of asylum applications, and uneven treatment of migrants in migrant custody and temporary holding facilities (Ibid.). Regional Protection Programmes (RPPs) are mentioned as measures aimed to improve refugee and asylum standards. Special attention is paid to border management: EU or, as the case may be, Schengen standards of so-called integrated border management

---

11 Negotiations are currently under way for an Association Agreement which will succeed the PCA. The signing of an association agreement would recognize Ukraine's progress in its political and economic development. In line with this association agreement, a free trade agreement is being negotiated as well. A so-called New Practical Instrument will replace the Action Plan.

12 The EU-Ukraine Action Plan has been replaced by the Association Agenda in 2010. It prepares the entry into force of the currently negotiated Association Agreement.

(IBM) are to be applied in Ukraine. Regarding Ukrainian compliance, the 2010 Progress Report observes that "Ukraine has not yet fully fulfilled the commitments in the Action Plan of the Association Agenda related to migration." (European Commission 2010: 13). Progress has been made concerning the implementation of the readmission agreement, border management, border demarcation, and the ongoing visa dialogue (Ibid.: 14).

By importing aspects of the EU's migration policy, Ukraine presents itself to the EU as a cooperative partner. The reasons of Ukraine to agree to import policies which may have unfavorable consequences, such as readmitting not only their own nationals but also third-country nationals, can only be explained within a broader framework to be outlined in the following.

Firstly, the exchange of visa facilitation for the EC readmission agreement as well as rewards for compliance through the upgrading to an associated partner country help to explain Ukraine's interest in satisfying the EU's demands. Secondly, Ukraine's aspirations to become an EU member state in the future may also be an incentive for its intense cooperation in matters of migration and other policies (Bobitski 2008). Both the rapprochement between the EU und Ukraine and Ukraine's objective of EU accession were strengthened by the Orange Revolution in 2004/2005 (Commission of the European Communities 2010) and secure borders can be seen as a prerequisite to become a future accession candidate (Uehling 2004: 101) [13]. Thirdly, Ukraine's close cooperation with the EU in matters of visa and border politics has to be interpreted as a strategy to compensate for negative effects of the 2007 Schengen enlargement and stricter border regimes with new EU member states. Resulting from the Schengen accession of neighboring EU member states in 2007 (Hungary, Poland, and Slovakia), visa policies changed in these countries. Former liberal travel regimes between these countries and Ukraine were submitted and adjusted to the Schengen *acquis* which, in practical terms, means that restrictions for Ukrainian citizens had to be introduced (Boratyński et al. 2006; Stefan Batory Foundation 2009; Trauner and Kruse 2008: 412). In order to benefit from eased visa rules, Ukraine committed itself to enhancing its border policies and making its border guard (SBGS) compatible with Schengen standards.[14] Fourthly,

---

13 Progress in negotiating the Association Agreement as laid out in the *3rd Joint Progress Report* and the monitored performance of Ukraine corroborate the assumption that Ukraine is highly interested in greater cooperation with the EU. Further steps which facilitate Ukraine's (partial) integration into the EU are to follow in 2010 with the planned negotiation of a Deep and Comprehensive Free Trade Area (DCFTA).

14 The *Joint Evaluation Report: EU-Ukraine Action Plan* states: "The EU and Ukraine cooperated closely on the reform of the State Border Guard Service based on the Service's development concept up to 2015, aimed at making the Service 'Schengen-compatible'." (Commission of the European Communities 2008: 6).

Ukraine's efforts for intensive cooperation regarding border management also have to be understood against the background of the shared and still partly demarcated borders between Ukraine and Russia. "Moscow's position [on the demarcation of the Ukrainian-Russian border; M. H.] is that the international borders of the former USSR should be left open to facilitate personal and commercial contacts between the countries of the former Soviet Union" (Gatev 2008: 101). Approximation to the EU could well be taken as a move away from Russia. However, interdependence with Russia may limit the EU's influence in Ukraine (Dimitrova and Dragneva 2009: 854).

Policy Transfer Processes and Externalization Effects

In order to analyze recent developments in Ukraine's migration and border policies, this section looks at the Europeanization of the country with respect to two modes of governance. A distinction will be drawn between rather involuntary, conditionality-driven modes of governance and softer modes of network governance. Both modes allow for the transfer of EU migration policies to Ukraine.

Negotiating Agreements on Readmission and Visa Facilitation

The transfer of EU migration policies manifests itself, *inter alia*, in the conclusion of the readmission and visa facilitation agreement between Ukraine and the EC. Core aspects of the EU return policy have been implemented in Ukraine through the EC readmission agreement which sets out the provisions on the return of third-country nationals to their home country or a transit country and defines which of these migrants are to be deported, and how. All EC readmission agreements contain the non-negotiable provision that transit migrants—that is, stateless individuals or rejected asylum seekers—are to be returned (Council of the European Union 2008: 4). Because of the obligatory inclusion of transit migrants in these agreements, negotiations are usually difficult and protracted (Roig and Huddleston 2007: 363). Countries which are strongly affected by transit migration, in particular, hesitate to conclude EC readmission agreements. As stated earlier, Ukraine is a highly-frequented transit country, which explains its unwillingness to conclude a readmission agreement in the past. The Commission addressed the problem concerning the readmission of transit migrants by offering a transitional two-year period in which Ukraine was not obliged to readmit such migrants until January 1, 2010.

Unsurprisingly, the process of negotiation had been lengthy. In June 2002, the Commission had been mandated by the European Council to effect negotiations of a readmission agreement with Ukraine. After three years of negotiation, the Commission, in need of a compensatory incentive, opened negotiations on visa facilitations (VFA) in November 2005 (Commission of the European Communities 2009a: 4). The aim of the VFA is to facilitate the issuance of short-term Schengen visas to a closely defined group of Ukrainian nationals. Bona fide travelers in particular benefit from these agreements. A clear distinction between certain categories of people is drawn: students and retirees are generally exempt from the visa fee, the purpose of the travel is relevant (visiting close relatives, education, etc.), as is the profession of the visa applicant. For example, truck drivers, researchers, and businessmen are eligible for eased access to Schengen visas. Apart from privileged access to Schengen visas for certain groups, visa fees for all Ukrainian applicants were lowered from €60 to €35. In addition, these agreements determine the time period in which visas have to be issued and reduce the number of documents required for application.

Generating a strong "shadow of hierarchy" (Scharpf 2000: 323ff.; Börzel 2008; Héritier and Lehmkuhl 2008), the EU made it clear that Ukraine could only benefit from visa facilitations if it accepted an EC readmission agreement. Since visa facilitations allow for an easier flow of people between third countries and the EU, they are conducive to trade and economic relations and are therefore very attractive and widely used to permit the conclusion of readmission agreements (Billet 2010; Coleman, 2009).[15] Ukraine's strong interest in visa facilitations was demonstrated by the fact that it introduced a visa-free travel regime for EU citizens on a unilateral basis in May 2005.[16] This act was intended to show Ukraine's willingness to cooperate with the EU concerning questions of visa facilitations. The negotiations over an EC readmission agreement and on visa facilitations were finally successfully con-

---

15 Interestingly, this *quid pro quo* approach of offering visa facilitations in exchange for readmission agreements is not applied to all third countries: In the case of Morocco, negotiations over visa facilitations are bound to the successful conclusion of a readmission agreement. In spite of this exception it can be argued that the EU follows a *quid pro quo* logic as it was outlined in the Hague Programme: "The European Council invites the Council and the Commission to examine, with a view to developing a common approach, whether in the context of the EC readmission policy it would be opportune to facilitate, on a case by case basis, the issuance of short-stay visas to third-country nationals, where possible and on a basis of reciprocity, as part of a real partnership in external relations, including migration-related issues." (Presidency Conclusions of the Brussels European Council 2004: 26).

16 Generally, VFA are reciprocal. Since Ukraine already lifted the visa obligation for EU citizens, the VFA is not relevant to EU citizens. In case of reintroduction of a visa obligation for EU citizens, the principles of the VFA would also apply to EU citizens.

cluded in 2007. The negotiation processes regarding the readmission agreement and the VFA were reflective of the strong conditionality used by the EU.

The EU principle of conditionality contains a quasi-hierarchic element in that it employs a very strong incentive which drives the externalization of EU migration policy. Ukraine receives no direct benefits from the readmission agreement itself. Rather, it is the combination, or the quid pro quo-logic with the agreement on visa facilitation which makes this deal attractive to Ukraine. Furthermore, Ukraine's general and overall compliance with EU demands has been rewarded by the rather unusual prospect of a visa-free travel regime for Ukrainian citizens: "A visa-free regime seems actually impossible for most of these countries [endorsing readmission agreements; M. H.]." (Billet 2010: 71). In the case of Ukraine, the VFA sets out the mid-term prospect of a visa-free travel regime.[17] In order to reach this visa-free regime, a visa dialogue was established in 2008.

Europeanization of Ukraine's Migration Policy Through Project-Based Network Governance

Complementing quasi-hierarchical structures and governance modes, several EU financial instruments provide the basis for extended *network* governance in collaboration with non-state and state actors. Along the lines of the network governance applied to EU member states (especially the newly-acceded member states), financial programs like AENEAS facilitate migration-related projects.[18] Core aspects of EU migration policy, such as standards of asylum and refuge and border management, are transferred to and implemented in

[17] It should be noted that VFA are not synonymous with visa liberalization. VFA are used to simplify, expedite, and reduce the cost of visa processing. VFA only apply to short-term visas. Other kinds of Schengen visas are not covered by VFA. However, VFA do not have any influence on the Schengen code and therefore do not affect the conditions on which visas are issued.

[18] The funding can be distinguished by geographical and thematic scopes. The EC funds relevant to Ukraine are, or have been, the AENEAS program for financial and technical assistance to third countries in the area of migration and asylum and its successors, the Thematic Programme on Cooperation with third countries in the areas of migration and asylum; TACIS (Technical Assistance to the Commonwealth of Independent States); and ENPI (European Neighbourhood Policy Instrument). The financial resources for these programs are provided by EuropeAid, an EU agency which implements the Commission's external aid instruments. The following empirical findings are based on an analysis of the EC financial programs related to migration in the period of 2006 to 2009 (AENEAS; its successor, the Thematic Programme on Cooperation with Third Countries in the Area of Migration and Asylum; TACIS; and ENPI, respectively).

Ukraine (and other ENP countries) through such network governance[19], which also is a softer mode of governance when compared to the mode of negotiation (Lavenex 2008) and lacks the strong applied conditionality of the previously mentioned "shadow of hierarchy".

The EU has an interest in pursuing this kind of governance for various reasons: Implementing an effective migration and asylum policy through network governance curbs migration to the EU. The EU's aim is actually to set up an environment in which multiplier effects can take place; for example, training programs for migration officers and personnel in detention facilities are intended to cultivate knowledge and standards in the treatment of migrants and refugees. The scope of many of these projects transcends ultimate goals and points to the future workings of a Ukrainian migration policy. Such projects are usually carried out by NGOs or intergovernmental organizations, such as the International Organization for Migration (IOM), the UN High Commissioner for Refugees (UNHCR), and the International Red Cross, or by NGOs, such as NEEKA, ECRE, and the Danish Refugee Council. This project-based governance constitutes an important aspect of network governance and accounts for a variety of policy transfers which will be explained in the following.

Border management and the "Schengenization" of Ukraine's border policies act as a cornerstone of EU-Ukrainian cooperation in accordance with the specific JHA Action Plan (Commission of the European Communities 2007). As already outlined above, Ukraine has become an important partner for the EU in matters of border management. Common interests concerning security issues also account for the EU-Ukrainian cooperation on border management.[20] Apart from that, Ukraine pursues its own interests in curbing illegal migration. Joint operations and support of the EU in the demarcation of its eastern border could reduce illegal migration to Ukraine and figures reveal that the Ukrainian border guards have actually apprehended more illegal migrants (Söderköping Process 2009). Since Ukraine is confronted with a growing influx of migrants, this becomes more and more appealing to the Ukrainian government.

Close cooperation between Frontex and the SBGS, which is based on a joint working agreement concluded in 2007, supports Ukraine's efforts to modernize the SBGS. Joint operations, such as the Five Border Project and

19 See Slaughter (2004: 52ff.) for an elaborated explanation of implementation networks and Lavenex (2008) on implementation networks within the external dimension of the EU migration policy.

20 As stated in the conclusion of the common Meeting on Justice, Freedom, and Security between the Troika of the European Union and Ukraine in 2009, Ukraine and the EU perceive "common challenges in the fight against organised crime, including trafficking in human beings, illegal immigration and other illegal activities which are of cross-border nature" (Council of the European Union 2009: 2).

Jupiter 2009, which involved training for Ukrainian border guards and Ukraine's participation in the European Patrol Network, show the close relation between Frontex and Ukraine. The aim of their growing cooperation is the transfer of good practices of participating border guards from member states to the SBGS in order to achieve its Schengen compatibility by 2015 and to enhance border controls.[21] In addition, several projects were developed to modernize and "Europeanize" the SBGS. The Huremas I and II projects, carried out by the IOM, sought to develop the management tools and practices needed to select qualified professionals, to provide training, and to set standards which "would allow Ukraine to be a full partner throughout Europe in maintaining open and secure borders." (IOM 2006) Aside from this very practical cooperation, the project was directed towards the modernization of Ukraine's law on border management (IOM 2009). EC funding was used to introduce integrated border management standards in Ukraine through joint training, legislative reforms, and, most importantly, by supplying modern technical equipment. Various border crossing points along the EU-Ukrainian border, such as Rava-Ruska, Jagodyn, Chop, and Uzghorod, were provided with modern border surveillance equipment through the BOMUK project.

With regard to *human trafficking*, the ninth annual *Trafficking in Persons Report* of the US Department of State (2009: 290) states: "Ukraine is a source, transit and, to a lesser extent, destination country for men, women, and children trafficked for the purposes of commercial sexual exploitation and forced labor. Forty-eight percent of the trafficking victims assisted by IOM and its local NGO partners in Ukraine in 2008 suffered sexual exploitation; three percent had been forced to beg; and 49 percentsuffered other forms of forced labor." The JHA Action Plan envisions measures to combat human trafficking and people smuggling (Commission of the European Communities 2007: 6). In order to prevent human trafficking, efforts are directed towards the implementation of the UN Convention against Transnational Organized Crime, which deals with human trafficking and people smuggling, among other things (United Nations Office on Drugs and Crime 2004). IOM has carried out anti-trafficking-projects in Ukraine[22] since 1998, focusing on the implementation of anti-trafficking laws by Ukrainian authorities as well as on supporting victims of human trafficking. Reintegration of victims through microcredits is one of the measures in dealing with human trafficking. EC funding supports these activities. In order to combat the root causes of human trafficking, the International Centre for Migration Policy Development (ICMPD) implemented an EC-financed project which aimed at

---

21 In addition, the close cooperation with Frontex aims to prepare Ukraine for the co-hosting of the European Football Championship in 2012 (European Commission 2010: 13).

22 [online] Available at: iom.org.ua/index.php?page=catalog&id=11 [Accessed June 10, 2010].

offering a long-term perspective against human trafficking.[23] Labor market-based measures have been driven forward by this project.

Return policies are another instrument of migration policy. Having concluded an EC readmission agreement, Ukraine is eligible to receive EC funding to implement return measures. Ukrainian policies concerning the return of illegal migrants and the effective implementation of the readmission agreement are supported by the EU both in financial and practical terms. Technical Cooperation and Capacity Building for the Governments of Ukraine and Moldova (GUMIRA) is one such project supporting the implementation of the readmission agreements through capacity building and consulting of Ukrainian authorities in place to deal with matters of readmission. Carried out by IOM, the project encompasses training on legal, technical, and administrative aspects of readmission, the development of a methodology for monitoring and evaluation of the activities of governmental bodies in the area of readmission, and awareness raising amongst civil servants dealing with readmission-related matters. Another issue concerns the implementation of recommendations and best practices for temporary accommodation and detention centers for migrants in providing training for the staff of the Ministry of Internal Affairs and the SBGS (with a particular focus on voluntary return, health care for migrants, human rights, asylum opportunities, and documentation). One part of this project is the establishment of a program to encourage migrants to return to their countries of origin voluntarily and to support the government in the implementation of a state program aimed to promote voluntary return. Cooperation with international and local NGOs such as NEEKA and Caritas, as well as with intergovernmental organizations such as UNHCR aims to protect the human rights of the migrants concerned. Other projects like Capacity Building in Migration Management, carried out by IOM, include voluntary assisted return as well. IOM cooperates with local NGOs to assist migrants in organizing and financing the voluntary return to their home countries. Measures to promote voluntary return have been of particular interest to Ukraine since the readmission agreement and improved control policies have been in force. Facing a potentially growing number of illegal and returned migrants poses challenges for the Ukrainian government. Returning them to their home or a transit country may be a viable solution.

With regard to *asylum and refugee policies* the EU, among others, may pursue the goal of implementing an externalization strategy to share the burden of migration in the future as well. The setting-up and improvement of existing asylum and refugee policies aims primarily to enhance the protection level of refugees and asylum seekers. At present, Ukraine cannot be considered a safe third country where core principles of international refugee protection, such as the principle of non-refoulement, are safeguarded (Ukrainian

---

23 [online] Available at: icmpd.org/696.html?&no_cache=1&tx_icmpd_pi1[article]=1116&tx_icmpd_pi1[page]=1120 [Accessed June 10, 2010].

Refugee Council 2010; European Commission 2010: 13). Allegations of inhuman treatment of asylum-seekers, a lack of refugee status determination procedures, and the phenomenon of xenophobia call for profound enhancement of asylum und refugee policies in Ukraine (Ibid.). In particular, the coming into force of the EC readmission agreement and the possible return of asylum seekers to Ukraine again raise serious concerns about the Ukrainian asylum system (Ukrainian Refugee Council 2010). Notwithstanding the fact that the return of recognized asylum seekers is not intended by the readmission agreement, there is concern that among the migrants returned to Ukraine there may be some in need for protection.[24]

The transfer of asylum policies clearly focuses on status determination procedures and, for example, the treatment of asylum seekers and refugees in accommodation facilities. It can be assumed that an effective and reliable status determination system is seen as a means to control immigration into the EU. The fact that a fair and well-working status determination system is regarded as a prerequisite for Ukraine's transition to becoming a safe third country shows that the EU is pursuing its externalization strategy because such a system would allow the EU to disclaim any responsibility for asylum seekers transiting Ukraine on their way to the EU. Moreover, the EU could send asylum seekers back to Ukraine if they transited it before entering the EU.

EC-funded Regional Protection Programmes (RPPs) and other initiatives are intended to close these policy gaps in the Ukrainian asylum and refugee policies. Established and run by the Danish Refugee Council and the Austrian Caritas, these RPP aim to build protection facilities in Ukraine and provide support to asylum and refuge seekers in Ukraine through legal advice or translation services.[25] Another focus is on the enhancement of refugee status determination. The overall aim of these RPP is to establish a sustainable infrastructure in Zakarpattya and other regions that are strongly affected by (transit) migration and mixed flows of migrants. The determination of the legal status of migrants in Ukraine has been supported by another project (ERIT), carried out by ICMPD, an intergovernmental organization assigned

---

24 "In practice, not only irregular migrants and failed asylum seekers are returned under such agreements, but also asylum seekers whose claim for asylum and protection needs have yet to be determined." (Human Rights Watch 2005: 11). UNHCR (2007: 13) points to the "risk of creating 'chain-refoulement' from the European Union or of an overburdening the nascent Ukrainian asylum system in the future" by the implementation of the readmission agreement.

25 The aim of these RPP is to build an asylum system and to improve the already existing policies. For the period analyzed, two RPPs were identified: i) Strengthening Asylum and Protection Capacity in Ukraine by Enhancing the Capacity of Governmental and Civil Society Stakeholders in a Participatory Approach and Cross-sector Cooperation and ii) Enhancing Capacities in the Area of Protection and Treatment of Refugees in Zakarpattya.

to migration management. Screening centers and a country-of-origin system have been set up and training for migration officers has been provided.

Accommodation and detention of migrants and refugees is a major problem in Ukraine and has been criticized by NGOs and international organizations like the Council of Europe. For example, the European Committee for the Prevention of Torture and Inhuman or Degrading Treatment or Punishment (CPT) issued a report on a visit to Ukrainian detention centers in 2009 and expressed concerns about the conditions of detention in temporary holding centers (CPT 2009). In response to this problem, Capacity Building in Migration Management and several other EC-funded projects were developed and implemented by IOM to provide support to detention facilities in Ukraine. Two migrant detention centers in the Volyn and Chernihiv oblasts have since been opened with the support of this project.

Another project addressed the *integration* of legally residing refugees into the Ukrainian society. The UNHCR conducted a project (Local Integration of Refugees in Belarus, Moldova, and Ukraine) to detect deficiencies in Ukraine's refugee integration policy. Based on the results of this project, an action plan on the integration of recognized refugees into Ukrainian society for the period until 2012 was developed and approved by the Cabinet of Ministers in July 2009 (United Nations High Commissioner for Refugees 2009).

Summarizing these findings on policy transfer and the use of governance modes, one effect of the policy transfer facilitated through network governance is an approximation of policies between Ukraine and the EU, both in legal and practical terms, with respect to border management, human trafficking, asylum, and migration. Whereas the negotiation mode of governance primarily accounts for the signing of the EC readmission agreement, convergence from Ukrainian policies to EU standards is prominently promoted via network governance. This mode of governance can be considered to be particularly effective in terms of capacity building and sustainability. Network governance and the participation of NGOs and other local non-state actors may help to promote standards in the Ukrainian society. NGOs like NEEKA and, most importantly, intergovernmental organizations such as UNHCR, ICMPD, and IOM, serve as executive actors in the transfer of policies.

Ambiguous Results of Ukraine's Europeanization and Its Impacts on Migrants

Most migrants coming to Ukraine find themselves in a challenging situation marked by violations of rights and a significant lack of rights, especially for irregular migrants (European Commission 2010; Amnesty International 2010; CPT 2009). To a certain extent, irregularity has to be seen as a by-product of the malfunctioning migration and asylum system in which determination procedures are not in compliance with international standards and only 3% of asylum seekers are granted asylum. The Europeanization of Ukraine's migration policies has been leading to ambiguous results for migrants in the country. It can be shown that the influence of the EU has both negative and positive effects on the situation of migrants in Ukraine. One consequence of the EU's externalization policy is that the situation of migrants in Ukraine is worsening because Ukraine becomes a trap and an unwelcoming last stop for transit migrants. However, the externalization and transfer of policies to Ukraine also lead to an improvement of the situation of migrants. This ambiguity will be addressed in the following subsections.

Resulting Constraints for Migrants in the "Buffer Zone"

The EU's externalization policy and Ukraine's willingness to cooperate closely on issues of border management and migration policy indirectly fuel immigration into Ukraine, leading to a growing immigration population living in Ukraine. Since the Schengen enlargement in 2007, Ukraine has seen an increasing number of transit migrants ending their journey in Ukraine due to increased border controls from the new Schengen members in the EU (Pylynskyi 2008).[26] At the same time, EU externalization policies lead to intensified border control by the Ukrainian side. The EC readmission agreement and the import of return policies further contribute to Ukraine's migration profile as an immigration country of second choice if readmitted migrants stay in the country (ECRE 2008: 57). From a migrant's perspective, Ukraine's convergence to European standards makes it significantly more difficult to enter and transit through Ukraine, let alone illegally cross the EU-Ukrainian border, making it more and more likely that migrants have to remain in Ukraine involuntarily and against their original intention. Ukraine's compliance with EU standards may prevent them from returning to their home countries since re-entry is becoming more and more difficult due to increased and modernized border controls and stricter policies on illegal migration.

These developments and, even more important, the fact that more and more transit migrants become stranded in Ukraine adds further fuel to an already tense atmosphere with growing xenophobia and hostility. Although Ukraine has been considered to be a relatively tolerant country since its inde-

26 Even in cases where transit migrants without proper travel documents are arrested in Ukraine, detention is limited to a maximum of six months, according to Article 32 of the Law of Ukraine on the Legal Status of Foreigners and Stateless Individuals. Migrants whose nationality and identity cannot be determined while in detention cannot be returned to their home country and are thus to stay in Ukraine.

pendence, this picture has changed due to a number of xenophobic incidents since 2006, when two Africans residing in Ukraine were murdered. The following years were marked by an increase in xenophobic and racist attacks, with more than 100 incidents of hostility and xenophobia reported in 2006 and 2007 (Tyshchenko 2008). In public debate, immigration is largely perceived as a security threat: "Public opinion sees immigration of foreigners as a major cause of criminal activities, terrorism, illegal transportation of human beings, drugs and weapons, the shadow economy and prevalence of dangerous and exotic diseases." (Malynovska and Kubanova 2008: 331). International and local NGOs and intergovernmental organizations frequently report on racism and racial crime against migrants in Ukraine (International Executive Committee of BMP Ukraine 2010: 3; Schiffer et al. 2010). The NGO Human Rights First (2008) claims that "[racial] and other bias-motivated violent crimes are dramatically on the rise in Ukraine. Individuals of non-European origin, immigrants and minorities are the most vulnerable to violent attacks, many of which occur in broad daylight." The migrant groups most affected by the growing xenophobic attitude are members of the so-called new minorities from Africa, Asia, and countries of the Caucasus like Chechnya (Ibid.: 41).

Despite an existing legal framework, the Ukrainian prosecutors and investigators "until now generally lack an explicit instruction and adequate training to fully investigate possible racial and other bias motivations behind violent attacks."[27] In its *2009 Country Reports on Human Rights Practices* on human rights violations in Ukraine, the U.S. Department of State states: "The media and domestic monitoring NGOs reported an increased number of protests against dark-skinned individuals, irregular migrants, and foreign students by locally based skinhead groups and neonationalist organizations. On November 28, the nationalist Svoboda party launched a national anti-immigrant campaign and conducted marches in all regions" (Department of State 2010). Immigrants are even faced with violence and the violation of their fundamental rights by state actors: Abuse of Somali refugees in March 2009 by members of the Ukrainian police and their reluctance to investigate the case have been reported (Schiffer et al. 2010: 48). Well aware of xenophobic tendencies in Ukraine, the EU supports measures which aim to strengthen civil society's efforts to combat xenophobia. For instance, the Diversity Initiative brings together local NGOs, diplomatic missions in Ukraine, organizations from the government sector, and interested individuals dealing with matters of racism and xenophobia in Ukraine.

As well as increasing xenophobia and racism, migrants and refugees in Ukraine face unfavorable social, economic, and human rights conditions (Düvell 2008). Ukraine still considers itself to be a country in political, eco-

---

27 [online] Available at: humanrightsfirst.org/discrimination/pages.aspx?id=155 [accessed June 10, 2010].

nomic, and social transition and is ill-equipped to offer acceptable living conditions to migrants. Refugees, asylum seekers, illegal migrants, and unaccompanied refugee children, in particular, have to be considered as vulnerable to the shortcomings of Ukraine's migration regime (European Commission 2010: 13). Bearing in mind that status determination procedures are still in their infancy, the illegal status of many migrants, among those many asylum seekers, is a striking feature of Ukraine's still deficient migration policy, which leads to severe problems and challenges in the lives of many migrants.

Accommodation and employment are major problems for migrants without proper documents. Irregular migrants and asylum seekers still face unbearable situations in detention facilities, although, thanks to international assistance, some progress has been made (CPT 2009). These often overcrowded facilities are run by the border guards and the treatment of migrants has been subject to heavy criticism. It is reported that the human rights of many migrants are seriously violated in these facilities (Düvell 2008a: 4; Pro Asyl 2009: 3f.; Amnesty International 2010: 336f.). According to Article 20 of the Refugee Law, only recognized refuges are eligible for accommodation and financial support (UNHCR 2007: 11), so illegal migrants are left to their own devices. Furthermore, there are still only a few accommodation facilities run by the state, so that many refugees and migrants are forced to rent apartments. Pro Asyl (2009) and other NGOs report that landlords often exploit the precarious situation of migrants and charge higher rents, resulting in overcrowded apartments and poor living conditions. Frank Düvell (2008: 6) further points out that the landlords' frequent unwillingness to provide written tenancy agreements to migrants leads to a vicious circle, because these documents are required to receive a statutory registration document.[28] Lacking a registration document is closely connected with irregular employment, since irregular migrants cannot obtain a tax number. Furthermore, the poor economic situation and xenophobic attitudes of employers make it even more difficult for migrants to enter the labor market. This situation forces many migrant to work illegally, such as in street trading, foodservice and agriculture (Pylynskyi 2008: 37), and in precarious conditions. Often, the money earned in this way does not even cover the basic necessities of life such as food, medicine, and rent (ECRE 2009: 71).

Another factor that hampers the integration of migrants into Ukraine is the issue of protracted diploma thesis defense procedures due to insufficient support of Ukrainian authorities in the recognition of diplomas. As a result, many migrants with secondary or higher education are employed in jobs for which they are overqualified. In addition, Ukrainian authorities do not offer

---

28 The former propiska system was officially abolished by a ruling of the Ukrainian Constitutional Court in 2001. A residency registration, which is mandatory for access to medical assistance in public hospitals or for obtaining a birth certificate, replaced this very restrictive *propiska* system (UNHCR 2007: 12).

sufficient language courses to immigrants, thus constraining their integration into their host country and the Ukrainian labor market. UNHCR's activities in setting up a refugee integration agenda in Ukraine show the policy gap migrants in Ukraine are faced with. Discrimination of migrants is another aspect of the deficient migration policy in Ukraine: While in Kiev access to school is free for refugees, the situation is rather different in other parts of Ukraine where, for example, Somali children have been denied access to education (Düvell 2008a: 3).

In view of these briefly outlined shortcomings, the EU externalization strategy has proved to be problematic. The EU-supported transformation into a "buffer zone" (Zimmer 2008) exacerbates the already difficult situation of migrants and refugees and it is to be feared that the situation will become even worse if border control measures become tighter. In addition, the full implementation of the EU readmission policies will contribute to a growing migration population.[29] Stricter border controls result in higher numbers of stranded transit migrants, which will prove particularly problematic if measures such as policies to combat xenophobia fail, or emerging civil society activities are not sufficiently supported by state authorities or donor agencies. Restrictions on accommodation, for example, are reinforced through the externalization processes and the effects of Ukraine's Europeanization. "So far, Ukraine is not geared up to this challenge and indeed, hosting refugees and migrants whose aspiration is to move west does not seem to be in the best interest of Ukraine. In other words, the problems we describe are largely a consequence of strict EU migration policies which puts Ukraine in a position to deal with a phenomenon it lacks the capacity to deal with." (International Executive Committee of Border Monitoring Project 2010: 3). The EU policies may thus even exacerbate existing problems related to accommodation, employment, integration, and the enjoyment of human rights of migrants. It remains doubtful whether the positive effects of the EU policies will counterbalance this effect in the future.

Balancing Negative Impacts?

The described shortcomings and severe deficiencies in Ukraine's migration system, the negative effects of its sectoral Europeanization, and the import of control measures have resulted in an urgent need to establish a system which respects the fundamental rights of migrants and refugees. State authorities still fail to protect migrants and, in particular, vulnerable groups such as asy-

[29] Figures on the implementation of the EC readmission agreements are not yet available. Future research should address the effects of the full entry into force of this agreement.

lum seekers.[30] Rather, the protection of these groups—originally a responsibility of the general public—is now provided by a highly active system of international and local NGOs and intergovernmental organizations. The EU-driven establishment of an asylum system, the empowerment of civil society actors concerned with providing support to migrants and asylum seekers, and capacity building in Ukraine all aim to mitigate these shortcomings. Ukrainian NGOs dealing with migration-related issues are usually brought together by intergovernmental organizations such as UNHCR. HIAS, Rokada, and NEEKA are some of the most commonly known Ukrainian NGOs which work on migration and refugee issues. In addition, Ukrainian Refugee Council and other umbrella organizations have been set up with the support of the Danish Refugee Council and with financial contributions from the EU. The establishment of organizations dealing with refugee and migration matters in Ukraine is actively supported and encouraged by the Europeanization of Ukraine's migration system. Unsurprisingly, most of the NGOs dealing with migration and refugee issues have been set up in the last few years, when the effects of Europeanization became noticeable (Schiffer et al. 2010: 57). With Ukraine having become an immigration country of second choice and an immigration country "by default" that is still not ready and/or willing to host (illegal) migrants and refugees in a way that respects human rights, international as well as national and local NGOs have gained an increasingly important role.

While the Ukrainian government seems rather indifferent to problems such as xenophobia and racism (Amnesty International 2008; Zimmer 2008; Schiffer et al. 2010: 53), the role of NGOs and intergovernmental organizations in fulfilling the responsibilities originally assigned to state authorities has been strengthened by EU support, leaving few incentives for state authorities to engage in protection policies. Accordingly, network governance plays a vital role in compensating for the deficiencies of Ukrainian authorities. The assumption of responsibilities by the NGOs and their vital role in protecting basic human rights are highlighted in a report on the functioning of detention centers issued by the CPT. The report describes the activities of the NGOs, which range from basic health care at detention facilities in Chop at the Ukrainian border to Slovakia and Hungary to providing access to legal support for detained refugees and asylum seekers (CPT 2009: 23). At the same time, the Ukrainian government and authorities are criticized for their lack of

30 The 2010 Progress Report of the European Commission (2010: 13) stresses that Ukraine, in particular, has failed to protect refugees and asylum seekers: "During 2009 there were certain violations of rights of refugees and asylum-seekers in breach of obligations under international human rights and refugee law, in particular the 1951 Geneva Convention on the Status of Refugees, notably with regards to deportation of migrants to countries despite risks of ill-treatment. Issues of the economic and social rights of asylum seekers and their access to the appropriate procedure remain to be addressed."

action in protecting migrants and refugees. In response to the CPT report, the Ukrainian side points out that substantial progress has been made thanks to the support of NEEKA, Caritas Austria, and other NGOs (CPT 2009a: 8). It is the financial support from the EU which enables NGOs to assume these responsibilities and it can be argued that this extended use of network governance makes it easy for Ukrainian authorities to disclaim and shift their own responsibility for fair treatment of migrants to non-state actors. Consequently, the role of the NGOs should be subjected to a critical assessment and the question arises as to whether it may actually discourage the Ukrainian state authorities from improving the migration system. In this light, the EU-induced reform of Ukraine's migration policies seems to obstruct rather than facilitate changes in the treatment of migrants by Ukrainian authorities.

Even though positive developments resulting from NGO activities have been reported (Schiffer et al. 2010: 23), the capacity of NGOs to assume responsibilities of the state has to be questioned, especially when considering their comparatively limited financial resources (Stewart 2009). This makes compensation for the authorities' failure nearly impossible and the activities of the NGOs seem like a drop in the ocean. Field research has even cast a dark shadow over the activities of some NGOs: Frank Düvell (2008: 7) reports on cases of corrupt NGOs and negative attitudes of migrants and refugees towards NGOs due to their close interaction with state authorities. Contracts between the border guards and some NGOs restrict other NGOs and lawyers from access to detained migrants and refugees (ECRE 2010: 13).

Another (indirect) result of Ukraine's Europeanization is a certain level of self-organization of migrants. As a group affected by this trend, migrants actively react to developments stemming from EU external governance within Ukraine. Self-organization can be perceived as an adaptation strategy to an environment which does not react sufficiently to a growing migrant population, ignores their needs, and even violates their rights. Organizing their interests promises better protection and visibility as a group with specific problems, needs, and interests. However, as a study by Stefanie Schiffer, Tetiana Katsberg, and Sabine Roßmann (2010: 57) makes clear, self-organization is still rare and in its early stages. Apart from NGOs which provide assistance to refugees, such as HIAS, the Social Action Centre–No Border Project, and the Chernihiv Human Rights Committee, only few migrant organizations have so far been established in Ukraine. While the diaspora of the so-called old minorities of Russians and Azerbaijanis, among others, is fairly well organized, the self-organization of the new minorities has begun only recently (Ibid.: 54). The African Centre and Berkat, Association of Koreans in Ukraine are examples of migrant organizations in Ukraine. In contrast to NGOs like NEEKA and the Danish Refugee Council, the activities of migrant organizations are not directly funded and supported by the EU. Facing financial and organizational constraints, many migrant organizations forge links to networks and umbrella organizations such as the Diversity Initiative and the newly-established Ukrainian Refugee Council, both of which receive support from the EU. Because of the lack of adequate funding, most of the refugee and migrants community organizations provide primarily non-material assistance to other migrants. Furthermore, they depend on voluntary efforts of their members. Due to these financial and material restrictions, the reach of their work is limited.

One of these refugee and migrant organizations, Berkat, provides legal advice to migrants, helps migrants to find accommodation, and supports the migrants and refugees in their efforts to enter the Ukrainian labor market. Other examples include Social Service of Assistance, an organization that focuses on the education of refugee children, and a group of students in the city of Vinnytsya, who set up a mentoring program for immigrated students (Ibid.: 65). NGOs providing assistance to refugees and migrants are located not only in Kiev and other large cities, but also in Ukraine's "hot spots" such as the Zakarpattya oblast to ensure that migrants receive support directly.

Migrant and non-migrant organizations in Ukraine are also involved in campaigns to raise awareness among the Ukrainian society of intolerance of migrants. One such campaign is "We have more in common than we think: the colour of the skin doesn't matter" (IOM 2009a), which involves so-called "living library events", where representatives of minorities and immigrants report on their experiences with xenophobia and racism in Ukraine.

Conclusion

This article explored the transfer of EU migration policies to Ukraine, specifically with regard to two major modes of governance. The negotiation mode of governance accounts for transfer by means of an applied *quid-pro-quo* logic: the EC agreement on visa facilitations and the prospect of closer EU-Ukraine cooperation as a result of the negotiation of an association agreement intended to put in place the core aspect of the EU's externalization strategy. Network governance is responsible for the transfer of several other aspects of EU migration policy. The Europeanization of Ukraine's migration policy through this governance mode becomes manifest in border and return policies, asylum and refuge, and anti-human trafficking and integration policies. In general, NGOs and other non-state actors, as well as intergovernmental organizations, implement aspects of EU migration policy in Ukraine and thus compensate for deficiencies in Ukrainian migration and asylum policies. Although pressure for compliance is not as obvious and direct as in the case of the EC readmission agreement, this mode of transfer is widely used and proves particularly effective in Ukraine's Europeanization. However, the multi-faceted role of non-state actors in the Europeanization process must be subjected to a critical assessment because these actors may reduce the government's commitment to reforming its policies—not least because intergovernmental organizations such as IOM and ICMPD in particular are directly involved in transforming Ukraine into an immigration country of second choice, which has negative implications for migrants and refugees.

While it is in the interest of the EU to transfer its policies to third countries such as Ukraine in order to keep migration out of its territory, these third countries cooperate for two main reasons: First, the import of migration policies and compliance with EU demands and standards are rewarded through closer political and economic relations with the EU, such as the negotiation of a Deep and Comprehensive Free Trade Area (DCFTA) and the prospect of future EU membership for Ukraine. Second, Ukraine's own interest in curbing illegal immigration explains its efforts to bring its migration policies in line with EU standards.

The results of the Europeanization of Ukraine's migration policy have proved to be ambiguous when it comes to the impact on migrants and refugees in Ukraine. On the one hand, the EU's influence leads to better protection of migrants and asylum seekers in Ukraine by correcting some shortcomings of Ukraine's migration policy; on the other hand, the EU externalization strategy transforms Ukraine into an immigration country, leading to virtually insurmountable barriers to migration to the EU. Already existing challenges, including xenophobic tendencies and deficiencies in Ukraine's migration policy, are reinforced by the EU-driven transformation of Ukraine into what could be called a "dead end". Positive effects of the EU externalization strategy are unlikely to fully compensate for the various problems and deficiencies in Ukraine's migration policy, which are partly caused by the EU's shift of control policies to Ukraine. Self-organization, as an adaptation strategy employed by some migrants in Ukraine, serves to address and mitigate these serious challenges. Concluding, one can say that the EU's influence seems to be highly problematic for the Ukrainian government, but particularly for migrants in Ukraine who are directly confronted with the negative effects of Europeanization.

References

Amnesty International (2008): Ukraine: Government must act to stop racial discrimination. [online] Available at: http://www.amnesty.org/en/library/asset/EUR50/005/2008/en/a2ae7885-5ed9-11dd-a592-c739f9b70de8/eur500052008spa.pdf [Accessed February 14, 2011].

Amnesty International (2010): Amnesty International Report 2010. The State of the World's Human Rights. [online] Available at: http://thereport.amnesty.org/sites/default/files/AIR2010_EN.pdf [Accessed 13 June 2010].

Barbé, E./Johansson-Nogués, E. (2008): The EU as a modest 'force for good': the European Neighbourhood Policy. In: International Affairs 84, 1, pp. 81-96.

Bendel, P. (2007): Everything under control? The European Union's policies and politics of immigration. In: Ette, Andreas/Faist, Thomas (ed.): Between Autonomy and the European Union – The Europeanization of National Immigration Policies. London: Macmillan, pp. 32-48.

Billet, C. (2010): EC Readmission Agreements: A Prime Instrument of the External Dimension of the EU's Fight against Irregular Immigration. An Assessment after Ten Years of Practice. In: European Journal of Migration and Law 12, 1, pp. 45-79.

Bobitski, N. (2008): Do Ut Des? The Need for True Reciprocity in the European Neighbourhood Policy. In: European Foreign Affairs Review 13, pp. 449-472.

Boratyński, J./Gromadzki, G./Sushko, O./Szymborska, A. (2006): Questionable Achievement. EC-Ukraine Visa Facilitation Agreement. [online] Available at: http://www.batory.org.pl/doc/ec-ukraine-visa-facilitation-agreement.pdf [Accessed 10 June 2010].

Börzel, T. (2008): European Governance – Verhandlungen und Wettbewerb im Schatten der Hierarchie In: Politische Vierteljahresschrift, Sonderheft 40/2007, pp. 61-91.

Boswell, Ch. (2003): The 'external dimension' of EU immigration and asylum policy In: International Affairs, 79, 3, pp. 619-638.

Bulmer, S./Padgett, S. (2005): Policy Transfer in the European Union. An Institutionalist Perspective. In: British Journal of Political Science 35, 1, pp. 103–126.

Clandestino Project (2009): Undocumented Migration in Ukraine. Policy Brief, July 2009. [online] Available at: http://clandestino.eliamep.gr/wp-content/uploads/2009/11/ukraine-policy-brief_july-091.pdf [Accessed 13 June 2010].

Coleman, N. (2009): European readmission policy. Third country interests and refugee rights. Boston: Brill.

Commission of the European Communities (2002): Communication from the Commission to the Council and the European Parliament. Integrating Migration Issues in the European Union's Relations with Third Countries', Brussels, COM (2002) 703.
[online] Available at: http://ec.europa.eu/justice_home/funding/2004_2007/doc/com_2002_703_final.pdf [Accessed 10 June 2010].

Commission of the European Communities (2007): Revised EU-Ukraine Action Plan on Freedom, Security and Justice. Challenges and strategic aims, [online] Available at: http://ec.europa.eu/world/enp/pdf/action_plans/ukraine_enp_ap_jls-rev_en.pdf [Accessed 10 June 2010].

Commission of the European Communities (2008): Joint Evaluation Report. EU-Ukraine Action Plan, March 2008. [online] Available at: http://ec.europa.eu/external_relations/ukraine/docs/ukraine_eu_joint_evaluation_2008_en.pdf [Accessed 10 June 2010].

Commission of the European Communities (2009): Implementation of the European Neighbourhood Policy in 2008. Progress Report Ukraine. SEC (2009) 515/2,

[online] Available at: http://ec.europa.eu/world/enp/pdf/progress2009/sec09_515_en.pdf [Accessed 10 June 2010]
Commission of the European Communities (2009a): Evaluation of the implementation of the European Community's visa facilitation agreements with third countries. SEC (2009) 1401.
Commission of the European Communities (2010): EU-Ukraine Association Agenda to prepare and facilitate the implementation of the Association Agreement. [online] Available at: http://ec.europa.eu/external_relations/ukraine/docs/2010_eu_ukraine_association_agenda_en.pdf [Accessed 10 June 2010].
Commission of the European Communities (2010a): List of the EU-Ukraine Association Agenda priorities for 2010. [online] Available at: http://ec.europa.eu/external_relations/ukraine/docs/2010_association_agenda_priorities_en.pdf [Accessed 10 June 2010].
Council of the European Union (2008): Council Conclusions on the evaluation of the Global Approach to Migration and on the partnership with countries of origin and transit, 2914th General Affairs Council meeting, Brussels, 8 December 2008. [online] Available at: http://www.eu2008.fr/webdav/site/PFUE/shared/import/1208_CAGRE/Council_Conclusions_Migration_EN.pdf [Accessed 10 June 2010].
Council of the European Union (2009): Meeting on Justice, Freedom and Security between the Troika of the European Union and Ukraine. Conclusions, Luxembourg 3 June 2009. 10602/09 (Presse 165). [online] Available at: http://register.consilium.europa.eu/pdf/en/09/st10/st10602.en09.pdf [Accessed 10 June 2010].
Dannreuther, Roland (2006): Developing the Alternative to Enlargement: The European Neighbourhood Policy. In: European Foreign Affairs Review 11, pp. 183–201.
Department of State (2009): Trafficking in Persons Report 2009[online] Available at: http://www.state.gov/documents/organization/123357.pdf [Accessed 10 June 2010].
Department of State (2010): 2009 Country Reports on Human Rights Practices – Ukraine. [online] Available at: http://www.unhcr.org/refworld/country,,,,UKR,,4b9e52ae80,0.html [Accessed 10 June 2010].
Dietz, B. (2007): Migration policy challenges at the new Eastern borders of the enlarged European Union: The Ukrainian case. Arbeiten aus dem Osteuropa-Institut München, Nr. 267, July 2007.
Dimitrova, A./Dragneva, R. (2009): Constraining external governance: interdependence with Russia and the CIS as limits to the EU's rule transfer in the Ukraine. In: Journal of European Public Policy 16, 6, pp. 853-872.
Dolowitz, D. P./Marsh, D. (2000): Learning from Abroad. The Role of Policy Transfer in Contemporary Policy-Making. In: Governance: An International Journal of Policy and Administration 13, 1, pp. 5–24.
Düvell, F. (2008): Ukraine – Immigration and Transit Country for Chechen Refugees. Research resource report 3. Oxford: COMPAS. [online] Available at: http://www.compas.ox.ac.uk/fileadmin/files/pdfs/Non_WP_pdfs/Transit_Migration_in_Ukraine/Ukraine_Chechens_Case_Study_3of3.pdf [Accessed 10 June 2010].

Düvell, F. (2008a): On the Fringes of Europe: Refugees in Ukraine. Central and East European Migration, Research Resources Report 2/3. [online] Available at: http://www.compas.ox.ac.uk/fileadmin/files/pdfs/Non_WP_pdfs/Transit_Migration_in_Ukraine/Ukraine_Refugees_2of3.pdf [Accessed 13 June 2010].

Düvell, F. (2010): Asylum Protection vs. Border Control: An Unattainable Balance? Evidence from Central and Eastern Europe and CIS Countries, Brief, EPC workshop, Brussels. [online] Available at: http://www.compas.ox.ac.uk/fileadmin/files/pdfs/Franck_Duvell/Asylum%20Protection%20vs%20Border%20Control_Duvell.pdf [Accessed 10 June 2010].

ECRE (2008): Country Report 2007. Belarus, Moldova, Russia, Ukraine. [online] Available at: http://www.ecre.org/resources/Policy_papers/1222 [Accessed 10 June 2010].

ECRE (2009): "Here to Stay?" Refugee voices in Belarus, Moldova, the Russian Federation and Ukraine.
[online] Available at: http://www.ecre.org/resources/ECRE_actions/1322 [Accessed 10 June 2010].

ECRE (2010): Ukraine Country Report 2009. Situation for refugees and asylum seekers. [online] Available at: http://www.ecre.org/files/ECRE_Report_Eng_with_cover_preview.pdf [Accessed 18 July 2010].

European Commission (2010): Implementation of the European Neighbourhood Policy in 2009. Progress Report Ukraine, SEC (2010) 524. [online] Available at: http://ec.europa.eu/world/enp/pdf/progress2010/sec10_524_en.pdf [Accessed 13 June 2010].

European Committee for the Prevention of Torture and Inhuman or Degrading Treatment or Punishment (CPT) (2009): Report to the Ukrainian Government on the visit to Ukraine carried out by the European Committee for the Prevention of Torture and Inhuman or Degrading Treatment or Punishment (CPT) from 5 to 10 December 2007, CPT/Inf (2009) 15. [online] Available at: http://www.cpt.coe.int/documents/ukr/2009-15-inf-eng.pdf [Accessed 10 June 2010].

European Committee for the Prevention of Torture and Inhuman or Degrading Treatment or Punishment (CPT) (2009a): Response of the Ukrainian Government to the report of the European Committee for the Prevention of Torture and Inhuman or Degrading Treatment or Punishment (CPT) on its visit to Ukraine from 5 to 10 December 2007, CPT/Inf (2009) 16. [online] Available at: http://www.cpt.coe.int/documents/ukr/2009-16-inf-eng.pdf [Accessed 10 June 2010].

Eurostat (2008): Recent migration trends: citizens of EU-27 Member States become ever more mobile while EU remains attractive to non-EU citizens. [online] Available at: http://epp.eurostat.ec.europa.eu/cache/ITY_OFFPUB/KS-SF-08-098/EN/ KS-SF-08-098-EN.PDF [Accessed 30 September 2009].

Evans, M., ed. (2004): Policy transfer in a global perspective. Aldershot: Ashgate.

Gatev, Ivaylo (2008): Border Security in the Eastern Neighbourhood: Where Biopolitics and Geopolitics Meet. In: European Foreign Affairs Review 13, pp. 97-116.

Haas, H. de (2007): Remittances, Migration and Social Development. A Conceptual Review of the Literature. United Nations Research Institute for Social Development, Social Policy and Development Programme Paper Nr. 34. [online] Avail-

able at: http://www.heindehaas.com/Publications/de%20Haas%20-%20 UN-RISD%20PP%202007%20-%20Remittances%20Migration%20and%20Develop ment.pdf [Accessed 10 June 2010].
Héritier, A./Lehmkuhl, D. (2008): Introduction. The Shadow of Hierarchy and New Modes of Governance. In: Journal of Public Policy 28, 1, pp. 1-17.
Human Rights First (2008): Hate Crime Survey 2008: Ukraine. [online] Available at: http://www.humanrightsfirst.org/pdf/fd/08/fd-080924-ukraine-web.pdf [accessed 10 June 2010].
Human Rights Watch (2005): Ukraine. On the Margins – Rights Violations against Migrants and Asylum Seekers at the New Eastern Border of the European Union. [online] Available at: http://www.hrw.org/en/reports/2005/11/29/ukraine-margins [Accessed 10 June 2010].
Human Rights Watch (2009): World Report 2010. [online] Available at: http://www.hrw.org/world-report-2010 [Accessed 10 June 2010].
International Executive Committee of Border Monitoring Project (BMP) (2010): Monitoring the implementation of social and human rights of refugees and other vulnerable migrants in the Border region of the European Union and Ukraine. Fact Finding Missions, Chop Detention Centre, March and April 2009 (Update January 2010). [online] Available at: http://bordermonitoring-ukraine.eu/files/2010/03/BMP_Chop_report_2010.pdf [Accessed 10 June 2010].
International Organization for Migration (IOM) (2006): Reinforcing the Human Resources Management of Ukraine's State Border Guard Service (HUREMAS). [online] Available at: iom.int/jahia/Jahia/pid/1979 [Aaccessed June 10, 2010].
International Organization for Migration (IOM) (2008): Migration in Ukraine: A Country Profile 2008. [online] Available at: http://publications.iom.int/book store/index.php?main_page=product_info&products_id=492 [Accessed 10 June 2010].
International Organization for Migration (IOM) (2009): Ukrainian Border Guards Enhance Border Management Legislation to Meet EU Standards. [online] Available at: iom.org.ua/index.php?page=news&type=events&id=339&idn=true [Accessed June 10, 2010].
International Organization for Migration (IOM) (2009a): New Campaign in Ukraine Encourages Youth to Embrace Multi-Culturalism. [online] Available at: iom.int/jahia/Jahia/media/press-briefing-notes/pbnEU/cache/offonce?entryId=25124 [Accessed July 11, 2010].
Kelley, J. (2006): New Wine in Old Wineskins: Promoting Political Reforms through the New European Neighbourhood Policy. In: Journal of Common Market Studies 44, 1, pp. 29-55.
Kohler-K., Beate/Rittberger, V. (2006): Review Article: The ‘governance turn' in EU studies. In: Journal of Common Market Studies 44, pp. 27-49.
Lavenex, S. (2008): A governance perspective on the European neighbourhood policy: integration beyond conditionality? In: Journal of European Public Policy 15, pp. 938-955.
Law of Ukraine on Legal Status of Foreigners and Stateless People (LSF) (1994): Law No. 3929-XII. 4 February 1994 (as amended 20 June 2007). [online] Available at: http://www.ecoi.net/file_upload/1504_1217246562_law-on-legal-status-of-foreigners-and-stateless-people.pdf [Accessed 10 June 2010].

Magen, A. (2006): The Shadow of Enlargement: Can the European Neighbourhood Policy achieve compliance? In: The Columbia Journal of European Law 12, pp. 383–427.
Malynovska, O. (2006): Caught Between East and West, Ukraine Struggles with Its Migration Policy. [online] Available at: http://www.migrationinformation.org/profiles/display.cfm?id=365 [Accessed 10 June 2010].
Malynovska, O./Kubanova, E. (2008): Ukraine. In: Hönekopp, Elmar/Mattila, Heikki (ed.): Permanent or Circular Migration? Policy Choices to Address Demographic Decline and Labour Shortages in Europe, pp. 301-338, [online] Available at: http://www.iom.int/jahia/webdav/site/myjahiasite/shared/shared/mainsite/published_docs/books/Permanent_circular_migration.pdf [Accessed 10 June 2010].
Petrov, Roman (2008): Exporting the Acquis Communautaire into the Legal Systems of Third Countries. In: European Foreign Affairs Review 13, p. 33-52.
Presidency Conclusions of the Brussels European Council (2004): The Hague Programme (Annex 1 to the Presidency Conclusions of the Brussels European Council, November 2004). [online] Available at: http://ec.europa.eu/justice_home/news/information_dossiers/the_hague_priorities/doc/hague_programme_en.pdf [Accessed 10 June 2010].
Pro Asyl (2009): Projekt zur Situation von Flüchtlingen in der Ukraine. [online] Available at: http://www.proasyl.de/fileadmin/proasyl/fm_redakteure/WIR_UEBER_UNS/Stiftung/Bericht_Ukraine_Projekt_Dezember_2008.pdf [Accessed 13 June 2010].
Pylynskyi, Y. (2008): Undocumented Migration. Counting the Uncountable. Data and Trends across Europe. Country Report Ukraine. [online] Available at: http://clandestino.eliamep.gr/wp-content/uploads/2009/10/clandestino_report_ukraine_final_1.pdf [Accessed 10 June 2010].
Roig, A./Huddleston, Th. (2007): EC Readmission Agreements. A Reevaluation of the Political Impasse. In: European Journal of Migration and Law 9, 3, pp. 363–387.
Scharpf, F. W. (2000): Interaktionsformen. Akteurzentrierter Institutionalismus in der Politikforschung. Opladen.
Schiffer, St./Katsberg, T./Roßmann, S. (2010): Hate Crime in Ukraine. Opfergruppen und Beratungsangebote zivilgesellschaftlicher Akteure. [online] Available at: http://www.european-exchange.org/fileadmin/user_upload/Hate_Crime_EVZ/Hate_Crime_Ukraine_2010_DE.pdf [Accessed 10 June 2010].
Schimmelfennig, F./Sedelmeier, U., ed. (2005): The Europeanization of Central and Eastern Europe. Ithaca, NY.
Slaughter, A.-M. (2004): A new world order. Princeton.
Söderköping Process (2009): Statistics. [online] Available at: http://soderkoping.org.ua/page12462.html [Accessed 30 September 2009].
Stefan Batory Foundation, ed. (2009): Changes in Visa Policies of the EU Member States. New Monitoring Report. [online] Available at: http://www.soros.org/initiatives/brussels/articles_publications/publications/visa-policies-20090531/visa-policies-20090531.pdf [Accessed 10 June 2010].
Stewart, Susan (2009): NGO Development in Ukraine since the Orange Revolution. In: Besters-Dilger, Juliane (ed.): Ukraine on its way to Europe. Interim Results of the Orange Revolution. Frankfurt: Peter Lang , pp. 177-194.

Trauner, F./Kruse, I. (2008): EC Visa Facilitation and Readmission Agreements: A New Standard EU Foreign Policy Tool? In: European Journal of Migration and Law 10, pp. 411-438.

Tyshchenko, Y. (2008): Inadequate migration laws and policies contribute to xenophobia. In: Kyiv Post, March 27, 2008. [online] Available at: kyivpost.com/news/opinion/op_ed/detail/28687/ [accessed July 5, 2010].

Uehling, G. (2004): Irregular and Illegal Migration through Ukraine. In: International Migration 42, 3, pp. 77-109.

Ukrainian Refugee Council (2010): The EU-Ukraine Readmission Agreement – Myths, Facts and Risks. [online] Available at: http://www.ecre.org/resources/Press_releases/1530 [accessed 27 July 2010].

United Nations High Commissioner for Refugees (2007): UNHCR Position on the Situation of Asylum in Ukraine in the Context of Return of Asylum-Seekers, October 2007. [online] Available at: http://www.unhcr.org/refworld/docid/472f43162.html [Accessed 14 June 2010].

United Nations High Commissioner for Refugees (2009): Action plan on integration of the recognized refugees into Ukrainian society for the period till 2012. [online] Available at: www.unhcr.org.ua/img/uploads/docs/Integration%20plan%20eng_2.doc [Accessed 10 June 2010].

United Nations Office on Drugs and Crime (2004): United Nations Convention against Transnational Organized Crime and the Protocols Thereto. [online] Available at: http://www.unodc.org/documents/treaties/UNTOC/Publications/TOC%20Convention/TOCebook-e.pdf [Accessed 10 June 2010].

Wichmann, N. (2007): The Intersection between Justice and Home Affairs and the European Neighbourhood Policy.
Taking stock of the Logic, Objectives and Practises. [online] Available at: http://shop.ceps.eu/BookDetail.php?item_id=1546 [Accessed 10 June 2010].

Wolff, S. (2008): Border management in the Mediterranean: internal, external and ethical challenges. In: Cambridge Review of International Affairs 21, 2, pp. 253-271.

Zimmer, K. (2008): Migrants and Refugees in the Buffer Zone: Asylum Policy in Ukraine, Focus on Central and Eastern Europe, March 2008. [online] Available at:
http://aa.ecn.cz/img_upload/6334c0c7298d6b396d213ccd19be5999/KZimmer_Ukraineasylumandmigrationpolicy.pdf [accessed 10 June 2010].

Turkey at the Crossroads Between the Middle East and the EU: Changing Border Control and Security Policies

Başak Bilecen-Süoglu

Introduction

Migration issues are at the top of the political agenda in Western Europe, and there has been a significant increase in right-wing electoral support in the past few years. The prospect of EU enlargement and the geographical expansion of its external borders to the east and the south are a great concern evidenced by the attention illegal immigration has been receiving in Western European media and political circles. Turkey is not only very important, but it is also an interesting actor which deserves of greater attention. "Given its geographical position at the crossroads of Asia, Africa, and Europe, Turkey faces irregular migration flows as both a destination and a transit country" (İçduygu 2006). The composition of these irregular flows include growing numbers of transit migrants heading for Europe or other advanced countries, clandestine immigrant laborers, asylum-seekers and refugees[1]. This article focuses on the Turkish context, highlighting the control measurements of irregular migration upgraded in accordance with the EU acquis. As has been stated in the latest EU progress report[2], there is a general recognition of the need to launch, modernize, and advance the laws, policies, practices, and administrative structures of Turkish authorities, particularly with regard to the issue of irregular migration. These policies and laws adopted will be investigated here.

In addition, this article provides an overall picture of the role Turkey plays in irregular migration from the Middle East to the EU in its position as a transit zone. However, the aim of this article is not only to describe the role of Turkey as a transit zone, but also, more importantly, to examine the Europeanization of its migration and asylum policies and the future trends with

---

1 "Transit migration can be defined as the movement of people entering a national territory, who might stay for several weeks or months to work to pay or to organize the next stage of their trip, but who leave the country to an onward destination within a limited period, for instance one year" (Düvell, 2006, cited in de Haas, 2008: 14).

2 Turkey 2009 Progress Report, accompanying the Communication from the Commission to the European Parliament and the Council, Enlargement Strategy and Main Challenges 2009-2010, [online] available at: http://ec.europa.eu/enlargement/press_corner/key-documents/reports_oct_2009_en.htm [Accessed on February 11, 2010].

respect to what has been done so far. To this end, this article is structured as follows: the Turkish case concerning irregular migration is introduced in the second part, followed by a definition of Europeanization and a detailed examination of how Turkey copes with its situation concerning EU accession and Turkish legislation, along with the transformations which have taken place in the areas of migration and asylum, visa policy, external border control, and geographical limitation. The article ends with a short conclusion and a summary of future developments regarding these issues.

Contextualizing the Irregular Migration Experience: The Turkish Case

"Turkey's prolonged experience of refugee and migratory movements, the fact that it is a large asylum seeker and irregular migrant-producing country, that it is a hub for other irregular migrants hoping to reach Europe and that it is engaged in a very important process of reform in the area of asylum and migration make it a particularly interesting case study" (Mannaert 2003: 1). Another study has also indicated that "Turkey is the main transit route for asylum seekers from countries such as Afghanistan, Iran, or Kurdish people from Turkey and Northern Iraq" (ILO 2004). There are four main factors identified in irregular migratory movements which make Turkey attractive and increase its role as a transit country. The first is that the political turmoil and clashes in neighboring countries force people to go to Turkey to seek better living conditions, security, and protection. Second, the country's role as a hub makes it an excellent transit area for migrants. Third, the EU's restricted admission policies have diverted migration flows to peripheral countries such as Turkey, and, fourth, the relative economic prosperity of Turkey make it a country of preference in the region (İçduygu 2004).

Another important reason for the large number of irregular transit migrants going to Turkey is the national immigration regulation. Turkey only accepts migrants who are either from European countries or of ethnic Turkish origin as asylum seekers. To put it another way, for example, "migrants from Iraq, Iran, and Afghanistan go through Turkey, which does not have readmission agreements with the EU member states for constitutional reasons, and thus does not accept the return of migrants who travel through Turkey en route to Europe" (Philip, Midgley & Teitenbaum 2002). This is known as "geographical limitation", included in the 1951 Geneva Convention Relating to the Status of Refugees. Therefore, such refugees are de facto accepted as transit migrants.

Irregular migratory flows to Turkey have been highly diversified in terms of the migrants' countries of origin, personal characteristics, and prospects. “Three types of irregular migrants can be identified in contemporary Turkey: economic migrants, who remain for some time before moving on to western or northern Europe; overstayers, who work illegally; and rejected asylum seekers” (Baldwin-Edwards 2005). The motivation of irregular migrants from the Middle East, Iran, Iraq and, to some extent, from Asia and Africa (such as Pakistan, Bangladesh, Sri Lanka, Nigeria, and Somalia) is partly economic and partly political. They enter Turkey as a transit country, living there for a while and planning to continue their journey illegally to more developed countries in the west (İçduygu 2006).

Another group of irregular migrants are from countries of the former Soviet Union, such as the Russian Federation, Moldova, and Ukraine, who enter Turkey legally, but stay and continue to work there after their entry visas have expired. In the western regions of Turkey, these migrants work for Turkish farmers and industrialists or as domestic helpers for middle- and upper-class families (İçduygu and Toktas 2002).

The third group of irregular migrants in Turkey are asylum seekers coming primarily from Iran and Iraq, whose asylum applications have been rejected or are still being processed (İçduygu 2006). These migrants are unwilling to go back to their countries of origin, preferring to stay in Turkey to try to make a living there or to migrate to another country. These three major groups of asylum seekers and economic migrants in Turkey often overlap. Both mobility categories originate from the same countries, both involve illegal activities such as entry and overstay, and both have similar motivations for departure (İçduygu 2005).

The Europeanization of Migration Policies in Turkey

Europeanization is the impact of the EU on its member and associate states. It is “the construction, diffusion and institutionalisation of formal and informal rules, procedures, policy paradigms, styles, ‘ways of doing things’ and shared beliefs and norms which are first defined and consolidated in the EU policy process and then incorporated in the logic of domestic (national and sub-national) discourse, political structures and public policies” (Radaelli 2000: 4, cited in Geddes 2007: 78). It is a top-down process of member states’ adaptation to the EU, which is different from European integration which involves a bottom-up process of channeling the influence of member states. Fundamentally, Europeanizaton is a three-step process involving: (a) the creation of a governmental system and specific policies at the European level; (b) the generation of constraints for domestic policies and processes of policy making in terms of adaptation resulting from the conflict between these national political structures and those at the European level; and (c) the adaption of national policies and politics to developments at the EU level (Faist and Ette 2007).

According to Bendel (2007), national immigration policies can—and should—have five goals: "(1) the restriction and control of immigration, (2) the protection of refugees, (3) the prevention of refugee movements, (4) the integration of migrants and (5) the attraction of different groups of migrants (for instance, the highly skilled)". However, with regard to these goals, "we have to admit that migration policies in the EU have, so far, concentrated on only one overarching aspect: restriction and control" (Bendel 2007: 46–47). Migration control plays a central role in the EU policy and politics of immigration and the Europeanization processes of migration policy, and so does the management of diverse migration flows. The Turkish migration policy of tightening border control is not so very different from that of the European Union. However, one should keep in mind that migration and asylum policies and practices are country-specific, involving a dynamic interplay of different components such as social, cultural, political, and economic norms and values.

Turkey has repeatedly been criticized for its lax immigration and border control policies, specifically with regard to the country being a major transit territory for non-Europeans coming to the EU. Hence, one of the main concerns of the EU, and one of the requirements for Turkey's membership, is to implement stricter exit and entry controls at its borders (Mannaert 2003). Turkey has made significant progress in developing preliminary migration management strategies since 2000, and has been in the process of making even more adaptations to the acquis communautaire in connection with its application for EU membership. The asylum and immigration policies of Turkey and the EU have been inextricably linked for decades. The adjustments to EU policy will include the establishment of a more consistent immigration policy, the removal of geographical limitation to asylum applications, and the modification of visa requirements. It is argued elsewhere that these transformations will enhance Turkey's control over movements in the region (Baldwin-Edwards 2005: 31).

There is general recognition of the need to launch, modernize, and advance the applicable immigration and asylum laws, policies, practices, and administrative structures of Turkish authorities, specifically with regard to the issue of irregular migration. As will be explained in this section, various steps have been taken towards achieving this goal, particularly in connection with the country's candidacy for accession to the European Union. As a candidate country for EU membership, Turkey is obliged to apply the EU standards of migration management and is considered to be a safe country where asylum claims can be filed, which could eventually result in "burden shifting" rather than "burden sharing" if the country fails to obtain full member status (İçduygu 2005 cited in van Liempt 2006). Given this, Europeanization in Turkey is directly linked to the prospect of EU accession. In all probability, Turkey will have to conform to EU demands to transform its immigration policy. Nevertheless, since the issue is highly politicized, the Europeanization of migration and asylum policies in Turkey is far from being an effortless, harmonious or smooth process. Indeed, in conjunction with other factors and mostly political issues at stake, there also is some opposition to transformation. Turkish authorities have complained that they are not given the appreciation they deserve for their efforts and resources expended in fighting illegal migration, and that the EU is treating Turkey differently than previous candidate countries with which readmission agreements were not signed until accession negotiations had already begun, which then also continued bilaterally. This different treatment has led Turkish officials to distrust the intentions of the EU, which has not been helped by the prospect of "burden shifting". In other words, authorities feel that they are left alone with the problem of returning irregular migrants to their countries of origin. Another reason for doubt is that the financial and technical support from the EU is considerably less than that provided to other third countries (Apap et al. 2004). The following subsections illustrate the steps taken to harmonize Turkish and EU policies.

Asylum and Immigration Legislation in Turkey

There is no provision in the Constitution of the Republic of Turkey concerning asylum issues, nor is there a specific law on immigration. Rather, Turkish refugee policy has been based on three key legal sources: the Law on Settlement, the 1951 Geneva Convention, and the 1994 Regulation.

According to the Law on Settlement, adopted in 1934, individuals of Turkish descent or culture are entitled to migrate, settle, and obtain refugee status. Article 3[3] defines "refugees" as individuals who come to Turkey seek-

---

3 Specifically, Article 3 states that "persons attached to Turkish culture who wish to come collectively and settle in Turkey, shall be accepted, respectively, upon the order of the Ministry of Internal Affairs on condition that the opinion of Ministry of Health and Social Assistance on condition that the opinion of the Ministry of Interior obtained (...) shall be called immigrants (...). Those persons who take shelter in Turkey in order to reside temporarily on account of compelling reasons without the intention to settle permanently shall be called refugee. In the event that refugees wish to settle in Turkey and notify their wish in writing to the highest civil governor of the place where they are located, they shall be treated as immigrants by the Ministry of Health and Social Assistance, provided that these refugees are not barred by Article 4. Other refugees shall be subjected by the Ministry of Interior to the provisions of the law of citizenship. The ways of accepting immigrants and refugees shall be set out in instructions issued by, respectively, the Ministry of Health and Social Assistance and Ministry of Interior." In accordance with the 2006 amendments of Law no. 5543,

ing asylum as a result of compulsion and who have the intention to stay on a temporary basis (Kaya, C. 2009). Between 1923 and 2005 almost two million ethnically Turkish people settled in the country under this particular law, which has had a direct impact on the management of regular migration flows (İçduygu 2007). However, the law has been criticized (Ulker 2007; 2008) for its assimilative design in accordance with the state's nationalistic tendencies during the initial nation-building phase as well as for their implementation in different localities. The founders of the republic promoted cultural (ethnic) homogeneity and highlighted the "Turkishness" of the state (Kirişçi 1996) by giving immigrants of Turkish descent and culture preferential treatment and allowing them to settle in Turkey, while at the same time severely limiting the rights of foreigners. The attitudes of the state were clearly reflected in the national legislation. "In fact, the Law on Settlement of 1934 is the major piece of legislation that sustains the conservative philosophy of various immigration- and asylum-related policies and practices in Turkey; and consequently it seems to be subject to renewal within the EU integration process" (İçduygu 2007: 286).

The second major legal source is the 1951 Convention which has already been mentioned in the previous section in relation to Turkey's geographical limitation. Turkey was one of the drafters and original signatories of this Convention, but signed it with both temporal and geographical limitations. When signing the Protocol Related to the Status of Refugees in 1967, Turkey lifted the temporal but not the geographical limitation, and today it is one of the last remaining countries to maintain this limitation. The implication of this strategy is that the protection Turkey offers to refugees is only temporary and that the refugees are expected to be resettled in another safe third country. Improvements regarding this issue will be explained in detail later in this article.

The third major legal source is the 1994 Regulation on Asylum, which addresses procedures and principles of migration management. Its five chapters cover general provisions; procedures and principles concerning individual aliens either seeking asylum in Turkey or applying for a residence permit in order to seek asylum from a third country; preventative measures to be taken against possible mobility and foreigners arriving in Turkey in groups to seek asylum; action and preventative measures to be taken when refugees are accepted and asylum seekers coming to borders or enter Turkish territory as groups; and common provisions (Kaya, C. 2009). The Regulation also defines the terms in accordance with UNHCR[4], which was a novelty in legisla-

---

the definitions which are not in conformity with international law have been abolished (Kaya, C. 2009: 34-35).

4 In Article 3 of the Regulation, "refugee" is defined as "an alien as a result of events occurring in Europe and owing to well-founded fear of being persecuted for reasons of race, religion, nationality, membership of a social group or

tion of this type. Moreover, Article 29 of the Regulation is an unequivocal acceptance of the principle of non-refoulement. Even so, neither the National Action Plan (NAP) nor the National Plan (NP) provide any guidance regarding the implementation of the principle.

Kemal Kirişçi argues that the Regulation appeared to be an improvement in terms of status determination, in that it led to the fulfillment of certain expectations which may have encouraged the Turkish government to lift the geographical limitation at the time. The adoption of the Regulation showed that the Turkish authorities were beginning to take a tougher stance on issues of asylum and irregular migration. Although the implementation of the Regulation is often criticized as inefficient (Frelick, 1997), in the same study Kirişçi expresses optimism that some of the problems associated with the Regulation and its implementation can be overcome by improving communication between the Turkish authorities and international organizations such as UNHCR (Kirişçi 1996).

Another important legal document is Circular Order no. 57 of July 22, 2006 (Circular on Transfer of Authority), prepared by the General Directorate of Security at the Ministry of Interior, aiming to fill the gaps in the legislation in conformity with the relevant EU directives, It explains the principles and procedures to be applied during the asylum application process as well as crucial changes in the types of social, financial, and healthcare support provided to asylum seekers by social service agencies and charitable organizations. The Circular serves particularly vulnerable groups, including unaccompanied minors, victims of torture and trauma, those in need of medical assistance, women with special needs such as pregnancy, and elderly persons with disabilities according to UNHCR standards. However, in practice in Turkey only the unaccompanied minors' procedures are regulated by another article. Another salient issue addressed in the Circular is the amendment to Article 6[5] of the 1994 Regulation to accelerate review procedures, but not only did it aim to shorten the period for appeal filed by individuals

---

political opinion, is outside the country of his nationality and is unable or, owing to such fear, is unwilling to avail himself of the protection of that country, or who, not having a nationality and being outside the country of his former habitual residence as a result of such events, is unable or, owing to such fear, is unwilling to return to it."—According to the definition provided in the same Article, an "asylum seeker" is "an alien who owing to well-founded fear of being persecuted for reasons of race, religion, nationality, membership of a particular social group or political opinion is outside the country of his nationality and is unable or; owing to such fear, is unwilling to avail himself of the protection of that country, or who, not having a nationality and being outside the country of his former habitual residence as a result such events, is unable or owing to such fear, is unwilling to return to it."

5 An alien whose claim has not been accepted may appeal to the relevant provincial directorate within 15 days. The appeal period may be shortened by the MOI when necessary to accelerate the decision making procedure.

whose application for asylum had been rejected, it also introduced more detailed provisions on this issue, ensuring that priority would be given to the accelerated applications. In other words, wherever judicial review is necessary, the legal right of the person will be safeguarded (for example, decisions will be taken to another administrative court). However, it has been argued elsewhere that, in order to work properly and efficiently, special courts should be established to deal with asylum issues, and that judges should specific receive training on asylum law and be given access to information about an appellant's country of origin (Kaya, I. 2009).

While the 1994 Regulation and the 2006 Circular are the most important instruments setting out the procedure of asylum and although the Turkish asylum system relies on on them, there is no statutory basis for either of them. To put it differently, they are written by administrative bodies rather than by the Parliament, which has the power to enact a law. Drafted by the Ministry of the Interior, neither of the two instruments is enacted as a law, so they may be subject to change by another administrative decision (Kaya, I. 2009). There is a clear need in Turkey for an asylum law and the continuance of its harmonization of regulation and implementation in accordance with the EU. While this section described the legislation in Turkey in the field of immigration and asylum, the next section will concentrate on the broader contemporary transformations undertaken by the Turkish authorities.

Recent Changes

To be more precise on the process, by the time of accession the candidate countries must apply the Schengen acquis completely, which is a two-step process. During the first phase, by the time of their accession to the EU, candidate countries have to meet minimum border control requirements and begin to prepare for full Schengen zone membership. In the second phase (post-accession), upon approval of the steps taken in the first phase and when it is agreed that the member state has become a full Schengen member, the member country's national borders are eliminated (Mitsilegas, 2002). Another issue that needs addressing at this point is the alignment of Turkey's visa policy with the common visa policy of the EU. In 2003, by way of the Accession Partnership Document (APD), the EU requested Turkey to align its visa legislation and practice with EU legislation in the medium term. (European Commission 2003) In addition to this request, the National Program for the Adoption of the EU Acquis (NPAA) set its priorities (National Program for the Adoption of the Acquis 2003). However, since it could not be fully accomplished, the same issue was put forward in the next APD (European Commission 2006). Turkey has recently taken a number of steps in the areas of justice, freedom and security at the legislative, policy, and practice levels.

Among the strongest motivations for Turkey to pass these legislative acts before 2004 were the meetings in December 2004, during which the decisions on opening the EU accession negotiations were taken. In the wider framework of Turkey's accession to the EU, harmonization of laws and policies with the European acquis covers the whole set of EU policies. Justice and Home Affairs is a significant yet reserved issue in this package. In the Accession Partnership (AP) strategy, the main issues for Turkey are Justice and Home Affairs in general and border management policies and fighting irregular migration in particular. These political issues are both essential and delicate since they involve issues of territory and sovereignty. At the same time, Turkey is aware that the EU is anxious about sharing borders with Syria, Iraq, Iran and countries of the Caucasus (Apap et al. 2004).

There are a number of other regulations already in place aimed at combating irregular migration relating, among other things, to the introduction of stricter punishment for smugglers and traffickers, changes in citizenship laws, and easier access to the labor market, all of which address different issues of irregular migration and its consequences. While stricter punishment for smugglers and traffickers is aimed at reducing illegal practices, citizenship laws and labor market regulations deal mainly with the consequences of illegal migration.

Migration and Asylum: Policy and Procedures

Turkey has developed a series of measures to specifically manage irregular migration. In June 2002, the Turkish government created the Task Force on Asylum, Migration, and Border Protection, which consists of representatives from the coast guard, the gendarmerie, the military, the Ministry of Interior, the Ministry of Foreign Affairs, the Undersecretary of Customs, and the Secretariat-General for European Union Affairs. Within this Task Force, working groups were established to perform legislative analysis. The Task Force has a major role in providing uniform implementation of existing legislation. In addition, it conducted studies and study visits concerning border protection, irregular migration, the Schengen visa regime, and asylum. After conducting these studies, the Task Force prepared strategy reports on each of the areas concerned, which were then negotiated with the European Commission in Ankara. Based on the results of this process, the government issued a series of proposals for twinning projects[6], which include action plans for the application of the strategy reports and offer training programs and resources for administrative capacity building, funded by the Accession Partnership for

6 See European Commission, Enlargement DG, Twinning; [online] Available at: http://ec.europa.eu/enlargement/how-does-it-work/technical-assistance/twinning_en.htm [Accessed February 14, 2011]

Turkey. Twinning projects[7] play a major role in pre-accession negotiations as "highly valuable instruments for targeted administrative cooperation to assist candidate countries to strengthen their administrative and judicial capacity and to implement the EU framework in their national systems" (Apap et al. 2004: 16). These projects are considered to be cornerstones and are designed to enhance institution building. They are then translated into action plans which provide more detailed information about the implementation phase and usually include a timeline. Despite considerable progress in this area, according to the Commission's report, it was not until nearly two years later (May 2009) that the Task Force convened again after the meeting held in summer of 2007 (Turkey Progress Report 2009), which indicates a certain slackening of commitment.

In September 2003, the Interior Ministry officials, along with the gendarmerie, cooperated with the non-governmental organization Human Resources Development Foundation (HRDF) and the Directorate-General of the Status of Women to organize social support for victims of trafficking until the time of deportation back to their countries of origin. This development shows that important changes are taking place in Turkey and is an example of collaboration between the bureaucracy and civil society (Apap et al. 2004).

At this point, it should be noted that the Turkish National Program (NP) on the Adoption of EU Acquis[8], put into force in 2003, which led to the development of the National Action Plan for Asylum and Immigration. The General Directorate of Security at the Ministry of Interior created the NAP for Asylum and Immigration, and it was approved by the Prime Minister in 2005. The NP provides details on the official initiation of the harmonization

7 The first twinning project was implemented in Turkey in 1998. Many of these projects were conducted under the direction of the Department of Justice and Home Affairs, which shows the importance attached to these issues by both sides. For instance, in 2003, five out of eighteen twinnings dealt with related issues such as enhancing the forensic abilities of the police, strengthening institutions in combating human trafficking, intensifying efforts against money laundering, financial sources of crime, and the financing of terrorism, visa policies, and practices. In 2004 additional projects were implemented relating to such issues as asylum, border protection, law enforcement, and migration (Kirişçi, 2007).

8 According to Article 24.1., "Initiation of Harmonization Process with the EU Legislation and Capacity Building in the Field of Asylum' has been identified as a priority in the Accession Partnership Document of 2003 and it is foreseen that administrative and technical capacity be improved particularly through the maintenance of works in developing accommodation and social support mechanisms for refugees. Following the enactment of the Draft Bill on Asylum, administrative arrangements shall be put into force and the harmonization process with the EU legislation shall continue." Document available online at: http://www.unhcr.org.tr/MEP/FTPRoot/Dosyalar/Anasayfa/EU%20Acquis%20Book_Eng.pdf.

process with the EU legislation in general and with regard to asylum issues in particular. It was last updated in 2008[9] and came into force with immediate effect. The new version is concerned not only with compliance with EU legislation but also with international standards. In order to comply with the EU acquis in the field of asylum, the NAP provides information about what needs to be done and when. According to the NAP, a national asylum law is required which should be passed by 2012, but no bills on this issue have yet been introduced. A regulation for the implementation of the planned asylum law will be authorized by 2011, which will replace the 1994 Regulation (see above).

In addition to the above, the Development and Implementation Office on Asylum and Migration Legislation and Administrative Capacity was created in October 2008, which provides the Undersecretary of the Ministry of the Interior with information, studies, projects and analyses of the legislative and administrative structure for integrated border management (IBM),. The office also has a role in drafting and implementing the National Action Plan on Asylum and Migration and the National Action Plan on the Adoption of the Acquis (NPAA). However, "the resources of this office are very limited compared with its tasks" (Turkey Progress Report 2009: 73).

Another step in fighting irregular migration which the EU expects Turkey to implement is the conclusion of readmission agreements with third countries of origin and neighboring countries. So far, agreements have been signed with Syria (September 2001), Kyrgyzstan (May 2003), and Romania (January 2004). While some countries have failed to respond to Turkey's requests regarding this matter, agreements with other nations are still under negotiation. However, what is most important is Turkey's obligation to have a readmission agreement with the European Union after the EU's long-lasting resistance for fear of experiencing a massive influx of undesirable immigrants. Negotiations began in March 2004, following pressure from the EU. Facing problems beginning and concluding negotiations on readmission agreements with most of the countries of origin of illegal migration as they did, Turkish authorities were distressed. This anxiety is quite understandable if one considers what position the country would be in if the EU were allowed to send back illegal migrants to Turkey, which then would be unable to guarantee their return to their countries of origin. Nevertheless, a bilateral readmission agreement was concluded with Greece in 2001, although its implementation proved to be complicated (Apap et al. 2004). Turkey also

---

9 According to Article 24.2 of the updated NP, the main goal is for Turkey to continue its "efforts (...) to implement the National Action Plan on Asylum and Migration including the adoption of a roadmap and preparations for the adoption of a comprehensive asylum law in line with the EU acquis with the establishment of an asylum authority and increased capacity for combating illegal migration in line with international standards."

signed a readmission agreement with Syria which seems to be working out rather well. Negotiations with Pakistan, Iran, and Libya have commenced and are ongoing. Signing an EC readmission agreement with Turkey is very important for the EU and a prerequisite for full membership. Negotiations were suspended in 2006, but resumed in January 2010. However, by the time this agreement would be concluded, other bilateral agreements between Turkey and third countries are expected to already be implemented (Turkey Progress Report 2009).

Even though the readmission agreements are being signed, deportations may prove difficult to execute in practice. "They are expensive and have a limited deterrent effect because expelled migrants tend to attempt to migrate again" (de Haas 2006). In accordance with readmission agreements, reception and readmission centers for smuggled and/or trafficked migrants are created in order to control them or provide assistance to them. However, an effective administrative, legal, and financial infrastructure has yet to be established (İçduygu 2005).

There are also improvements regarding geographical limitation in Turkey. The UNHCR has been criticizing geographical limitation on the grounds that "the application of refugee law should be universal. A refugee should be granted protection on the merits of his or her individual claim without discrimination based on country of origin" (UNHCR 1997 press release). However, there are several factors affecting the decision of Turkey not to abolish this particular clause. According to Turkish officials, neighboring states in the Middle East are, for political reasons, particularly prone to producing refugees, which would result in Turkey becoming a country of asylum. Like many European countries, Turkey perceives the situation as a threat to national security and authorities are concerned that the country would probably not be able to handle a large influx of asylum seekers and illegal migrants. Geographical limitation is therefore believed to be a crucial safeguard in Turkey's migration management policy. National migration laws have been discouraging non-Turkish immigrants from entering Turkey. Nevertheless, Turkey has adopted a National Action Plan which envisages the abolition of geographical limitation by 2012, on the condition that the legal and institutional arrangements for asylum and the understanding on "burden sharing" with the EU are in place by that time (UNHCR 2007).

Turkey has also been collaborating with international and regional bodies to fight irregular migration and the use of forged and stolen documents, including the Center for Information, Discussion, the Exchange on the Crossing of Borders and Immigration (CIREFI), and the Early Warning System. In addition, Turkey has participated in activities organized by the Global Commission on International Migration and the International Migration Policy Dialogue of IOM. IOM was given full diplomatic status in 2004 and Turkey became a full member of the organization. Turkey has also been taking part in the Berne Initiative, the Mediterranean Transit Migration Dialogue, and the Bali Process (Kirişçi 2008). The Turkish government has a long history of collaboration on various issues with The International Catholic Migration Committee (ICMC) and UNHCR (Mannaert 2003).

Visa Policies

For quite a long time, Turkey had liberal visa policies. The Turkish Passport Law (Law no. 5682 of July 24, 1950) established the conditions for issuing entry visas to foreigners. Until recently, citizens from forty countries—among them Iran, Morocco and Tunisia—did not require a visa to enter Turkey and were exempt from visa requirements for three months (Icdugyu 2007).

Particularly between 2002 and 2005, Turkey's visa policies were tightened to comply with the exclusive EU Schengen requirements. Between the years 2000 and 2001, visa requirements were introduced for Kazakhstan, Bosnia, Bahrain, Qatar, the United Arab Emirates, Kuwait, Saudi Arabia, and Oman. Visa requirements were introduced for another thirteen countries in July 2003 (Indonesia, South Africa, Kenya, The Bahamas, the Maldives, Barbados, Seychelles, Jamaica, Belize, Fiji, Mauritius, Grenada, and Saint Lucia) and for Azerbaijan in November of the same year. By the end of 2004, Turkey was requested to put another six countries on the visa list, but was reluctant to oblige the request due to historical and cultural ties, particularly with Bosnia and Macedonia with which a visa free period of up to 60 days was agreed on (Kirişçi 2007).

However, in 2005, Turkey began to introduce reciprocal and more open visa policies for its neighbors. A series of bilateral visa exemption agreements were concluded with neighboring countries including Lebanon, Albania, Jordan, Brunei, Kosovo, Libya, Qatar, Syria, and, most recently in May 2010, Russia, which led to increased mobility between Turkey and these visa-exempt countries. The current Turkish government perceives visa-free travel as necessary to achieve better economic integration in the region, which is favorable for the Turkish economy (Evin et al. 2010).

Another issue is the sticker- or stamp-type visas that are still issued at the borders, while airport transit visas and the new Turkish visas with better security features are yet to be introduced nationwide. There are also different sticker-type visa regulations for each country. For example, a visa of this type can be issued for three months for nationals from Belarus, Russia, and Ukraine, but for only one month for citizens of Azerbaijan, Moldova, and Jordan and for fifteen days for people from Georgia. Regulations are generally stricter for countries which are perceived as posing a high risk of potentially sending a large number of immigrants (İçduygu 2007). Even so, as indicated by the Commission, all Turkish visas, passports, and travel documents must be issued fully in compliance with EU security standards and must contain, among other things, biometric identifiers (Turkey Progress Report 2009).

According to the European Commission's latest progress report of 2009, little progress has been made in the implementation of a consistent visa policy in Turkey which would cover all the citizens of the EU. At this junction, Turkey needs to adjust its positive and negative visa lists in accordance with the EU. Turkish visa policy is based on the principle of reciprocity, meaning that Turkey requires visas from citizens of countries which require visas for Turkish citizens. However, in order to adjust to the EU acquis, Turkey aimed to formally put an end to visa-less travel for citizens from countries on the negative list of the EU and instead introduced more liberal policies for neighboring countries, which presents somewhat of a dilemma.

External Border Management

The harmonization of Turkey's border management policies with those of the EU will be beneficial for Turkey's national security. Geographically, however, it is not an easy task for Turkey to control its extensive land borders (2,949 km) and coastlines (8,330 km). Moreover, "Turkey's border with Iran and partly Iraq is very mountainous and particularly vulnerable to uncontrolled passages. Enhancing Turkey's capacity to control its eastern borders during the pre-accession period will remain among the toughest challenges" (Kirişçi 2005: 360). Nevertheless, there is an awareness that improvements are necessary.

According to the latest EU report of 2009, limited progress has been made in the areas of external border control and Schengen acquis, especially in the implementation of the National Action Plan on integrated border management and in the determination of a consistent roadmap. In addition, a recognized apparatus to observe and supervise the implementation of the Plan does not exist as yet either.

After the creation of the new Office on Asylum and Migration, the Task Force on External Borders was reorganized and has convened every two months since the beginning of 2009. Border crossing points are still being modernized. A specialized department of border security studies was established within the Police Academy, with 48 enrolled students. Turkey has also demonstrated its willingness to work with the external border management agency Frontex.[10]

[10] Frontex was established by the Council Regulation (EC) 2007/2004 of 26 October, 2004 establishing a "European Agency for the Management of Operational Cooperation at the External Borders of the Member States of the European Union" in order to secure the external borders of the EU through the

However, collaboration between border management agencies and authorities is still lacking, particularly between police and customs enforcement agents. The EU has recognized a need to design a new civilian, non-military border law enforcement agency under the direction of the Ministry of the Interior (Turkey Progress Report 2009).

Concluding Remarks

The influx of irregular migration from the Middle East, Russia, and Ukraine to Turkey and from there to the EU has been one of the main concerns of the EU. The late former Director-General of ICMPD, Jonas Widgren, voiced this concern clearly when he said: "What if Turkey, as a Candidate country to the European Union, having recently committed herself (as a principle) to the Schengen control system, would abrogate from that in the interest of free flows from her unstable neighbours to the East and South? An unthinkable situation." (Conference Proceedings of Council of Europe 2002: 84) Turkey is under continuous pressure from the EU to establish more proactive legislation and practices in the area of migration and asylum and is therefore in the process of enacting and implementing new laws in the hope of becoming a full member of the EU.

As discussed above, however, the process of achieving policy convergence is not a very smooth one, but rather depends on the overall negotiations and politics. Despite a number of achievements made by Turkey, the country's current migration and asylum policies are still considered to be very liberal, especially in the light of new developments such as the increase in the number of neighboring countries with visa-free arrangements. Pressure from the EU will definitely continue, which will force Turkey to tighten border control, introduce stricter visa regulations, and conclude readmission agreements both with other third countries and the EU, although the success of these measures seems doubtful. Unlike in previous years, particularly in the period 2000–2005, Turkish authorities are now reluctant to comply with the measures and practices imposed by the EU, especially in the area of migration and asylum. This is due mainly to Turkey's perception of not being able to gain full membership in the near future, especially after the disap-

coordination of the operative collaboration of the member states, supporting the member states in the training of national border personnel, establishing common directives for the education of national border personnel, carrying out risk analysis, monitoring the research concerning the control of the external borders, assisting the member states in situations that require stronger technical and operative support, and the organization of repatriation missions of migrants (Council of the European Union, 2004).

pointing negotiations in December 2004. Moreover, when the political and economic instabilities in the neighboring countries are taken into account, it is highly likely that both legal and illegal migration will continue, which would add further fuel to the debate. As a consequence—and as a precautionary measure—Turkey will not lift the geographical limitation to the 1951 Geneva Convention in forthcoming years, but rather will hold on to that clause as a means of political leverage.

It is important to note that, despite its efforts to align its national asylum and migration policies with those of the European Union, there is no guarantee that Turkey will ever become a full member of the EU. The carrot for Turkey may be precious and highly valuable, but the stick makes it a little too far out of reach. If Turkey adapted its migration and asylum policies without ever becoming a full member of the EU, it could turn into a shelter for many migrants who have tried to enter the EU unsuccessfully. Turkey would then be left alone with the problem of dealing with the resulting difficulties such as financing issues, instability of Turkish society, and further debates on integration. As a condition to lifting the geographical limitation, Turkey is therefore seeking a guarantee from the EU that it will receive support in dealing with the burden of accepting refugees and asylum seekers from non-European countries and eventually be granted full EU membership.

Despite its reluctance to harmonize its migration and asylum policies and the resulting difficulties, Turkey has changed drastically under the pressure from the EU. However, it should also be acknowledged that, despite the promising achievements at the policy level, the transformations were not quite so fundamental at all levels, but were actually limited to accepting new values and practices. This process could be considered as partial Europeanization, as has been noted in other studies (see, for example, İçduygu, 2007). Europeanization is a political process in which various interests are negotiated at various levels, which are often imposed by the EU in a top-down process and occasionally met with reluctance by Turkey. This situation sometimes causes both sides to reconsider specific issues such as humanitarian issues, politics, sovereignty, and security concerns. Nevertheless, migration-related issues should not just be seen as a part of EU accession period in the short term and policies should not be adopted just for the sake of it. Rather, migration issues should be seen and treated as issues in their own right and measures should be implemented efficiently, especially given Turkey's significant role in the migration flows.

The issue of migration is not limited to the national level, but involves various levels and actors. With regard to the situation of irregular migrants, there will be improvements in the form of more efficient reception centers and better living conditions if Turkey continues its efforts to deal with issue of migration more considerately both with the support of the EU and for its own sake. Implementing the policies and working in cooperation with civil society associations and international organizations such as UNHCR will enhance Turkey's ability to deal with the issue of irregular migration and its consequences. Nevertheless, some authors have expressed concern. Mannaert (2003) notes that "in the area of social support services provision such as housing, healthcare, counselling, legal advice and training, Turkey is seriously underdeveloped. Following even a positive appreciation of their application, asylum seekers are assigned to live in one of 25 'satellite' cities, usually in poor neighbourhoods and in cheap accommodation. Although in theory refugees and asylum seekers are entitled to work and receive social assistance in Turkey, in practice it is very difficult to obtain work permits and social support programmes are virtually non-existent" (Mannaert 2003: 8). Another current study, in which 31 refugees were interviewed in various cities in Turkey, argues that the legislative changes are based on considerations of national security and that they are often rather poorly implemented. Examples of this include the arbitrary registration of temporary asylum claims; the difficulties asylum seekers face when trying to obtain residence permits or leave their city of residence to travel within the country; the temporary nature of assistance; the challenges in finding accommodation in satellite cities; the extreme difficulties most refugees living in satellite cities face in obtaining formal work; the non-committal and arbitrary allocation of funding from social security and charity funds; and the almost non-existence of healthcare funds for migrants (Biehl 2009). There is a clear indication that these policies are poorly implemented. Therefore, with regard to the prospect of becoming a full member of the EU, the main objective must be to ensure better and efficient implementation of these policies to protect migrants, asylum seekers, and refugees.

There are still research and policy gaps to be filled at the societal level. After looking at the problems in Western European countries, it can be said that one of the major challenges Turkey will soon have to deal with concerns the integration of migrants into society. There are currently no active integration policies in place, and most types of immigration are seen as temporary. Although most of these issues are usually covered in the media sooner or later, the Turkish society will also face the challenges and impacts of migration in their everyday lives and will soon recognize the importance of integrating those asylum seekers in order to maintain a harmonious society. The issue will attract greater attention when people begin to realize that the society they are living in is changing drastically and is becoming much more multicultural than expected. These issues may appear on the agenda of political parties in Turkey some day, as has been the case in the EU for many years. But so far, this has not yet happened. There is still an urgent need to raise awareness of the issue among both authorities and Turkish society. In the near future the question of national identity—the question of who is considered to be Turkish and who is not—will pose an even greater challenge to both society and the state.

References

Apap, J./Carrera, S./Kirişci, K. (2004): 'Turkey in the European Area of Freedom, Security and Justice', EU-Turkey Working Paper 3, Brussels: Centre for European Policy Studies, pp.1-55.

Arslan, C. (2003): Göçmen Kaçakçılığı Suçları (Crimes of Human Smuggling), Yargıtay Dergisi (Journal of Supreme Court) 52, 1, pp. 113-145.

Baldwin-Edwards, M. (2005): Migration in the Middle East and Mediterranean, University Research Institute for Urban Environment and Human Resources, Panteion Univeristy, Athens, Greece, Paper prepared for the Policy Analysis and Research Programme of the Global Commission on International Migration, [online] Available at: http://www.gcim.orgattachements/RS5.pdf [Accessed July 30, 2006].

Bendel, P. (2007): Everything under control? The European Union's policies and politics of immigration, In: Faist, Thomas/Ette, Andreas (eds.): Between Autonomy and the European Union. The Europeanisation of National Immigration Policies and Politics. London: Palgrave Macmillan, pp. 43-67.

Biehl, K. (2009): Migration 'Securitization' and its everyday implications: an examination of Turkish asylum policy and practice. CARIM Best Participant Essay Series 2009/01.

Council of Europe (2002): Conference on 'Irregular Migration and Dignity of Migrants: Co-operation in the Mediterrenean Region, 3-4 October 2001. Athens.

Council of the European Union (2004): Council Regulation (EC) No 2007/2004 of 26 October 2004 establishing a European Agency for the Management of Operational Cooperation at the External Borders of the Member States of the European Union. [online] Available at: eur-lex.europa.eu/LexUriServ/LexUriServ.douri= OJ:L:2004:349:0001:0011:EN:PDF [Accessed February 2, 2010].

De Haas, H. (2008): Irregular Migration from West Africa to the Maghreb and the European Union: An Overview of Recent Trends. IOM Migration Research Series, No. 32, Geneva.

De Haas, H. (2006): Trans-Saharan Migration to North Africa and the EU: Historical Roots and Current Trends, Migration Information Source. [online] Available at: http://www.migrationinformation.org/Feature/display.cfm?id=484 [Accessed June 11, 2009].

European Commission (2003): Accession Partnership with Turkey. Brussels, 19 May 2003. [online] Available at: http://www.deltur.cec.eu.int/english/e-g-countries-01.html [Accessed June 5, 2009].

European Commission (2006): Accession Partnership with Turkey. Brussels, 23 January 2006. [online] Available at: www.abgs.gov.tr/dokumanlar/apd/Turkey_APD_2006.pdf [Accessed June 5, 2009].

Europol (2005): Legislation on Trafficking in Human Beings and Illegal Immigrant Smuggling. [online] Available at: http://www.eipa.eu/files/File/Migration/Europol%202005%20-%20Legislation%20on%20Trafficking%20in%20Human%20Beings%20and%20Illegal%20Immigrant%20Smuggling.pdf [Accessed June 13, 2006].

Erzan, R. (2009): The Impact of the Global Crisis on Illegal Migration and Remittances: The Turkish Corridor, CARIM Analytic and Synthetic Notes 2009/38, Series on the Impact of the Economic Crisis, Demographic and Economic Module.

Evin, A./Kirişçi, K./Liden, R./Straubhaar, T./Tocci, N./Tolay, J./Walker, J. (2010): Getting to Zero: Turkey, Its Neighbors and the West, Transatlantic Academy.

Faist, T./Ette, A. (2007): Between Autonomy and the European Union. The Europeanisation of National Immigration Policies and Politics. London: Palgrave Macmillan.

Frelick, B. (1997): Barriers to Protection Turkey's Asylum Regulations. In: International Journal of Refugee Law 9, 1, pp. 8-34.

Geddes, A. (2007): The Europeanisation of what? Migration, asylum and the politics European integration. In: Faist, Thomas/Ette, Andreas (eds.): Between Autonomy and the European Union. The Europeanisation of National Immigration Policies and Politics. London: Palgrave Macmillan, pp. 68-99.

Havinga, T./Böcker, A. (1999): Country of asylum by choice or by chance: asylum-seekers in Belgium, the Netherlands and the UK. In: Journal of Ethnic and Migration Studies 25, 1, pp. 43-61.

İçduygu, A. (2008): Rethinking Irregular Migration in Turkey: Some Demo-Economic Reflections, CARIM Analytic and Synthetic Notes 2008/72, Irregular Migration Series, Demographic and Economic Module.

İçduygu, A. (2007): EU-isation matters: Changes in immigration and asylum practices in Turkey. In: Faist, Thomas/Ette, Andreas (eds.): Between Autonomy and the European Union. The Europeanisation of National Immigration Policies and Politics. London: Palgrave Macmillan, pp. 284-314.

İçduygu, A. (2006): The Labour Dimensions of Irregular Migration in Turkey, CARIM Research Report 2006/05.

İçduygu, A. (2005): Turkey and International Migration, İstanbul: SOPEMI Report for Turkey.

İçduygu, A. (2004a): Demographic Mobility and Turkey: Migration Experiences and Government Responses. In: Mediterrenean Quarterly 15, 4, pp. 88-99.

İçduygu, A. (2004b): Transborder Crime between Turkey and Greece: Human Smuggling and its Regional Consequences. In: Southeast European and Black Sea Studies 4, 2, pp. 294-314.

İçduygu, A./Toktas, S. (2002): How do Smuggling and Trafficking Operate via Irregular Border Crossing in the Middle East? Evidence from Fieldwork in Turkey. In: International Migration 40, pp. 25-54.

ILO (International Labour Organisation) (2004): Forced Labour, Migration and Trafficking in Europe, ILO's Special Action Programme to Combat Forced Labour. [online] Available at: http://www.ilo.org/dyn/declaris/DECLARATIONWEB.DOWNLOAD_BLOB?Var_DocumentID=3241 [Accessed April 8, 2006].

Kaya, C. (2009): Procedural rights under Turkish Law in the light of the EU asylum law. [online] Available at: www.adalet.gov.tr/english/e-journal/PROCEDURAL_RIGHTS.pdf [Accessed February 16, 2010].

Kaya, I. (2009): Reform in Turkish Asylum Law: Adopting the EU Acquis? CARIM Research Reports 2009/16, Robert Schuman Centre for Advanced Studies, San Domenico di Fiesole (FI): European University Institute.

Kirişçi, K. (2008): Managing Irregular Migration in Turkey: A Political-Bureaucratic Perspective. CARIM Analytic Series 2008/61, Robert Schuman Centre for Advanced Studies, San Domenico di Fiesole (FI): European University Institute.

Kirişçi, K. (2007): Border Management and the EU-Turkish Relations: Convergence or Deadlock. CARIM Research Report 2007/03.

Kirişçi, K. (2005): A Friendlier Schengen Visa System as a Tool of "Soft Power": The Experience of Turkey. In: European Journal of Migration and Law 7, pp. 343-367.

Kirişçi, K. (1996): Is Turkey Lifting the 'Geographical Limitation'? The November 1994 Regulation on Asylum in Turkey. In: International Journal of Refugee Law 8, 3, pp. 293-318.

Mannaert, C. (2003): Irregular Migration and Asylum in Turkey, New Issues in Refugee Research. Working Paper No. 89, UN Refugee Agency (UNHCR) Evaluation and Policy Analysis Unit.

Meese et. al. (1998): Multidisciplinary Research on the Phenomenon of Trafficking in Human Beings from an International and National Perspective. A Pilot Study with Poland and Hungary. Ghent: University of Ghent.

Mitsilegas, V. (2002): The implementation of the EU acquis on illegal immigration by the candidate countries of Central and Eastern Europe: challenges and contradictions. In: Journal of Ethnic and Migration Studies 28, 4 pp. 665-682.

National Action Plan (NAP): [online] Available at: www.egm.gov.tr [Accessed February 14, 2011].

National Program for the Adoption of the Acquis (2003): Official Gazette 25178 (24 July 2003). [online] Available at: http://www.abgs.gov.tr/NPAA/up.htm, [Accessed September 2, 2009].

Penninx, R. (2002): Human Smuggling and Trafficking of Migrants: Types, Origins, and Dynamics in a Comparative and Interdisciplinary Perspective. Institute for Migration and Ethnic Studies (IMES): Project Proposal to Nederlandse organisatie voor Wetenschappelijk onderzoek (NWO) for the programme "European Collaborative Research Project in the Social Sciences". [online] Available at: http://www.temaasyl.se/upload/Human%20smuggling.pdf [Accessed April 10, 2006].

Philip, M./Midgley, E./Teitelbaum, M. (2002): Best Practice Options: Turkey. In: International Migration 40, 3, pp. 119-131.

Salt, J. (2000b): Trafficking and Human Smuggling: A European Perspective. In: International Migration, Special Issue 1, 38, 3, pp. 31-56.

Salt, J.& Hogarth, J. (2000): Migrant Trafficking and Human Smuggling: A Review of the Evidence with Case Studies from Hungary, Poland and Ukraine. IOM: Geneva.

Turkey 2009 Progress Report: Accompanying the Communication from the Commission to the European Parliament and the Council, Enlargement Strategy and Main Challenges 2009-2010. [online] Available at: http://ec.europa.eu/enlarge

ment/press_corner/key-documents/reports_oct_2009_en.htm [Accessed February 11, 2010].
Turkish Ministry of Foreign Affairs: [online] Available at: www.mfa.gov.tr [Accessed March 2, 2011].
Turkish Ministry of Interior (MOI), General Directorate of Security, [online] Available at www.egm.gov.tr [Accessed March 2, 2011].
Ulker, E. (2008): Assimilation, Security and Geographical Nationalization in Interwar Turkey: The Settlement Law of 1934. In: European Journal of Turkish Studies, Thematic Issue N°7, Demographic Engineering – part I. [online] Available at: http://www.ejts.org/document2123.html [Accessed February 14, 2011].
Ulker, E. (2007). Assimilation of the Muslim communities in the first decade of the Turkish Republic (1923-1934). In: European Journal of Turkish Studies. [online] available at: http://www.ejts.org/document822.html
United Nations Convention against Transnational Organized Crime and Its Protocols (2001) [online] Available at: http://www.unodc.org/pdf/crime/a_res_55/res5525e.pdf [Accessed April 5, 2006].
UNHCR Turkey (2007): Turkey Briefing Note.
UNHCR (1997) PRESS release,
UNHCR welcomes Latvia lifting geographical restriction on asylum. [online] Available at: http://www.unhcr.org/3ae6b81366.html [Accessed February 17, 2009].
Van Liempt. I. (2006): Navigating Borders: An Inside Perspective into the Process of Human Smuggling. Amsterdam: Amsterdam University Press.

Turkish legislation
1994 Regulation on Asylum.
The 1934 Law on Settlement, No 2510.
The 1950 Passport Law, No. 5682.
The 1964 Citizenship Law, No 403.
The 1950 Law related to the Residence and Travel of Foreigners, No.5683.
The Law on the Work Permit of Foreigners, No. 4817.
Application Regulation of the Act on Foreign Work Permit, No. 25214, Official Gazette on 29.08.2003 Circular numbered 57.

Part Two: Experiences from the U.S. migration regime

Undocumented Immigration between the U.S. and Mexico: The Complex Development of Militarized Borders and Social Responses

Avital Bloch and Ma. Alejandra Rocha Silva

Introduction

This essay examines the undocumented immigration from Mexico to the United States from the 1990s to the present. The discussion focuses on Mexicans, since the numbers of Mexican immigrants far exceed those of immigrants from other regions of the world. The economic disparity between Mexico and the U.S. and the long border that separates them have resulted in millions of Mexicans immigrating illegally to the U.S. The focus of this essay is on the ever-more complex barriers and harsh border policies, through which the U.S. authorities, as well as civil groups, seek to reduce illegal entry and increase deportation of undocumented migrants residing in the U.S. The essay provides an analysis of the human, economic, and legal pressures with which Mexican communities are confronted, concluding with a discussion of the current state of the debate on anti-illegal immigration, which reached its climax following the passage of Arizona's Support Our Law Enforcement and Safe Neighborhoods Act, known as SB 1070, one of the strictest anti-illegal immigration measures in the last decades.

Immigration to the United States: History and Numbers

The U.S. has never ceased to be a nation of immigrants. Starting with the colonies in the 17th century, English and Dutch immigrants, later joined by Germans and other Western Europeans, started a new society. The native Indian population was displaced, Africans were brought in as slaves, and the new American nation was defined as white Anglo-Saxon. In the 19th and early 20th centuries, the first large waves of immigrants from Ireland and Central, Eastern, and Southern Europe arrived, who were perceived as being different from the early settlers. The initial concept of identity that guided U.S. society in the 19th century was centered on the assimilation of new immigrants into the Anglo-American culture, which found expression in the term "melting pot." By the end of the century, the large numbers of immigrants of diverse ethnic background arriving in the U.S. met considerable resistance by the descendants of the original settlers. Early on, Chinese immigrants were the group that was affected most by ethnically-based rejection, which eventually resulted in the passage of the Chinese Exclusion Act of 1882. This growing anti-foreign "nativism" culminated in the Johnson-Reed Act of 1924, which limited the number of newcomers, created a "national origins quota system" for each nationality already residing in the U.S., and introduced the category "illegal alien." The Border Patrol was created to guard the Mexican border and undocumented entry was criminalized (Hernández 2010: Ch. 1-4; Ngai 2005: Ch.1; Schrag 2010: Ch. 2-5).

As immigrant groups demonstrated that assimilation would not be a rapid process, the national structure of diversity now emphasized "pluralism." New groups were allowed to maintain their particular traditions in their private sphere, while being obligated to follow the public Anglo-European culture and political principles and assimilating into the mainstream majority over time. Pluralism dominated ethnic thinking up until the 1970s. The arrival of new waves of immigrants from developing countries in Latin America (mainly Mexico), Asia, and the Middle East followed changes in immigration policy, which were reflected in the Immigration and Nationality Act of 1965, which abolished the National Origins Formula that had been in place since 1924. As liberation and equal rights ideologies of racial and ethnic movements in the U.S. gained influence and the non-European foreign-born population increased in the 1980s, a new concept of diversity emerged. Multiculturalism, as it was now called, expanded the rights of ethnic minorities to ensure greater respect for, and the inclusion of, their particular cultures in the dominant Anglo-American culture without pressing for immediate integration. Among the immigrants thus included in the multicultural model were other non-European groups, Mexican Americans, native Mexicans, and other Hispanic and Latino American national origin groups (such as from Cuba and the Dominican Republic).

Mexicans were part of the population of the Southwestern United states following the annexation of Texas and California in 1845 and 1846, respectively, and the Mexican Cession of 1848. Migration across the border continued, and in the 20th century the need for field laborers in agriculture, especially in California, brought about the Bracero Program, which existed from 1942 to 1964. This program recruited poor male peasants who, based on the accord between Mexico and the U.S., were later to return to Mexico. However, many of them stayed in the U.S, while illegal immigration continued (Calavita 1999; Ngai 2005: Ch. 4). When the Bracero program ended, Mexico and the U.S. maintained guest worker programs and a policy of migration tolerance, which Mexico then turned to its advantage, using emigration as an economic safety valve to let portions of its lowest economic stratum go north. Eventually, the Immigration Reform and Control Act of 1986 (IRCA) legalized three million undocumented immigrants under a general amnesty and the status quo of immigration prevailed until the U.S. imposed new limitations in the 1990s (Bustamante 2000), and even more after the September 11 attacks.

Statistics on immigration for the year 2000 indicated that of the total of close to 31 million foreign-born residents in the U.S., a little over 9 million (i.e. 29% of all foreign-born residents) were from Mexico, nearly 3 million from the Caribbean, and 2 million from Central America, as well as over 8 million from Asia and nearly 5 million from Europe (U.S. Census Bureau 2000). In 2007, the number of immigrants reached an all-time high of almost 40 million. More than half of those who have entered the U.S. since 2000 are illegal aliens (Camarota 2007). According to the U.S. Census Bureau, in 2007 over 29 million people of Mexican origin were living in the U.S., which was equivalent to 64% of all the Hispanics in the U.S. The fast growth of the Mexican population in the U.S. began in 1990, when close to 63% of the present Mexican population of the U.S. entered the country. As of 2007, 40% of all Mexicans living in the U.S. were born in Mexico. While in the past most of the immigrants settled in the U.S.-Mexico borderlands, in recent years they have also gone to the Northwestern, Midwestern, and Southern Atlantic states. However, as of 2007, 36% of Hispanics, almost all of whom are of Mexican origin, lived in California and Texas, while 43% lived in New Mexico, the state with the highest concentration of Mexican immigrants. Between 2000 and 2005, California's unauthorized immigrant population grew by 13% and the number of Hispanics by over 16%. In the same period, the number of undocumented Mexicans living in Texas increased by 50%. California, Texas, and Florida account for nearly half of all unauthorized Hispanic immigrants, although between 2000 and 2006 a large increase in the illegal immigrant population was also recorded in Georgia, Washington, and Arizona. In addition, the demographic composition of Mexicans has changed from rural farmers to a larger proportion of men and women from urban areas who are employed in services, manufacturing, and small businesses. In any case, over 20% of the population of Mexican origin residing in the U.S. live in poverty (Pew 2009: 1-3; U.S. Census Bureau 2000; 2005).

It is estimated that in the early 1970s Mexican nationals made up over 90% of the illegal immigrant population, but by 2002 their numbers had decreased significantly, due to an increase in the numbers of other illegal Latinos, who now represented about 25% of the undocumented population, and the steady influx of illegal immigrants from Asia, Europe, and Africa (Sadowski-Smith 2008: 792–798). Between 2000 and 2005, 85% of Mexicans entering the country did so illegally (Tuirán 2006a). From 2000 to 2006, according to the Office of Immigration Statistics, the number of unauthorized immigrants increased by 69%, which makes undocumented Mexicans the largest group of illegal immigrants (57%) in the U.S. At the beginning of

2009, the Department of Homeland Security, which is in charge of immigration matters, estimated the total number of undocumented immigrants to be between 10.8 and 12 million. In 2007 and 2008, in the wake of the general economic downturn in the U.S., this number decreased to 11.8 million and 11.6 million, respectively, which resulted in, among other things, increased unemployment among Mexican-born immigrants and a reduced influx of new illegal immigrants (Associated Press 2010a; Preston 2009a). Even so, according to data from 2005, Mexico is also the primary source country of new legal immigrants and newly naturalized citizens (Gelatt and Meyers 2006), but of course these immigrants represent a small percentage compared to the vast number of illegal undocumented Mexicans entering the country, and even to the number of Mexicans who are eligible for naturalization (DeParle 2009).

Social and Cultural Attitudes Toward Mexico and Mexicans

Since the 1990s and even more so since the September 11 attacks, immigrants have been increasingly met with suspicion, and not everyone in the U.S. has been happy with liberal multiculturalism, an approach traditional nationalists and conservatives view as a threat to the national culture and traditions of citizenship posed by inordinately powerful minority cultures. The general tolerance for non-Europeans with a darker skin has decreased over the years. Of course, the growing resistance to the concept of multiculturalism should be seen in relation to the sheer number of illegal Mexican and Latin immigrants residing in the U.S. However, it would be an oversimplification to say that this phenomenon is a manifestation of racism. While critics of immigration have objected to the heavy burden that undocumented immigrants place on public services and welfare, the most commonly voiced argument is that illegal immigrants take jobs from both the native-born majority and the non-native minorities, although this claim has been widely refuted by economic research.

Whatever the merits of the economic arguments, the illegality of immigrants has been at the center of the debate. U.S. society maintains a strong tradition that emphasizes the "rule of law" and the centrality of the legal procedures in all aspects of life, exemplified by the large number of questions the Supreme Court takes on to decide over their constitutionality and the multitude of legal suits regarding social behavior, government's work, and institutional functioning. Even for people who are in favor of legal immigration, the issue of immigrants living and working illegally in the country is a genuine concern, yet underlying negative attitudes toward undocumented immigrants are essentially the result of racially, culturally or socially constructed perceptions of national origin and skin color. The populist Tea Party movement emerging since 2009 strongly reflects the prevailing anti-foreigner mood. Its white middle class supporters, who consider themselves "All-Americans," are motivated by social status concerns and racial anxiety. Their feeling is that the country no longer belongs exclusively to them and its traditional social and cultural fabric is threatened, for in the multicultural/social scheme of things immigrants and minorities have made strides in society that disturb them (Brinkley 2010; Moser 2010; Skerry and Fernandes 2006).

There is a fear among these groups and other traditional and conservative Americans that the nation's ethnic makeup has been changing due to the growing influence of apparently "inassimilable" groups, such as Mexicans, who are often seemingly "invisible" poor, underclass people living in in rural areas, cities, and suburbs. Right-wing anti-immigration supporters encourage people to think of Mexicans immigrants as people who import poverty, refuse to learn English, arrive in relentless waves, naturalize late, and integrate slowly (Eviatar 2006). In addition, the culturally constructed national image of Mexico has been stigmatized as being "alien," inferior, wild, and contaminated. Sentiments such as these have had a profound impact on the way Americans perceive their immigrant neighbors: dangerous, violent, criminal, delinquent, involved in drug trafficking, sexually depraved, corrupt, ungovernable, and therefore undeserving of Western-style citizenship (Barajas Escamilla 2005: 171; Horowitz 2001; Judis 2006; Ramos García 2002: 63-70; Velázquez García 2008: 47-50, 56-60). Racial anxiety has increased as a result of the publicized projections that non-whites in the U.S. will become the majority of the population in a matter of a few decades. Since 2000, the number of immigrants has been growing by almost one million a year. The Census Bureau predicts that white Americans will become a minority, accounting for only 46% of the population (DeParle 2009; Roberts 2009; U.S. Census Bureau 2000).

Even though Mexicans and Hispanics are classified as white, in the general racially-based color-consciousness prevalent in the U.S. they are still distinguished from whites of European background and targeted as racially inferior by other whites. Of rural and working class origin, less educated, and poor, in terms of class prestige they are located at the lower end of the social scale. Despite their number and visibility in areas where large numbers of immigrants reside or work, Mexicans are easily disregarded. Even legal aliens and naturalized citizens of Mexican origin are not always accepted as "real" Americans. Indeed, the term "illegal immigrant" itself reflects the idealization of legality and the vilification of unauthorized Mexicans associated with illegality (Paspalanova 2008). The social perceptions of color give rise to "racial profiling," that is, the assumption that all Mexicans are illegal aliens because of their skin color, language, and social class.

Many Americans view Mexicans as non-citizens and foreigners, a perception which increases the Mexicans' social and legal vulnerability with regard to privileges of citizenship and constitutional protection on U.S. territory. The state still reserves the classic sovereign right to determine who is a national citizen, despite the recent globalized human rights paradigm of international standards and the attainment of "social citizenship", both of which go beyond the traditional concept of legal citizenship (Bustamante 2001; Dow 2007: 533-544; Koulish 2009; Kretsedemas 2008: 553-554, 561).

In this context, critics of immigration require the cloak of legality so as not to appear racist. Immigration advocates, on the other hand, talk about legalizing unauthorized immigrants but evade the debate about the delicate social and cultural intricacies of immigration, some of which do not sit well with anti-immigration groups (Jencks 2007; Rosenblum 2003; Skerry and Fernandes 2006). In reality, most Americans are unfamiliar with the complex immigration laws and see the issue primarily as a dichotomy between the concepts of "legal" and "illegal". Not only do they lack the understanding that entering the country legally as an immigrant is extremely difficult, they are also unaware of the various ways many Mexicans—even immigrants who are already on U.S. territory—use to obtain legal status. The courts usually grant legal status on a case-by-case basis based on factors such as long-term residency, marriage to a legal resident alien, permanent residency in the U.S., or a place in the country an immigrant may have earned over time through work and social involvement. This is part of a legal tradition of flexibility which blurs the line between immigrants being considered legal or not (Motomura 2009).

The American public is fairly evenly divided on the current issue of immigration (Archibold and Thee-Brenan 2010; Cortina 2007: 14, 17, 19; Pew 2009). Pro-immigrant groups, principally liberals and younger people, argue that, aside from the fact that the U.S. needs immigrant workers, the immigrants also generally obey the law, help to keep jobs in the U.S., revive old neighborhoods, enrich multiculturalism, join unions, consume products, pay taxes, and thus contribute to social security. These groups also realize that, once naturalized, a good number of Mexicans gain upward mobility, move on to better jobs, take economic risks, intermarry, and receive formal education. Anti-immigrant conservatives, on the other hand, point to the alleged problems of cultural difference, illegality, demographic threat, and social disruption caused by immigrants (Cave 2010; Eviatar 2006; Winston 2006).

California was the first state to resort to local anti-immigrant measures, passing Proposition 187—commonly known as the "Save Our State" (SOS) initiative—as early as 1994. Arguing that California was unable to bear the enormous costs of immigration, the state prohibited undocumented aliens from using health care, welfare, and other public social services. Many critics saw Proposition 187 as "institutional racism" (Bustamante 2001: 7). Historically, the realization of the California Dream has indeed always been a privilege the white middle class (Saler 2010). Prejudice against non-white Americans runs deep, its roots dating back to the time when the state passed the drastic anti-immigration Chinese Exclusion Act of 1882 and the anti-Japanese California Alien Land Law of 1913 (Bloch and Ortoll 2010). In 2004, ten years after Proposition 187, the State of Arizona passed Proposition 200, which denies immigrants who are unable to provide proof of citizenship access to public benefits and the right to vote. Of course, anti-immigration measures are not foreign to Arizona either. In the 1920s and 1930s, Mexicans and Native Americans were socially discriminated against as non-whites, and Japanese immigrants were forcibly removed from the borderland region by Anglo-Americans (Benton-Cohen 2009: 2-15; Weber 1986: 79-81). While Proposition 187 was eventually found unconstitutional and Proposition 200 is still being challenged legally, xenophobic attitudes still prevail in the borderland.

Mexicans and the Characteristics of Their Diaspora

Culturally, the long Mexican-American border is a symbol of illegality, social and cultural division, and mistrust, as well as a symbol of legal and transnational connection and communication. The gateway with the largest movement of merchandise and people (3.4 million) per year in the world (Meneses 2005: 123), the border is, indeed, not only a symbolic divide but also a physical place of social interaction. Many scholars have pointed to a complex sphere of cross-border activity in which ethnic, linguistic, religious, and artistic exchanges take place (Kearney 1999). Residents, families, business people, missionaries, artists, students, musicians, and others used to be able to pass the border unhindered. Many of them have settled illegally on the U.S. side of the border and those who did not succeed in crossing the border as undocumented immigrants remain permanently in the Mexican border towns and cities. Ideas, concepts, and assets are exchanged as well as a result of this form of mobility, reinforcing the idea of trans-border Mexican and Mexican-American national/ethnic communities. Given this, the 1,969-mile long border, though still functioning as a national boundary, should also be seen as fluid, deterritorialized, and non-dichotomous.

The Mexican "diaspora," however, is geographically spread beyond the borderlands and reflects current notions and practices of globalization and bi-nationalism manifested in various phenomena. For example, there are more than 600 hometown associations of Mexicans in the U.S. (known as "clubs," *clubes de oriundos*) registered in 30 American cities, through which Mexican-Americans and immigrants maintain economic, cultural, and political contact with their home communities, sending remittances, sponsoring cultural events, and influencing local political affairs (Fitzgerald 2000; Orozco et al. 2003). At the national level, the National Association of Latino Elected Officials has been involved in issues that are of mutual interest to both countries. Discussion forums, bilateral commissions, memoranda of understanding, accords, and inter-parliamentary commissions attest to an institutionalized dialogue between the U.S. and Mexico (Cano and Delano 2006: 27-39; García-Acevedo 2003).

The Mexican government has been interested in enhancing relations with the diasporic Mexican community. In 1989, Mexico's National Institute of Migration (INM) set up the Programa Paisano (Countryman Program) to provide assistance to immigrants and Mexican U.S. residents who visit Mexico and protect them from abuse by Mexican border officials. Through this program, Mexico demonstrates its recognition of constant migratory movement. While Mexico's policies have proved that it favors the continuation of emigration, it has also shown itself willing to define and protect the communities in the U.S. as a component of the "Mexican global nation," despite hostility expressed by some Mexicans toward emigrants heading to the U.S. In 1990, implementation of the Mexican Communities Abroad Program (PCME) began and offices of the Agency for the Support of Migrants and Their Families (OFAM) were established in Mexican consulates, operated by the IMM in collaboration with eleven federal ministries, to deal with emigration issues (Secretaría de Relaciones Exteriores 2000). This was followed by the creation of the Presidential Office for Mexicans Abroad and an Advisory Council of the INM in 2000, the latter of which is composed of over 150 representatives of the Mexican communities in the U.S. The objective of these bodies is to channel migration-related issues through Mexican government agencies. The outreach reflects sensitivity to Mexican migrants and Mexico's interests in their growing economic power and the benefits of emigration, primarily in the form of remittances for Mexico (García-Acevedo 2003; Imaz 2007: 64-66). Recently there have also been attempts to establish academic cross-national relations. Some Mexican state universities have started study programs for immigrant students in the hope that, being educational institutions, they will be rewarded with support from their communities in the U.S.

Another proof of the Mexican government's desire to maintain the idea of a transnational polity united with its diaspora and to retain the loyalties of its citizens was the legalization of dual citizenship for Mexicans residing in the U.S in 1996. In light of the belief in multiculturalism and the perception of how globalization operates, American elites have come to understand that even naturalized immigrants do not necessarily wish to sever their ties with their original identity and citizenship. At the same time, Mexico has decided to treat undocumented emigrants living in the U.S. as Mexican citizens, thus emphasizing their non-citizen status and reinforcing social marginalization in the north. In 2005, nearly ten years after the passage of the nationality law, the details of extraterritorial voting rights were approved and took effect for the first time during the 2006 presidential election (Cano and Delano 2006: 29; García-Acevedo 2003). However, the Federal Electoral Institute (IFE) reported that a very small number of Mexican citizens who reside in the U.S. voted in the Mexican presidential election; fewer than 36,000 registered to vote, of whom a little over 28,000 actually voted. In spite of that, Mexico's approach has resulted in a transnational "external citizenship," which helped fulfill expectations regarding cross-border attachments (Bauböck 2003: 715; Calderón 2004; Carbado 2005: 636-639; Félix 2008: 618-621; Neuman 1996).

While the cross-border relationships refer to a national/ethnic communal identity, they do not always imply continuation and unity. Second and third-generation residents in the U.S. become more and more distant from their Mexican roots and eventually integrate into mainstream society. Mobility in the borderland may also have conflicting results. In El Paso, Texas, for example, where many former residents of Ciudad Juárez, Chihuahua have settled, a distinct identity has developed. The residents on the U.S. side have developed an American identity and distance themselves from Mexico. Feeling superior because they live in the U.S., they now look down on Mexicans in Ciudad Juárez, and even go so far as to adopt the attitudes of American conservatives by supporting anti-immigration measures. At the same time, *juarences*, the residents of Ciudad Juárez, despise the Mexicans living across the border who consider themselves members of a superior social class. Another example of conflicting identity is that of the Border Patrol. The officers, usually of Mexican descent, play a communicative role (by speaking Spanish with Mexicans at the border), but their work also generates conflict, as evidenced by complaints about their discriminatory behavior (Hill 2003; Spener 2001; Vila 2000: Ch. 1-5; 2005). Phenomena such as these reflect the social and cultural forces in great flux along the national boundaries.

U.S. Federal and Local Anti-Immigration Laws, Border Control Policies, and Militarization

While, thanks to family, cultural, and political relations, the border has never been closed completely, anti-immigration sentiments in the U.S have prevented free movement and mass legalization of undocumented immigrants. For years, supporters of anti-illegal immigration policy have attacked Congress's failure to enact comprehensive immigration reform. In the 1990s, with no other solution in sight, the perception of cultural polarization between the two countries regarding illegal crossings motivated the U.S. to reinforce parts of the physical border (Delacroix and Nikiforov 2009: 105-106), with several operations being put in place by the Clinton administration. In 1993, Operation Blockade was launched at the checkpoint between El Paso, Texas and Ciudad Juárez, Chihuahua (later renamed Operation Hold the Line due to its military connotations). One year later, Operation Gatekeeper was implemented in the border region between Tijuana, Baja California and the suburbs of San Diego, California, which included the erection of the first border wall between the two cities. In the same year, Operation Safeguard established security measures between the two Nogales—Sonora and Arizona—and in 1997, Operation Rio Grande was implemented along the river between Laredo, Texas and Nuevo Laredo, Tamaulipas, all the way to Brownsville, Texas near the Gulf of Mexico (Bustamante 2001; Meneses 2005: 116; Nevins 2002).

The increasing anti-immigrant sentiments and practices are explained by the post-9/11 atmosphere and the War on Terror declared by then-President George W. Bush. According to the national defense strategy, weak national borders were perceived as potentially vulnerable to terrorist infiltration, and border security and illegal immigration have been defined as issues of national security. The earliest measure of this kind enacted by the government, the USA PATRIOT Act of 2001, reduced legal restrictions on law enforcement inside the country to facilitate the detection of terrorist activities and undocumented immigration. The attempt of the U.S. government to enforce these harsh security measures worldwide reflected its desire for global hegemony. The measures, which included operations and agreements regarding intelligence and border and transport security, were implemented by the newly-created Department of Homeland Security (DHS) in 2003, under the direction of the then-Secretary of Homeland Security, Michael Chertoff. The functions of what used to be the State Department's Immigration and Naturalization Service (INS) were divided into separate new agencies; the investigative and enforcement functions were transferred to Immigration and Customs Enforcement (ICE) and U.S. Citizenship and Immigration Services (USCIS), and the former Border Patrol (BP) was incorporated into U.S. Customs and Border Protection (CBP).

Since the institutional restructuring, the number of BP agents increased from 4,000 in 1993 to 12,000 in 2006 and over 18,000 in 2008. By 2009, the total number had grown to 20,000 (Preston 2009d). So-called Smart Border agreements were signed with strategic partners Canada in 2001 and Mexico in 2002. The Enhanced Border Security and Visa Entry Reform Act was passed in the same year (Benítez and Rodrígue 2006; Emmerich 2003: 28-30). Mexico, in turn, implemented Operation Sentinel (2003-2006), which employed 18,000 federal armed troops to detain emigrants trying to leave the country at the border. Other bilateral national security programs included the 2005 Security and Prosperity Partnership of North America, the 2006 Improve Public Safety, and the 2008 Mérida Initiative for transnational regional security, which includes training Mexican personnel (Anguiano and Trejo Peña 2007: 49-51).

One of the more extreme measures to restrict illegal crossings taken in the mid-1990s was the erection of a 10-foot welded metal fence, which extends along a 14 mile-long stretch of the above-mentioned San Diego–Tijuana divide, the region with the largest influx of undocumented immigrants (100,000 per year). In light of the removal of the Berlin Wall as a metaphor for the fall of totalitarianism and the rise of unrestricted movement across Europe, the erection of the fence by the U.S. met with some public opposition. Even so, more high-tech reinforcements were added to the fence, including sensors and night vision technology such as infrared cameras. In 2007, as the border debate reached a new climax, the Secure Fence Act was passed. The initial stretch was proposed as a model for extending it along the entire border and resembled the security barrier Israel started to build in 2006 at the border with the Palestinian territories. The so-called Tortilla Wall was planned to be finished by the end of 2008, but by early 2010 only about 650 miles were completed, with just over a hundred miles on the Sonora-Arizona border (Meneses 2005: 117-118; U.S.-Mexico Border Fence 2010).

One feature of the policy changes is the application of new high technologies in the borderlands, including pulsed fast neutron analysis for scanning vehicular traffic, which has been in use since as early as the 1990s. In the early 2000s, Smart Border introduced bridges with intelligence gathering technologies, such as the Automated Biometric Identification System (ABIS). ABIS uses electronic biometrically enabled ID cards, called *micas* by migrants, that are given to legal residents and the inhabitants of the Mexican borderland inhabitants for crossing the border. Holders of these cards may travel as far as 215 miles into U.S. territory for a maximum duration of 72 hours. The cards contain information on physiological biometric characteristics, including fingerprints, hand geometry, handwriting, voice, and iris recognition. Guided by the anti-terror, anti-crime state of mind of a "risk society," the database contains 90 million records collected by the DHS and the FBI's National Crime Information Center (Ackleson 2005: 138-139, 144-148; ICE n.d.).

In 2004, the first unmanned air vehicle (UAV) equipped with a surveillance camera—the RQ-4 Global Hawk—was flown at 300–400 feet above the border. The private, anti-illegal immigration citizen group that flew it, the American Border Patrol, claimed to have provided information to the BP. The DHS has also considered using a UAV (the MQ1 Predator) along with an extending network of ground sensors (Notimex 2004; Opción, 2010; Sherman and Rivers 2003). In 2007, as part of the Secure Border Initiative, the government contracted with the Boeing Company to produce radar and motion satellite sensors to be installed along the first 50 miles of the Sonora-

Arizona divide. However, due to a delay caused by technological limitations, the project, originally intended to be implemented in 2011, will not be operative before 2014 (Billeaud 2010; Barrapunto 2006; Kroft 2010; www.texasborderwatch.com; www.virtualvigilence.org). The Secret Border Initiative, which is part of the Mérida Initiative, also planned to add X-ray technology and inspection scanners to the 25 helicopters that are already in operation (Mendoza 2010).

Border control has become de-territorialized: it no longer just serves the traditional function of surveillance at the actual site of the national border, but has extended its focus to other regions further inland, because most undocumented immigrants have succeeded in penetrating far into the U.S. This shift of focus is also reflected in the use of webcam networks by vigilantes to monitor the border from a distance. Since 2008, over 100,000 internet users have volunteered to use such virtual border patrol systems to support the Texas Border Sheriff's Coalition. As soon as they observe any suspicious movement around the border, they email the authorities (Luscombe 2009). In response, migrants have not shied away from using low-cost technology. The so-called Transborder Immigrant Tool signals the locations of patrols, water, and aid groups through a cell phone converted into a GPS satellite navigator (Notimex 2009). With cell phones now popular even among the poorest migrants, modern technology has stepped in to help them in the wilderness.

A significant aspect of the deterritorialization of immigration management includes the detection of undocumented workers anywhere in the U.S. who use fraudulent social security cards. In the past, carrying a forged ID card—punishable a federal offense—did not lead to prosecution because workers who were caught with such cards could plead guilty to a lesser charge. This has changed as a result of tougher enforcement and the use of information technologies, including the E-Verify program. Established in 2007, E-Verify is an internet-based system that checks employee information against social security and DHS databases. Except for federal contractors and the state of Utah, participation is voluntarily, which is also the reason why the program is considered to be inefficient; of the 7 to 8 million employers in the U.S., only 184,000 use E-Verify. Fewer than 10% of hired employees have been processed through the program and just a small percentage of unauthorized workers were denied employment. Some employers only obtain verification for what they consider "foreign looking" applicants, which means that there is ethnic profiling going on among employers. Many companies justify their practice of employing illegal workers for longer periods of time, stating that it would be discriminatory to lay them off after so many years (Associated Press 2010b, 2010c; Bacon and Hing 2009; Hanson 2009; Jencks 2007; Liptak and Preston 2009; Preston 2008, 2009b). The traditional method of conducting raids has also been used more frequently since the 1990s and there has been a six-fold increase in the number of illegal employees who are apprehended each year (Coleman 2007: 65). Raids and audits are used to pressure businesses to dismiss undocumented immigrants and deter employers from hiring new ones. Although they fear that their licenses might be revoked, employers still take chances employing low-paid, unauthorized workers (Camarota 2009; Hanson 2009). It is of no surprise, then, that companies have started lobbying against such federal measures in Washington (Lewis 2009; McKinley 2009; Preston 2008, 2009c).

Although the U.S. government has justified its anti-undocumented immigration policies as a component of the War on Terror, the racially-motivated rejection of immigrants by some sectors of the population is still strong. The extra-legal activities of paramilitary citizen organizations on the border reflect right-wing, white supremacist, and extra-governmental traditions on the southern frontier. In 2001, the small paramilitary Border/Ranch Rescue in Texas and the Civil Homeland Defense patrol in the Tijuana-San Diego border stretch started reporting illegal crossings to the authorities (Kennedy 2009; Trujeque 2007: 144-146, 153-154). In 2004, the armed Civil Homeland Defense Corps of Arizona was established, which transformed into the controversial Minuteman Project a year later, named after the colonial militia active in Massachusetts during the American Revolutionary War. Founded as a response to the BP's alleged inefficiency, the group received some public support, but by 2007 had lost the wide media coverage it had enjoyed in the years previous (Anti-Defamation League 2010; Ayres 2006; Gilchrist and Corsi 2006; Krieger 2008; Winston 2006; http://www.minutemanhq.com). At the height of its activities the group was evidence of the tough militarization and masculinization of border control. The BP's work bears military characteristics as well: armed agents driving around in armored "Humvees" and riding through the hills on horses, tracing the movements of detected migrants. Thus, traditional American male machismo has been harnessed and channeled into sophisticated technologies used to control the vast space and stop immigration, whereas those whom the militia would describe as feminized urban liberals see immigration as a natural and positive human activity (Coleman 2007: 54–60; Buff 2008: 531; http://search.cbp.gov/query.html).

The increasing transfer of security control from federal authorities to local agencies has been one of the most notable transformations in immigration policy. Although immigration issues are officially handled by the federal government and ICE as its centralized authority, the above-described changes were the result of public dissatisfaction with the way the federal system had been handling the issue of illegal immigration in the past. According to constituencies in various states and municipalities, it is not that the BP has been ineffective, but, given the constant flow of immigrants, the results expected of the overworked agents are far from being achieved (Bosquez 2010). A lack of agreement between the political parties and the civil sectors has prevented Congress and recent administrations from enacting comprehensive immigration reform. The last attempt to pass federal legislation on issues of immigration was made in 2005, in the form of the Border Protection, Antiterrorism, and Illegal Immigration Control Act (H.R. 4437), which was successfully passed in the House of Representatives but failed to pass the Senate. Drafted by several House Republicans, particularly from immigrant states such as Arizona, California, and Florida, it reflected the wish to implement federal reform, but without amnesty, while including provisions for stronger control at the border and in the interior. H.R. 4437 reflected a federalized approach, and its failure just reinforced local action. The government has transferred some of its control functions to eager local enforcement agencies, which now act as a somewhat informal arm of government (Schrag 2008). In the southern states, the insistence on local action has been based on the "state rights" tradition, which justifies "inherent authority" to act alone if federal interest contradicts that of the state (Kretsedemas 2008: 556, 564; Ong 2006).

Especially after the defeat of H.R. 4437 in 2007, various additional state and local laws and ordinances have been enacted in favor of shifting federal immigration-related responsibilities to lower levels of government. The enforcement of local immigration laws is defended by the federal executive's policy agenda, albeit as temporary laws. Indeed, the latest administrations have supported the expansion of the immigrant labor market, and localized legislation has been used to demonstrate that the federal government is taking a tough stance on immigration, to later justify federal reform that would legalize more aliens and allow them to work (Kretsedemas 2008: 562–568). The newly created Section 287 (g) of the Immigration and Nationality Act (INA) permits agreements of cooperation between the Secretary of the DHS and state or local law enforcement agencies "to perform a function of an immigration officer in relation to the investigation, apprehension or detention of aliens in the United States" to increase safety and security. Through contracts, local law enforcement agencies have cooperated with ICE to combat specific challenges in their communities. Since 2006, over 65 such agreements have been entered into with local sheriffs and chiefs of police. ICE has trained over 800 officers in several states, who are reported to have identified some 70,000 undocumented individuals (Cole 2009; Kennedy 2009; Preston 2009b). The increased number of local governments readily collaborating with ICE situate the border at any location security dictates. Thus, the traditional logic of fixed territoriality marked by the national border has been disrupted and the border has become a shifting and expanding space populated by local patrols (Coleman 2007: 56-58).

Since being in the country illegally has become a punishable offense, local authorities have been taking action on their own. Not only do they arrest individuals for visa violations, which is defined as a misdemeanor or—where regulations are violated for the purpose of illegal immigration—as a crime, but also for minor violations, such as traffic violations, petty theft, prostitution, drug possession, and shoplifting (Coleman 2007: 65). This regime was originally introduced in 1988 for "criminal aliens" who committed serious offenses, but the 1990 and 1994 Immigration Laws and the 1996 IIRAIRA considerably broadened the definition of "crime" and expanded the list of felonies (Kanstroom 2007: 226-228). The 2008 ICE Secure Communities initiative was designed to locally facilitate the identification of immigrants who violated the law. Local law enforcement agencies use the Automated Biometrics Identification System (IDENT), which contains fingerprints and immigration status information on some 30,000 immigrant inmates of federal and state prisons. In the past, access to this system was restricted to FBI personnel. Now law enforcement agencies are even authorized to hold suspects in detention. Thus far, Secure Communities has been implemented in California, Oregon, Michigan, Texas, Arizona, Florida, North Carolina, Maryland, Virginia, Illinois, and Hawaii (Editorial 2009a; ICE n.d.; McKinley 2009).

When arrested, undocumented individuals are detained and eventually deported, regardless of their country of origin. This is the most extreme measure currently taken by the government. The deportation of Mexican immigrants from the U.S. is by no means a recent phenomenon. Unconstitutional forced "repatriations" of 300,000 Mexican nations occurred in the 1930s, another 280,000 were forcibly removed in 1949, and during Operation Wetback in 1954, about one million Mexicans were forced out of the southwestern U.S. by land and sea (Balderrama 2008; Buff 2008: 534–535; Garcia 1980). A few decades later, detention and deportation policies were expanded, especially under DHS Secretary Michael Chertoff after the September 11 attacks. According to the federal government, there are currently about 32,000 immigrants being held in 350 local jails and private prisons that are operated as detention facilities (Bernstein 2009b; Dow 2007). Between 1995 and 2007, somewhere between 6,000 and 27,000 individuals were being held in detention centers at any given day (Dow 2007). Between 1999 and 2008 their total number reached 1.4 million as a result of increased workplace raids and reports received from landlords, hospitals, schools, and local police (Bernstein 2009b). In 2008 alone, over 370,000 individuals were detained (Bernstein 2009a).

Executive orders and laws have allowed even legal aliens to be subjected to "mandatory" or "administrative" detention and deportation, the official legal argument being that detention is a punitive measure but is not equivalent to imprisonment. Although comparatively few of the detainees are U.S. citizens, between 2004 and 2009 the ICE held between 3,500 and 10,000 detainees who had already gained U.S. citizenship, half of whom were deported back to their country of origin (Liptak and Preston 2009; Stevens 2008). The DHS sees deportations as an appropriate "orderly process" to handle illegality, although previously, through judicial review, the courts had often implemented "discretionary relief": legal options to avoid deportation, such as waivers, grace periods, military service, paying taxes, business ownership, or citizen spouses or children (Coleman 2007: 58-61; Kanstroom 2007: 226-228; Neuman 1996: 118-138). The debate over the constitutionality of current deportations is taking place as the courts' legal options such as judicial reviews have become limited.

Critics point out that detained aliens receive worse treatment for minor offenses than regular prisoners who have citizen rights. These immigrants are not terrorists, of course, but, due to their special legal status, may be considered as such. The DHS defines them as a risk to the community, so they can be detained for months, sometimes years, while their cases are indefinitely delayed (Bernstein 2009a; Buff 2008: 529-530; Coleman 2007: 60-62; Dow 2007; Puente 2007). The detention centers are located in remote and sometimes hidden areas across the country. The detainees are transferred there secretly in unmarked, windowless vans driven by armed agents who often choose not to wear uniforms, making identification impossible. Many individuals facing deportation hearings do not have a lawyer to defend them and enable them to stay in contact with their families, and they may indeed become invisible and nameless. The general public is unaware of the system and the effects of secrecy and disappearance create feelings of terror that are reminders of conditions in authoritarian regimes (Bernstein 2009b; Stevens 2009; 2010; Talavera et al. 2010).

The DHS refuses to enact legal standards for the treatment of detainees. Conditions at the detention facilities are reported to be abysmal, and neglect, abuse, and inadequate medical care are rife. Between 2003 and 2008, 30 detainees died, almost all of them Hispanic, possibly as a result of inadequate medical care (Editorial 2009b; Goldstein and Priest 2008a; 2008b; 2008c; 2008d). According to critics, control and supervision over the system are seriously lacking, because the centers are sub-contracted to private companies (Bernstein 2009a; Editorial 2009c). The American Civil Liberties Union (ACLU) sued ICE in 2007 for inappropriate conditions at the for-profit T. Don Hutto Residential Center for asylum seekers in Austin, Texas, a former medium-security state prison. The government sub-contracted it to Corrections Corporation of America, the largest private jail management company in the U.S. ACLU attacked the center's practice of separating family members, placing children behind razor wires, and denying access for families subsequent to conviction (Bernstein 2009a; Talbot 2008).

ICE keeps insisting on detaining families, but following the substantial criticism of the facilities, President Barack Obama declared in 2009 that he intended to transform the prisons into a humane, "truly civil detention system" (Bernstein 2009a). U.S. Secretary of Homeland Security Janet Napolitano announced a plan to eliminate the abuse, convert hotels and nursing homes into detention centers, centralize and digitalize the system through outsourcing, and make the facilities appropriate locations for all categories of detainees. She also mentioned taking the serious felons out of the facilities and reducing the number of the rest by possibly using electronic bracelets for released inmates as an alternative. The new ICE unit in charge is the Office of Detention Policy and Planning, which promises to insure improvements, inspection, and investigation of grievances (Bernstein 2009a; Editorial 2009c; 2009d; ICE 2009; Talbot 2008).

Most detainees are eventually deported. Deportation procedures are handled by a national center which coordinates the deportation of aliens upon their release from prison. The number of deportees per year has increased at least six-fold since the 1990s. Between 2005 and 2007, the number of deported Mexicans went up by 25%, with over 136,000 deportees in 2007 (*El Mañana* 2008). In 2008, U.S. immigration courts ordered the deportation of over 134,000 undocumented immigrants from various countries. During the next year judges heard more than 300,000 cases, and in 2010, at the time of the writing of this article, there are over 228,000 cases still pending from 2009. The immigration court system in the U.S. is severely backlogged (Bernstein 2010; Coleman 2007: 65; Jencks 2007; Kennedy 2009; Krestedemas 2008: 556; Preston 2009b, 2009d; Salinas 2007). In 2009 alone, about 95% of all detainees were deported (Bernstein 2009a).

Social and Humanitarian Effects of Adversity and Pro-Immigrant Action

The tightened control mechanisms have had serious social and humanitarian effects, disrupting the historical and traditional relations between Mexicans, Americans of Mexican origin, and immigrants living on the U.S. side of the border (Ackleson 2005: 141-142). The new policies implemented by the DHS have led to a "Berlinization", creating historically connected, but now separate cities on either side of the U.S.–Mexican border, such as the two Nogales; Tijuana and San Diego; Ciudad Juárez and El Paso; and Mexicali and Calexico. Transborder commerce, shopping, and visits without the intention of emigration to the U.S. have been impeded and the formerly linked neighborhoods are becoming increasingly disconnected from one another (Emmerich 2003: 8–11; Mendoza 2010). It is as though a "low intensity war" has occurred, a reminder of Europe's sealed menacing borders during the Cold War. The northern regions of Mexico have experienced a significant decline in tourism and serious social problems created by migrants who, upon being returned by the U.S. authorities, settle in the border towns. Employment is scarce, crime has risen, and the current brutal war between drug cartels and the government only exacerbates these problems (Hernández

2008). At home, the Mexican government is criticized for lacking security policies that would include a social development agenda and response to problems that threaten Mexico's public and national security (Barajas Escamilla 2005).

In the U.S., where more resident aliens have been rushing to naturalize in order to secure citizenship and avoid harassment, fewer people are discovered crossing the border, indicating a decline in the number of migrants who enter the country illegally.

The zero-tolerance policy at the border since the construction of the Tijuana–San Diego fence and the implementation of the security technologies has also brought about radical changes in the crossing routes of undocumented Mexicans. The new paths to Arizona now run through the Mexican state of Sonora, the Yuma desert, and Imperial County, California. Unlike in the past when Mexican emigrants knew the old routes well, immigrants coming to the U.S. today have much less experience and knowledge and are forced to choose dangerous routes which involve brutal conditions: far away from cities, very high and very low temperatures, longer distances, and a shortage of food and water (Anguiano and Trejo Peña 2007: 51-52, 56-63; Tuirán 2006b). For a few years, the probability of being captured along the new routes decreased from 33% in 1997 to 19% in 2004, the reason being that the BP did not patrol these areas (Tuirán 2006a). After some time, however, the intensified controls and more frequent patrols which were extended to the desert region began to discourage immigrants from crossing the border. The weak U.S. economy had an impact as well. In 2009, the number of border seizures had dropped by 23% from 2008, when the BP apprehended close to 724,000 individuals. Between 2007 and 2008, the number of seizures decreased by 18%. There was a total decline in the number of apprehended immigrants of 39% between 2005—the year when the number was 1.2 million—and 2008, when the number was the lowest in 34 years (Latino 4 U 2008; Wilson and Singer 2009).

Between the years 2000 and 2004, the annual average of 99 casualties from 1995 and 1997 increased to 411, which is equivalent to an increase in the death rate from 1.5 per 10,000 crossing attempts in 1999 to 3.7 in 2003, which was followed by a decrease to 2.8 in 2004 (Tuirán 2006a). The BP and Mexico's Ministry of Foreign Relations estimate that between 1993 and 2002 the total number of migrant deaths exceeded 3,000. The years 2008/2009 saw an increase in casualties by at least 7%, half of them occurring in the Tucson area (*Almargen* 2010; Meneses 2005: 113-118). At the same time, the number of immigrants rescued by the BP increased to nearly 2,500 individuals in 2000 over about 1,040 in the previous year (Meneses 2005: 119-121; Preston 2009d; Wilson and Singer 2009).

People smugglers hired by Mexican immigrants to lead them to their destinations—commonly known as "coyotes" or "polleros"—play an important role in facilitating migration along the clandestine routes. Owing to the increased border control, between 1997 and 2003 the demand for their services quadrupled (Andreas 2000: Ch. 3, 5; Andreas 2001). Reports from 2005 indicate that there are as many as 400 coyote organizations specializing in specific routes. Their job involves a complicated multi-stage process. In the first stage clients are recruited in the main emigration regions in Mexico. In the second stage, those who arrive at the collecting point are smuggled across the border. This is done by a different coyote. In the third stage, the undocumented immigrants are handed on to still others who take them to safe houses by van, where they are turned to the hands of interested employers who pay the coyote in return. The division of functions is designed to lower the coyotes' risk and increase their profits (García Vásquez et al. 2007: 104-107; Meneses 2001; Salt and Stein 1997).

While migrants who hire coyotes usually benefit from their protective service, they also face various perils. They might receive wrong instructions about weather, topography, distances, and dangerous areas. Many vulnerable migrants die of dehydration, drown or freeze to death, die from snake bites, in train and car accidents or from suffocation in the sealed vans. Others get lost or are caught by border patrol when the polleros abandon them in critical situations. More and more polleros put profit over safety and get involved in crime. Some of them rob or even kill immigrants or rape women; these smugglers are known as *asaltapollos* (assaulting polleros) (Archibold 2010a; Coronado and Orrenius 2007: 40-43, 46, 52-55; Meneses 2005: 122-123, 126). People smuggling has become a highly lucrative business. In addition to the regular charges, which may be anywhere between US$2,000 and US$6,000 per individual, depending on the risk involved, items sold to migrants, rooms rented in safe houses, and shuttle transport also yield high profits. Many youths, therefore, get involved in this cross-border business; there are indeed entire towns dedicated to it, and many families who reside on both sides of the border collaborate in the contraband operations (Andreas 2001; García Vásquez et al. 2007: 105; Meneses 2005: 126). However, the coyotes do not operate as a mafia and their description in the media as villains is mostly unjustified (Barajas Escamilla 2005: 171; Spener 2008: 130-133, 136-152).

Mexico's abusive border authorities are partially responsible for the hazardous conditions of illegal border crossing. Human rights commissions have reportedly received a host of complaints about abuse, kidnapping, and blackmailing by officers of the notorious Mexican Preventive Federal Police and the Grupo Beta (Beta Group), an INM force that was originally established to assist and save migrants. (INM 2010; Lacey 2010b; Pacheco 2005).

The Grupo Beta agents are trained in searches, first aid, rescue, human rights defense, and social assistance (INM 2010). In 2005, the Mexican Foreign Ministry published the *Guía del Migrante* (The Migrant Guide) to in-form emigrants about the perils of illegal emigration and their rights once they arrive in the U.S. The Guide was met with criticism from the U.S. for allegedly interfering with American domestic affairs (Cano and Delano 2006). In the U.S., Arizonan humanitarian organizations such as No Más Muertes (No More Deaths) and Humane Borders help save migrants by providing them with maps, water, food, and transportation, and despite the heavy criticism the Border Patrol received in the past, its Search, Trauma and Rescue team has been operating satisfactorily since 1998 (Pacheco 2005; Reyes 2010).

Communities and civil organizations in both Mexico and the U.S. have been criticizing the border policies for the last two decades and have been offering help to migrants. Pro-immigrant groups in Mexico's borderland currently run 14 homes for deportees and undocumented would-be emigrants who have been returned to the border, including women, children, and adolescents. Casa del Migrante (House of the Migrant), founded by the Catholic Church in Tijuana in 1987, over 20 years ago, reports that every year 6,000 people pass through to receive shelter, food, and medical care (La Jornada 2010; Salinas 2005; http://migrante.com.mx/Tijuana.htm). In Sonora, the state government-run Camino a Casa (The Way Home) programs maintain several shelters which tended over 36,300 children between 2004 and 2009. In 2008, Hidalgo, a state which sends many of the cross-border migrants, adopted the Camino a Casa program (see http://www.camino-a-casa.org; http://www.borderhealth.org; www.hidalguia.com.mx).

However, these activities conducted by communities and civil organizations are little more than a drop in the ocean. Arrests and deportations have instilled terror in foreign-born residents, causing more undocumented individuals to go underground and avoid driving, seeking medical care, sending their children to school, and looking for work (Buff 2008: 531-532; Traub 2009). Thousands of unauthorized immigrants have already returned to Mexico voluntarily, in some cases permanently, not only because of rising unemployment resulting from the recent economic crisis and the ban on employing immigrant workers, but also for fear of being arrested (El Mañana 2008). Some of the undocumented immigrants can no longer visit their families they left behind in Mexico, and many may have to stay in the U.S. indefinitely because the trip back has become unacceptably dangerous. In its 2008 report *Forced Apart*, Human Rights Watch documented that "families are often separated when some family members, even children, are deported while the rest of the family are allowed to stay." There have even been cases of families whose chose to return to Mexico and leave their U.S. citizen children behind. This problem may be exacerbated because the number of "mixed status families" residing in the U.S. has increased since 2009. There are 3 million families with children where at least one spouse is an illegal immigrant, and 2.3 million families with undocumented parents have at least one child who is a U.S. citizen by birth (DeParle 2009; Gonzalez 2009; Human Rights Watch 2007; Puente 2007).

The restrictive immigration policies have drawn considerable criticism and inspired controversy. The Sanctuary Movement, a campaign initiated by dozens of churches in Los Angeles in the early 1980s, was intended for Central American immigrants who were fleeing violent conflict in politically turbulent countries but could not obtain asylum in the U.S. Sanctuary's activism was based on the Judeo-Christian tradition of offering asylum in churches and synagogues as places for worship and refuge. The movement grew to become a national coalition dedicated to comprehensive immigration reform and humanitarian support for immigrants whom the movement considers to be victims of U.S. policies. Sanctuary claims to have protected tens of thousands of people since its foundation (Badillo 2006).

In 2006, Cardinal Roger Mahony of the Archdiocese of Los Angeles stated he would instruct his priests to disregard the provisions of H.R. 4437, which would have criminalized providing humanitarian aid to illegal immigrants. Following his lead and building on the achievements made since the 1980s, the current New Sanctuary Movement continues to protect families facing deportation whose cases are fraught with legal contradictions and clearly the result of grave injustice (www.newsanctuarymovement.org). Churches in several American cities have declared themselves as safe havens for immigrants and adopted ordinances of non-cooperation with federal law enforcement agencies (Coleman 2007: 65). Philadelphia went even further by deliberately facilitating the settlement of immigrants in the city. All of the organizations involved in the coalition have expressed strong criticism of the detention practices. Various groups in New York City, such as Human Rights First, Detention Watch Network, Families for Freedom, and Immigrant Defense Project provide detainees with legal aid and fight for alternatives to detention (www.detentionwatchnetwork.org).

The immigrant rights grassroots movement, which emerged in the U.S. in response to H.R. 4437 in 2006, was outraged at the proposed stricter immigration policies. The bill was condemned as being exploitative and abusive, followed by massive street protests on May Day 2006 (Pallares and Flores-González 2010). In over one hundred U.S. cities, tens of thousands of legal and illegal Mexican and Hispanic workers and students skipped school and work to participate in "A Day Without Immigrants" demonstrations. Waving American and Mexican flags, they emphasized their new transnational identity, legality, and social legitimacy in the U.S. By marching together they intended to blur the line between the concepts of legal and illegal immigrants and point out that the boundaries that separate them are illegitimate and absurd. The movement calls for amnesty, but is also intended to give visibility to undocumented immigrants and overcome the prevalent notion that they constitute a foreign and problematic sector in society (Costanza-Chock 2008; Hamilton 2006; Skerry and Fernandes 2006).

The clash between pro-civil rights critics and local anti-illegal immigration supporters came to a head very recently. In April 2010, Arizona SB 1070 was passed. Governor Janet Napolitano, who was in office from 2003 to 2009, had authorized state officers to act as ICE officers and increased the size of the Border Patrol. The new law goes even further, accommodating strong anti-immigrant sentiments and preference for local policies displayed in the state (Archibold and Steinhauer 2010; Weisberg 2009). In part the sentiments resulted from the fact that the Mexican population of Arizona had ballooned from 19% in 1990 to 25% in 2000. At present, 2 million Hispanic U.S. citizens live in the state. The illegal population grew by 52% between 2000 and 2006 and is now estimated to be at 430,000 to 460,000. Concentrated along the crossing strip, illegal immigrants represent about 30% of the state's population. In Phoenix, the largest city of Arizona and once dominated by Anglo-Americans, the immigrant population has increased from 20% to about 34% (Archibold 2010b; 2010e; Pew 2009).

This increase is explained by the fact that Arizona has become the principal gateway to the U.S. and a major destination for undocumented immigrants from Mexico and Central America. Many white Arizonans—and not just the Minuteman movement—who still defend a Western frontier tradition of gun possession and vigilantism, have become worried about the changes which they perceive as the "Mexicanization" of the state and the rapid transformation of Arizona into some kind of "Mexifornia." Residents have expressed concern about Mexicans not speaking English, putting up Mexican flags, competing for businesses and jobs, and committing vandalism, crime, and smuggling (Archibold 2010b; 2010e; Archibold and Steinhauer 2010; Coronado and Orrenius 2007: 40–42; Judis 2006; Preston 2010a; Velázquez García 2008).

SB 1070 authorizes state authorities to demand proof of legal entry and stay in the U.S. "when practicable" and on a basis of "reasonable suspicion." Illegal presence in Arizona is a state crime, in addition to being a violation of federal immigration laws, and is therefore a cause for arrest. The principal innovations of the law in comparison to more than 220 laws and ordinances enacted in Arizona and 48 other states are that it gives broader authority to arrest suspects and allows citizens to sue the state if the law is not enforced (Archibold 2010b; Preston 2008). For the 70% of Arizonans who support the law, the main argument is that it is necessary because the federal government has not acted adequately to resolve a problem that Arizonans did not create (Archibold 2010b; 2010c; 2010d), also claiming that in 2009 alone immigration control cost the state US$2.7 billion (Fox and Friends, 2010).

The Prevailing Public Opinion and Concluding Remarks

Arizona SB 1070 brought the controversy over immigration to a head, demonstrating the divisions over the issue. Nationally, views on immigration and the new law are mixed: 51% of Americans think it was a good decision to pass the bill because Washington had failed to act on the issue; 9% even feel it does not go far enough; 78% think that more should be done along the border; and 45% support fundamental changes in the immigration system. On the critical side, 36% stated that the law goes too far; 50% think that it encourages ethnic profiling; 57% believe that immigration law should be federal law; 29% think that the law may reduce illegal immigration into Arizona; 29% believe that it might serve as a deterrent; and 19% think that the law would help reduce crime (Archibold and Thee-Brenan 2010; Rich 2010). Some observers believe that since the law provides that the state can be sued if it fails to arrest undocumented migrants, the intention of its adherents is to press Congress to introduce tougher federal reform. Thus far, however, President Obama has sent 1,200 National Guard troops to the border and promised US$500,000 in funds to cover the costs of additional border control (Archibold 2010e; Jacoby 2010).

The critics of SB 1070 condemn it as discriminatory and harmful to the civil rights of immigrants and citizens alike, who may be harassed and subjected to ethnic profiling (Cathcart 2010; Preston 2010b). Several days after Governor Jan Brewer signed the bill, she made changes to the law, explicitly prohibiting the practice of racial profiling, although the effectiveness of this provision is doubtful (Archibold and Thee-Brenan 2010). Another argument brought forward against the new Arizona law is that immigration should be exclusively a federal matter. Only federal agents are authorized to decide who can be a citizen or alien, and yet Arizona enforces its own statutes (Motomura 2010). Massive protests started as soon as the law was passed. Latino associations, labor unions, civil rights groups, and African American and Jewish organizations took to the streets on May Day 2010 (Preston 2010b). President Obama, Secretary of Homeland Security Napolitano, and the Mexican President Felipe Calderón expressed concern about the law. Commercial, academic, and tourist boycotts of Arizona have been announced both in Mexico and the U.S. The federal government sued Arizona over the new immigration law and the state's appeal in response is still pending (Archibold 2010g; 2010h; Inside Higher Ed 2010; Lacey 2010a; Preston 2010c). For now, the quarrel between critics and supporters is continuing. The future of immigration control and legislation remains uncertain and is indeed unknown at this point.

As this article has shown, the issues related to undocumented immigration from Mexico to the U.S. in the last two decades have become increasingly complex. In comparison to previous periods when crossing the border was relatively easy, in recent years border control has been reinforced through advanced technologies, patrol mechanisms, and physical barriers. Anti-immigration policies also include devices, methods, and laws enforced in areas away from the actual border itself, such as workplace raids, arrests, and deportation. The strict legislation was enacted in response to the negative attitudes toward illegal immigration, especially in the Southwest and since the September 11 attacks, and to the intense anxiety about security that undocumented entries have caused in the past. The zero-tolerance policy has forced migrants to take dangerous routes, shaken the stability of legal and illegal aliens of Mexican origin, and disturbed the traditional relationship between the communities on both sides of the border.

References

Ackleson, J. (2005): Border Security Technologies: Local and Regional Implications. In: Review of Policy Research 22, pp. 137–155.

Almargen (2010): Cruzan menos indocumentados a EU, pero mueren más en el intento, 26 January. [online] Available at: http://almargen.com.mx/notas.php? IDNOTA=925&IDSECCION=Diario&IDREPORTERO=La%20Redacci%F3n. Last visited 2 Febraury 2010 [Accessed February 14, 2011].

Andreas, P. (2000): Border Games: Policing the U.S.-Mexico Divide. Ithaca, N.Y.: Cornell University Press.

Andreas, P. (2001): The Transformation of Migrant Smuggling Across the U.S.-Mexican Border. In: Global Human Smuggling: Comparative Perspectives, edited by David Kyle and Rey Koslowski. Baltimore, Md.: Johns Hopkins University Press, pp. 107-125.

Anguiano, M. E./Trejo Peña, A. (2007): Políticas de seguridad fronteriza y nuevas rutas de movilidad de migrantes mexicanos y guatemaltecos. Liminar: Estudios Sociales y Humanísticos 5, 2, pp. 47-65.

Anti-Defamation League (2010): The Minutemen. [online] Available at: http://www.adl.org/Extremism/minutemen.asp [Accessed 3 November 2010].

Archibold, R. C. (2010a): Immigration aids Focus on Shuttle Vans. In: New York Times, April 15.

Archibold, R. C. (2010b): Immigration Bill Reflects a Firebrand Impact. In: New York Times, 19 April.

Archibold, R. C. (2010c): Arizona's Effort to Bolster Local Immigration Authority Divides Law Enforcement. In: New York Times, April 21.

Archibold, R. C. (2010d): U.S.'s Toughest Immigration Law is Singed in Arizona. In: New York Times, April 23.

Archibold, R. C. (2010e): Growing Split in Arizona Over Immigration. In: New York Times, April 25.

Archibold, R. C. (2010f): Obama to Send 1,200 Guard Troops to Mexico Border. In: New York Times, May 25.

Archibold, R. C. (2010g): Foes and Supporters of New Immigration Law Gather in Arizona. In: New York Times, May 29.
Archibold, R. C. (2010h): Judge Blocks Key Parts of Immigration Law in Arizona. In: New York Times, July 28.
Archibold, R. C./Steinhauer, J. (2010): Welcome to Arizona, Outpost of Contradictions. In: New York Times, April 28.
Archibold R. C./Thee-Brenan, M. (2010): Poll Shows Most in U.S. Want Overhaul of Immigration Laws. In: New York Times, May 3.
Associated Press (2010a): DHA: the Number of Illegal Immigrants in U.S. Fell. In: New York Times, February 9.
Associated Press (2010b): Report: E-Verify Misses Half of Illegal Workers. In: New York Times, February 25.
Associated Press (2010b): Hiring Illegal Immigrants May Lead to Jail in Utah. In: New York Times, February 26.
Ayres, Ch. (2006): Tombsone Vigilantes Ride Shotgun to Keep the Strangers Out. In: The Times, April 1.
Bacon, D./Ong Hing, B. (2009): Rights, Not Raids. In: Nation, 18 May.
Badillo, D. (2006): Latinos and the New Immigrant Church. Baltimore, Md.: Johns Hopkins University Press.
Balderrama, F. E. (2005): The Emergence of Unconstitutional Deportation and Repatriation of Mexicans and Mexican Americans as a Public Issue. In: Radical History Review 93, pp. 107-110.
Barajas Escamilla, M. de Rosario (2005): Review of Seguridad nacional y fronteriza. In: Ramos, José Ma./Woo, Ofelia: Frontera Norte 17 (July–December), pp. 167-172.
Barrapunto (2006): [online] Available at: http://ciberderechos.barrapunto.com/ar ticle.pl?sid=06/06/02/2046232 [Accessed 5 June 2010].
Bauböck, R. (2003): Towards a Political Theory of Migrant Transnationalism. In: International Migration Review 37, pp. 700–723.
Benítez, R./Rodríguez, C. (2006): Seguridad y Fronteras en Norteamérica. Del TLCAN a la ASPAN. In: Frontera Norte 18, pp. 7-28.
Benton-Cohen, K. (2009): Borderline Americans: Racial Division and Labor War in the Arizona Borderlands. Cambridge, Mass.: Harvard University Press.
Bernstein, N. (2009a): U.S. to Reform Policy on Detention for Immigrants. In: New York Times, August 6.
Bernstein, N. (2009b): Reports Find Lapses in Immigration Detention System. In: New York Times, December 3.
Bernstein, N. (2010): Database Tracks Immigration Court Crush. In: New York Times, March 12.
Billeaud, J. (2010): El muro virtual se tambalea. In: El Universal, February 4.
Bloch, Avital/Ortol, Servando (2010): The Anti-Chinese and Anti-Japanese Movements in Cananea, Sonora, and Salt Lake River, Arizona, During the 1920 and 1930s. In: Americana: E-Journal of American Studies in Hungary 1 (spring). [online] Available at: http://americanaejournal.hu/vol6no1/bloch-ortoll [Accessed 29 October 2010].
Bosquez, V. (2010): Q & A: Interview with David Spener. mySA, 14 February. [online] Available at: http://www.mysanantonio.com/entertainment/books/Review_Clandestine_Crossings.html [Accessed 4 May 2010].

Brinkley, A. (2010): The Party of Me. In: New York Times, April 15.
Buff, R. (2008): The Deportation Terror. In: American Quarterly 60, pp. 523-551.
Bustamante, J. A (2000): Migración irregular de México a Estados Unidos: 10 años de investigación del proyecto Cañón Zapata. In: Frontera Norte 12, pp. 7-50.
Bustamante, J. A. (2001): Proposition 187 and Operation Gatekeeper: Cases for Sociology of International Migrations and Human Rights. In: Migraciones Internacionales 1, pp. 7-34.
Calavita, K. (1999): Inside the State: The Bracero Program, Immigration, and the INS. New York: Routledge.
Calderón, Leticia, ed. (2004): Votar en la distancia. La extensión de los derechos políticos a migrantes: experiencias comparadas. Mexico City: Instituto Mora.
Camarota, S. A. (2007): Immigrants in the United States, 2007: A Profile of America's Foreign-Born Population. Center for Immigration Studies, November. [online] Available at: http://www.cis.org/articles/2007/back1007.html [Accessed 6 August 2010].
Camarota, S. A. (2009): Wages Will Go Even Lower. In: New York Times, March 18.
Cano, G./Delano, A. (2006): The Mexican Government and Organized Mexican Immigrants in the United States: A Historical Analysis of Political Transnationalism (1848-2005). In: Journal of Ethnic and Migration Studies 3, 5, pp. 695-725.
Carbado, D. W. (2005): Racial Naturalization. American Quarterly 57, pp. 633-658.
Cathcart, R. (2010): Los Angeles Archbishop Speaks Out Against Immigration Law. In: New York Times, 1 May.
Cave, D. (2010): A Generation Gap Over Immigration. In: New York Times, May 17.
Cole, D. (2003): Driving While Immigrant. In: Nation, May 22.
Coleman, M. (2007): Immigration Geopolitics Beyond Mexico–US Border. Antipode 39, pp. 54-76.
Coronado, R./Orrenius, P. M. (2007): Crime on the U.S.-Mexico Border: The Effect of Undocumented Immigration and Border Enforcement. In: Migraciones Internacionales 4, pp. 39–64.
Cortina, Jerónimo (2007): La unitalla no les queda a todos: la opinión pública con respeto a la inmigración. In: Istor: Revista de Historia Internacional 7, pp. 9-21.
Costanza-Chock, S. (2008): The Immigrant Rights Movement on the Net: Between 'Web 2.0' and Comunicación Popular. In: American Quarterly 60, pp. 851-864.
Delacroix, J./Nikiforov, S. (2009): If Mexicans and Americans Could Cross the Border Freely. In: Independent Review 14, pp. 101-133.
DeParle, J. (2009): Struggling in Suburbs Where Failing Means Fitting In: New York Times, April 19.
Dow, M. (2007): Designed to Punish: Immigrant Detention and Deportation. In: Social Research 74, pp. 533-544.
Editorial (2009a): Hope and Worry on Immigration. In: New York Times, June 5.
Editorial (2009b): Detained and Abused. In: New York Times, August 1.
Editorial (2009c): Salvaging Immigration Detention. In: New York Times, October 6.
Editorial (2009d): Wrongs Paths to Immigration Reform. In: New York Times, October 12.
El Mañana (2008): Era sólo un sueño; regresan a México, July 7.
Emmerich, G. E. (2003): México-Estados Unidos: Frontera eficiente, pero no abierta. In: Frontera Norte 15: 7-33.

Eviatar, D. (2006): Nightly Nativism. In: Nation, August 28.
Félix, A. (2008): New Americans or Diasporic Nationalists? Mexican Migrant Reponses to Naturalization and Implications for Political Participation. In: American Quarterly 60, pp. 601-624.
Fitzgerald, D. (2000): Negotiating Extra-Territorial Citizenship: Mexican Migration and the Transnational Politics of Community. La Jolla: Center for Comparative Immigration Studies Monographs, University of California, San Diego.
Fox and Friends (2010): Fox Television, May 18.
Garcia, J. R. (1980): Operation Wetback: The Mass Deportation of Mexican Undocumented Workers in 1954. Westport, C.T.: Greenwood Publishing Group.
García-Acevedo, M. R. (2003): Politics Across Borders: Mexico's Policies Toward Mexicans in the United States. In: Journal of the Southwest 45, pp. 533-555.
García Vásquez, N. J./Guadalupe Gaxiola, E./Guajardo, A. (2007): Movimientos transfronterizos México-Estados Unidos: los polleros como agentes de movilidad. In: CONfines 3, pp. 101-113.
Gelatt, J. and D. Meyers (2006): Legal Immigration to United States Increased Substantially in FY 2005. Fact Sheet #13, Migration Policy Institute, October.
Gilchrist, J./Corsi, J. R. (2006): Minutemen: The Battle to Secure America's Borders. Los Angeles: World Ahead Publishing.
Goldstein, A./Priest, D. (2008): System of Neglect: As Tighter Immigration Policies Strain Federal Agencies. The Detainees in Their Care Often Pay a Heavy Cost. In: Washington Post, May 11.
Goldstein, A./Priest, D. (2008): In Custody, in Pain: Her Health Problems Worsening as She Fights Deportation. A U.S. Resident Struggles to Get the Medical Care She Needs. In: Washington Post, May 12.
Goldstein, A./Priest, D. (2008): Suicides Point to Gaps in Treatment: Errors in Psychiatric Diagnoses and Drugs Plague Strained Immigration System. In: Washington Post, May 13.
Goldstein, A./Priest, D. (2008): Some Detainees Are Drugged For Deportation: Immigrants Sedated Without Medical Reason. In: Washington Post, May 14.
Gonzalez, D. (2009): A Family Divided by 2 Worlds, Legal and Illegal. In: New York Times, April 26.
Hamilton, A. (2006): A Day Without Immigrants. In: Time, May 1.
Hanson, G. (2009): Two Very Different Groups Seeking Work. In: New York Times, March 18.
Hernández, G. (2008): Zona fronteriza reciente deportación de migrantes. In: Proceso, October 2.
Hernández, K. L. (2010): Migra! A History of the U.S. Border Patrol. Berkeley: University of California Press.
Hill, S. (2003): Metaphoric Enrichment and Material Poverty. In: Vila, P. (ed.): Ethnography of the Border. Minneapolis: University of Minnesota Press, pp. 141-165.
Horowitz, C. F. (2001): An Examination of U.S. Immigration Policy and Serious Crime. Center for Immigration Studies, April. [online] Available at: http://www.cis.org/articles/2001/crime/toc.html [Accessed 30 November 2009].
Human Rights Watch (2007): Forced Apart: Families Separated an Immigration Harmed by United States Deportation Policy 19, 3(G). [online] Available at:

http://www.unhcr.org/refworld/docid/46a764862.html [Accessed 1 December 2009].
Instituto Nacional de Migración (INM) (2010): Grupo Beta de protección a migrantes. [online] Available at: http://www.inm.gob.mx/index.php/page/Grupo_Beta [Accessed September 1, 2010].
Imaz, C. (2007): Percepciones de la migración en México y Estados Unidos. Metapolítica 51, pp. 62–67.
Immigration and Customs Enforcement (ICE) (n.d.): Secure Communities. [online] Available at: www.ice.gov/secure_communities [Accessed 16 April 2010].
Immigration and Customs Enforcement (ICE) (2009): Fact Sheet: 2009 Immigration Detention Reforms. [online] Available at: http://www.ice.gov/news/library/fact sheets/reform-2009reform.htm [Accessed 2 Febraury 2010].
Inside Higher Ed. (2010): 2 Mexican Universities End Exchanges With Arizona, 10 May. [online] Available at: http://www.insidehighered.com/news/2010/05/10/qt [Accessed 10 May 2010].
Jacoby, T. (2010): Immigration's Birmingham. In: New York Times, April 15.
Jencks, Ch. (2007): The Immigration Charade. In: New York Review of Books 54, September 27.
Judis, J. B. (2006): The Fight over Immigration is a Fight over Identity: Border War. New Republic, January 16.
Kanstroom, D. (2007): Deportation Nation: Outsiders in American History. Cambridge, Mass.: Harvard University Press.
Kearney, M. (1999): Fronteras fragmentadas, fronteras reforzadas. In: Mummert, Gail (ed.): Fronteras fragmentadas: género, familia e identidades en la migración al norte. Zamora: El Colegio de Michoacán, pp. 559-571.
Kennedy, R. (2009): Texas Mayor Caught in Deportation Furor. In: New York Times, April 5.
Koulish, R. (2009): Immigration and American Democracy: Subverting the Rule of Law. New York: Routledge.
Kretsedemas, Ph. (2008): Immigration Enforcement and the Complication of National Sovereignty: Understanding Local Enforcement as an Exercise in Neoliberal Governance. In: American Quarterly 60, pp. 553-573.
Krieger, Z. (2008): The Minutemen Turn on Each Other. In: New Republic, November 19.
Kroft, S. (2010): Watching the Border. 60 Minutes, CBS Television, January 8.
La Jornada (2010): Migración: Directorio del migrante en México. [online] Available at: http://www.jornada.unam.mx/migracion/?seccion=directorio-mexico [Accessed July 22, 2010].
Latino 4 U (2008): Inmigrantes regresan a casa. La crisis merma el empleo y los ingresos, October 31.
Lacey, M. (2010a): The Mexican Border's Lost World. In: New York Times, August 1.
Lacey, M. (2010b): Migrants Going North Now Risk Kidnapping. In: New York Times, October 18.
Lewis, N. A. (2009): Immigration Officials to Audit 1,000 More Companies. In: New York Times, November 20.
Liptak, A./Preston, J. (2009): Justices Limit Use of Identity Theft Law in Immigration Cases. In: New York Times, May 5.

Luscombe, R. (2009): Patrol Watches Texas-Mexico Border: From Pub in Australia. In: The Guardian, March 23.
Ngai, M. (2005): Impossible Subjects: Illegal Aliens and the Making of Modern America. Princeton, N.J.: Princeton University Press.
McKinley, J. C. (2009): Debate Intensifies Over Deportations. In: New York Times, July 26.
Mendoza, A. (2010): Habrá mayor vigilancia en la costa fronteriza. In: Diario San Diego, February 4.
Meneses, G. A. (2001): Migra, coyotes, paisanos y muertitos: sobre la analiticidad y el sentido de ciertos factores de la migración clandestina en la frontera norte. In: El Bordo 7, pp. 27-41.
Meneses, G. A. (2005):. Violencias asociadas al cruce indocumentado de la Frontera México—Estados Unidos. In: Nueva Antropología 65, pp. 113-129.
Moser, B. (2010): Who Is 'We the People'? In: New York Times, April 15.
Motomura, H. (2009): A History of Legal Flexibility. In: New York Times, April 22.
Motomura, H. (2010): Impulsive Extremism. In: New York Times, April 15.
Neuman, G. L. (1996): Strangers to the Constitution: Immigrants, Borders, and Fundamental Law. Princeton, N.J.: Princeton University Press.
Nevins, J. (2002): Operation Gatekeeper: The Rise of the "Illegal Aliens" and the Making of the U.S.-Mexico Boundary. New York: Routledge.
Notimex (2004): Se estrella avión espía en frontera con México, March 25.
Notimex (2009): Ofrecen tecnología a indocumentados para cruzar frontera sin riesgos, November 22.
Ong, A. (2006): Neoliberalism as Exceptions: Mutations in Citizenship and Sovereignty. Durham, N.C.: Duke University Press.
Opción (2010): Fuerza aérea de EU vigilará la frontera, 10 November. [online] Available at: http://www.revistaopcion.com/web/tag/dea/ [Accessed 10 November 2010].
Orozco, G./González, E./Díaz de Cossío, R. (2003): Las organizaciones mexicano-americanas, hispanas y mexicanas en Estados Unidos. Mexico City: Instituto Nacional de Migración/Centro de Estudios Migratorios/Fundación Solidaridad Mexicano-Americana.
Pacheco, A. L. (2005): Cruzar la frontera norte, riesgo mortal. CIMAC Noticias, 20 September. [online] Available at: http://www.cimacnoticias.com/noticias/05sep/05092001.html [Accessed 20 January 2010].
Pallares, A./Flores-González, N., eds. (2010): ¡Marcha! Latino Chicago and the Immigrant Rights Movement. Urbana: University of Illinois Press.
Paspalanova, M. (2008): Undocumented vs. Illegal Migrant: Towards Terminological Coherence. In: Migraciones Internacionales 4, pp. 79-90.
Pew Hispanic Center (2009): Hispanics of Mexican Origin in the United States, 2007. Fact Sheet, September 16, pp. 1-4.
Preston, J. (2008): Employers Fight Tough Measures on Immigration. In: New York Times, July 6.
Preston, J. (2009a): A Slippery Place in the U.S. Work Force. In: New York Times, March 22.
Preston, J. (2009b): Firm Stance on Illegal Immigrants Remains Policy. In: New York Times, August 4.

Preston, J. (2009c): Immigration Crackdown with Firings, Not Raids. In: New York Times, September 30.
Preston, J. (2009d): Detentions at Border Are Down. In: New York Times, November 26.
Preston, J. (2010a): Work Force by Highly Skilled Immigrants. In: New York Times, 15 April.
Preston, J. (2010b): Latino Groups Urge Boycott of Arizona Over New Law. In: New York Times, 6 May.
Preston, J. (2010c): Federal Government Sues Over Arizona Immigrant Law. In: New York Times, 6 July.
Preston, J. (2010d): Lawyers Back Creating New Immigration Courts. In: New York Times, 9 February.
Puente, L. (2007): HRW: Deportaciones sumarias en EU, de migrantes con documentos. In: Proceso, 27 July.
Ramos García, J. M. (2002): Seguridad pública fronteriza: Gestión, contexto y redefinición de políticas. In: Frontera Norte 14, pp. 47-81.
Reyes, A. (2010): Desierto de Arizona: El cementerio de los inmigrantes. Suite101.Net, 3 February. [online] Available at: http://desiertos.suite101.net/article.cfm/desierto-de-arizona [Accessed 20 September 2010].
Rich, F. (2010): If Only Arizona Were the Real Problem. In: New York Times, May 2.
Roberts, S. (2009): Projections Put Whites in Minority in U.S. by 2050. In: New York Times, December 18.
Rosenblum, M. R. (2003): The Political Determinants of Migration Control: A Quantitative Analysis. In: Migraciones Internacionales 2, pp. 161-169
Sadowski-Smith, C. (2008): Unskilled Labor Migration and the Illegality Spiral: Chinese, European, and Mexican Indocumentados in the United States, 1882-2007. In: American Quarterly 60, pp. 779-804.
Saler, M. (2010): The Golden State? Commentators Continue to See California as a Beacon, for Better or Worse, of the Future, Even as It Remains Stubbornly Sui Generis. In: Times Literary Supplement, January 29.
Salinas, J. A. (2005): Cambia EU política de deportaciones. In: Proceso, 1 July.
Salt, J./Stein, J. (1997): Migration as a Business: The case of Trafficking. In: International Migration 35, pp. 467-494.
Schrag, P. (2008): Divided States. In: Nation, January 7.
Schrag, P. (2010): Not Fit for Our Society: Immigration and Nativism in America. Berkeley: University of California Press.
Secretaría de Relaciones Exteriores (2000): Programa para las Comunidades Mexicanas en el Exterior (PCME) 1990–2000. Mexico City: SRE. [online] Available at: http://www.paisano.gob.mx [Accessed September 11, 2010].
Sherman, K. B./Rivers, B. P. (2003): UAVs for Border Patrol? In: Journal of Electronic Defense 26, pp. 20.
Skerry, P./Fernandes, D. (2006): Fixing the Immigration Debate. In: New Republic, May 8.
Spener, D. (2001): Review of Crossing Borders, Reinforcing Borders: Social Categories, Metaphors, and Narrative Identities on the U.S.-Mexico Frontier, by Pablo Vila. In: American Journal of Sociology 106 (January), pp. 1191-1192.

Spener, D. (2008): El apartheid global, el coyote y el discurso de la migración clandestina: distinciones entre violencia personal, estructural y cultural. In: Migración y desarrollo 10, pp. 127-156.
Stevens, J. (2008): Thin ICE. In: Nation, June 23.
Stevens, J. (2009): Secret Courts Exploit Immigrant. In: Nation, June 16.
Stevens, J. (2010): America's Secret ICE Castles. In: Nation, January 4.
Talavera, V./Nuñez, Guillermina G./Heyman, J. (2010): Deportation in the U.S.-Mexico Borderlands: Anticipation, Experience, and Memory. In: de Genova, Nicholas/Peutz, Nathalie (eds.): The Deportation Regime: Sovereignty, Space, and the Freedom of Movement. Durham, N.C.: Duke University Press.
Talbot, M. (2008): The Lost Children: What do Tougher Detention Policies Mean for Illegal Families? In: New Yorker, March 3.
Traub, A. (2009): Getting Tough on Exploitation. In: Nation, November 17.
Trujeque, J. A. (2007): Minutemen Project: segregación y activismo antimigratorio. In: Andamios: Revista de Investigación Social 3, pp. 137-172.
Tuirán, R. (2006a): México y el debate migratorio en Estados Unidos. In: Foreign Affairs Latinoamérica 6, pp. 10-22.
Tuirán, R. (2006b): La reforma migratoria pendiente. In: Migraciones Internacionales 3, 4, pp. 161-174.
U.S. Census Bureau (2000): Census 2000. Summary File 3. [online] Available at: www.census.gov/prod/cen2000/doc/sf3.pdf [Accessed 13 March 2010].
U.S. Census Bureau (2005): Facts for Features. 8 September. [online] Available at: http://www.census.gov/newsroom/releases/archives/facts_for_features_special_editions/cb05-ff14-3.html [Accessed March 26, 2010].
U.S.-Mexico Border Fence/Great Wall of Mexico Secure Fence (2010): [online] Available at: http://www.globalsecurity.org/security/systems/mexico-wall.htm [Accessed October 3, 2010].
Velázquez García, M. A. (2008): La construcción de la imagen de México en Estados Unidos desde una perspectiva de riesgo. In: Frontera Norte 20, 39, pp. 37-67.
Vila, P. (2000): Crossing Borders, Reinforcing Borders: Social Categories, Metaphors, and Narrative Identities on the U.S.-Mexico Frontier. Austin: University of Texas Press.
Vila, P. (2005): Border Identifications: Narratives of Religion, Gender, and Class on the U.S.-Mexico Border. Austin: University of Texas Press.
Weber, D. J. (1986): Turner, the Boltonians, and the Borderlands. In: American Historical Review 1, 91, pp. 66-81.
Weisberg, J. (2009): Program Under Fire. In: Nation, October 14.
Wilson, J./Singer, A. (2009): How the Recession's Affecting Immigration. In: New Republic, November 18.
Winston, A. (2006): Ground Zero for Immigration. In: Nation, August 18.

Evaluating Recent U.S. Immigration Control Policy: What Mexican Migrants Can Tell Us

Wayne A. Cornelius[1]

Introduction

In recent years the United States has plunged into its fourth major debate on immigration policy since the early 1980s. The debate that went on from 1980 to 1986 gave us the Immigration Reform and Control Act of 1986, which legalized 2.7 million undocumented migrants who were already in the country but failed to provide a legal entry option for most of the future migrants, nor did it provide an effective mechanism to keep undocumented migrants out of the workplace. In the 1990s, another immigration policy debate brought about the Illegal Immigration Reform and Immigrant Responsibility Act of 1996 which, among other things, sought to discourage immigration by limiting access to basic human services even for legally admitted immigrants, while almost eliminating judicial discretion and legal due process in the deportation of unauthorized immigrants. Fierce battles were joined over immigration policy in 2006, 2007, and 2010, but in all cases legislative action was blocked by hostile coalitions dominated by Republican members of Congress.

The opponents of legalizing undocumented immigrants, expanding opportunities for legal temporary and permanent immigration, and other liberalizing measures have shown little interest in evidence-based policymaking, preferring to invest ever more resources in border and interior enforcement efforts with little or no regard for the efficacy of such investments. There is much to be learned, however, from the ways in which the current U.S. immigration control strategy has affected (or failed to affect) the behavior of Mexican migrants, who constitute by far the largest component of unauthorized immigration to the United States. This chapter summarizes what we know about the actual experience and perceptions of Mexican migrants to the United States, through extensive field research in migrants' communities of origin and destination. It also identifies the consequences that continued investment in a failed immigration control strategy is likely to have.

The field research reported in this chapter was conducted between 2005 and 2010 in three high-emigration communities in rural Mexico (in the states

1 An earlier version of this paper was presented as the Fourth Annual Pastora San Juan Cafferty Lecture at the School of Social Service Administration, The University of Chicago, October 1, 2009.

of Jalisco, Oaxaca, and Yucatán) and in the U.S. cities to which they are linked through migration. The Mexican research sites were purposively selected to maximize variation on three dimensions: the length of the community's history of migration to the United States; the level of social and economic development and/or poverty; and the ethnic composition (mestizo vs. indigenous). The U.S. research sites were determined by the principal destinations of migrants leaving the Mexican research sites: Los Angeles, California; Orange County, California; San Diego, California; the San Francisco Bay area; and Oklahoma City. Each year between 2005 and 2010, binational field research teams were assembled and trained by the Center for Comparative Immigration Studies at the University of California, San Diego and its partner institutions in Mexico. A total of 4,884 Mexicans were interviewed for this project, on both sides of the border, using standardized questionnaires. In addition, more than 1,500 hours of qualitative life-history interviews were conducted. Migrants with considerable U.S. experience were interviewed, as well as those with no such experience but who were potential first-time migrants.

The research delved deeply into the motivations, perceptions, migration strategies, and actual experiences of Mexican migrants, both in crossing the border and in living and working in the United States. The resulting data paint a sobering picture of what has been accomplished during the post-1993 period of heightened immigration control efforts: a period in which the United States "got serious" about border enforcement for the first time and stepped up immigration enforcement in the interior of the country—in workplaces, neighborhoods, and public spaces of all kinds (Cornelius/Lewis 2007; Cornelius et al. 2007; Cornelius et al. 2009a; Cornelius et al. 2009b; Fitzgerald et al. 2010)[2].

Fortifying the Border with Mexico: The Main U.S. Strategy of Immigration Control

Since President Clinton started the ongoing border enforcement build-up in 1993, in an effort to insulate himself from charges of "softness" on illegal immigration and enhance his chances for reelection in 1996, the United States has sharply increased its spending on this approach to immigration control (Dunn 2009)[3]. Budgets for both border and interior enforcement have

2 The survey and ethnographic data gathered by the Mexican Migration Field Research and Training Program (MMFRP).

3 The early (1993–1998) phase of this border enforcement build-up, in which "concentrated border enforcement operations" were launched in and around major U.S. border cities, is well documented in Dunn 2009.

grown rapidly, especially in the period since 2003 (see Figure 2). The Border Patrol has more than quintupled in size, to approximately 20,000 agents, and the overall budget for policing the southwestern border has increased by the same proportion. The U.S. Congress routinely appropriates more money for border enforcement than the executive branch requests.

The latest enhancement of the fortified U.S. border with Mexico is the Secure Border Initiative, otherwise known as the "virtual fence." An electronic barrier utilizing high-tech surveillance and communications towers built initially along two stretches of the Arizona border, this project was supposed to cover all but about 200 miles of the southwest border by 2014, at a projected cost of US$6.7 billion (not including maintenance costs), but it has essentially been abandoned by the Barack Obama administration because of design flaws and performance failures.

Figure 1: U.S. government spending on border enforcement and interior enforcement, Fiscal Years 2003–2010 (in billion US$)

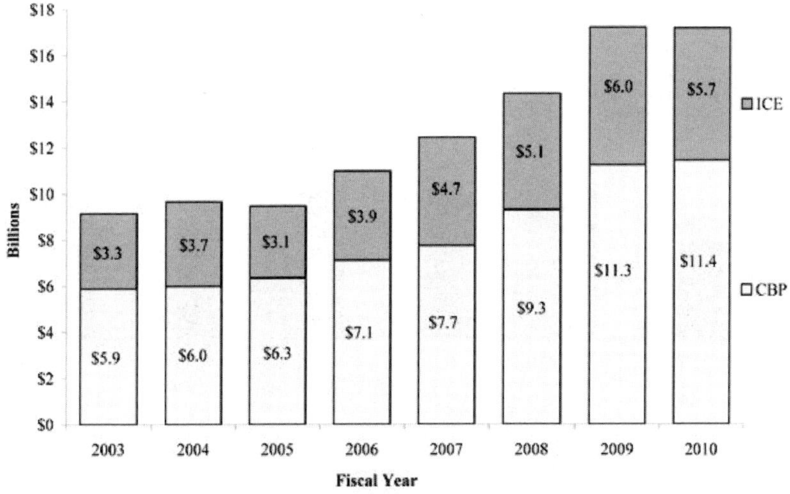

Source: U.S. Department of Homeland Security, Budget-in-Brief for Fiscal Years 2005–2011. [ICE: U.S. Immigration and Customs Enforcement; CBP: U.S. Customs and Border Protection]

The U.S. government contends that investments in border enforcement since 1993 are finally paying off: Apprehensions made by the Border Patrol have dropped sharply since 2007, to levels not seen since the early 1990s. But is this the correct metric of success? Apprehension statistics only tell us about migrants who get caught. Our field interviews show that fewer than half were caught, even once, during their most recent trip to the border. Moreover, apprehension statistics say nothing about migrants who are caught on the first try but keep trying until they succeed. Our field interviews reveal that nearly all migrants who are caught on the first try eventually make it into the United States, usually on the second or third try, without returning to their place of origin In most of the years covered by our field research, the eventual success rate was 97–100 percent (see Figure 3). The record of the last 16 years clearly shows that determined economic migrants cannot be stopped by putting more obstacles in their path: They will detour around them, climb over them, tunnel under them, and cut through them.

Figure 2: Apprehension rates and eventual success rates among unauthorized Mexican migrants to the United States

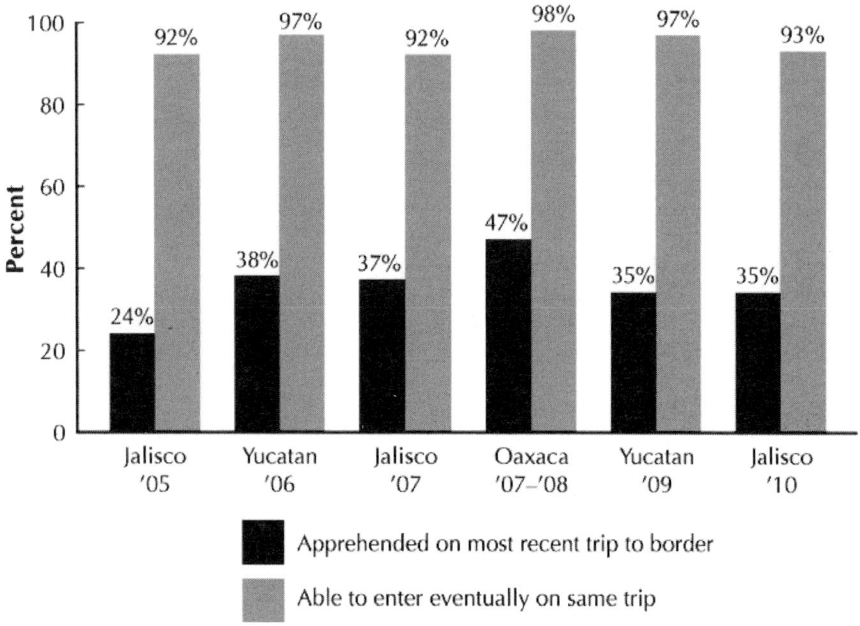

Source: Mexican Migration Field Research Program, Center for Comparative Immigration Studies, University of California-San Diego, annual surveys in Mexican migrant-sending and U.S. receiving communities, 2005–2010.

Stronger border enforcement has greatly increased the demand for the services of professional people smugglers. Nine out of ten undocumented migrants we interviewed in 2009 had hired a people smuggler, or coyote, to assist them in their most recent border crossing. Coyote fees have more than tripled during the period of tighter border enforcement, from a median fee of $861 before 2001 to $3,000 in 2010.[4] In fact, border enforcement discourages migration mainly by making it costlier to hire a people smuggler. Some would-be migrants cannot afford them—usually people who do not have relatives in the U.S. who are already well-established enough to lend them the money. And once they get to the U.S., undocumented migrants now need to work nearly 400 hours to earn enough money to pay off their coyote-related debt.

But it is the combination of higher coyote costs and the lack of jobs in a contracting U.S. economy that has reduced illegal migration in recent years. Far fewer new U.S.-bound migrants have left Mexico since 2007, but that is primarily because jobs were not waiting for them in the United States (see Figure 3). Our interviews with migrants from Yucatán and Jalisco in 2009 and 2010 showed that even "green card" holders who are legally entitled to enter the United States were less likely to be planning migration than in previous years, a clear indication that the lack of an assured job in the United States is discouraging would-be migrants, regardless of their legal status. But going to the United States is not being permanently discarded as an option; it is only being delayed.

Tougher border enforcement has produced a considerable amount of what the U.S. military would call "collateral damage." Since 1993, the United States government has created the deadliest land border in the world, with 6,678 documented fatalities among migrants attempting to cross the border—perhaps twice that many, if bodies not yet discovered were to be included in the count. On average, more than one migrant dies along the southwestern U.S. border every day. Twenty-three times more border-crossing deaths have been recorded along the U.S.–Mexican border since 1995 than occurred at the Berlin Wall during its 28 years of existence.

The slow-motion death march occurring along the U.S.-Mexico border is directly attributable to the U.S. strategy of concentrated border enforcement, which funnels would-be migrants into increasingly remote and life-threatening terrain. Virtually all high-emigration towns in Mexico have one or more graves occupied by migrants who perished in border-crossing attempts. The residents are well aware of the dangers. In our field interviews among Mexican migrants and potential migrants in 2009 we found that 44 percent knew someone who had died trying to cross the border, but that knowledge does not discourage them from going north.

---

4 Data in 2010 U.S. dollars. Source: Field studies conducted by the Mexican Migration Field Research and Training Program, Center for Comparative Immigration Studies, University of California-San Diego, 2005-2010.

U.S. Interior Enforcement: The "Immiseration Approach" to Immigration Control

What impact do workplace raids, neighborhood sweeps, traffic stops, mass-transit surveillance, local housing ordinances, and the like have on undocumented migrants and would-be migrants? In recent years, this approach to immigrant control has been championed by anti-immigration politicians and advocacy groups, who call it "attrition through enforcement," but it might also be called the "immiseration approach" to immigration control.

In essence, this involves making life in the U.S. so difficult for unauthorized immigrants that they will give up and go home voluntarily, or "self-deport." If migrants cannot be discouraged from coming here in the first place, then our immigration control policies should be crafted in ways that diminish incentives for settling permanently in the U.S.: excluding migrants from labor and housing markets, limiting their access to basic human services, denying them driver's licenses, making it more difficult for them to rent an apartment, and generally raising their anxiety levels.

Fifteen years have passed since California voters passed an "immiseration"-type ballot measure, Proposition 187 (see the article by Bloch/Rocha Silva in this book), which would have denied education and all but emergency health care to undocumented immigrants had it been upheld by the federal courts. There is still no scientifically reliable evidence that access to tax-supported social services or any other public benefit actually influences decisions to migrate internationally or to settle in destination countries. This holds true cross-nationally. Among OECD countries in general, the data show that economic migrants and asylum-seekers do not choose destinations based on considerations of short-term welfare maximization. What matters is migrant networks—ties with friends or family in the destination country—and relative employment opportunities. These are "structural" pull factors that are beyond the reach of immigration policymakers.

In the United States, denying jobs to people unauthorized to work is the main focus of interior enforcement. A widely touted proposal to strengthen workplace enforcement, championed by U.S. Senator Charles Schumer, chairman of the Immigration Subcommittee of the Senate Judiciary Committee, relies on a biometric, tamper-resistant ID card, in which the bearer's fingerprints, a digital photograph, and other personal identifying information would be embedded. Such a card would be issued to every legal resident in the United States. Those who present the card to an employer could be hired; those without such a card would be shut out of the labor market. All employers would be required to participate in this new electronic employment eligibility verification system. But how likely is it that such a system would make it so difficult for undocumented migrants to get a job that they would leave the United States, or discourage them from coming here in the first place?

This is what we know from field research: Workplace enforcement instills a great deal of fear among undocumented immigrants, but it does not affect their decisions to migrate to the United States, or decisions about whether to stay here. In our 2009 survey of Mexican migrants, those who had personally witnessed a workplace raid, or had a relative or friend who had been arrested in such a raid, were actually more likely to be planning to migrate to the United States this year than those who had no experience with workplace enforcement. And, there virtually no difference between the two groups in terms of how they perceived the difficulty of getting a job in the United States. Thus, we find that worksite enforcement has no appreciable effect on the propensity to migrate.

Senator Schumer's proposal, which he sees as the cornerstone of comprehensive immigration reform, raises numerous issues of cost and feasibility (Balch 2010; Mitsilegas 2009)[5]. If successfully implemented, a biometric card-based employment eligibility system would keep undocumented migrants out of some jobs in some formal-sector businesses, but it is unlikely to make them completely unemployable in the United States. Indeed, the most certain consequence of such a system would be to push more undocumented migrants into the underground economy, where they would not be paying taxes and where they would be more vulnerable to exploitation.

Even if the verification system is "mandatory," some percentage of employers will not use it, because it is not in their economic interest to limit their access to the immigrant labor pool. In our 2009 survey of Mexican migrants, we asked those living in the United States at the time of the interview whether their current employer had asked them for some form of documentation when they sought a job. One third had not been asked to produce any proof of legal residence, and three out of five of our interviewees reported that their most recent U.S. employer probably knew, or knew for certain, that they were not authorized to work in the U.S., regardless of the documents presented upon hiring. If, in the future, the Immigration and Customs Enforcement agency fields a veritable army of inspectors to enforce a new employment eligibility system, the number of employers who choose to ignore it will be reduced, but that level of enforcement is unlikely to be achieved, especially in the small-business sector, because it would be too disruptive to the lives of too many native-born Americans.

More generally, even if they are not influencing migration or settlement decisions, interior enforcement activities are creating a climate of fear in im-

---

5 Interest in biometrics to control unauthorized immigration has also been growing in the European Union. Similar issues of cost, technical feasibility, efficacy, and unintended consequences have been raised about this approach in the EU and United States contexts.

migrant communities. In our 2009 survey of Mexican migrants we asked the interviewees, "What does a person living without documents in the U.S. worry about most?", mentioning seven specific types of behavior that could expose such a person to the risk of deportation. We found that what our interviewees were worried about most was the risks of driving a car, going to a hospital, going to work, and walking in public.

The risks associated with driving a car have been increased in recent years by a rising incidence of random traffic stops. We were surprised to find that more than one out of four (26 percent) of Mexican immigrants interviewed by our research team in 2010 had been stopped by police and questioned about their immigration status during the preceding 12 months. That is even higher than the Pew Hispanic Center found in a national sample of Latinos interviewed in 2009, and it reflects the growing incidence of local police stops of immigrants in southern California, where our field interviews were conducted. The fact that driving with a broken tail light can now put one directly on the road to deportation does indeed strike fear into the hearts of undocumented immigrants. But, in our field studies we have found no evidence that U.S. interior enforcement efforts were actually discouraging potential migrants from going north, or from putting down roots in the United States once they get here.

Interior enforcement does influence how immigrants go about their daily lives, and whether they would expose themselves to public authorities. For example, over one third (37%) of our U.S.-based migrant interviewees in 2009 said that they would not report a crime if they observed it. Interior enforcement causes considerable anxiety in immigrant communities. In a 2007 national survey by the Pew Hispanic Center, two thirds of Latino immigrants in the U.S. said that they were worried about the possibility of a deportation hurting their family. Even among Latinos who are U.S. citizens, about one third feared it could happen to a relative or friend who lacks legal status. Their concerns are well-founded: The proportion of mixed-legal-status families in our immigrant population is growing rapidly. The Pew Hispanic Center has estimated that the number of children in the United States who have at least one undocumented parent increased from 3.8 million to 5.1 million between 2000 and 2009. For these children, the apprehension of a parent represents a huge threat to their well-being.

The anti-immigration movement in the United States has seized upon recent Census Bureau data showing a slight decrease in the total number of foreign-born people in the U.S. from 2007 to 2008 as proof that undocumented immigrants are not, after all, permanently attached to their lives in this country. If that is the case, these groups argue, the United States does not need a legalization program to deal with the roughly 11 million undocumented immigrants now estimated to be living in the United States: Let "attrition through enforcement" take its course, and step up enforcement to hurry the process along. Moreover, it is much easier, politically, to justify denying basic human services to undocumented immigrants if they are seen as transients rather than potential or *de facto* permanent settlers in the United States.

But the mass return migration to Mexico that anti-immigration activists have lauded is wishful thinking on their part. The Pew Hispanic Center's estimates, based on the Census Bureau's monthly Current Population Survey, show that the total stock of Mexicans in the United States—legal and undocumented—has plateaued (see Figure 4). Most importantly, there is no evidence on the ground, in Mexico, of a large-scale return migration from the United States. National-level survey data from Mexico show no appreciable increase in the number of migrants returning home from the U.S. in the 2007–2009 period.

Figure 3: Estimates of the number of unauthorized immigrants from Mexico residing in the United States, 2000–2009 (in millions)

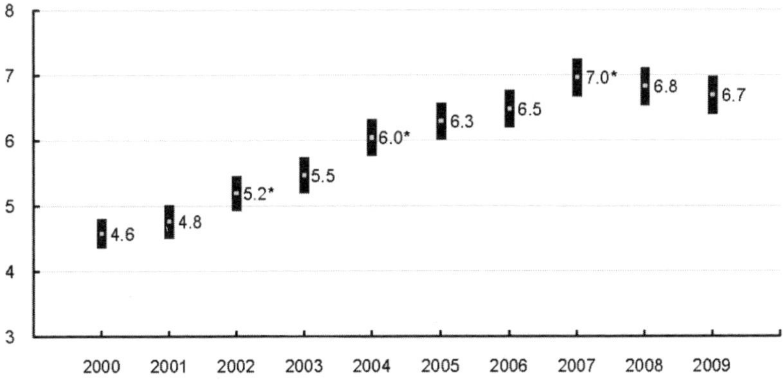

Source: Pew Hispanic Center, Washington, D.C., estimates based on a residual methodology applied to annual supplements to the Census Bureau's Current Population Survey. Note: Bars indicate low and high points of the estimated 90% confidence interval. *Change from the previous year is statistically significant.

This is powerful evidence of the tenacity of Mexican migrants to keep their hard-won foothold in the U.S. labor market, coupled with the lack of economic options in Mexico. It also reflects what Waldinger and Porzecanski have called the "caging effect" of border enforcement: Mexicans already working in the United States are acutely aware of the costs and dangers of clandestine migration (Waldinger/Porzecanski 2009). These are powerful incentives to wait out the current U.S. economic downturn rather than make a temporary journey back to Mexico. The psychology at work here is that the next trip to the U.S. would be even more costly and more risky than the trip that got them here.

By making it more costly and more risky for heads of families to visit their dependents in Mexico, tougher border enforcement has only strengthened the incentive to reunify families on the U.S. side of the border. As a result, there are millions of Mexican women and children living in the United States today who would not otherwise be here. There are many factors, in addition to border enforcement, now favoring long-term residence, if not permanent settlement, in the United States. Accordingly, it can be assumed that new migrants leaving Mexico in the future will be much more likely to stay in the United States once they get here than were their fathers or grandfathers. U.S. social policies, such as access to health care and education, should reflect that assumption.

Conclusions

The key findings of the field research reported in this chapter can be summarized as follows:

- Border enforcement discourages new migration mainly through its effect on "coyote" fees, creating a stronger demand for people smugglers. The direct effects of border enforcement-related knowledge and perceptions on the probability of migration among Mexicans are relatively weak, mostly statistically insignificant determinants of migration propensity.
- The financial crisis of 2007–2010 has strongly discouraged new migration from Mexico, both legal and unauthorized, by changing the cost-benefit calculus of migration. But many potential migrants are only postponing migration until the U.S. economy improves. The recession has, however, reduced the capacity of some would-be migrants to go north because U.S. relatives can no longer pay for people smugglers to assist them.
- In recent years, tougher border enforcement has been deterring unauthorized crossings only in combination with the weak labor demand in the United States. Potential migrants' perceptions of border-crossing difficulty and danger have remained basically the same since 2007, but their perceptions of the U.S. labor market have changed dramatically.
- There is no evidence that border fortifications are keeping unauthorized migrants out of the United States. Mexican migrants' success rates have been remarkably stable over time and across very differ-

ent sending communities. More than 60 percent still get in on the first try, and more than nine out of ten of those who were apprehended once succeed in entering on the same trip to the border.

- There has been no large-scale exodus of Mexican migrants from the United States due to the financial crisis. The fear of losing their U.S. jobs if they return home for even a brief period, along with the high cost of being smuggled back into the country, has led migrants already in the United States to stay where they are.

As we assess the outcomes of U.S. immigration control policies, it is crucial to keep in mind that major changes in immigration law and policy are huge experiments in behavior modification. To have their intended effects, they must induce millions of immigrants, potential immigrants, their relatives in both sending and receiving countries, and the employers who hire them to change their behavior in significant ways. All so-called immigration reforms are only as good as the assumptions they make about human behavior.

This simple truth tends to get lost in complex econometric modeling exercises, but policymakers ignore it at their peril. Many elected officials believe—or wish their constituents to believe—that the U.S. government actually has the capacity to intervene in international migration flows in ways that yield the expected outcomes and minimize the unintended consequences—hence the broad, bipartisan consensus existing in the U.S. Congress that more spending on border security will yield greater control over clandestine immigration. This is a tremendous—and generally unwarranted—assumption given the historical record in the United States and abroad, which shows that private market forces and demography almost invariably trump the effects of government interventions in international migration.

The United States, like all major labor-importing countries, needs a sense of humility and a strong dose of realism in approaching the challenge of reforming its national immigration system. The point of departure should be a recognition that it is the economic conditions in the United States and Mexico that fundamentally determine whether a potential migrant will invest thousands of dollars and risk his life in the desert to get into the United States, not the obstacle course that is being built at the U.S.–Mexico border. And even if a virtual fence were to be built all the way from San Diego to Brownsville, there would not be enough Border Patrol agents on the ground to keep large numbers of migrants from getting through. The probability of apprehension would still be well below 100 percent, which is a gamble that most migrants are willing to take.

The business cycle is the most effective instrument to control unauthorized immigration to the United States that has ever been invented. The Great Depression of the 1930s is the only thing that truly kept Mexicans from migrating to the United States during the last 100 years; it brought new immigration from Mexico down to essentially zero. Similarly, field interviews conducted for this project in rural Mexico in early 2009 show that the U.S. economic crisis of 2007—2010 has done far more to reduce illegal immigration than anything that the U.S. Government has done in the last 16 years. And if history is any guide, the northbound flow from Mexico will rebound as soon as the U.S. economy recovers to the point that labor-intensive firms are hiring again.

The fundamentals of Mexican-to-U.S. migration have not changed: The real wage differential between Mexico and the United States for most low-skilled jobs is still at least 8:1; Mexico's job creation rate is far below that of the U.S., even in the best of times for Mexico's economy; and there is a huge potential for family reunification migration. Nearly two out of every five people living in Mexico has at least one close relative in the United States, and the proportion of Mexicans with close U.S. ties rises to about 85 percent in small Mexican towns that have high emigration rates.

Whether the next wave of Mexican migrants to the United States comes legally or illegally is up to the U.S. legislators. If they once again fail to enact comprehensive immigration reform, including measures that significantly expand opportunities for both temporary and permanent legal immigration, Mexicans will still come, paying more to people smugglers and taking greater risks with their lives. And unless the United States turns itself into a police state in the name of immigration control, at least some U.S. employers will continue to hire undocumented migrants who show up at their door. That is the reality, but whether the U.S. politicians can grasp it and respond appropriately remains to be seen.

References

Balch, A. (2010): Managing Labour Migration in Europe: Ideas, Knowledge, and Policy Change. Center for Comparative Immigration Studies, University of California, San Diego, Working Paper No. 184, January 2010. [online] Available at: http://ccis.ucsd.edu/wp-content/uploads/2010/02/WP184.pdf [Accessed 04-02-2011]

Cornelius, W. A./Lewis, J. M., eds. (2007): Impacts of Border Enforcement on Mexican Migration: The View from Sending Communities. La Jolla, Calif.: Center for Comparative Immigration Studies, University of California, San Diego/Boulder, Col.: Lynne Rienner Publishers.

Cornelius, W. A./Fitzgerald, D./Fischer, P. L., eds. (2007): Mayan Journeys: The New Migration from Yucatán to the United States. La Jolla, Calif.: Center for Comparative Immigration Studies, University of California, San Diego/Boulder, Col.: Lynne Rienner Publishers.

Cornelius, W. A./Fitzgerald, D./Hernández-Díaz, J./Borger, S., eds. (2009a): Migration from the Mexican Mixteca: A Transnational Community in Oaxaca and Cal-

ifornia. La Jolla, Calif.: Center for Comparative Immigration Studies, University of California, San Diego/Boulder, Col.: Lynne Rienner Publishers.
Cornelius, W. A./Fitzgerald, D./Fischer, P. L./Muse-Orlinoff, L., eds. (2009b): Mexican Migration and the U.S. Economic Crisis: A Transnational Perspective. La Jolla, Calif.: Center for Comparative Immigration Studies, University of California, San Diego/Boulder, Col.: Lynne Rienner Publishers.
Dunn, T. J. (2009): Blockading the Border and Human Rights: The El Paso Operation that Remade Immigration Enforcement. Austin, Texas: University of Texas Press.
Fitzgerald, D./Alarcón Acosta, R./Muse-Orlinoff, L., eds. (2010): Recession Without Borders: Mexican Migrants Confront the Economic Downturn. La Jolla, Calif.: Center for Comparative Immigration Studies, University of California, San Diego/Boulder, Col.: Lynne Rienner Publishers.
Mitsilegas, V. (2009): Borders, Security, and Transatlantic Cooperation in the Twenty-First Century. In: Givens, Terri E./Freeman, Garp P./Leal, David L. (eds.): Immigration Policy and Security: U.S., Eueropean, and Commonwealth Perspectives. New York, London: Routledge, pp. 148-66.
Waldinger. R./Porzecanski, R. (2009): Caged: Expatriate Voting and Its Limits. Dept. of Sociology, UCLA (unpubl.).

Economic Policy Matters: Incentives that Drive Mexicans Northward

Kathleen Staudt and Sergio García

The United States has long been considered a nation of immigrants. No matter what region you refer to, only a tiny fraction of the country's population of 308 million would respond affirmatively to the question: "Were your ancestors born in this country?" Waves of immigrants from Europe, Africa, Asia, and Central and South America settled in the U.S. In 1890-1920, an era of high levels of immigration, 20% of the labor force was foreign born, compared with the most recent estimate of 15% (US Census 2007). Laborers were desperately needed in a growing industrial economy that was expanding westward. With more 38.3 million immigrants living in its territory, the U.S. has accepted more immigrants than Russia (12 million) or Germany (10.1 million) (UN 2005 figures, cited in Council on Foreign Relations 2009: 12). During the 1990s, a period of economic prosperity in the U.S., immigrants from Mexico and other countries supplied much of the demand for labor. The trilateral North American Free Trade Agreement (NAFTA) solidified ties among strong trading partners and the implicit move toward a more integrated labor force. However, no common North American immigration policy exists.

During the second half of the 20th century, Mexico was the largest source of immigrants to the U.S. This hardly comes as a surprise, considering that Mexico lost half of its pre-war territory after the 1848 Treaty of Guadalupe Hidalgo, ceding most of what is now the Southwestern United States. Until the establishment of the Border Patrol in 1925, Mexicans often crossed borders between both countries to find employment. Border control enforcement waxed and waned, depending upon the demand for labor in the U.S. Southwest. In the period 1942-1964, under the U.S. Bracero guest worker program, as many as six million Mexicans supplied much-needed agricultural labor to the war economy and in other jobs in the subsequent economic growth (Delano 2006). Many stayed in the U.S., starting families with children who already were U.S. citizens by birthright and acquiring citizenship themselves.

After the Mexican Revolution of 1910, in the name of *tierra y libertad* (land and liberty), the exploitation of the country's abundant natural resources (such as oil) and the land reform of the 1930s under President Cárdenas produced remarkable economic growth (commonly referred to as the "Mexican miracle"), which continued into the 1960s. However, the growth was not coupled with equity, despite the redistributive rhetoric of Mexico's dominant party, the Institutional Revolutionary Party (PRI), which generated one of the sharpest income inequalities in the world and the Americas: a Gini coefficient[1] of 0.481, compared with 0.408 and 0.326 for the U.S. and Canada, respectively (UNDP 2009: Table M, with 2007 figures). In 1980, Mexico's recession, debt crisis, and entry into the General Agreement on Tariff and Trades (GATT) laid the groundwork for the subsequent free trade regime enshrined in the North American Free Trade Agreement of 1994. Meanwhile, in the U.S., after the 1986 Immigration Reform and Control Act (IRCA) granted amnesty and pathways to citizenship for undocumented immigrants, millions of immigrants entered the U.S. without authorization. Many secured jobs and settled in with their families, preparing for long-term residence and perhaps hoping for another amnesty. After the 1990s, estimates put the figure at 12 million undocumented immigrants, despite the relative harshness of the Illegal Immigration Reform and Immigrant Responsibility Act of 1996 (IIRIRA) (Staudt and Capps 2004). Thus, the relative ease of obtaining employment, coupled with the ineffective immigration law and border control, did not deter migration.

In this paper, we examine Mexican immigration to the U.S. in the 1990s and beyond, focusing on a broad range of national policies and the particular institutions in which they are crafted in both Mexico and the United States. We argue that the long-held U.S. political values that celebrated "bureaucrat bashing" in the 1980s Reagan era and the limited government regulation during the prosperity of the Clinton era in the 1990s generated a demand for low-cost labor, which was supplied by Mexican immigrants. Mexico's policies and the PRI's unfulfilled promises—given persistent poverty which affected half the population, low wages, and the destruction of small-scale farming operations—drove migrants northward. We argue that these macro-level policies in both countries do far more to explain undocumented immigration than the U.S. immigration policy, including the border control policies and their enforcement (on the ineffectiveness of border control enforcement in deterring unauthorized immigration, see Cornelius, this volume). We predict that as North America enters the second decade of the 21st century, the pursuit of potentially contradictory priority goals of economic development and security—amid complex political institutions and values—will con-

1 According to policy analysts Kraft and Furlong (2010: 272), the Gini coefficient is "a way of demonstrating a nation's income equality and inequality. Income equality is represented by a forty-five degree line, on which each percentage of the population is making the same percentage of the income. As a curve deviates away from the forty-five degree line, it shows an increase in income inequality. The implicit interpretation of the curve is that if a few people are making a large percentage of the income, more people are put at risk of poverty".

tinue to shape migration behavior, the rhetorical political minefield of national U.S. immigration reform, and the snail pace of bilateral negotiations on immigration or a North American mobility strategy.

In the body of this paper, we analyze a variety of public policies that shape emigration and immigration, for there is no single consistent economic policy in these two fragmented federal systems of government. Rather, a *laissez faire* template of political and economic values, rather than coherent centralized economic policy, guides labor supply and demand. The Obama administration, amid highly polarized partisan debates, weakly challenged the anti-regulation atmosphere, given the near-collapse of major U.S. economic sectors in 2008 and thereafter. The post-2008 recession generated unusually high unemployment rates in this free-trade regime, further de-industrializing the U.S. and undermining "citizen" workers. In this chapter, we take a political institutional approach to explain the dysfunctions of coherent public policy.

Our outline for this chapter covers the following topics. First, we examine political values, ideologies, and political institutions as long-term determinants of public policy choices. Second, we examine economic and related policies of Mexico as the largest sending country. Third, we analyze the extent of authorized and unauthorized migration from Mexico, along with the politics of recent efforts at immigration reform in the United States. We close with reflections and recommendations for policy reforms.

Institutional Analysis: Long-term Determinants of Public Policy Choices

In this section, we will focus on institutional factors which explain macroeconomic policy in terms of political values, institutions, party issues, and bureaucracies themselves. The analysis also reveals the increasingly profitable privatization and contractor arrangements associated with maintaining the status quo of unreformed immigration policy—a policy disconnected from economic policy choices.

Political Values and Ideologies

In the United States, great value is placed on freedom and limited government control in a capitalist market economy. Government size, growth, and regulation are viewed with dismay, given both the tax burden associated with supporting civil servants and bureaucracy and the limits to freedom—particularly corporate freedom—that regulation implies. The privatization of public services, through contracts with private corporations, resonates not only with voters, but also with the lobby groups that represent industries with stakes in lucrative contracts. Private corporations pay big money to re-elect their allies in Congress, including border congressmen like Silvestre Reyes (Barry 2009). One key growth industry from unauthorized immigration involves private, for-profit prisons and detention centers that create jobs in regions where they are situated, per-detainee fees to local governments strapped for financial resources, and dividends for investors (Staudt 2009).

In the U.S., the single-member electoral system drives two-party rather than multi-party competition, the latter more common in proportional representation systems with their incentives to seat more ideological parties in proportion to the percentage of votes obtained. Historically, in two-party, single-member systems in the U.S., both parties have aimed toward centrist positions, with the left-of-center Democrats promoting a more proactive government and the right-of-center Republicans promoting more limited, business-friendly government, except for the core commitment to strong military, war, and defense budgets and their private-sector contractors. The so-called wedge issues, such as abortion and immigration, complicate party lines. In high-polarization partisan periods, such as the current one, such issues may stall change.

In Mexico, the multi-party system presents challenges to political leadership and the problem-solving capacity of the state. Loaeza (2006) notes that while the multi-party feature of Mexican political system is one of the most palpable accomplishments of democratization, it has also been one of the main obstacles to policy decision-making. There has been no single-party majority in the Chamber of Deputies since 1997, as once was the case for more than seventy years. In 2000 and thereafter, neither the center-right National Action Party (PAN) nor the center-left Institutional Revolutionary Party (PRI) held a majority of the seats in Mexico's congress. Other parties, such as the left-wing Party of the Democratic Revolution (PRD), the Green Party and the Workers Party, are also represented. The multi-party characteristics of the legislature in Mexico have hindered the ability to pass laws and implement new policies. In addition, the Mexican political system does not allow the reelection of legislators, which hinders the possibility of building seniority and expertise. Moreover, Loaeza (2006) notes that since legislators cannot hope for a direct reelection once their term is over, they depend on the political parties to be considered for future candidacy in upcoming elections. This makes block party voting a common feature of the Mexican system.

U.S. identity politics also figure into party positions. By identity groups we mean Latino, African American, and Asian and Pacific American groups, with corresponding "caucuses" in the U.S. Congress. The largest and growing minority group consists of Latinos, including citizen voters, non-voting permanent residents, and undocumented immigrants. While Latinos typically vote for Democrats, Republicans have been courting this constituency as well, as evidenced during George W. Bush's term as governor and also his attempts at immigration policy reform in 2004, with the failed bipartisan Kennedy-McCain bill. George W. Bush spoke to crowds in broken Spanish and hired *mariachi* bands at Latino campaign events in what critics viewed as a cynical ploy. Party politicians have become notably more polarized since 2004. There has been a growing rift between the two main wings of the Republican Party; the limited-government, pro-business moderates differ from the xenophobic right wing on various issues, including immigration reform. While most business constituencies seek access to immigrant labor and are resolved to some regulation, they are less visible advocates than they could be, given underlying voter suspicions about job loss to the global economy and home foreclosures in the still minimally-regulated financial-industrial complex.

In Mexico, identity politics differ. One significant difference is the identity of transnationals, including those dual citizens who can vote in both the U.S. and Mexico. The Mexican legislation in 2005 granted Mexicans residing abroad the right to vote. The Federal Electoral Institute (IFE) reports that 35,763 Mexican living in the United States were registered to vote in the 2006 election, and 28,335 actually did so. Although Mexicans in the United States typically vote for the Democratic Party, which is largely considered center-left, in the Mexican elections the majority (about 60 percent) of this tiny constituency (U.S.-based Mexicans who vote in Mexican elections) voted for the conservative PAN. Such inconsistency reaffirms the initial message sent by Mexican immigrants by first "voting with their feet" and then voting against the PRI.

Political Institutions

Unlike many centralized European governments, the federal systems of both the U.S. and Mexico divide authority between national (federal), regional (state), and local (municipal) levels, often with complex negotiations and formulas associated with intergovernmental relations. Each state government—50 in the United States and 31 in Mexico (plus the Federal District)—has its own political cast of characters, institutions, taxing and spending authorities. According to the Migration Policy Institute (MPI), a non-partisan think tank, each year U.S. state legislators introduce more than 1,000 bills dealing with immigration, but fewer than 20% are actually enacted into law (2008), which is typical in the U.S. legislative process. We would also note that state and local courts have bureaucratic stakes in the large caseloads they address, a burdensome responsibility but one associated with increased budgets and staff, including reimbursements from the federal government.

There is no central planning unit or national plan with coherent, relatively stable economic policy in U.S. federal government. Given the enduring political value of "limited government," the introduction of such institutional machinery would be challenged as anti-market or even creeping socialism—a "red-baiting" term akin to "communist" during the Cold War. Of the fifteen cabinet-level federal executive branch departments, each with a myriad of agencies and programs, two are primarily focused on economic policy: the Department of Commerce and the Department of the Treasury, although others also affect economic policies and jobs. The White House and Congress also have budget offices and economic advisors. The Board of Governors for the independent Federal Reserve System, informally known as the Fed, (equivalent to a central bank) makes monetary policy. But the U.S., without coherent industrial or jobs policies, pushes a wide variety of ever-changing contradictory policies based on the prevailing political winds and the ever-present elections, for members of the House of Representatives serve only two-year terms and if they wish to be reelected, must constantly behave and vote accordingly. One of the most famous examples of this type of contradiction is the provision of subsidies to farmers amid free-trade regimes, which includes subsidies to tobacco farmers, while simultaneously deterring cigarette smokers, given the costs of these drugs to health programs and premature deaths, with the concession of warning labels that the Surgeon General deems smoking dangerous to health.

Policy direction changes with each new presidential administration through the political appointment process. The legislative branch, through the Senate, scrutinizes and approves high-level appointees such as cabinet secretaries and the Chairman of the Federal Reserve. With presidential terms of four years, and incumbents being limited to only a second term, the president, his cast of political appointees, and policies can change markedly at the end of a presidential term. Thus, people refer to presidential political eras, such as the Reagan (1981-1988), Clinton (1993-2000), Bush (1989-1992 and 2001–2008, referring to father and son, respectively), and Obama eras.

Like the U.S., Mexico has no central planning, but unlike in the United States, this is due to the historically strong central government. Until the 1980s, Mexico's institutional arrangement involved highly centralized executive power which implemented government functions with the state as the principal agent of modernization (Loaeza 2006). Thus, the state assumed central responsibilities in the promotion and implementation of the model of development. In 1982, Mexico faced a major financial and political crisis which reduced the state capacity for political leadership. The prevailing situation in the country was desperate: inflation reached 100 percent and the public sector deficit was 16 percent of the gross domestic product. As a result of the 1982 economic crisis, the need to design a national development plan arose.

The Immediate Economic Reorganization Program (PIRE) was the first line of commitment to strategic planning with short- and long-term perspectives. Many goals were established in this program, including the lowering of inflation by reducing the public deficit from 16 percent to 8 percent through spending cuts and strengthening sources of income (Lomelí 2007). As part of the PIRE, President Miguel de la Madrid presented the National Development Plan, which established national objectives, strategies, and priorities for his administration. The National Development Plan of Mexico has been set out by all subsequent Mexican presidents with their objectives and strategies in each administration. While it represents the commitment that the federal government provides to the citizens for accountability, there is neither an enforcing agency to ensure the accomplishment of such commitments nor a central agency to oversee whether goals have been accomplished. Rather, it is assumed that all agencies and even local governments will comply with the plan set out by the federal government. This seems unlikely under a highly polarized political system and with a lack of political will to compromise. Moreover, without a formal civil service and with the change in direction from administration to administration there is little, if any, incentive to comply with Plan goals when there is a high possibility that new goals will be established with a new administration and different people will hold different positions.

Mexico: Sending Country Policies

In this section we focus on several public policies that drive migrants to move northward for higher wages, in particular on agrarian reform; regional trade (NAFTA); inequality, poverty, and low wages; tax reform failures; and law enforcement flaws in a system yet to guarantee the "rule of law." The basic political institutions in Mexico and the public policies shaped in these institutions have created dynamics that foster the intended and unintended consequences of stimulating migrants from Mexico to make risky journeys northward toward unauthorized entry into the United States.

Scholars suggest that Mexico became democratic during the 1990s (see Magaloni 2006; Smith 2005), with growing civil society activism, electoral reforms, and victories for candidates from three major political parties. During the 1990s, for the first time since the "Mexican miracle," Mexico experienced macroeconomic stability (Orrentius 2006). In addition, according to Anaya Muñoz (2009: 503), moderate poverty fell from 63.7% to 51.7% and extreme poverty fell from 34% in 1998-2000 to 20.3% in 2002. Despite the slight drop in poverty, under conditions like these people "vote with their feet" to seek higher wages; over the last few decades Mexico has lost at least

10 percent of its prime-working age labor force (Randall 2006). While many of those who leave the country are low-skilled workers, Mexico loses professionals as well, estimated at 20,000 annually since 2000, up from 15,000 annually in the 1990s, which is referred to as the "mounting cost of brain drain" (Paterson 2009). This exodus has dramatically increased from Ciudad Juárez at the northern border, the world's murder capital in 2009–10 (see later section). Conversely, in 2003 more than $13 billion were transferred from the United States as remittances, which now represent the second largest source of income in Mexico, just after oil exports and above tourism (Randall 2006). That figure grew to $24 billion in 2007, an amount greater than the official foreign direct investment (FDI) (Zepeda et al. 2009: 10). Mexico has an interest in maintaining the exit of workers; their absence avoids political demands for more living wage jobs. Remittance senders have moved from once being referred to as traitors who deserted their country to heroes who supply needed capital (Castañeda 2007: 21).

Agrarian Policies

Towards the end of the 1970s, Mexican social and economic policies sought to create a stable modern labor force financed to a lesser extent by the government (Roberts and Escobar Latapi 1997). The system was developed to cover different aspects and needs of a changing society. However, these policies were focused mostly on urban development; few of the policies implemented covered the rural workers. In fact, these policies favored those in formal and stable jobs (Mesa Lago 1978). Subsidies for transportation and housing in the big cities provided incentives for entrepreneurs to locate their industries in the cities (Roberts and Escobar Latapí 1997). In addition, the reform to the IMSS (social security) and the creation of INFONAVIT (housing) and ISSSTE (social security for state workers) sought the participation of the private sector and clearly favored the urban areas. These distributive policies led to rapid urbanization. Hence, the massive population flows during the 1970s to urban areas were able to generate enough formal jobs to internal migrants, reducing the push factors for international migration (Escobar Latapí and Roberts 1991; García 1988; Gregory 1985; Oliveira and Roberts 1994). Indeed, until 1980 the concern was with internal migration; the policy in relation to international immigration was actually a "policy of no policy" (Delano 2006). The Bracero Program was the exception to this policy, but economic reasons pushed the government to negotiate such a program (Delano 2006). Most programs were in fact focused on protecting the migrants (Roberts and Escobar Latapí 1997; Delano 2006), although corruption ensued, as money deducted from workers' pay as ostensible savings and then deposited in the Banco de México never made its way to the workers upon their return to Mexico (Casteñeda 2007: 54).

By the end of the 1980s, rural stagnation was evident. What had changed was the basic structure that once motivated the creation of an economic and social system in which agriculture was pivotal to maintaining political and economic stability. The policies that led Mexico to achieve food self-sufficiency also led to stagnation in the agrarian system. President Carlos Salinas de Gortari (1988-1994) offered to modernize the *ejido* (communal landholdings) through "privatized joint ventures—without fundamentally altering the *campesino* (peasant farmer) way of life" (Franko 1999: 298). This policy only made official what had already been happening; that is, peasants legally rented their land. Even worse, confronting a problem of opportunity cost, *campesinos* were finally able to sell the land that would allow them to survive for a couple of years (Morett Sánchez 2003). Whether they sold to developers or larger landowners, peasants lost a key asset.

Technically, Salinas' offer to modernize the *ejido* represented an improvement because the *campesinos* were now free to improve their lands, but, predictably, it was the wealthy who bought up most of the available land. With no land, the *campesinos* were forced to either work for someone else in the land they previously owned or to migrate. According to Morett Sánchez (2003), 80% of former *ejido* members have migrated. This figure is consistent with data provided by the National Population Council (CONAPO); the annual net influx of migration to the United States has grown from an average of 26,000 to 29,000 people to more than 300,000 people in the 1990s. According to Zepeda et al. (2009: 13), in the early 2000s, this figure increased by half a million annually, whereas agricultural employment rates in Mexico dropped from 8.1 million in 1993 to 5.8 million in 2008, due to the exodus of 2.3 million workers. It would seem that Mexico exports valuable people.

Thus, as the Berlin Wall fell and former socialist countries moved toward capitalism, President Carlos Salinas de Gortari joined the global momentum and reversed Mexican revolutionary principles in several areas—political, economic, and even religious. Salinas reversed the course of revolutionary anticlericalism, struck at most of the all-powerful unions, and privatized most companies formerly owned by the state. In addition, he reversed the principles of the Revolution in the countryside. As Salinas declared in a 1992 speech, "In the past land distribution was a path of justice; today it is unproductive and impoverishing" (quoted in Morett Sánchez 2003). This set the stage for fulfillment of what seemed to be one of Salinas' ultimate goals: the inclusion of Mexico into the North American Free Trade Agreement (NAFTA).

Trade Policy

With NAFTA in place for fifteen years, by 2009, scholars in both countries have started to question the value of this trade policy, especially with regard to the creation of sustainable jobs at living-wage levels. On the surface, NAFTA seemed to benefit Mexico: trade and foreign direct investment (FDI) increased threefold, inflation was reduced and productivity increased—indicators that might well have actually resulted from Mexico's drastic 1994-95 devaluation of the peso, which cheapened wages and thereby increased FDI and export growth during unprecedented U.S. economic prosperity (Zepeda et al. 2009: 12). Most of the NAFTA-created jobs were in manufacturing, particularly in the *maquladoras* (export-processing factories concentrated along the U.S.-Mexico border), but these jobs are linked to the upturns and downturns of the U.S. economy. For example, the decline of the U.S. automobile industry put automobile harness factory workers into serious jeopardy (Miker Palafox 2010).

Scholars have drawn stark conclusions regarding NAFTA's inability to create jobs. "With roughly one million Mexicans entering the labor force each year, the NAFTA model has failed to deliver what Mexico needs the most" (Zepeda et al. 2009: 10). Without immigration to the U.S., Mexico might have faced explosive political consequences. Indeed, drug cartels offer lucrative albeit high-risk income to thousands of young men unable or unwilling to work in unstable *maquiladora* employment for a wage of $40 per week, as we will discuss below in the section on Mexico's inability to maintain public safety and functional law enforcement institutions.

A binational team of scholars at the Pardee Center for the Study of the Longer-Range Future at Boston University notes that a "trade agreement is no substitute for a coherent national development strategy" and "increasing trade and foreign investment will not alone generate dynamic economic development" (Pardee 2009: 2). In yet another insightful conclusion, UC Berkeley professor Harley Shaiken calls the new phenomenon that developed under NAFTA "high-productivity poverty;" low wages do not translate into purchasing power that stimulates the production of consumer goods (quoted in Malkin, 2009: 1A: 4). Stark inequalities between both countries prevail: the GDP per capita is $45,592 in the U.S., but only $9,715 in Mexico (UNDP, 2009: Table M). As of 2010, the legal minimum wage per day in Mexico is $4, at current exchange rates, while the hourly minimum wage in the U.S. is $7.25. Economic migrants are well aware of these differences, prompting migration.

Wage Policy: Real-Wage Stagnation

Despite a social revolution and redistributive rhetoric, Mexican public policy shaped an economic structure wherein half the population lives in "moderate" poverty and a fifth of the population lives in extreme poverty. Poverty levels increased from 52.4 percent in 1994, when NAFTA was signed, to 69 percent in 1996. Between 1998 and 2002, the poverty rates dropped slightly after the Institutional Revolutionary Party (PRI) lost its 71-year control over the presidency and executive branch of government to the conservative National Action Party (PAN) and after the left-wing Party of the Democratic Revolution (PRD) triumphed in Mexico City, the largest urban concentration and bellwether for the nation. However, it is worth noting that shortly thereafter poverty rates increased again, from 42.6 percent in 2006 to 47.4 percent in 2008. Zepeda et al. (2009) note that by opening its economy, the Mexican government made the assumption that it would increase FDI, that foreign companies would source from domestic companies while increasing their capital and technology, and that such increases in technology would lead to an increase in productivity and efficiency which would make domestic firms more profitable and eventually have a spillover effect. Unfortunately, Zepeda et al. note, "a significant portion of FDI went into buying domestic firms rather than establishing new facilities which does not increase the stock of capital" (2009: 8). Moreover, the poor credit system, along with the poor infrastructure, forced many domestic companies to go out of business. Also, FDI in manufacturing has not been sourced from domestic companies as assumed initially; rather, they import components to add some value and export them. Eventually, some firms did become more productive and efficient, but that only allowed domestic firms to require less labor and in the aftermath, the spillover effect became smaller and reduced the rate at which poverty levels dropped.

Slight improvements in living conditions in Mexico have not been enough to reduce great emigration flows. The minimum wage in Mexico divides the country into three zones with a difference of approximately 3 pesos ($0.25) per day (with 57.46, 55.84, and 54.47 pesos being equivalent to about $4 per day based on exchange rates at the time of this writing), which, even after adjusting for differences in prices and exchange rates using purchasing power parities (PPPs), is equivalent to just about $0.72 per hour (Immervoll 2007). Although these wage differentials can certainly stimulate some internal migration within Mexico, the reality of the labor market makes the United States a more attractive destination.

The Mexican economy has rarely produced enough employment for its growing population. In the bid to attract foreign investment and decentralize its industry, Mexico initiated the Border Industrialization Program in the mid-1960s. Simultaneously, the country began to attract more foreign investment from firms seeking low-cost labor. At its high point in 2000, Mexico's largest border city Ciudad Juárez employed a quarter of a million workers in export-processing factories. At the U.S.-Mexico border, hundreds of export-processing factories owned by U.S. (75% of the total), Canadian, Japanese and European firms pay little more than Mexico's legal minimum wage plus benefits (see selections in Staudt, Monárrez, and Fuentes, 2010). In manufacturing, figures from 2007 document that U.S. manufacturing jobs pay 5.8 times more than those in Mexico, a higher differential than in 1993 (Zepeda et al. 2009: 14). Under free trade regimes, the home countries of these foreign investors and the global community are free to pay wages that perpetuate highly disparate inequalities between both nations.

Even though wages are only slightly higher, real minimum wages have fallen 25 percent (Zepeda et al. 2009: 14). Despite this, real wages are still higher than what they would be had there been no emigration. Orrentius (2006) points out that Mexican emigration is a self-selected processes in which the people at the lower and higher ends of the income distribution scale usually do not migrate, the former because of a lack of resources and the latter because skills are usually not transferable. This dynamic forces the supply of labor to shift inward which in turn pushes wages up. The neoclassical models predicting that wages in different regions equalize after cost-of-living adjustment is driven precisely by the assumption of a perfectly mobile labor force.

Tax Policy

Mexico has historically been an inefficient tax collector, with about 15 percent of Mexico's GDP in tax collection, compared with 36% in OECD countries. Zepeda et al. (2009: 9) note that Mexico still obtains 30% of its revenue from the state-owned petroleum company and that the rich pay little tax. According to data from the United Nations Public Administration Network (UNPAN), tax revenue in 2000 was 16.1 percent of the GDP, while in the same year Canada collected 36.4 and the U.S. 28.3 percent, and other Latin American developing countries such as Brazil and Chile collected 29.3 and 19.1 percent, respectively. According to Mayer-Sierra (2006), Mexican governments in general, despite their rhetorical redistributive ideology, have faced resistance when they try to promote tax reforms and that tax rates for consumption in the U.S. are actually lower than in most developed countries. Because of the high concentration of wealth, an increase of taxes would affect mainly the richest 10 percent of the country, who contribute about 37 percent of the taxes collected.

Although most income collection comes from the wealthiest minority, this figure does not reflect the reality of the Mexican wealthy, who, helped by a weak and deficient tax administration, simply seek legal advice to minimize their tax obligations or take their investments outside the country (Mayer-Sierra 2006; Przeworki 1998). Indeed, the weak tax structure undermines the ability of the Mexican government to create an infrastructure that could retain the influx of immigrants. Thus, those who might benefit from a tax reform—i.e., from more tax collected from the wealthy for redistributive purposes—are either politically dispersed or politically underrepresented. The change of the composition in the legislative power after 2000 has been unable to achieve a profound tax reform due to a lack of a party majority in Congress (Mayer-Sierra 2006).

Lack of Public Safety, Insecurity, and Problematic Law Enforcement Institutions

The lack of public security is another factor that drives migrants northward. Police at the municipal and state levels have long operated with impunity, making many residents reluctant to report crime. Immediately adjacent to the United States (the largest drug-consuming population), Mexican drug cartels have become major suppliers in this lucrative trade (Payan 2006). Corruption is deeply embedded in law enforcement institutions (see selections in Cornelius and Shirk 2007). According to Transparency International, which produces an annual Corruption Perceptions Index on a 1-10 scale from high to low corruption, 2009 scores show Mexico at 3.3, the United States at 7.5, Canada at 8.7 (and Germany at 8).

Migrants flee from poverty, impunity, and a lack of security. Their journeys are fraught with crime, including rape and theft from official and criminal sources (see selections in Staudt, Payan and Kruszewski 2009). Harsh U.S. border control policies, including blockades in the major urban areas of El Paso, Texas and the Southern California/San Diego area, have funneled migrants toward less populated desert regions where heat and lack of water have led to approximately 300 "policy-induced deaths" (Staudt 2009: Ch. 1) annually, or a total of 4,600 deaths since the early 1990s (when counting identified bodies). Thus, with only weak commitment to the rule of law in Mexico, coupled with the economic and wage magnets pulling migrants northward, immigration continues.

The U.S.-Mexico border has been a major gateway for drug trafficking into the United States. For decades, with a nod from corrupt forces in government, the border center point of Ciudad Juárez became the infamous location of femicides (i.e., misogynist rape-mutilation murders), with little response from police forces (Staudt 2008). With an overall annual homicide rate running at 200–300, after 2007 the number of execution-style murders skyrocketed to 1,600 in 2008 and 2,600 in 2009. Despite (or perhaps because of) Mexico's military presence, the city of 1.5 million people became the world's murder capital, worse than Baghdad. Both the U.S. and Mexico have responded with border militarization strategies and Juarenses have begun to flee, including middle-income residents and small business owners, with numbers estimated to be 30,000–100,000 people and a quarter of empty housing stock.

Migrants with money to invest are eligible for special U.S. visas and a fast track to legal permanent residency. Others blend in to the shadows with local visas (ostensibly for shopping in the borderlands), travel visas, and/or undocumented status—hoping for the violence and impunity to end or for immigration reform in the United States.

Authorized and Unauthorized Migration from Mexico: Why Reform?

Figures on immigration—or "numeric metaphors" which can serve as a powerful force for political pressure, as Deborah Stone (1997) notes—fuel debates among both proponents and opponents of immigration and the reigning coalition of political representatives in the U.S. Congress and state legislatures. According to recent figures from the Office of Immigration Statistics, 8.15 million legal permanent residents (i.e., legal immigrants) are eligible to naturalize as citizens, 34% of them born in Mexico (U.S. Department of Homeland Security 2007: 3, 4) and 11.6 million unauthorized immigrants lived in the U.S. in 2008, a slight decrease from 2007, 61% of whom are from Mexico. Among the fifty states, the two largest states of residence for unauthorized immigrants are California and Texas, at 2.85 and 1.68 million, respectively (U.S. Department of Homeland Security 2008: 3, 4). Both documented and undocumented immigrants are workers, taxpayers and consumers of commercial products and public benefits.

Policy analysts frequently use cost-benefit or efficiency arguments to make or contest their cases for policy choices. According to a study from the Congressional Budget Office (CBO), unauthorized immigrants work in the formal labor force (as opposed to the underground, informal economy), pay taxes, and approximately half of them pay into the Social Security system, even though an underground market in identity documents means that some are paying into accounts other than their own. That same CBO document indicates that unauthorized immigrants may burden state and local government more, given the U.S. constitutional delegation of many government functions to those levels (U.S. Congressional Budget Office 2007). The burdens fall heaviest on education funding and schools (Ibid.). However, the results of the CBO study may be challenged on the grounds that it fails to account for property taxes and state income taxes that provide primary funding for schools. Also, it must be noted that many immigrants' children were born in the United States and therefore are U.S. citizens by birth. Finally, many negative externalities are borne by undocumented immigrants themselves who, for example, avoid reporting crime or seeking health care due to anxieties about putting their households at risk of deportation.

A more detailed study conducted by the Texas State Comptroller's office (2006) in the second-largest immigrant-receiving state, goes beyond the CBO approach of cost-benefit analysis in public service terms to the overall impact on economy. While acknowledging the burdens on local property taxpayers (in a state without a state income tax), the Comptroller's careful study shows that the overall state economy benefited by $17 billion due to the presence of undocumented immigrants. It must be noted that this study was released just a month after a highly contentious gubernatorial election with five candidates (in a plurality system) in which the State Comptroller was a candidate who echoed the same hard-line anti-immigrant border control message as her competitors. In elections with citizen-only voters, it is often convenient to scapegoat non-citizen populations.

The U.S. undergoes major immigration reforms every ten or twenty years, with minor reforms in between. The previously mentioned IRCA of 1986, developed during the Reagan administration in a bipartisan manner, provided both for amnesty if undocumented residents could show evidence of residency within a certain time period and, ostensibly, for employer sanctions if people are hired without legal authorization to work. This dramatic policy change was the first time that the principle of employer burdens had been established, with legal consequences. However, the enforcement of employer sanctions was extremely limited and underfunded. Moreover, in an advanced capitalist economy like the U.S., a cottage industry developed in false documents. "Market" solutions for policy failures had long been fine-tuned arts.

In 2000, with the simultaneous elections of Presidents Bush and Fox in the U.S. and Mexico, respectively, negotiations were in motion for a bilateral immigration approach. Such an approach was long overdue, given the importance of Mexico and the U.S. not only as major trading partners, but also as—in migration terms—the major sender and recipient countries in North America (see discussions in Castañeda 2007). However, with the tragedy of the attacks of September 11, 2001 (informally referred to as "9/11"), negotiations came to a halt, and the U.S. moved toward shoring up its borders and against pursuing immigrant-friendly policies. In fact, one and a half months after the incidents of September 11, President Bush brought security and immigration issues together in the Homeland Security Presidential Directive 2, "Combating Terrorism Through Immigration Policies," issued October 29, 2001. An era of sharp increases in border security budgets, staff, and harsh enforcement began. Irresponsible media commentators linked immigrants with terrorists in an atmosphere of public fear.

Military planning and institutions supplemented North American free trade cooperation in the name of the Security and Prosperity Partnership. The U.S. Northern Command (USNORTHCOM), created in October 2002, established a security space larger than North America, from the Caribbean to the Arctic Sea. After the Bush administration ended, the Partnership diminished, although the North American heads of state (Canada, Mexico, and the U.S.) meet annually at trilateral summits, the last of which took place in Guadalajara, Mexico in 2009. A North American Union (NAU) (see Staudt and Coronado 2002), complete with mobility for people and commerce, a common currency, and funding for pockets of poverty, seems distant. Obstacles remain, among them sovereignty concerns, high levels of inequality, and xenophobic racism. However, trade relations remain important, with militarized notions of security lurking in the background, from bilateral agreements between the U.S. and Canada to the Mérida Initiative between the U.S. and Mexico, which aims to supply technology and training to Mexico in its "War on Drugs" in the trilateral North American region.

Toward the end of his first term, President Bush favored a temporary guest worker program with revenue-generating fees and fines, and a bipartisan effort to support immigration reform was launched in the U.S. Senate under the McCain-Kennedy bill in 2004. Meanwhile, the extreme right wing of the Republican Party developed harsh anti-immigrant measures, authored by Wisconsin Congressman James Sensenbrenner and passed by the U.S. House of Representatives as H.R. 4437. More "politics of fear" took hold, the media lumping together crime, terror, and drugs and politicians using the large figure of 12 million undocumented immigrants to suggest that the U.S. could not control its borders. Sensenbrenner's bill not only called for deporting all undocumented immigrants, but also for penalizing those who assisted them. These threats to human rights and freedoms in themselves produced backlash, as large proportion of the public questioned the ever-growing intrusion of government into their daily lives and a possible police state atmosphere, perhaps resulting in the criminalization of teachers, non-profit staff, and clergy. An important political value remained: limited government intrusion into people's personal lives.

Business had substantial stakes in the large low-cost labor force immigrants provide. According to the U.S. Chamber of Commerce, which opposes extensive workplace enforcement,

"Experts estimate there may be as many as 10 million undocumented workers throughout the country who are working hard and performing tasks that most Americans take for granted but won't do themselves, in such industries as construction, landscaping, health care, restaurants and hotels and others. The combination of a need for workers and an inadequate immigration system has caused an unacceptable status quo. By not creating adequate legal avenues for hiring foreign workers and not addressing the status of workers already here, Congress and this administration are not fully safeguarding the economy for the future" (cited in Texas Conservative Coalition Research Institute 2007).

Currently, the U.S. Chamber of Commerce's position celebrates the contributions of immigrants to the U.S. economy and promotes immigration reform to include a pathway to legalization for law-abiding residents. It is critical of the current impasse, citing "delays, backlogs, and disruptions in our immigration and border management systems that impede the movement of legitimate cargo and travelers across U.S. borders."

After 2004 and especially 2008, partisan politics in the U.S. Congress became more polarized, and moderate Republicans and conservative Democrats aimed to assuage and appease the xenophobia in parts of the public and media, who were still smarting after the September 11 attacks. New York Senator Schumer's enforcement-oriented immigration reform bill of 2007 failed, but as Mexican, U.S.-based political scientist Jorge Castañeda notes, "once they were defeated, the concessions to the right wing remained and were put in effect, while the substance of the reforms disappeared" (Castañeda 2008: 131). The only congressional achievement of the era was the Secure Fence Act of 2007, authorizing the multi-billion dollar construction of nearly 700 miles of border wall, which turned out to be a boon to private, for-profit building and defense contractors, like the increased budgets for Department of Homeland Security to purchase surveillance equipment. Elsewhere, Staudt, Payan, and Dunn (2009) have analyzed the "Border Security Industrial Complex," (BSIC) developing the language from former President Eisenhower's parting warnings about the "military-industrial complex". U.S. militarization strategies offer a market niche for contracted enforcement and detention facilities while maintaining the appearance of limited government.

While segments of the economy, and certainly the security-oriented bureaucratic agencies, benefited from the fear and the ensuing budgetary increases and private contracts, it became clear that policy action was necessary. Under the harsh enforcement years since the September 11 attacks (and, some could argue, since the Immigration Reform and Control Act of 1986), many human rights abuses occurred, including deportations of non-criminals, workplace raids, a growth in for-profit detention facilities, family separations, and deaths in detention facilities (Staudt 2009). Valiant non-profit organizations filed charges and spread awareness of offenses, but human rights have little traction in U.S. domestic politics.

With the presidential and party transition that took place with the election of Obama in 2008, a new era began in 2009, as the U.S. economy started its slow recovery from recession and unemployment, yet continued the weary war economy, defense and related private contractor expenses. New political constituencies emerged, but immigration policy reform was put on hold while addressing the election priorities of bank and automobile industry restructuring, health-care policy reform, and the expansion of war on yet another front (Afghanistan), leaving immigration reform for 2010 or thereafter. It is up to the weak human rights and the strong business constituencies (the latter being reluctant to push immigration too visibly) to cultivate bipartisan support for immigration policy change.

Concluding Reflections

In the U.S. and Mexico, there is no single economic policy on which to focus. Rather, multiple economic policies have impacts on migration to the United States and on the extent to which ever-changing immigration laws are enforced. In this complex institutional and political environment, economic policies continue to attract and stimulate migration.

In this chapter, we have analyzed public policies that motivate Mexicans to migrate northward to the United States. There are more motivations for people to migrate than to stay: agrarian policies which render small-scale farming unviable, public investment that favors urban over rural areas, a lack of political will to collect taxes that redistribute income more fairly to ensure decent wages for the majority, and a lack of public security, coupled with dishonest and corrupt law enforcement institutions. Mexican immigrants seek to enter an economic system that draws them through a multiple set of attractive policies and practices: demand for labor, available jobs, unenforced employer sanctions, and limited government enforcement that favors business autonomy and allows people to live in the shadows, albeit with risks of deportation, detention, and family separation.

It has been possible for millions of migrants to settle in the United States and become lawful permanent residents. Many await an immigration reform that offers a pathway to citizenship or genuine economic development and institutional reforms in Mexico to enable their return. U.S. immigration policies represent a necessary, but insufficient deterrent to the northward movement of immigrants from Mexico. Control-oriented policies strengthen bureaucracies and their budgets but cannot totally regulate people's movement in face of the economic policies and practices stressed in this chapter.

The policies fail to solve problems. Policies are deeply rooted in the contexts of both states, in which seemingly irrational policies and practices emerge and sustain.

The most important policy recommendation from this analysis is to address the extreme inequalities within Mexico and between Mexico and the

United States. Thus, policy solutions would involve national, binational, and trilateral North American policy reform and transformation. As long as half or more of the Mexican population lives in poverty, higher wages will remain a magnet that draws people northward. The current minimum wage in Mexico is artificially low. Foreign investors are all too eager to take advantage of low labor costs, perhaps ready to relocate business to China and elsewhere if wages increase. However, the country's proximity to the U.S. and its population of 111 million end consumers are good reasons to raise Mexican minimum wages and the wages that North American-based global corporations pay in Mexico. The more Mexico is enabled to grow economically, with more equity, the greater the likelihood that Mexicans will avoid perilous journeys and a precarious life in fear as illegal workers in the United States.

In the U.S., business interests often prevail, regardless of which party is in power. The Council on Foreign Relations (2009) concludes that the ultimate security is economic prosperity, and public policies will emerge to enhance economic growth in North America. Time will tell whether political and institutional factors will continue the prevailing impasse in public policies that drives migrants and draws immigrants: the short-term benefits of low-cost and immigrant labor to U.S. corporations and the continuing delays in the Mexican government's efforts to reduce poverty, raise wages, and secure everyday safety for the country's citizens.

References

Anaya Muñoz, A. (2009): Mexico after the institutional revolutionary party. In: Forsythe, D. P (ed.): Encyclopedia of Human Rights, Vol. 3.

Barry, T. (2009): National security business on the border: Former border patrol chief Silvestre Reyes now a major player in new military, intelligence, and homeland security complex. [online] Available at: www.americaspolicy.org. [Accessed October 2009].

Castañeda, J. G. (2007): Ex-Mex: From migrants to immigrants. New York: The New Press.

Castañeda, J. G. (2008): Morning in Latin America: The chance for a new beginning. Foreign Affairs, 87, 5, pp.126-138.

Cornelius, W./Shirk, D. (2007): Reforming the Administration of Justice in Mexico. Notre Dame: University of Notre Dame Press.

Council on Foreign Relations (2009): U.S. Immigration Policy. Independent Task Force Report No. 63: Jeb Bush and Thomas F. McLarty III. New York: Council on Foreign Relations.

Delano, A. (2006): De la „no intervención" a la institucionalización: la evolución de las relaciones estado-diáspora en el caso mexicano. In: Gutiérrez, C. G. (ed.):

Relaciones estado-diáspora: perspectivas de América Latina y el Caribe. Mexico City: Miguel Ángel Porrúa.
Escobar Lapatí, A./Roberts, B. (1991): Urban stratification, the middle classes and economic change in Mexico. In: González de la Rocha, M./Escobar Latapí, A. (eds.): Social responses to Mexico's econoomic crisis of the 1980s. La Jolla: Center for U.S.-Mexican Studies.
Federal Electoral Institute (IFE). [online] Available at: www.ife.org.mx [Accessed March 2, 2011].
Franko, P. M. (1999): The puzzle of Latin American economic development. New Jersey: Rowman & Littlefield.
Frederick S. Pardee Center for the Study of the Longer-Range Future (2009): The future of North American trade policy: Lessons from NAFTA. Center Task Force Report, No. 1, November 2009. University of Boston. [online] Available at: www.bu.edu/pardee/task-force-report-nafta [Accessed January 11, 2010].
García, Brigada (1988): Desarrollo Económico y Abstracción de Fuerza de México: 1950-1980. Mexico City: El Colegio de México.
Gregory, P. (1985): The Myth of Market Marginality. Baltimore: Johns Hopkins Press.
Immervoll, H. (2007): Minimum wages, minimum labour costs and the tax treatment of low-wage employment. Discussion Paper No. 2555. Bonn: Institute for the Study of Labor (IZA).
Kraft, M. E./Furlong, S. R. (2010): Public policy: politics, analysis, and alternatives. Washington, D.C.: CQ Press.
Loaeza, S. (2006): Los problemas de la consolidación política en México. In: Randal, L. (ed.): Reinventar México: estructuras en proceso de cambio. Perspectiva política, cocial y económica. Mexico City: Siglo XXI.
Lomelí, P. G. (2007): Plan Nacional de Desarrollo. Dossier. Revita Bien Común 150, Junio.
Magaloni, B. (2005): The demise of Mexico's one-party dominant regime: Elite choices and the masses in the establishment of democracy. In: Mainwaring, S./ Hagopian, F. (eds.): The third wave of democratization in Latin America: Advances and setbacks. Cambridge: Cambridge University Press.
Malkin, E. (2009): Nafta's Promise, Unfulfilled. In: New York Times, March 24, A1, 4.
Mayer-Sierra, C. E. (2006): Cambios en los factores determinantes de las políticas tributarias. In: Randall, L. (ed.): Reinventar México: Estructuras en proceso de cambio. Perspectiva política, social y económica. Mexico City: Siglo XXI.
Mesa Lago, C. (1977): Modelos de seguridad social en América Latina. Estudio comparativo. Buenos Aires: Ediciones SIAP.
Migration Policy Institute (2008): State Responses to Immigration: A Database of All State Legislation. [online] Available at: www.migrationpolicy.org. [Accessed June 10, 2008].
Miker Palafox, M. (2010): Global production and precarious labor: Harness production in Ciudad Juárez. In: Staudt, K./Fuentes, C./Monárrez, J. E. (eds.): Cities and citizenship at the U.S.-Mexico border: The Paso del Norte metropolitan region. New York: Palgrave Macmillan.
Morret Sánchez, J. C. (2003): Reforma agraria: del latifundio al neoliberalismo. Mexico City: Plaza y Valdés.

Oliveira, O./Roberts, B. R. (1994): Urban growth and social structure in Latin America, 1930–1990. In: Bethell, L. (ed.): Cambridge History of Latin America, Vol VI. Cambridge: Cambridge University Press.
Orrenius, P. M. (2006): La emigración de México a Estados Unidos efectos económicos e impacto en la política. In: Randall, L. (de): Reinventar México: Estructuras en proceso de cambio. Perspectiva política, social y económica. Mexico City: Siglo XXI.
Paterson, K. (2009): The Mounting Brain Drain. Frontera News Service (March 9, 2009).
Payan, T. (2006): The three U.S.-Mexico border wars: Drugs, violence, and homeland security. New York: Praeger.
Pew Hispanic Center (2006): The size and characteristics of the unauthorized migrant population in the U.S.: Estimates based on the March 2005 Current Population Survey. [online] Available at: http://www.pewhispanic.org/files/reports/6I.pdf [Accessed November 7, 2007].
Przeworki, A. (1998): El estado y el ciudadano. In: Política y gobierno 5, 2 (Spring).
Randall, L. (2006): México se reinventa. In Randal, L. (ed.): Reinventar México: Estructuras en proceso de cambio. Perspectiva política, social y económica. Mexico City: Siglo XXI.
Roberts, B./Escobar Latapí, A. (1997): Mexican social and economic policy and emigration. In: Bean, F. D. et al. (eds): At the crossroads: Mexican migration and U.S. policy. New Jersey: Rowman & Littlefield, pp. 47-78.
Smith, P. H. (2005): Democracy in Latin America: Political change in comparative perspective. New York. Oxford University Press.
State of Texas (2006). Undocumented immigrants in Texas: A financial analysis of the impact to the state budget and economy. Austin: Comptroller of Public Accounts. [online] Available at: www.cpa.state.tx.us [Accessed September 2010].
Staudt, K. (2009): Violence at the border: Broadening the discourse to include feminism, human security, and deeper democracy. In: Staudt, K./Fuentes,C./Monárrez, J. E. (eds.): Cities and citizenship at the U.S.-Mexico border: The Paso del Norte metropolitan region. New York: Palgrave Macmillan, pp.1–27.
Staudt, K./Capps, R. (2004): Con la ayuda de dios? El Pasoans manage the 1996 welfare and immigration law reforms. In: Kretsedemas, P./Aparicio, A. (eds.): Immigration welfare reform and the poverty of policy. Westport, CT: Greenwood.
Staudt, K. /Fuentes, C. /Monárrez, J. E. (2010): Cities and citizenship at the U.S.-Mexico border: The Paso del Norte metropolitan region. New York: Palgrave.
Staudt, K./Payan, T./Dunn, T. (2009): Closing reflections: Bordering human rights, social democratic feminism, and broad-based security. In: Staudt, K./Payan, T. /Kruszewski, Z. A. (eds.): Human Rights Along the U.S.-Mexico Border: Gendered Violence and Insecurity. Tucson: University of Arizona Press, pp. 185-202.
Staudt, K./Payan, T./Kruszewski, Z. A. (2009): Human rights along the U.S.-Mexico border: Gendered violence and insecurity. Tucson: University of Arizona Press.
Stone, D. (1997): Policy paradox: The art of political decision-making. New York: W. W. Norton.
Texas Conservative Coalition Research Institute (2007): State approaches to illegal immigration. Updated following the 80th Texas Legislature.

Transparency International (2009): Corruption Perceptions Index 2009. [online] Available at: media.transparency.org/imaps/cpi2009 [Accessed February 15, 2010].
United Nations Development Programme (2009): Human Development Report. New York: Oxford University Press.
UNPAN: Basic Data on Government Expenditure and Taxation (1990-2002). [online] Available at: www.unpan.org/tabid/456/ItemID/181/language/en-US/Default.aspx [Accessed February 14, 2011].
U.S. Congressional Budget Office (2007): The Impact of Unauthorized Immigrants on the Budgets of State and Local Governments. Washington, D.C.: CBO.
U.S. Chamber of Commerce: Immigration. [online] Available at: www.uschamber.com/issues/index/immigration/default. [Accessed December 20, 2009].
U.S. Department of Homeland Security (2007): Estimates of the legal permanent resident population in 2007. Office of Immigration Statistics.
U.S. Department of Homeland Security (2008): Estimates of the unauthorized immigrant population residing in the United States: January 2008. Office of Immigration Statistics.
Zepeda, E./Wise, T. A./Gallagher, K. P. (2009): Rethinking trade policy for development: Lessons from Mexico under NAFTA.
Carnegie Endowment for International Peace. [online] Available at: carnegieendowment.org/files/nafta_trade_development.pdf [Accessed January 11, 2010].

Part Three: “Illegality” Discourses and Spaces of the Political

Caught in Mobility: An Ethnographic Analysis of the Context of Knowledge Production on Migration in Southeast Europe

Sabine Hess

The Production of the Transit Migration Dispositif

At the beginning of the new millennium, the countries of Southeast Europe were not only one of the hot spots of international migration to Northern and Western Europe, they also became destinations for migrants themselves (Icduygu 2003). Even so, public and political attention in the European Union has focused primarily on undocumented so-called transit migrants who are usually portrayed as single young males entering the country irregularly, basically left at the mercy of people smugglers and forced to work in the illegal labor market (Icduygu 2003; IOM, 1995). Political efforts by the EU to create more effective policies to protect its outer borders have invariably been directed at this particular category of migrants. During the EU summit in Seville in 2002, the EU even threatened Turkey with sanctions, if the government did not take more serious actions to combat undocumented transit migration (Hess/Karakayali 2007). Now, following the analytical finding of the "mixed nature of the new migration flows" (Van Hear et. al. 2009: 6f.), the EU's political efforts tend to aim at placing anonymous transit migrants into the distinct political categories of asylum seekers, solicited labor migrants, victims of trafficking, and irregular migrants, the latter of these groups, in particular, being associated with illicit migration projects in line with the EU (im)migration policies. Due to their diffuse, blurred, and unknown nature (in regard to time and space) and their presumed intention to migrate further north or west, transit migrants appear to be one of the most sought-after groups. This concerns academic migration research on the new European border regions, as well as the border control system and its "will to knowledge," to use a Foucauldian phrase describing the interrelation of the new modes of governance and knowledge production (Foucault 2004). Based on the critical analyses of contemporary maps of illegal immigration by the Canadian political scientist William Walters, this could even be considered as "the birth of something new—a dispositif formed around the time, space, economy and culture of transit" (Walters 2009: 25).

This article attempts to develop a different analytical perspective on this topic, focusing on the political and scientific context and conditions of knowledge production with respect to (transit) migration processes. Specifically, the article starts with a reflection on the particular context and conditions of knowledge production we found in Turkey in 2002, when we started our two-year research project "Transit Migration" (2007), an interdisciplinary research project which ran from 2001 to 2004, focusing on the Europeanization of migration policies and, particularly, the formation of the European border regime in Southeast Europe, specifically Turkey, Greece, and the Balkans. In the course of our research project we were faced with various problems, some of them unexpected, first and foremost being the fact that at that time the category of transit migrants did not exist in the public discourse on migration in Turkey and therefore was not regarded as a problem. This situation emphasized the political importance of knowledge production in the area of transit migration and was a decisive factor for us to develop our specific approach called "ethnographic regime analysis," which will be explained in detail below. This analysis clearly shows that the context of the implementation of the EU migration policies in Turkey is characterized by a multitude of different national and international, governmental, intergovernmental, and private actors who try to reach consensus concerning the fact that migration needs to be regulated. The article will show that this is mainly done based on a specific discursive and knowledge-based policy. The overall aim of this analysis is to evaluate the scientific usefulness of the concept of transit migrants.

By drawing on our ethnographic insights into the biographies and strategies of migrants, the article concludes with another analytical conceptual suggestion. Particularly against the background of the recent debate in (radical) geography on global processes of reterritorialization and restructuration of socioeconomic and political/institutional spaces in the age of globalization (Brenner 1997), the article argues for the concept of "precarious transit zones". These transit zones are to be understood as the conflict-ridden products of the practices of both migrants and the European border regime. By drawing on the constructivist understanding of the border regime as developed during "Transit Migration"—as opposed to theorizations of the border as a purely exclusionist political mechanism—, the border regime is defined as a catalyst in a new zoning of territories, economies, rights, and subjectivities. Thus, the paper also shows that the transit policies of the EU cause certain boomerang effects as the newly labeled "transit countries" learn to use this categorization for their own power games.

"Transit Migration": An Ethnographic Regime Analysis

"Transit Migration" was an interdisciplinary research and exhibition project conducted as part of a national exhibition entitled "Project Migration", which was held in Cologne, Germany in 2005 to celebrate the 50th anniversary of the first guest-worker contract with Italy (Kölnischer Kunstverein 2005; www.transitmigration.org). Being a group of political scientists, sociologists, cultural anthropologists, and artists, interdisciplinarity was both a curse and a blessing when we started to construct our multi-sited research project on the Europeanization of migration policy. Specifically, we wanted to study the new migration realities on the southeastern fringes of Europe, in Turkey, Greece, and the Balkans. As cultural anthropologists, we first tried to convince the participants from the other disciplines of the advantages of our ethnographical, actor-centered research approach, which we deemed best suited to bring home the vibrant picture of migrant agency and subjectivity—an imagery we thought would work best to dispel the misconceptions of the hegemonic narrative of plight, victimhood, and dead bodies washed ashore on the Mediterranean coasts, which still dominates public debate. However, bewildered by our "nosing around" in the inner city areas of Istanbul, Athens, and Belgrade in an attempt to track the movements of migrants, the political scientists and sociologists tried to shift our analytical focus to the political discourses and the institutional and programmatic settings which they expected to find in Brussels, Berlin and on the Internet. In short: due to problems with the mainstream theorizations of the European border regime—particularly with those exclusively emphasizing its restrictive and repressive aspects—and unexpected developments during the course of our field research, we tried to combine all of these in an approach for which we coined the term "ethnographic regime analysis".

Our theoretical starting point was the fact that the erection of metaphorical and physical walls in Europe and elsewhere[1] did not seem to hinder migration movements. Despite the massive reinforcement of the borders of the EU and its member states in recent years, migration nevertheless occurred and still occurs today, altering the socioeconomic geography of border zones, urban areas, and the cultural fabric of societies. Against this background, our research project attempts to analyze the Europeanization of migration policy, specifically the formation of the European border regime, by using an approach which considers this Europeanization as a social, conflictual process of negotiation on diverse scales and with a multitude of actors involved (Transit Migration Forschungsgruppe 2007). In this context, we preferred the concept of "migration regime" over the classical system theories because it allowed us to include a multitude of actors whose practices relate to each other but are not ordered in the form of a central logic or rationality. Thus, using the term "regime" makes it possible to understand regulation as an ef-

1 For example, along the Rio Grande on the US-Mexican border, between Saudi Arabia and Yemen, Saudi Arabia and Iraq, Costa Rica and Nicaragua, India and Pakistan (through Kashmir), the Kingdom of Bhutan and India, and between Israel and Palestine.

fect of social practices, rather than presupposing it in a functionalist manner. The concept of "regime", then, implies a space of conflict and negotiation. By using this term, we also took the concept of practice seriously, in that we applied a practice-orientated understanding of policy in line with the latest approaches of the anthropology of the state (Trouillot 2001; Sharma/Gupta 2006). Aware of the gap between theory (academic papers and action plans) and practice (the implementation of such action plans), we tried to find ways to localize the Europeanization processes and analyze the actors, practices, technologies, and discourses involved in the process in specific social situations, which included using the method of participant observation.

Working as a team, we were able to apply an approach of "multi-sited ethnography" (Marcus 1995), thus covering not only different countries in Southeast Europe but also different social and local settings. This allowed us to work with a high level of cross-national comparison. "Multi-sited ethnography," as defined in Marcus' seminal study, was a very suitable operationalization of our regime approach. He described it as a radical, constructivist (1995: 105), theoretically driven but also imaginative "exercise in mapping terrain" (Ibid.: 99). His constructivist reformulation of the object of study—the "field", in anthropological terms—not as a pre-given, but emerging in the process of research (also understood as an imaginative practice) suited our analytical task to redefine the concept of "border" as a space of negotiation of diverse actors. This operationalization also involved a diagonal research orientation, as opposed to the classical dichotomies of micro versus macro, structure vs. agency, and bottom-up vs. top-down. The social anthropologists Cris Shore and Susan Wright have called this diagonal approach "studying through", that is, "tracing the ways in which the different actors, discourses or technologies create new webs and relations of power" (Shore/Wright 1997: 14).

Against the background of these general methodological and theoretical remarks, we drew on critical theories of bordering (Lahav/Guiraudon 2000; Guiraudon 2001; Walters 2002; Bigot/Guild 2003; Rigo 2005). Given that these researchers no longer conceive of (the European) borders as continuous lines, but as fragmented, diffused, stretched, and highly stratified "border zones", we had to abandon the concept of "walls" and similar metaphors for borders (Andreas/Snyder 2000) in favor of a concept that defines borders as structurally perforated systems or regimes. However, this process of border displacement and externalization should not be understood as a sovereign act whereby states extend power or competence based on an abstract claim for hegemony and control; rather, it has to be conceptualized as an effect and result of struggles, where the regime of mobility control is itself challenged and driven by fluid, clandestine, multidirectional, and context-dependent forms of mobility (Sciortino 2004). At first glance, this may seem like the kind of attempt to glorify migrant ruses and tactics that is often found in transnational studies on migrant practices, defining transnational space as a "counter-hegemonic space of resistance" (Appadurai 2000)[2]. However, understanding migration as a movement that possesses knowledge, follows its own rules, and collectively organizes its own praxis is a central epistemological starting point for us to theorize on the border regime. This, we hoped, would allow us to develop a theory of the border regime that no longer conceptualizes the movement of migration as the poor or heroic "other" of the border policies, but instead considers it to be a central immanent driving and structuring force (Hess/Tsianos/Karakayali 2009).

This article draws on this theorization and research experience in three ways. First, the ethnographic regime analysis which examined the various actors, discourses, and practices concerned with governing migration[3] was beneficial in that it highlighted the construction of what could be called the "transit migration management dispositif". Thus, this is an approach which includes, in a reflexive way, the condition of its own knowledge production, which will be outlined below. Second, our ethnographic approach is interested not only in the migrant narratives and biographies, but also in their role as a central source of situated theorization from the perspective of migration. Therefore, the second part of the article is focused on using the migrant narratives to develop the concept of "precarious transit zones". Third, in the conclusion of this article we will comment on our constructivist and productive understanding of the European border regime as a "space-producing policy", in line with the theorization of rescaling by radical geography, as mentioned above.

---

2 Transnational migration studies were of great importance to us because they focused on the trajectories of migrants and their strategies in coping with border realities. However, many of these studies regard transnational migration strategies as creative resistance against the restrictive migration policies of EU member states. This implies an understanding of the border regime as an exclusionist project that is bound to fail. We think this concept fails to recognize the productive dimension of the border regime (Hess 2005; Transit Migration Forschungsgruppe 2007).

3 These categories were also the organizing categories of our "virtual cartographies of European migration governance", abbreviated as "MigMap", which contain four analytical artistic maps of the actors, main discourses, routes/histories, and practices of the European border regime. "MigMap" was one of the main results of the close cooperation between art and cultural production and science. For further information, see www.transitmigration.org/migmap/home_map1.html.

Migration Policy in Turkey: The Context of Knowledge Production

Foucault's reflections on the interrelation of power and knowledge clearly show that the scientific practices of naming and conceptualizing are not innocent but have far-reaching objectifying effects, particularly so in the highly politicized field of migration. In this regard, the situation in the years 2001 and 2002 was the perfect setting for our research. This period, which can be described as the globalization of migration management rationality[4] (see critical remarks by Düvell 2002; IOM 2004), was one of the rare historical occurrences when cross-border movements of people had not yet been perceived as an issue and therefore had not yet become objects of governance.

When we started our research in 2001, hardly anyone in Turkey seemed to understand what we wanted to accomplish, which was to do research on the lives and strategies of international migrants traversing these countries on their way to Europe. In fact, we made so many unsuccessful attempts to explain our research interest that we began to feel as if we were hunting a ghost. But we had already seen many of these migrants in the inner city areas of Istanbul and in the so-called reception camps on the Greek islands in the Aegean Sea. It was not until we told people that we wanted to do research on *mülteciler* (the Turkish word for "refugees") that they suddenly became interested in our project and started to give us useful advice. This initial communication problem was neither due to our scientific jargon nor to a lack of knowledge among the people we talked to. Rather, it was simply due to the fact—and this is particularly interesting from an epistemological point of view—that the codified category now known as "transit migrants" did not exist in the public discourse in Turkey and was only marginally used in scientific debate at that time. It was only during the course of our research and due to a specific political process that this discursive figure was introduced. It emerged in the context of the period of Turkey's EU pre-accession since 2000 with the *Accession Partnership Document* (APD), which forced Turkey, among other things, to implement the so-called Schengen acquis without a clear prospect of proper accession negotiations (Kirisci 2003: 80).

One of the first organizations to commission studies on the subject was the International Organization for Migration (IOM), one of the globally leading agencies in the field of migration management (Düvell 2002; MigMap

4 The globalization of the "migration management rationality" is best exemplified in the global range of activities of the International Organization of Migration itself, the major globally active intergovernmental organization in the field of migration, which was one of the driving forces behind the formulation of the policy of "migration management" (IOM 2004). Another important example of the globalization of this rationality is the establishment of the Global Commission on International Migration by the UN in 2005.

Actors 2009). These studies provided estimates, statistical data, and information on central routes which are still referred to in more recent research projects and country information sheets (IOM 1995; Icduygu 2003; Hess/Karakayali 2007). In providing scientific evidence to the EU, these studies were significant milestones towards the recognition of Turkey as a major transit country, in that they included a vividly detailed description of the social realities behind the term "transit country", specifically the variety of migrant practices, the social and kin networks involved, the people smuggling industry, the dangers of trafficking, and the situation of the vast illegal labor market in the big cities of western Turkey. But there is also an institutional/power side to the studies because they helped the IOM to recommend itself to the EU Commission as the second leading migration management organization in Turkey (next to UNHCR). At that time, the EU Commission was about to introduce the Schengen regulations, "help" to set up institutions, codify law and train Turkish personnel, all of which are classic aspects of capacity building programs. UNHCR, with its long history of working in Turkey and a fairly clearly defined policy on asylum procedures[5], was a natural partner organization for the EU, not only in developing specific training programs, but also, in respect to public discourse, in raising awareness for the need to act along with the European asylum regulations (Hess/Karakayali 2007).

As a result, the UNHCR and the asylum discourse were able to find a material basis in the existing (albeit tiny) field of human rights activism. On a related note, IOM first had to set the migration management agenda and build up consensus on the issue of irregular transit migration. It did so by trying to describe irregular transit migration as a security issue, focusing on the irregularity of the majority of migrants and the people smuggling rackets. Richard Black, in his critical reading of IOM's scientific contribution, concludes that "they generally tended to emphasize the organization's public concerns with the link between migration and organized crime, drug-running and prostitution" (2003: 43). This, as Black and other critical researchers such as Didier Bigo and Elspeth Guild (2005) have observed, "reflects a wider literature that has placed the study on illegal migration firmly within a security framework—exactly where states themselves prefer to see it" (Black 2003: 43). However, throughout our research we had the impression that IOM did not really succeed with this kind of problematization because informality was already a central feature of the Turkish labor market and the right-wing nationalist discourses have always been focused on internal threats. The other, more successful discursive strategy employed by IOM was

5 For further reading on Turkish asylum policy, see Kirisci (2003).

to label human trafficking[6] the ultimate human rights violation in the area of irregular migration. Here, IOM was able to mobilize the support of NGOs.[7]

This knowledge practice of IOM in the case of Turkey shows that the governance of migration is deeply bound up with the problem of knowing and categorizing it and conceptualizing it as a problem. Foucault (2004), among others, has described this problem as a general, central scheme at the core of the new art of governance, which he defined as "biopower" (Pieper/Karakayali/Tsianos 2007). The term "biopower" denotes the change of objectives of the modern state power by increasingly addressing every sphere of life and the entire population of a national territory in a caring, activating and optimizing way in order to accumulate wealth. The political scientists William Walters and Sandro Mezzadra have extended this argument to include the EU's specific mode of governance of migration, which they define as "domopolitics" (Walters 2004; Mezzadra 2009). The neologism "domopolitics" is derived from the Latin verb *domare*, meaning "to tame" or "to domesticate". According to Walters and Mezzadra, this term best describes the rationality of the EU migration policy, which does not attempt "to arrest mobility, but to tame it" (Mezzadra 2009: 218), to strategically use mobility and immobility, which is not to say that migrants should be stopped or excluded, as has often been claimed, rather that they should be included in a highly selective manner. We argue that this type of policy needs equivalent new modes of knowledge production, in short, a new way of "knowledge governance".

One central characteristic of this new knowledge governance is the increasing diffusion and dissolution of the boundaries between scientific and applied research and its political application, following the increased activities of the research departments of operational institutions such as the European border control agency Frontex, IOM, the Vienna-based International Centre for Policy Development (ICMPD), and the German Federal Office for Migration and Refugees in connection with IMISCOE and other joint scientific research projects. Another characteristic is the increased importance of what we would like to call "intermediary" knowledge processing agencies, such as IOM, ICMPD, and other national private or semi-private, state-run think tanks within the migration management architecture (Georgi 2007),

---

6 That was the second area on which IOM commissioned research, which was conducted by the Turkish social scientist Sema Erder. However, IOM eventually removed the study from its website because, as the author told us in an interview, it was not in line with the rationalities of IOM, which in her case meant that she had failed to describe Turkey as a hot spot of trafficking, a claim she found herself unable to substantiate.

7 It is interesting to note that the two leading discourses the EU used to introduce and legitimize the implementation of its border regime in Turkey were both in the language of "human rights". In this study, the constitutive discourses of the contemporary border regime were mapped based on MigMap Discourses (2009).

"intermediary" referring to their specific strategic orientation in terms of their practices and image policies within the multi-level governance of migration. This qualifies them to advise states and bring them together through conferences and seminars. By the same token, these organizations are able to approach NGOs to draw on their knowledge and facilitate cooperation with state institutions on issues such as counter-trafficking and asylum policy (Hess 2009).

The problem of knowledge production on migration as a central basis for policy regulation has been exacerbated even more since the introduction of the new EU migration policy, the European Commission's "Global Approach to Migration" (Commission of the European Union 2007). Its new central governing logic of the "migratory routes concept", in particular, leads to a global geographical extension of the EU migration policy. The control and knowledge of migratory routes traversing the entire African continent and the former Soviet republics have been identified as the key issue of new migration governance. Thus, the Commission Communication of 2007 states: "However, applying the Global Approach to the Eastern and South-Eastern regions neighbouring the EU according to the concept of 'migratory routes' also requires consideration of countries of origin and transit further afield" (Commission of the European Union 2007). Therefore, the definition of a space as "transit" is coupled with a reduction of state sovereignty and renders the space as an object of risk analysis conducted by such diverse agencies as the EU, Europol, the United Nations Office on Drugs and Crime (UNODC) and Frontex, the latter being authorized to initiate and legitimize specific interventions, as its operations along the coast of Senegal show. In this process the definition of "risk" has changed; since the porosity of the border is taken into account, it is no longer the act of crossing the border itself that is the object of governance, but rather the movement itself which, as can clearly be seen in the new so-called i-Map, an interactive map of migration routes focusing on the African continent originally developed by ICMPD, Europol, and Frontex (i-Map 2009)[8]. In the above-cited Commission Communication, the increased need for knowledge production is described as follows: "In applying the Global Approach, a comprehensive analysis is required of legal and illegal movements, global labour supply and demand, labour migration and the management of economic migration, and the need for international protection. Migratory routes, trends and potential changes of routes also need to be examined" (Commission of the European Union 2007).

Given this structural background, this power-knowledge relation must be the top priority on the research agenda of transit migration. In sharp contrast

---

8 A very interesting subject to analyze is the future development of the i-Map, now that more and more organizations such as UNODC and UNHCR and several countries have joined the project and the geographic scope is about to be broadened to also cover Eurasia and Southeast Europe.

to this increased political focus on undocumented "transit migration" are the rather vague, blurred and diffuse social realities that lie behind this term. Indeed, while conducting research for our "Transit Migration" project and visting the main migrational quarters of Istanbul—places where diverse migration strategies overlap—it became unclear to us as to which of the migrants we spoke with could actually be categorized as transit migrants. The next section will introduce an alternative analytical suggestion of how reflexive social and cultural science research on transit migration can use its empirical insights. In it, we will argue against a reproduction of the governmental logic of categorizing and defining the movements of migration during and after of our research project and instead call for a reflexive twist of our analysis to scrutinize the constitution of the border-knowledge regime itself.

Precarious Transit Zones: "Caught in Mobility"

Starting the theorization from the perspective of migration means trying to meet the migrants in their daily lives and listening carefully to their narratives. These encounters with numerous migrants in Istanbul, along the Aegean coast, and in the Greek and Serbian metropolises showed that it is quite impossible to give a precise definition of the term "transit migrants" with respect to time and space. What we encountered in our multi-sited ethnography and during our cross-national comparison were precarious temporary settlement and increased circulation in the wider border regions.

Given this, it is safe to say that crossing another border definitely does not change the status of a transit migrant. Most migrants we met in Southeast Europe had to cross several borders as irregular migrants, almost all of them impoverished *sans papiers*, who were forced to travel on the ground[9]. As is often the case, some of the migrants we met in Istanbul had crossed the same border several times, repeatedly crossing the border to Greece and being sent back by the Greek border guards. Others told us of a bewildering zigzag trajectory, moving to and fro through the entire region from Syria to Eastern Europe and even the Caucasus countries further beyond. Many have attempted it repeatedly, traveling for months which stretched into years as people were deported or clandestinely pushed back over one of the national borders at night—which, incidentally, seemed to be a common practice among Turkish border guards at the Syrian border—but the migrants still keep trying.

Others reported that while in transit they heard rumors that a law had changed or a new reception camp had been built somewhere, which would at least promise rest, food, shelter, and perhaps an opportunity to finally obtain

9 This social fact has produced a specific bias in our sample.

legal status. Yet even the Dublin Convention, the SIS System, and the third-country regulation, all of which were originally intended to immobilize this movement, had the opposite effect. For example, very few people we met in the Greek reception camps were applying for asylum, simply because they knew that they would not be able to travel on if they did. With no other alternative, they opted for irregularity, which in effect meant that after three months in a camp they were given a release permit requiring them to leave the country within two weeks in a "direction of their own choice". We interpreted this policy as a catalyst of irregularization and transit migration, but not as a means to stop the movements (Panagiotidis/Tsianos 2007).

But settlement and forms of (social and economic) integration cannot be understood as the opposite of being in transit. Rather, the meaning of being in transit is extended to pending, suspended forms of transit existence or, to put it another way, to precarious provisional forms of settlement. For example, when we spoke with Ali[10] from Iran nothing hinted at a transit existence. He knew Russian very well, so he was able to sell textile products to Russian cross-border traders, who have been coming to Laleli, a district of Istanbul, by the hundreds since the end of the Cold War to buy and sell products on the local markets. During his transit trip Ali had fallen in love with a Moldavian women who commuted between Iran and Turkey as a domestic migrant worker. Ali and his Moldavian wife decided that, for the time being, Turkey would be the best compromise for both of them. But Ali had not forgotten that he was actually still in transit, on his way to his uncles in Sweden and that if an opportunity presented itself he would use it. So, he lived his life in constant interim arrangements, a phenomenon we know from the studies on the early years of the guest-worker system in Germany. He apparently felt most at home in the highly globalized context of his textile shop, where he was desperately needed because of his language skills, so he felt very secure, despite the fact that he was irregular.

Another case of precarious settlement suddenly turning into a new phase of transit was that of Rahman, whom we met at an UNHCR asylum camp in the outskirts of Belgrade. Unlike Ali, he had thought that he really had settled down in Belgrade with his Bosnian girlfriend and their little child. From a legal standpoint, they were living in highly precarious circumstances, yet they still somehow felt at home until Rahman was arrested in a sweeping series of raids following the assassination of Zoran Djindjić, the former President of Serbia, in 2000. These raids led to the arrest of so-called terrorists as well as many migrants without proper documents. Not being lawfully married to his girlfriend, Rahman's only chance to get out of the deportation prison—which was only recently opened thanks to IOM—was to apply for asylum, which he had not actually wanted to do. He had to stay at the camp for several months while his application was being processed. When we met

[10] All names are aliases.

him he told us that most of his fellow detainees had already left the camp on their own and moved on because the situation was unbearable. He actually considered doing the same, the only problem being that he still had personal ties to Belgrade.

The third category of precarious sedentary or pending transit existence is the traditional one, where migrants continually try to travel on but end up in one or another of the large cities in Southeast Europe and their informal economies for ten years or more (see also Bas 2005). Mike, one of the African migrants we met in Istanbul, stayed there for 11 years after having lived in Lebanon for a while. With the beginning of the civil war Lebanon was getting too "hot", so he and a friend decided to move on. They came to Turkey via Syria with only €2,000 to their name. After several attempts to get to the north—with fake passports and visas to Poland and Hungary which were rather costly—they ran out of money. The money black irregular migrants could earn with odd jobs in the informal economy was barely enough to survive. Mike was arrested several times, but each time was able to escape, depending on luck, money or some ruse or other[11]. We met him shortly after his release from arrest after having been caught traveling on a minibus close to the Aegean coast. At that time, he was trying to set up a small business with reggae music, using the latest tourist hype in Istanbul. Although he seemed to feel quite at home there, he described his situation highly metaphorically as being "caught in mobility". Or, as he said on another occasion: "Europe is a great prison."

Considering these diverse ethnographic, biographical accounts, we found it very hard to define which of these individuals should be regarded as transit migrants, asylum seekers or labor migrants. However, what the various unsteady, non-linear, flexible, and mobile migration biographies did show was the emergence of a highly "precarious transit zone"[12]. The production of such a precarious transit zone can be understood as a spatialized social effect of the EU border regime, but also as an effect of the migrants' own objectives and strategies: to exploit informal labor markets and make use of networks or nodes of migration-related knowledge and communication and transport technologies. In sharp contrast to the intended function of tightening border control, the European border regime, as we have seen, does not stop the

---

11 A few examples: One day, the whole group of arrested migrants feigned serious illness. After one ill migrant had already died in police custody, all the others were released. On another occasion, he told officials that he was married to a pregnant migrant woman, who was also bein held in custody. Since the police did not want to keep pregnant women in custody, he was released.

12 This interpretation is consistent with the notion of the construction of a "buffer zone" (Wallace/Sidorenko 1999) as transit countries turn into indefinite waiting rooms for migrants due to the externalization of the European border regime. However, the term buffer zone again implies the immobilization of the movements, which, as we intend to demonstrate, is not the case.

movements; in fact, it keeps people caught in mobility and transforms border regions into zones of increased circulation. What the border regime actually does is restrict the social, economic, and political rights of migrants, thus irrationalizing peoples' movements as it is interrupting their plans and is re-directing the trajectories of their movements. This description is consistent with theories of global restructuration and rescaling of economic and political processes of regulation (Brenner 1997; Ferguson/Gupta 2005), which, in the last 200 years[13], have manifested themselves in the form of the nation states. At present, in reaction to different processes of globalization resulting from the (obviously unstoppable) migration movements, the European border regime seems to be accelerating a process of fragmentation and stratified zoning of what was once, in regard to the application and articulation of rights, consistently thought of as national territory. Vivid examples of this form of zoning in Germany are the establishment of local "exterritorial holes" as part of the widely used "airport procedure" for asylum seekers and the extended definition of "border zone", which may include train stations and federal highways where border police have special rights to check documents. It can also mean regional constructions, such as the protection zone in Northern Iraq or even the establishment of national protectorates like Kosovo. In the area of migration, the policy of zoning is also reflected in the political construction of "transit countries" and "transit routes", as just shown, which are then subjected to a whole range of special control programs and technologies, which result in new forms of reduced or transnationalised state sovereignty (Ong 2005).

This must be linked with a discussion on new modes of citizenship; Aihwa Ong (1999) notes a highly hierarchical form of "flexible citizenship" as a corresponding form to this spatial rationality, while Etienne Balibar prognoses a new "European apartheid" in which some inhabitants of the EU have no political and social rights whatsoever, as is already the case with illegalized migrants (Balibar 2005). Based on her research on the development strategies of South Asian countries like Indonesia and Malaysia, Ong also describes the process of zoning, generally speaking, as a new mode of neoliberal governance, demonstrating how these countries try to become competitive on a global scale by establishing a specific mix of governmental practice and forms of repression of various segments of their populations:

> "In both cases [of Indonesia and Malaysia; S. H.], governments have become flexible in their management of sovereignty, so that different production sites vary in their mix of legal protection, controls, and repressive regimes. Citizens in zones that are differently articulated to global production and financial circuits are subjected to different kinds of

---

[13] Brenner also mentions a new "glocal state" as an effect of these processes of reterritorialization. The state does not vanish; rather, it is redimensioned and reterritorialized on various scales which no longer conform to the national framework nor form a homogeneous enclosed national totality (Brenner 1997: 17).

surveillance, and in practice enjoy different sets of civil, political, and economic rights" (2005: 94).

This policy introduces a new governmental rationality which she describes as "graduated sovereignty" (Ibid. 2005: 100). This implies new "state-transnational networks", in which specific aspects of state power and regulation are delegated to other, "foreign" actors (Ibid.: 85), a process just outlined above for the area of migration policy. In addition, this policy corresponds with a new biopolitical rationality, which, according to Aihwa Ong, is expressed in a continuing process of fragmentation of citizenship. This fragmentation partly reinforces existing ethnic/racial and gendered relations of inequality but, as Ong also shows, also implements new relations consistent with the positionality of the segments of population in relation to the global forces of neoliberal capitalism[14] (Ibid.: 86).

A research agenda focusing on the new geopolitical effects and the space-making quality of Schengen-Europe would need to further scrutinize the specific legal, social, and economic infrastructure underlying these "precarious transit zones" of stratified rights. In addition to the border regime and the history of migration, the following factors can be identified as further constitutive elements: the regulation of the labor market and the informal economy, the existence of camps and detention centers and the specific historical and contemporary connections between countries.

However, as Feruccio Pastore (2008) has recently been able to demonstrate, there is apparently also another side to the story, which could be called the boomerang effect of the externalization policy of European migration control policy. Pastore has shown how the peripheral countries themselves use and exploit the "transit card" in order to become eligible for specific programs and funding from the EU, IOM and other organizations and to get a say in the new global migration management architecture. It would seem that the global south can now use the construct of "transit migration" to threaten the north and, in a similar sense, as an international bargaining chip. This development turns the situation upside down, revealing the historical force of migration, a force which migration research should take much more seriously than the primarily functionalist or structuralist approaches have done in the past.

14 For the case of Malaysia Ong shows that the state government grants more rights to immigrants with internationally transferable skills than to Malaysian citizens to attract and motivate immigrants, whereas segments of the autochthonous population who are classed as economically inactive face severe repression and reduction of rights.

Concluding Remarks

The analysis of the condition and context of the implementation of the EU migration policy in Turkey has shown that these political efforts depended partly on the construction of a specific migration-knowledge regime, since in the early years of the new millennium the EU was faced with the same situation as we were as researchers. The situation was simply that the regulative category of "transit migration" was not yet known in public discourse in Turkey at that time, so migration was not considered to be an issue that needed to be regulated. It was only in the wake of the knowledge work of such intergovernmental and "intermediary" agencies as UNHCR and IOM and the studies these organizations commissioned that this regulatory category and discursive figure emerged. However, as shown in this article, it emerged in a specifically coded version as "irregular transit migration" and, thus, as a "security issue", which some critical scholars in the area of migration have defined as a "migration-security nexus" or the "securitization of migration" (Bigo 2005). This knowledge practice of IOM and similar agencies shows that the governance of migration is deeply bound up with the problem of knowing and categorizing it, and of conceptualizing it as a "problem". This, in turn, shows the increased importance of such knowledge producing and knowledge processing agencies within the multi-level governance structure in the area of migration management, which is even greater since the introduction of the new EU migration management policy of the "Global Approach". However, these analytical findings should also caution migration researchers not to unwittingly reproduce this regulatory political rationality by our academic knowledge production.

With regard to the recent research agenda on "transit migration", the empirical findings obtained by taking a closer ethnographic look at the strategies and biographies of migrants call the scientific practice of classifying migrants as transit migrants into question even more. Our encounters with migrants in the border regions of Southeast Europe showed that it is quite impossible to give a clear definition of "transit migrants" with respect to time and place. Many of the migrants we talked to preferred to live in a situation that can be described as "precarious and provisional forms of settlement" or "pending and suspended forms of transit existence", although many of them were caught in a somewhat ambivalent mode of mobility.

But what these flexible and mobile biographies of migrants—some of whom were forced to live a life on the move due to the effects of the border regime—have shown is the emergence of highly "precarious transit zones" in the European border regions. The emergence of these zones of reduced personal rights and increased mobility cannot simply be attributed to the political or economical rationalities of the states and agencies involved in this "transit migration management dispositif" but must be understood as a conflict-ridden process in which the forces and desires of migrants are one of the major factors. The emergence of such zones of reduced social, political and economical rights, which results in a marked fragmentation of national territories, is not just discussed by radical geography as a central feature of a rescaling of economic and political regulatory spaces in the age of new modes of global governance. Cultural anthropologists such as Aihwa Ong analyze such processes of fragmentation of citizenship rights as a central mode of neoliberal governance.

In this respect, rather than doing the job of defining the objects of control for the controlling bodies, migration research should use its analytical skills and expertise to help to understand these new ways of power and governance, also with respect to migration governance. An ethnographic regime analysis starting with a thorough theoretical and ethnographic understanding of the migration-knowledge regime and a consequent inductive approach seems particularly suited to finding an analytical path through the new social realities.

References

Andreas, P./Snyder, T., eds. (2000): The Wall around the West. New York/Oxford.

Andrijasevic, R, Bojadzijev, M, Hess, S et. Al. 2005, Turbulente Ränder: Konturen eines neuen Migrationsregimes im Südosten Europas, Prokla, Migration 35, 3, pp. 345-362.

Appadurai, A. (2000): Grassroots Globalization and the Research Imagination, Public Culture, Alternative Globalization, Capitalism, Cosmopolitanism 12, 1, pp. 1-19.

Balibar, E. (2003): Sind wir Bürger Europas? Politische Integration, soziale Ausgrenzung und die Zukunft des Nationalen. Hamburg: Hamburger Edition.

Bas, B. (2005): In Transit. In: Esen, O. /Lanz, S. (eds.): Self service city Istanbul. Berlin: b-books Verlag.

Bigo, D./Guild, E. (2005): Policing in the name of freedom, in Controlling frontiers. In: Bigo, D./Guild, E. (Eds.): Free movement into and within Europe. London: Ashgate, pp. 1-13.

Black, R. (2003): Breaking the Convention: researching the 'illegal' migration of refugees to Europe. In: Antipode 35, pp. 34-54.

Brenner, N. (1997): Globalisierung und Reterritorialisierung: Städte, Staaten und die Politik der räumlichen Redimensinierung im heutigen Europa. In: WeltTrends, 17, pp. 7-29.

Burawoy, M. (2000): Introduction: Reaching for the Global, in Global Ethnography. In: Burawoy, M./Blum, J./George, S. et. al. (eds.): Forces, Connections, and Imaginations in a Postmodern World. Berkley/Los Angeles/London: University of California Press, pp. 1-40.

Commission of the European Union (2007): Applying the global approach to the Eastern and South-Eastern regions neighbouring the EU, COM (2007) 247 [online] Available at:
http://eur-lex.europa.eu/LexUriServ/LexUriServ.do?uri=CELEX:52007DC0247:EN:NOT [Accessed May 16, 2007].

Düvell, F. (2002): Die Globalisierung des Migrationsregimes. Berlin/ Hamburg/Göttingen: Verlag Schwarze Risse.

Ferguson, J./Gupta, A. (2005): Spatializing States: Toward an Ethnography of Neoliberal Governmentality. In: Xavier, I. (ed.): Anthropologies of Modernity. Malden: Wiley, pp. 105-134.

Foucault, M. (2004): Geschichte der Gouvernementalität, vol. 1, Sicherheit. Territorium, Bevölkerung. Suhrkamp: Frankfurt am Main.

Georgi, F. (2007): Migrationsmanagement in Europa. Eine kritische Studie am Beispiel des Centers for Migration Policy Development. Saarbrücken: VDN-Verlag.

Grillo, R. (2001): Transnational Migration and Multiculturalism in Europe. Oxford ESRC Transnational Communities Working Paper WPTC-01-08 [online] Available at: www.sussex.ac.uk/migration/profile1090.html [Accessed May 30, 2008].

Guiraudon, V. (2001): De-nationalising control. Analysing state responses to restraints on migration control. In: Guiraudon, V./Joppke, C. (eds.): Controlling a new migration World.London: Routledge, pp. 29-64.

Gupta, A./Ferguson, J. (1996): Discipline and Practice: "The Field" as Site, Method, and Location in Anthropology. In: Gupta, A./Ferguson, J. (eds.): Anthropological Locations. Boundaries and Grounds of a Field Science. Berkeley/ Los Angeles/ London: University of California Press, pp. 1-46.

Hess, S. (2009): „Man schickt doch auch nicht eine Ersatzbraut zum Altar". Zur Konfliktualiät der neuen Formen des Regierens in und von Europa. In: Welz, G./Lottermann, A. (eds.): Projekte der Europäisierung. Frankfurt: Universität Frankfurt, Institut für Kulturanthropologie, pp.181-196.

Hess, S./Karakayali, S. (2007): New Governance oder die imperiale Kunst des Regierens. In: Transit Migration Forschungsgruppe (ed.): Turbulente Ränder. Neue Perspektiven auf Migration an den Grenzen Europas. Bielefeld: transcript Verlag, pp. 39-56.

Hess, S./Karakayali, S./Tsianos, V. (2009): Transnational migration: Theory and method of an ethnographic analysis of border regimes.
Sussex Center for Migration Research. Working papers [online] Available at: http://www.sussex.ac.uk/migra tion/1-3-3.html [Accessed November 30, 2009].

İçduygu, A. (2003): Irregular Migration in Turkey. IOM Migration Research Series no. 12, Genf.

I-Map (2009): [online] Available at: https://www.imap-migration.org/index2.html [Accessed November 30, 2009].

IOM - International Organisation for Migration (1995): Transit Migration in Turkey. Genf.

IOM (2004): Migration Management in Southeast Europe. Objectives for 2005. Wien.

Kölnischer Kunstverein, ed. (2005): Projekt Migration. Köln: Dumont Verlag.

Lahav, G./Guiraudon, V. (2000): Comparative Perspectives on Border Control: Away from the Border and Outside the State. In: Andreas, P./Snyder, T. (eds.): The Wall around the West. New York/Oxford: Rowman & Littlefield, pp. 55-77

Marcus, G. E. (1995): Ethnography in/of the World System. The Emergence of Multi-Sited Ethnography. In: Annual Review of Anthropology 117, pp. 95-117.
Mezzadra, S. (2009): Bürger und Untertanen. Die postkoloniale Herausforderung der Migration in Europa. In: Hess, S./Binder, J. et al. (eds.): No integration?! Kulturwissenschaftliche Beiträge zu Fragen von Migration und Integration in Europa. Bielefeld: transcript Verlag, pp. 207-224.
MigMap: [online] Available at: www.transitmigration.org/migmap/home_map1.html [Accessed November 30, 2009].
Ong, A. (1999): Flexible Citizenship. Durham: Duke University Press.
Ong, A. (2005): Graduated Sovereignty in South-East-Asia: In: Xavier, I. (eds.): Anthropologies of Modernity. Malden: Wiley, pp. 83-104.
Panagiotidis, E./Tsianos, V. (2007): Denaturalizing „Camps“: Überwachen und Entschleunigen in der Schengener Ägäis-Zone. In: Transit Migration Forschungsgruppe (Ed.): Turbulente Ränder. Neue Perspektiven auf Migration an den Grenzen Europas. Bielefeld: transcript Verlag, pp. 57-86.
Pastore, F. (2008): (Irregular) Transit Migration in the European space: Theory, Politics and Research Methodology. [online] Available at: http://www.compas.ox.ac.uk/fileadmin/files/pdfs/Non_WP_pdfs/Tranist_Migration_in_Europe__Koc_University_/Outline%20IMISCOE%20Transit%20Conference.pdf [Accessed November 30, 2009].
Pieper, M./Karakayali, S./Tsianos, V., eds. (2007): Empire und die biopolitische Wende. Frankfurt: Campus Verlag.
Rigo, E. (2005): Citizenship at Europes Borders: Some Reflections on the Post-colonial Condition of Europe in the Context of EU Enlargement. In: Citizenship Studies 9, 1, pp. 3-22.
Sciortino, G. (2004): Between Phantoms and Necessary Evils. Some Critical Points in the Study of Irregular Migrations to Western Europe. In: IMIS (ed.): Migration and the Regulation of Social Integration, IMIS-Beiträge 24, Osnabrück, pp. 17-43.
Sharma, A./Gupta, A., eds. (2006): The Anthropology of the State. Malden/Oxford: Wiley.
Shore, C./Wright, S. (1997): Policy. A new field of Anthropology. In: Shore, C./Wright, S. (Eds.): Anthropology of Policy. London: Routledge, pp. 3-42.
Transit Migration Forschungsgruppe, ed. (2007): Turbulente Ränder. Neue Perspektiven auf Migration an den Grenzen Europas. Bielefeld: transcript Verlag.
Trouillot, M.-R. (2001): The Anthropology of the State in the Age of Globalization. In: Current Anthropology 42, 1, pp. 125-138.
Van Hear, N./Brubaker, R./Bessa, Th. (2009): Managing Mobility for Human Development: The Growing Salience of Mixed Migration. Human Development Research Paper 2009/20. United Nations Development Programme (UNDP).
Wallace, C./Sidorenko, E. (1999): The Central European Buffer Zone. In: Giordano, C. (Ed.): Europäische Ethnologie–Ethnologie Europas. Fribourg: Universitätsverlag, pp. 123-169.
Walters, W. (2009): Anti-Political Economy: Cartographies of „Illegal Immigration” and the Displacement of the Economy. In: Best, J./Paterson, M. (eds.): Cultural Political Economy. London: Routledge.
Walters, W. (2004): Secure Borders, Safe Haven, Domopolitics, In: Citizenship Studies 8, 3, pp. 237-260.

Walters, W. (2002): Mapping Schengenland: Denaturalizing the Border, Environment & Planning. In: Society & Space 20, 5, pp. 561-80.

The Limits of Hospitality. Undocumented Migration and the Local Arena: The Case of Lampedusa

Heidrun Friese

Dans les civilisations sans bateaux les rêves se tarissent

Michel Foucault

Mapping the Fields

One of the most vital and politically contested questions of our time is how to hospitably welcome migrants and refugees. The island of Lampedusa has been one of Europe's borderlands since the late 1990s and has become a site of transit for undocumented migrants and refugees. Despite the fact that most of the undocumented migrants in Italy are overstayers arriving by overland routes and/or at airports and that a larger number of undocumented migrants arrived at the shores of mainland Sicily, the tiny island close to the Tunisian mainland, along with the Spanish enclaves of Ceuta and Melilla, became one of most powerful symbols of failing European migration policies, of technocratic utopias of migration and border management and the limits of hospitality.

Defining the boundaries of Europe has always been a contested endeavor. Although freedom of movement has generally increased for citizens of the European Union as a result of the Schengen Agreement, external borders are becoming increasingly surveilled and practices of hospitality are being restricted. At the same time, the exterritorialization of European borders across the Mediterranean to North Africa and the sub-Saharan states—and thus the former colonies—affirms European borderlands in a way that articulate the highly ambivalent relations to foreigners and non-members of the European (political) community. Whereas the right to mobility is guaranteed in the Universal Declaration of Human Rights,[1] the various aspects of a mobile, transnational world are becoming rather troubled

On one hand, it has been emphasized that "humanity on the move" (Bauman 2007), the transnational movement of people weakens borders and

---

1 Art. 13 divides the freedom of movement into three separate rights—namely, to leave a country, to return to one's own country and to have freedom of movement and residence within the borders of each state. Similar EU objectives are expressed in Art. 8a, 1 of the Treaty of Maastricht and reinforced by the 1997 Treaty of Amsterdam. However, there is a radical disjuncture between the freedom of exit and the freedom of entry.

the sovereignty of nation-states. In such views, the border becomes a constantly negotiated and contested site, a site of porosity allowing for multiple transfers, translation and various *Grenzgänger*. A strand of thought suggests that nation-states are becoming obsolete and advocate a cosmopolitan order and the free movement of people. On the other hand, borders and the "re-inscription of space" (Gupta 1992) promote increasing apprehension and lead to overdetermination and their ubiquity of borders (Balibar 2004). Thus, the proliferation of multiple and shifting borders, and practices of their *gouvernmentalité* (Foucault) are intrinsic to the processes of globalization. The growing movement of goods, commodities, capital, and media around the globe is by no means the end of borders. Rather, it is the result of the crisis of the classical relation between the nation-state, its territory, and political membership. In short, it is a re-shaping of the Westphalian order.

Mobilities and practices of hospitality have always been part of historical symbolizations, political struggle, and processes of demarcation. Historically, hospitality has been an ethical and religious duty, a sacred commandment to accommodate foreigners and to assign them a place in the community, however ambivalent. Hospitality (from the Latin *hostis/hospes*, friend and enemy) allows for welcoming an Other. At the same time, however, it fosters several tensions: it embodies generosity, engagement, a common place and it "harbors a trace of its double—hostility" (Honig 2008: 111) and the tension between (political, social, and cultural) membership and exclusion. In short, the semantics of hospitality engage fundamental questions about social, political, and ethical spaces. With the development of the modern nation-state, these tensions have been inscribed into the processes of political deliberation, legal procedures, and administrative regulations that re-articulate the ambivalences of hospitality and put aliens in a position which is neither friend nor enemy. The Westphalian concept of national sovereignty and the strengthening of the modern nation-state transformed the languages and politics of hospitality. However, they still entail the Westphalian "grammar" (Benhabib 2008) and the constitutive tensions between (political) membership, belonging and exclusion, between universalism and particularity, between the sovereign territorial nation-state and cosmopolitan, universalistic norms, and between ethical obligation and administered law that make up the modern state.[2]

Contemporary transnational mobility led to re-articulations of borders and to a complex map of borderlands that shape the limits of hospitality. In the following, I advocate a shift in perspective: First, I suggest that current discourses and powerful policies of migration intended to promote "effective

2 These remarks are based on the findings of an ongoing multi-sited research project on "The Limits of Hospitality", generously funded by the German Research Foundation (DFG). For a detailed account of the historical semantics of hospitality and its tensions, see Friese (2009; 2010).

border management"[3] reiterate in historically specific ways, the basic tensions of hospitality and modes of dealing with those who are marked as non-members of a given political community. These technocratic efforts articulate the ambivalence between inclusion and exclusion and, ultimately, between friend and foe (already identified by Carl Schmitt as the basic feature of "the political").

Second, I argue for a perspective that takes into account the complex and contradictory configurations which make up current policies and political discourse. Some strands of political activism ontologize migrants as victims—of the state, global capitalism, trafficking, racialization, and so on—who need to be rescued through solidarity and political good will. Others see mobility as a threat to welfare, security, political stability and, cultural identity to be effectively contained and "managed".

Third, to gauge the complexity of current border-regimes I suggest engaging the local arena, its various practices, (institutional) actors, and conflicts. Locals are not "stubborn racists" who need to be taught proper and tolerant behavior, just as mobile people are neither passive victims, as humanitarian discourse would have one believe, nor "the new revolutionary subjects" and heroes of disappointed hope ("Africans will save Italy").[4] In the proposed perspective, migrants are *actors* struggling to carry out personal projects and strategies of mobility in powerful contested juridical, social, and political circumstances. Taking these various actors into account, what will be advocated is a *grounded cosmopolitism* and thus a constant, even antagonistic, reworking of the ethical demand to welcome foreigners and the politics of hospitality.

Such a twofold argument will be outlined in four steps. Based on anthropological fieldwork conducted on the islands of Lampedusa and Sicily, routes taken by undocumented migrants will be sketched. Following this, taking account of the fact that the routes of the immigrants are shaped by various legal impasses, the complex border regime and its agents will be delineated. In order to grasp the limits of hospitality, the various local conflicts and economic interests associated with transborder agency and mobility as

---

3 Even recent efforts of "joint migration management" between the EU and African countries reiterate such semantics. Metaphors are far from being innocent. Just as the language of hospitality is associated with semantics of the gift—which begs the question: who gives and who receives, the host or the hosted?—we speak of "sending" and "receiving" countries. Do nation-states "send" human beings? Who is the "sender" and who the "recipient"?

4 A view expressed by Mangano (2010) and others after the deplorable incidents in the town of Rosarno in January 2010. After a violent attack on a black worker by local youths, the community of undocumented migrants reacted and the riots that followed were seen as a heroic fight against the "N'drangheta", a criminal network the locals do not dare to challenge. Such a view perpetuates the old topos of the stranger as liberator (Friese 2004).

well as the "struggle for recognition" (Honneth 1994) and common contest that opens up a transnational space of the political will be addressed.

Routes and Dwelling

For centuries, travel and trade shaped the Mediterranean world, connecting the desert and the sea. With reference to Arjun Appadurai (1990), the Mediterranean can be considered as a "seascape" allowing multiple connections. After the settlement of Lampedusa in 1843, trading and fishing made it possible for people from Lampedusa to establish busy relations with other countries in the Mediterranean region (namely, Tunisia, Libya, Algeria, Greece, Malta, and the countries bordering on the Adriatic Sea). Historically a safe refuge for escaped slaves and a mythical meeting place of religions, the island is still well-connected to its surrounding region today.[5]

The passage of undocumented migrants arriving on Lampedusa is usually "extraordinarily long and complex, involving multiple relationships often of an exploitative character, various transit points, especially in major cities" (Urry 2007: 36). These border-crossing journeys involve periods of increased mobility and interspersing periods of precarious dwelling, with immigrants having to rely on extended networks of solidarity and hospitality of family members, friends, companions of the journey, and diasporic communities.

Current overland routes taken by undocumented migrants from sub-Saharan countries run along the old caravan routes and itineraries of the slave trade, bifurcating in Agadez, Niger, into routes leading to Libya, Algeria, and Tunisia. Whereas in former times boat people continued their journey from the Tunisian coast to reach Lampedusa, for a while Libya became a major site of departure for the flimsy boats. The recent bilateral agreement between Italy and Libya (2009) closed down this route, if only temporarily, and in spring 2010, the first boat people were again intercepted and rescued off the coast of Lampedusa.

Most undocumented migrants originate from regions affected by economic crisis, political rigidity or endemic warfare and are subject to asymmetric inclusion/exclusion from global processes. The majority of boat people arriving on Lampedusa are from North Africa (Morocco, Algeria, Tunisia, Libya), the Horn of Africa (Somalia, Eritrea, Ethiopia, Sudan), the Middle East (Egypt, Palestine, Lebanon), Sub-Saharan Africa (Ivory Coast, Ghana, Togo, Liberia, Sierra Leone, Nigeria), and, to a lesser extent, from South Asia (Bangladesh, Pakistan, India, Sri Lanka) (see Table 3).

---

5 For a history of Lampedusa, see Friese (1996).

Table 3: Declared Nationalities (2000–Sep 21, 2009)

	North Africa	Horn of Africa	Middle East	Sub-Saharan	South Asia
2000	1,801	43	329	65	311
2001	2,233	539	510	117	194
2002	3,805	2,794	1,271	2,757	3,773
2003	1,615	3,951	3,540	2,066	1,110
2004	952	2,384	8,826	389	940
2005	5,657	3,531	1,113	2,115	1,096
2006	10,957	3,811	4,341	1,643	619
2007	4,005	4,857	4,698	2,949	341
2008	9,847	9,663	2,227	11,658	1,126
2009	1,795	2,640	415	2,378	182
Total	42,667	34,213	27,270	26,137	9,692

Source: Ministero dell'Interno (compiled by H. Friese).

Young men in particular feel themselves entangled in a double bind because they cannot realize personal aspirations and feel stuck in their countries of first citizenship. In addition, group pressure to prove manliness and the ability to surpass difficulties raise—often highly unrealistic—expectations to be successful, have a good life in Europe and return with the desired objects and symbols of consumer society. In the societies of the Maghreb, so-called *harraga* (young immigrants who cross from North Africa to Europe) developed a "burning" desire (*harga*) to undertake the enterprise and to reach a mythical Europe, "the promised land, flowing with milk and honey"—and personal liberation. This gave rise to a new forceful popular genre of ready-made *harga* films and *rai/rap* songs, which are disseminated via YouTube, promoting the social *imaginaire* of a generation that has no future prospects.

However, access to spatial (and, eventually, social) mobility entails other forms of injustice, inequality, and exclusion. Mobility and transnational practices require economic resources, sometimes massive investments in the future of migrating family members, and it is a well-known fact that migrants do not belong to the poorest and subaltern strata of their country of first citizenship. After all, migrants must be able to raise exorbitant sums to pay various *passeurs* for the complex journeys (at the time of writing this essay, the market price to traverse the sea is around US$1,000). Transnational mobility also requires appropriate survival skills, a certain amount of personal resources and capabilities related to gender, age, body strength, skills, imagination, adaptability, and practical reason, as well as the activation of informal networks of family ties, relatives, friends, diasporic communities, and so on.

Contrary to common belief (a belief so dear to European politicians), organized human trafficking is not usually involved when people decide to depart. "Migrants do have agency" and are not just passive victims of (post-) modern slave traders. Smugglers-"often (former) fishermen" (de Haas 2007:25)-are usually connected through dynamic networks rather than a rigid criminal or Mafia-like organization and are paid for their services. However, smuggling still relies on bribery and corrupt police and officials, and the paths and routes – an uncanny longue durée and a disturbing historical memory – of the slave trade[6], changed all that much.

Once these men (and to a far lesser extent women and minors) decide to depart on their journey, they encounter European legal systems that impose a variety of limits to their freedom of movement and their ability to stay. These legal maps and border regimes shape the everyday relationships between the new arrivals and the residents of the local communities, shape the spaces assigned to (undocumented) aliens, open or close doors to opportunities, and often lead to yet another period of remaining stuck, living in precarious dwelling, and moving on to other places which seem to present more promising alternatives.

Border Regimes and Legal Impasses

Practices of (limiting) hospitality which have become an integral part of organized solidarity, cannot be adequately understood without reference to the specifics of national and international immigration law, which shape the everyday relationships between new arrivals and local residents, provide and define the spaces assigned to foreigners and non-citizens, and open or close doors of opportunities for immigrants.

At the same time, the implementation of migration policies determines the status of the new arrivals, because illegality, like citizenship, is a (legal) concept which orders the relations to the state and the political order (De Genova 2002: 422). Borders, citizenship, and legal status contribute to the "production of illegality" (De Genova, 2002) and the strategies of day-to-day survival.[7]

6 See Chebel, 2007; Tangu Kwenzi-Mikala, 2003; Abdel Ghaffar, 2008. I intend to address this question elsewhere.

7 The notion, as understood in this context, covers several different phenomena, including people who deliberately decide to be brought across national borders, overstayers, and people who enter a marriage of convenience. The term is contested and highly controversial. The opposition is based on the notion that the terms "illegal" and "irregular" cannot be sensibly applied to a person. Smuggling can also "be illegal, but *licit*, or socially accepted" (de Haas, 2007:4). For a discussion on irregular migration, see Bogusz, 2004; Chavez, 1991; 1992; Jordan/Düvell, 2002; 2003.

Along with international treaties such as the Geneva Conventions and Protocols, the formal status of undocumented migrants and their rights and duties in Italy is governed by Act n. 40 (Legge Turco-Napolitano 1998). It sets out the general principles of immigration policies (Art. 1.1), the "rights and duties" of aliens (Art. 1.2.), the regulations for immigration, stay, and expulsion (Arts. 2, 1-9), "border controls and measures against illegal immigration" (Arts. 2, 10-17), "humanitarian issues" (Arts. 2, 18-20), "working permissions" (Arts. 2, 21-27), family reunification (Arts. 2, 28-33), health issues, "social integration", and "intercultural education", and establishes so-called Reception Centers (Centri di accoglienza Art. 40). This act and its subsequent amendment (Legge Bossi-Fini 2002) articulate the language of hospitality and its ambivalence between "friends" and "enemies" In the language of Italian immigration law, foreigners are considered guests (*ospiti*) who are received, accommodated, taken care of, but also controlled.

As well as national legislation, a complex system of international agreements needs to be taken into consideration. At the EU summit in Thessaloniki in 2003, the UK proposed the establishment of *transit processing centers*, suggesting the exterritorialization of border management. Although this proposal was rejected, it was later taken up by Germany, the UK, and Italy, despite the opposition of France and Spain, at the meeting in Florence in October 2004. The Commission then piloted five projects under the direction of Justice and Home Affairs (JHA) concerning already existing centers in Tunisia, Libya, Algeria, Morocco, and Mauritania and the laws governing asylum in these countries. These proposals were included in the The Hague Programme (2005/C 53/1), which, in cooperation with the UNHCR, commissioned a study concerning the establishment of such centers.

Current political designs draw adjacent border zones and borders beyond borders, (legal) no man's land blocking "exit" and "entry" (Bauman 2007:45) that maps the modalities of hospitality as well. These designs promote two types of action in containing movement and undocumented migration by shifting borders beyond European borders while increasing border control. In order to discourage unwanted mobility, cooperation in efforts to control illegal immigration to the Mediterranean region have been strengthened. The Western Mediterranean Dialogue on Migration involves representatives from Algeria, France, Italy, Malta, Mauretania, Morocco, Portugal, and Spain. Proposals of transit processing centers suggest exterritorialization of the border management.

"In recent years, irregular migration from sub-Saharan Africa to North Africa and Europe has received extensive media attention. Alarmed by these images, the issue has also been put high on the policy agenda of the EU and its member states, which have exerted pressure on North African countries to clamp down on irregular migration occurring over their territory through increasing border controls, toughening migration law, re-admitting irregular sub-Saharan migrants from Europe and deporting them from their own national territories." (de Haas 2007: 1)

In line with these efforts, Italy and Libya committed to strengthening their bilateral relations in August 2007, and in October of the same year the EU lifted its arms embargo on Libya, allowing the country to buy state-of-the-art surveillance technology and speedboats and to train border police. Recently, another agreement between Italy and Libya became operative, allowing joint patrols to close down these routes (Ministero dell'Interno, Dec. 29, 2007). However, recent evidence shows that routes have changed and Tunisia and Egypt have once again become countries of transit.

In addition, the Warsaw-based European Agency for the Management of Operational Cooperation at the External Borders of the Member States of the European Union (Frontex) was established in 2004. The agency is "intelligence driven" and provides cooperation in the surveillance of frontiers and additional "border management systems" to member States (Frontex).[8] In 2005, the European Commission adopted the so-called "Return Directive" which provides "common rules concerning return, removal, use of coercive measures, temporary custody and re-entry" (Commission of the European Communities 2005). In 2008, the Commission "presented a Communication on the creation of a European Border Surveillance System (EUROSUR), with the main purpose of preventing unauthorized border crossings".[9] Frontex is mentioned in the recent Italian-Libyan protocol and its representatives carried out a mission in Libya in 2004, visiting several detention camps for undocumented migrants: "Conditions of detention in different sorts of camps visited vary greatly, from relatively acceptable to extremely poor" (European Commission 2005: 5). A second Frontex mission was undertaken in 2007 in an effort to strengthen cooperation in border management (Frontex 2007).

This legislation creates various legal and ethical tensions: between the universal rights to freedom and asylum and the restrictions to movement, as well as between humanitarian aid and rescue from distress and surveillance and policing. Along with this, there are various legal impasses, inconsistencies, and legal fictions. Although in principle boat people have the right to non-refoulement, as stipulated in the 1951 Refugee Convention, people on the high seas who should enjoy freedom of movement are often intercepted,

---

8 On June 18, 2008, the Working Arrangements establishing a framework for cooperation between Frontex and UNHCR were signed (Frontex 2008).

9 The aim is "to build a space of free and secure travel through collective responsibility and solidarity. The objective should be to ensure a Schengen space which will continue to allow secure border-free-travel for citizens and travelers to 24 countries in Europe while improving border security" (European Commission 2008). On December 16, 2008, the European Parliament and the Council of the European Union adopted a Directive "on common standards and procedures in Member States for returning illegally staying third-country nationals" (European Commission 2008).

detained, and eventually repatriated without any chance to formulate requests for asylum (an illegal practice that has been denounced by various agencies and NGOs).

Access to the sea—and thus actions regarding boat people—is subject to customary international law: The United Nations Convention on the Continental Shelf (Geneva 1958/1964) and the United Nations Convention on the Law of the Sea (UNCLOS Montego Bay 1982) distinguishes between territorial sea (12 nautical miles or 22,224 km), contiguous zone (24 nautical miles or 44,448 km), continental shelf, and international waters (the latter Convention ratified by Italy in 1995). Accordingly, different tasks are assigned to the various military and civil corps on Lampedusa: the naval forces act in international waters, the *Guardia di Finanza* within the 24-mile zone, while the Coast Guard is basically engaged in search-and-rescue missions (SAR), based on the Maritime Search and Rescue Convention of 1979. Recently, Malta and Italy articulated contrasting interpretations of SAR zones, subsequently causing confusion as to which country is to accommodate people rescued from unseaworthy boats. However, according to rules and regulations, competent authorities have to assist the endangered without regard to nationality, status, or circumstances and to transfer these persons to a safe place; they are obliged to help if a ship is obviously not adequate for "the international transport of humans" and the engaging state has to take care that neither the "security of passengers, nor that of ships is being endangered." In addition, the Italian naval code, the *Codice navale,* provides sanctions for failure to assist persons in danger.

If there is *sirocco* or *libeccio* (southerly/south-westerly winds), the boats usually make it across the Mediterranean sea, with *maestrale* or *tramontana* (northerly/north-westerly winds) they are wrecked, fishers on Lampedusa told me. Rescuing people from life-threatening situations—a matter of course and part of every fishermen's ethos—has become highly problematic in view of the various new laws against what may now be construed as "human trafficking". Rescuing other people can now jeopardize the livelihood of many and will therefore likely to be left to the Coast Guard (the confiscation of the Cap Anamur in July 2004 and recent legal action against the crew of a Tunisian boat are striking examples). In recent times, it is not rare for fishermen to find drowned people or human limbs in their nets and throw them back into the sea to avoid trouble with the authorities and official checks which may prevent them from working for several days. However, I was assured that no one would watch a shipwreck—"siamo gente di mare" ("we are men of the sea")—"one might ask why should I lose some catches? But one would not leave them in that condition, one would call the authorities." In some situations, such intervention can be rather difficult, especially if one were to venture beyond the licensed zone. More than one fisherman told me that he had to call relatives, who in turn called the Coast Guard and reported the exact position of the boat in distress.

"The exact death toll will probably never be known, as some flimsy vessels disappear without [a] trace" (Spindler 2007). According to the Italian monitoring organization Fortress Europe, at least 2,486 people drowned in the Strait of Sicily, 1,525 went missing and 64 people drowned between Annaba (Algeria) and Sardinia in 2006. Despite the slight decrease in arrivals in 2007, the death toll had doubled—an increase that was due to the fact that boats were increasingly smaller and unsafe and odysseys became longer.[10]

As well as administrative tasks such as checking licenses and controlling arriving ships, the responsibilities of the Costal Guard basically include two primary fields of operation: policing and humanitarian aid and rescue. The local station in Lampedusa is manned by forty officers who—"with great sacrifice"—strive to provide a 24-hour service. The *Settima Squadriglia Guardia Costiera* coordinates the various missions. The experienced commander in charge of SAR missions sees his work as being basically humanitarian.[11] Indeed, what officers see during such operations is not always easy to stomach and the dramatic scenes are likely to be recalled. "The first time I was highly impressed, it was an emotional and unsettling sight," the chief of the local station told me. "One never really gets used to it, but after a while there is a certain routine." Boats are intercepted either by fishermen, officers who perform regular checks of the area in boats or helicopters, or boat people who call their relatives for help. "Accounts of the procedure have spread and often it is in their self-interest to get rescued, sometimes they destroy motors in order to be captured," the officer said. "Usually, they are really relieved." In case of an alarm, the headquarters in Palermo and Rome determine the appropriate course of action. Once the boat people have been brought to the shore, they are lined up and checked by collaborating teams from Doctors Without Borders and either flown out to Palermo hospitals or brought to the Center. These operations are marked by the ambivalences of policing and saving human lives, of ethical imperatives and control, and of the tensions

---

10 [online] Available at: fortresseurope.blogspot.com/2006/02/nel-canale-di-sicilia.html [Accessed : January 10, 2008]. This circumstance was already true for the slave trade of the Mediterranean middle passage. The new steamships were more easily to control and thus were hardly used for the transport of slaves (Wright 2007: 134-5).

11 The *Settima Squadriglia Guardia Costiera* is an organizational aggregation resulting from experiences with massive migration from Albania. These temporary aggregations have been transformed into a permanent unit which, since 1997, is based on Lampedusa and is in charge of SAR missions. As a result of an inter-ministerial decree (Jul. 14, 2003), these missions are coordinated by the headquarters in Palermo (Direzione dei Servizi Centrali per l'immigrazione istituita presso il Ministero dell'Interno) which became a sort of stage-director coordinating the navy, the police, the *Guardia di Finanza,* and the *Carabinieri*.

and aporias between the Law of hospitality and the laws that governs and regulates it.

National and international treaties, laws and regulations do not just determine who is to be considered as an irregular migrant and which space is assigned to them, they also define the various actors who arrange the reception of the boat people on a day-to-day- basis: the Coastal Guard and security forces, the employees of the Center, the local municipality and political forces, the members of local voluntary organizations, the representatives of humanitarian organizations (UNHCR, OIM), NGOs (such as Doctors Without Borders), political activists, and the representatives of the migrant communities.

The limits to hospitality are not just designed by legal fictions, but also become apparent in the complex and ambivalent situations created by local practice and the political and social circumstances. Thus, the border regime encompasses a highly complex institutional structure with various legal requirements and different (local) actors with various (corporate) traditions and values that respond to different demands and belong to different national and supranational frames of reference which combine day-to-day action and routines.

The Local Arena as Borderland

According to the ethos shared by all fishermen, unconditional aid and hospitality has to be offered to those who are endangered or shipwrecked. Without asking for name or nationality or noting skin color, the first boat people who arrived on Lampedusa were taken care of by local volunteers and even *Carabinieri* hosted boat people at home. Later, also due to increasing numbers of new arrivals, this spontaneous local hospitality became institutionalized and, with the institution of the Reception Center in 1998, a matter of political clientelism and economic interests. Between 2000 and 2009, more than 100,000 boat people approached the island (see Table 4).[12]

[12] In 2007, the municipality of Lampedusa e Linosa had 6,136 residents and 2,220 families (Source: Movimento della popolazione 1994–2007, Ufficio anagrafe, Comune di Lampedusa e Linosa, H. Friese)

Table 4: Undocumented migrants approaching Lampedusa e Linosa (LeL) and Sicily

Year	LeL	Sicily
2000	447	2,782
2001	1,105	5,505
2002	10,011	18,225
2003	8,891	14,017
2004	10,497	13,594
2005	15,890	22,939
2006	18,495	21,400
2007	12,177	16,875
2008	31,252	34,540
2009	2,823	7,418
Total	111,588	157,295

Data for 2009 as of Sep. 21, 2009; Source: *Ministero dell'Interno* (comp. by H. Friese)

Professionalization changed the relationship between new arrivals and local solidarity significantly, transforming gestures of hospitality into institutional reception and so-called "good practice". Whereas the first boat people to arrive on Lampedusa were hosted by local families who perceived them as individuals, boat people have now become "invisible" in two senses of the term: with the institution of the center, the *clandestini* have become a phantom presence on the island and are rendered to an absent presence. Upon arrival on the island, these migrants are immediately taken to the reception center, which they are not allowed to leave until they are flown out. They are virtually rendered invisible in an extraterritorial and segregated place, a space of "inclusive exclusion" (Agamben 1995), a "heterotopic" space of transition (Foucault 1994), a site of rites of passage and incorporation into the sovereignty of the state that reflects the ambivalence of hospitality:

"Before the newcomers who apply for admission to another social site are given access (if access is given) to a new wardrobe where the dresses appropriate to the new site and for that site reserved are stocked, they need to be bared (metaphorically as well as literally) of all and any trappings of their previous belonging; a quarantine is needed in the space-not-space of 'betwixt and between', where no socially forged and approved weapons are on offer and none is permitted. In the purgatory of the intermediate 'nowhere space' that separates the plots in the world sliced into plots and conceived as aggregation of spatially separate plots, the site is cleaned for the construction of a new belonging." (Bauman 2002).[13]

13 I will give a more detailed account of these rites elsewhere. There is a meticulously crafted set of means of first reception. According to the regulations (*Direttiva generale in materia di Centri di Permanenza Temporanea ed assistenza ai sensi dell'articolo 22, comma i del D.P.R. 31 agosto 1999, n. 394*), people are entitled to three meals (breakfast, lunch, and dinner) which are

The Italian immigration law that instituted reception centers articulates the language of hospitality and its ambivalence between "friend" and "enemy": foreigners are considered "guests" (*ospiti*) who are received, accommodated and taken care of, but, as potential enemies, have to be controlled and kept under surveillance. Originally an exceptional, fenced and secret site, the camp is being extended beyond its borders, making distinctions between inside and outside obsolete. Lampedusans constantly complained about the increasing "militarization", increasing surveillance (of infractions of law by locals as well) and the conversion of the island into a prison that indeed creates a "zone of indistinction".

Along with this, the local arena is made up of several *economical conflicts* which are sometimes intertwined with racial stereotyping that link the problematic perception of undocumented migrants and economical conflicts.

Historically, the local economy was based on the sponge and fishing industries, but with the decline of the sector, tourism became a major economical resource. Whereas in the 1980s seven enterprises processed local oily fish, such as sardines, anchovy, and mackerel, and usually hired local women, four of the companies are now closed. The sector's past was characterized by a surplus on the market causing the prices for the product to go down—we all recall the spectacular protest in the 1990s when fishermen dumped tons of fresh fish into local streets. Today, the local fishing industry is faced with an alarming crisis and the canning industry no longer processes the local product: "Nowadays, fish arrives from Greece, Spain, and Peru", as a fisherman sarcastically commented. The crisis of this pillar of the economy is causing a change in the social relationships that were connected to the boats and the seasonal rhythm of the activity: the organization of the crews, the relationships with the partners who own and operate the boats, relationships with traders and other regions, and the division of work ashore.[14]

In 2007, 91 boats were licensed for local fishing and around 500 families made at least part of their living from this activity. To reduce the fleet, the

---

provided in the Mensa and possibly respect religious convictions, and medical aid and medicine ("prescribed by medical staff"). The kit given to boat people includes items of personal hygiene such as soap, shampoo, razors, toothpaste, and toothbrush, and feminine hygiene items. In addition, new arrivals have to be provided with blankets, sheets, pillows, handkerchiefs, and, if clothing is not adequate, clothes and underwear ("dry-cleaned, in good condition and suitable for local climatic conditions"). Every ten days the "foreigner" (*straniero*) is given the right "to make phone calls, post letters (max. 10) and telegrams (max. 20 words) which may not cost more than five Euros." They are allowed to buy Italian or foreign newspapers and journals ("as long as they are locally available") as well as additional clothing and cigarettes, at own expenses. "These items are bought by the staff of the center". Immigrants who do not possess the necessary financial means may apply for funding from the competent prefect.

14 For a detailed account, see Friese (1996), Chapter 4.

EU finances the scrapping of boats. The remaining local fleet is basically used for inshore fishing within the six-mile zone and has to face national and international competition (by the fleets of the Sicilian city of Mazara del Vallo and South Korea, respectively). These fleets are considerably bigger and technically better equipped than the local boats which cannot expand their radius of action to Greece or Turkey because they are not licensed for fishing outside the six-mile zone.

The local fishing industry is no longer competitive on a globalized market. Structural handicaps, such as higher prices for diesel fuel and the lack of efficient transport aggravate the situation. The main reason for the crisis, however, is the dramatic over-fishing of the Mediterranean Sea that opened another arena of conflict. Whereas Lampedusans once fished along the Tunisian shores, Tunisians started to approach Italian national waters and, thus, the traditional fishing grounds around the island—the past, it would appear, is catching up with them. The structural crisis of the sector increasingly leads to quarrels about the violation of national borders. Local fishermen feel assaulted by Tunisian fishermen—irregular border commuters—and complain "to be left alone", that is, not to be *recognized as subjects* by politicians and public authorities.

> "Today Lampedusan fishery traverses one of the most critical moments of its existence; this is due to the extraordinary development of the Mazares' fleet of dragnets trawling close to the island and choosing it as a point of unloading the catch. Moreover, the crisis is due to the incredible development of the Maghrebinian fleet which almost daily approaches our territorial waters. It is no[t] rare to watch them throwing their nets undisturbed at four or five nautical miles from the coast of Lampedusa or next to Lampione."[15]

"They are a lot better equipped than in former times and go for a catch despite bad weather. We wouldn't even go out at a wind speed of 8 knots", I was told. "They are about to ruin us. They use dragnets, which we are no longer allowed to use, and we can't get past them because their nets would ruin the boat propellers, they present an insurmountable barrier." Local fishermen also complain that "they use small-mesh nets" which are no longer permitted by the EU, so "they catch everything."[16] In short, "they do everything we are not allowed to do."

---

15 Letter of the *Associazione Pescatori Lampedusa* to the Ministry of Agriculture, the *Comando Generale delle Capitanierie di Porto*, and the municipality of Lampedusa e Linosa (September 29, 2000).

16 In November 2006, after three years of tough negotiation—and after Italy had rejected a compromise in 2005—a European agreement was settled that aims at harmonizing fishery and at safeguarding the resources and ecosystems of the Mediterranean region. Fishermen have to keep a distance of at least 1.5 nautical miles (in Italy they the allowed distance is 0.7 nautical miles if water depth is at least 50 m). Fishing with dragnets is still allowed if a distance of 3 nautical miles (and a water depth of at least 50 m) is respected. From July 2007 on, the mesh has to be at least 40 mm (for square mesh) and 50 mm for other mesh. Subsidiaries are granted for conversion of the costly nets. In addition,

Fishermen complain that the Coast Guard does not prevent violations of national waters and remains inactive. The local association of fishermen (*Associazione Pescatori Lampedusa*), founded in 2000 and representing 200 members (and thus almost all enterprises on the island), has written several letters of protest, demanding that adequate measures be taken "to avoid unpleasant and violent incidents" and "the over-fishing of the *pesce azzurro*, at least in territorial waters."[17] However, the responsible authorities played down the issue and refused to act.

The association was not successful in raising public awareness of the issue and its members felt not recognized as (political) subjects. Below is the reply from the former President of the regional government, Salvatore Cuffaro (who recently resigned and, in 2008, was charged for aiding and abetting Mafia activities):

> "The regional Government has been and is willing to protect the sea from excessive exploitation in a way that its richness may constitute a patrimony accessible to everyone. However, such an engagement necessitates a strong support from the Ministry, following a logic of active dialogue with other countries of the Mediterranean."[18]

The position is quite clear: without strong support from the Ministry in Rome and cooperation of the adjacent Mediterranean countries the region is unable to resolve the issue. Fishermen have come to the conclusion that the authorities remain inactive to avoid diplomatic difficulties and that ultimately economic and political interests are at stake. "They tell us, 'let these poor people work', and they will not act until the first person dies." There already have been violent incidents with Tunisian boats: in May 2001, the Coast Guard captured a Tunisian boat 11 nautical miles off the coast (and thus in territorial waters) and confiscated 20 tons of fish, which were given to local restaurants).[19]

Whereas in former times the fleet of Mazara del Vallo had been the main object of complaint, now Tunisia became the antagonist. Fishermen from Sicily feel the effects of over-fishing as well. Basically run by Tunisian crews, the fleet of Mazara, a town with a consistent Tunisian population that started settling in the 1960s, reaches out as far as Turkey and Greece to catch

---

measurements have been introduced for each species: sardines, for example, must be at least 11 cm long. (See *SFOP* Informa, Strumento Finanziario di Orientamento della Pesca (*SFOP*), n. 3, Nov. 2006. However, compliance is hardly ever checked and many fishermen continue fishing even outside the open season.

17 Letter of the *Associazione Pescatori Lampedusa* to the Ministry, *Ministero delle Risorse Agricole e Forestali*, the *Comando Generale delle Capitanierie di Porto*, and the municipality of Lampedusa e Linosa (September 29, 2000).

18 Letter of the President of the Region of Sicily, prot. No 5552 (March 5, 2003).

19 Pro Memoria of the *Associazione Pescatori Lampedusa* (May 30, 2001).

giant red shrimp because the stock in their traditional fishing grounds is exhausted.

The structural crisis of the sector leads to quarrels at borders and to classical conflicts over scarce resources.[20] Local fishermen feel assaulted by Tunisians and abandoned by politicians and public authorities. The opinion that "everything is done for the clandestine whereas we're abandoned and nobody cares" is heard quite often and the symbolic relationship between Tunisian fishers and the "clandestine", "Arabs" or even "Albanians" is easily established:

– "We are ruined by these people, they should not be allowed to enter, and they even fish in stormy weather. As you see, today we are blocked and didn't go for a catch, and they do. The Coast Guard doesn't intervene; they are allowed to do whatever they want. In your country [Germany] authorities enforce the law and things like that don't happen!"
– "What about the people from Mazara?" I asked.
– "That's another question! They are like us, they have to work. But these Arabs are about to ruin us, they rob people and sell drugs. The Government should be kicked. They allow them to enter. They don't go to Libya because they would be shot, so they come here. They ruin local tourism, that's negative publicity and people think they roam in the streets. But they don't cause trouble. People don't even notice. Now they've created a new structure..."

Yet another arena of conflict has been established. Since the boom of the 1980s, the tourism industry has become one of the main economic pillars of the small community. In recent years, as many as 50,000 tourists have visited Lampedusa, making the hospitality industry the main source of income for the island.[21] The fear that media coverage and the visibility of the clandestine (i.e., the invisibles) could harm tourism is used in populist rhetoric, and not just in times of local elections. Media attention leads to an astonishing dialectic of visibility and invisibility. Populist rhetoric seeking to represent those who do not feel recognized and represented in the (local) political sphere aside, reception of boat people has become an integral part of a powerful political arena with a highly clientelist network that connects Lampedusa with the regional and national social and political context. Reception has also become a rather lucrative business. What is at stake are public works and commissions, subsidies, jobs, and the control of land and public resources.

Due to severe overcrowding, the original reception center had to be expanded. During the construction of the new center fierce local conflicts arose

---

20 Libyan authorities confiscated a boat and detained eight crewmembers from Mazara which was located 45 nautical miles off the coast in the Gulf of Sidra, an area considered by Libya as an "exclusive economic zone." The Italian Minister of Foreign Affairs intervened. (Source: ANSA, Feb. 1, 2008.)

21 There is a vast body of literature on this topic. For a recent account of the relation of hospitality und tourism, see contributions in German Molz and Gibson (2007).

about the designated site. One local faction favored a new building (in a rather obvious attempt to sell land), while the opposition favored the use of existing barracks that would cause a minor environmental impact.[22] Due to public protest, the construction of a new building was prevented. The new center, however, was built in a protected area and was technically illegal, as was the new site for the confiscated boats. With the arrival of the boat people, another serious ecological problem emerged: the disposal of the vessels. Hard-sided and inflatable boats reaching the island are confiscated by the *GdF* and kept at the local dump. The triennial plan of the municipality included €550,000 for the "establishment of a provisional depot for the nautical relicts of the extracommunitarians" which was funded by the Civil Defense Department (*Protezione Civile*). Ironically, the site, which has been planned for only 30 boats, was soon shut down by the authorities because it was built without authorization and no report on its ecological compatibility had been submitted—incidentally, it is located by a road with a picturesque panoramic view. In 2004, Civil Defense was tasked to deal with this "emergency", allowing it to circumvent rules for public commissions (the head of the department, Guido Bertolaso, recently came under national critical public scrutiny). His deputy identified a new site for the boat dump and the *Edilmeccanica G. Campione S.r.l* in Agrigento won the public tender. The company is part of the group controlled by Giuseppe Campione, a politician "rumored to be involved in Mafia activities" (Senato della Repubblica, 2004). However, because it was badly constructed, part of its walls crumbled in 2006. In 2007, the company *SEAP* was provisionally commissioned to scrap the boats. This contract was revoked by Civil Defense in 2008. *SEAP* appealed this decision and won the case in December 2009. In April 2009, a public tender worth €350,000 was released (Protezione Civile, March, 30, 2009), and in December 2008, the site was burnt down—certainly not unintentionally, given that setting fire is a common Mafia warning. In the meantime, Sergio Vella, the general administrator at *SEAP* and a personal friend of the Italian Minister of Justice, Angelino Alfano (PdL) from Agrigento, accused the mayor of Lampedusa of corruption and to have received €70,000 in bribe. The mayor was taken into custody in July 2009 and removed from office. (He was subsequently released and returned to office in August. The accusations are still being investigated.)

The "cemetery of boats" was a very impressive site (Friese, 2007). In 2007, more than 200 boats and inflatable boats were piled up, as a worker at

[22] The new center was financed by the Ministry of the Interior (the costs amounted to ca. €14 million). However, the mayor complains that the center management has not paid for water, waste disposal, and service since 1998 and that the €7 million the municipality received from the Region of Sicily is by no means sufficient to cover the overall cost.

the site estimated. Locals wondered why boats were not sold at public auctions like in Malta: “I could never afford a boat. I would be happy to get even a small one for €2,000 or €3,000 and here new boats are left to rot”, he told me, also raising doubts about the whereabouts of the outboard motors: ”They divide them among themselves”, he suspected, “I’ve never seen any up here. There is a black market, but what can we do? The laws are made by those who rule...” Even if motors are nicely piled up in the former NATO LORAN station, this case is symbolic of the economic interests and clientelist modes that are an intrinsic part of this business.

In 2007, two cooperatives associated with the leftist Legacoop, which has close ties with the leftist trade union, formed a consortium, *Lampedusa Accoglienza* (“reception”), and won the public bid to run the new center. Since Tangentopoli (the anti-corruption movement that shook the foundations of the Italian political system in the early 1990s) around 40% of public commissions are assigned to consortiums. Given that participation in the procedure requires the kind of (legal and financial) means small cooperatives can rarely afford, the usual procedure is that several individual coops form a consortium, with the Legacoop serving as a formal umbrella that participates in public tenders. However, the outcome dissatisfied not only antiracist groups. Exponents of the regional Legacoop told me that the two cooperatives in question—*Blu Coop* of Agrigento and *Sisifo* of Catania—had already sealed the deal before the tender was released and thus had excluded other regional competitors. In addition, the political affiliations and clientelist relations of both coops, which are more or less run by “family and friends”, are well-known. Indeed, although the procedure was legally correct, the affair sheds a light on how reception has become a business in which personal interests are intertwined with clientelist political networks.

After publication in the newspaper Manifesto (April 1, 2007), antiracist groups occupied the head offices of Legacoop in Bologna and Palermo, arguing that cooperatives should reflect the tradition and values of trade unions and the workers’ movement and therefore should not support the detention system. They also criticized that the coops had won the public tender by undercutting their competing bidder Misericordia, which previously ran the facility, by more than 30%. In order to render financial transactions more transparent and to avoid further waste of public resources, the Ministry of the Interior limited the expenses for every “guest” to €50 per day. Misericordia offered €50, another Sicilian coop, Connecting People, offered €37, and *Lampedusa Accoglienza* offered €33. The Vice-President of *Sisifo*, a member of the then-existing party *La Margherita*, which has since merged into the Democratic Party, stated that their calculation was around €2 million per year, that they would do a marvelous job and that service would not suffer. However, the center was no longer a Center of Temporary Stay (CPT) but was converted into a Center of First Reception and Aid (CPA), which means, at least in theory, that new arrivals were not to stay there for more than 72 hours.

Financing having become a serious issue, the Praesidium Projects 1, 2, and 3 were renewed in 2008. The project is a joint collaboration between the International Organization for Migration (IOM), the Italian Red Cross, and UNHCR on Lampedusa. The aim of the projects was to "improve reception" and services for unaccompanied minors. The Ministry of the Interior requested €395,935 from the European Commission (European Commission ARGO). In order to promote "an increase in communication between immigrants and the Ministry of Interior", to streamline procedures for the identification of migrants, and to reduce "clashes between different ethnic groups and between immigrants", the Ministry requested another €371,827,60 (European Commission ARGO).

Apparently, the Sicilian Mafia became interested in local business as well. In 2008, for the first time, the *Direzione Investigativa Antimafia* mentions a Mafia "family" in Lampedusa e Linosa (DIA, 2008:29). Even more astonishing alliances have been established since. In August 2003, Ganat Tewelde Barhe (a young woman born on January 1, 1980 in Asmara, Eritrea and known as "Madame Genette") was arrested and, in February 2004, was extradited from Libya and flown to Rome where her sister lives. She had fled from Eritrea and worked for a few years as a housemaid in Tripoli before trying to cross the Mediterranean Sea in 2000. She failed, but came to know a high-ranking Libyan *passeur*. Her headquarters was a bar in Zuwarah, a port city near the Tunisian border from which most boats departed. Barhe is considered to have been one of the main "travel agents" in the region. She was convicted on human trafficking charges and sentenced to four years in prison. Thanks to a general amnesty in August 2006, she was released, applied for asylum, and was brought to the CPT of Ragusa, Sicily. While in prison, she reportedly became friends with a fellow inmate, Maria Rita Carmela Falsone, the sister of Giuseppe Falsone, one of the heads of the Sicilian Mafia, who was arrested in June 2010. While waiting for her application to be decided, she married into this important Mafia family and became the wife of Falsone's brother Calogero, thus acquiring Italian citizenship which automatically saved her from deportation. Since 2008, she has lived near Livorno, where she is part of the Sicilian community (DIA 2009: 37).

However, the ongoing militarization of the island was widely noticed. Even though the US interception facility had been closed, the border regime brought many security staff (some *Carabiniere* did - to the regret of some - even mingle in local affairs) and were accommodated in hotels. This was met with polemic attention, although the opposition was probably partly fueled by jealousy because some hotel owners received a steady income while others did not.

With the establishment of the center, the first volunteers had been replaced and were not considered for the new paid jobs. The locals also generally felt excluded from decision-making, participation, and representation. As decisions are made elsewhere, hospitality is no longer a practice involving the local community, but a contested matter of exclusion, negated participation, conflicting notions of justice, and struggles for recognition.

Opening a Space of the Political

In January 2009, boat people forced open the gates of the overcrowded facility to protest against their treatment and imminent deportation, resulting in the facility being burnt down. Chanting "Freedom! Freedom!" and "Grazie Lampedusa", hundreds of people joined the demonstrating residents who had founded the association S.O.S. Pelagie and were protesting plans by the government and the Minister of the Interior, Maroni (Lega Nord) to convert the center of first reception and aid (CPA) into a center of identification and expulsion (CIE). The protest opened a shared space of contest, allowing to press for participation in political decision-making, the implementation of (international) legal norms and the debate on conflicting notions of (distributive) justice. The borderlands and the limits of hospitality became a site of engagement, solidarity, and antagonistic political practice. Hospitality became a site of contestation and a site where different disjunctures became apparent, disjunctures between sovereignty, the self-determination of a (political) community, belonging and citizenship on one hand and rights to democratic political participation and cosmopolitan norms on the other.

Representations of the migrants' "ontological victimhood", as proposed by humanitarian discourse and some political activism, point to the (imperfect) duty to support the endangered. However, it neither challenges the powerful discursive fields and the general perception of undocumented migration as a social threat and a problem of public welfare and supposed security, nor the democratic paradox of membership and exclusion. "The concept of hospitality is bound to generate conflicts and passionate arguments", and "it is inevitably linked to the daily practices of ordinary citizens" (Rosello 2001:6). Articulating tensions between the global and the local spheres, it is rooted in specific historical contexts in which local, national, and supranational actors are interwoven. The local setting, its various agents, interests, and conflicts promote these tensions in a specific way and reiterate the ambiguity of hospitality that results from the mobility of agents and their personal dreams and aspirations. Technocratic utopias of efficient "management," lack of recognition, political exclusion, and restrictions to local participation promote further limits to the hospitable welcome of an Other. At the same time, however, the local protest opened up a pluralist transnational political space in which so-called ordinary citizens and so-called undocumented migrants together expressed their demands and expectations. Hospitality became a site of contest and a political space that criss-crossed common concepts of citizenship, the demarcation of aliens, and the inclusion/exclusion divide. Without being rooted, without reference, and without political participation of the local arena and its various actors renewed concepts of hospitality and transnational, cosmopolitan justice will just remain a normative and theoretical academic exercise.

References

Abdel Ghaffar M., A (2008): Sudanese trade in black ivory: Opening old wounds. UNESCO. [online] Available at: portal.unesco.org/culture/fr/ev.php-URL_ID=38507&URL_DO=DO_TOPIC&URL_SECTION=201.html [Accessed February 14, 2011].

Agamben, G. (1995): Homo sacer: Il potere sovrano e la nuda vita. Torino: Einaudi.

Appadurai, A. (1990): Disjuncture and difference in the global cultural economy. In : M. Featherstone (ed.): Global culture: Nationalism, globalization and modernity. London: Sage, pp.295-309.

Balibar, É. (2004): Europe as Borderland. The Alexander von Humboldt Lecture in Human Geography. University of Nijmegen, November 18, 2004. [online] Available at: socgeo.ruhosting.nl/colloquium/Europe%20as%20Borderland.pdf [Accessed February 14, 2011].

Bauman, Z. (2002): The fate of humanity in the post-Trinitarian world. In: Journal of Human Rights 1, 3, pp. 283-303.

Bauman, Z. (2007): Humanity on the move. In Liquid Times. Living in an age of uncertainty. Cambridge: Polity.

Benhabib, S. (2008): Another cosmopolitanism: Hospitality, sovereignty and democratic iterations. Expanded Tanner Lectures with commentaries by Jeremy Waldron, Bonnie Honig and Will Kymlicka. Oxford: Oxford University Press.

Bogusz, B. (2004): Irregular migration and human rights: Theoretical, European and international perspectives. The Hague: Nijhoff.

Chavez, L. R. (1991): Outside the imagined community: Undocumented settlers and experiences of incorporation. In: American Ethnologist 18, pp.257-78.

Chavez, L. R. (1994): The power of the imagined community: The settlement of undocumented Mexicans and Central Americans in the United States. In: American Anthropologist 96, 1, pp.52-73.

Chebel, M. (2007): L'esclavage en terre d'Islam. Un tabou bien gardé. Paris: Fayard.

De Genova, N. P. (2002): Migrant "illegality" and deportability in everyday life. In: Annual Review of Anthropology 31, pp.419-47.

de Haas, H. (2007): The Myth of Invasion: Irregular Migration From West Africa to the Maghreb and the European Union. IMI Research Report, University of Oxford.

Direzione Investigativa Antimafia (2008): Relazione del Ministro dell'Interno al Parlamento sull'attività svolta e sui risultati conseguiti dalla Direzione Investigativa Antimafia. 2° semestre. [online] Available at: interno.it/dip_ps/dia/semestrali/sem/2008/1sem2008.pdf. [Accessed February 14, 2011].

Direzione Investigativa Antimafia (2009): Relazione del Ministro dell'Interno al Parlamento sull'attività svolta e sui risultati conseguiti dalla Direzione Investigativa Antimafia. 1° semester. [online] Available at: interno.it/dip_ps/dia/semestrali/sem/2009/1sem2009.pdf [Accessed February 14, 2011].

Düvell, F., Pastore, F., de Haas, H. et al. (2008): Transit, migration and politics: Trends and constructions on the fringes of Europe. [online] Available at: compas.ox.ac.uk/fileadmin/files/pdfs/Non_WP_pdfs/Reports_and_Other_Publications/Duvell%20transit%20IMISCOE%20report.pdf [Accessed February 14, 2011].

European Commission, Sep. 1 (2005): Proposal for a Directive of the European Parliament and of the Council on common standards and procedures in Member States for returning ollegally staying third-country nationals (presented by the Commission), COM(2005) 391 final, 2005/0167 (COD)SEC(2005) 1057. Brussels.
[online] Available at: ec.europa.eu/justice_home/fsj/immigration/fsj_immigra tion_intro_en.htm [Accessed February 14, 2011].

European Commission (2005): Technical mission to Libya on illegal migration 27 Nov-6 Dec 2004. Report. [online] Available at: http://www.statewatch.org/news/2005/may/eu-report-libya-ill-imm.pdf [Accessed February 14, 2011].

European Commission, Feb. 13 (2008): A comprehensive vision for an integrated European border management system for the 21st century. Press Release. [online] Available at: europa.eu/rapid/pressReleasesAction.do?reference=IP/08/215&format=HTML&aged=0&language=EN&guiLanguage=en [Accessed February 14, 2011].

European Commission, Dec. 24, 2008. Directive 2008/115/EC on common standards and procedures in Member States for returning illegally staying third-country nationals, as published in the Official Journal (L 348 of Dec. 24, 2008). European Commission, Towards a common European Union immigration policy. [online] Available at: ec.europa.eu/justice_home/fsj/immigration/fsj_immigration_intro_en.htm [Accessed February 14, 2011].

European Commission ARGO – External borders, asylum, visas and immigration No. JLS/2006/ARGO/GC/10. [online] Available at: http://ec.europa.eu/justice/funding/2004_2007/argo/funding_argo_en.htm [Accessed February 14, 2011].

European Commission ARGO – External borders, asylum, visas and immigration No. JLS/2006/ARGO/GC/09. [online] Available at: http://ec.europa.eu/justice_home/funding_2004_2007_argo/doc/projects_selected_details_2006_en.pdf [Accessed February 14, 2011].

Foucault, M. (1994 [1984]): Des espaces autres. In: Dits et écrits, Vol. IV. Paris: Gallimard, pp.752-62.

Friese, H. (1996): Lampedusa. Historische Anthropologie einer Insel. Frankfurt am Main: Campus.

Friese, H. (2004): Spaces of hospitality. In A. Benjamin and D. Vardoulakis (eds.): Politics of Place, Angelaki. Journal of the Theoretical Humanities, 9, 2, pp.67-79.

Friese, H. (2007): Partire. Photoessay. [online] Available at: web.mac.com/hfriese/heidrun_friese/photoessays.html [Accessed February 14, 2011].

Friese, H. (2009): The limits of hospitality. In: Dikec, M./Clark, N. H./Barnett, C. (eds.): Extending hospitality: Giving space, taking time. Paragraph 32, 1, pp. 51-68.

Friese, H. (2010): The limits of hospitality. Political philosophy, undocumented migration and the local arena. In: Friese, H./Mezzadra, S. (eds.): Borderlands. Migration and social theory. European Journal of Social Theory 10, 3, pp. 299-333.

Frontex (2007): Frontex-led EU illegal immigration technical mission to Libya 28 May–5 June 2007. [online] Available at: frontex.europa.eu/newsroom/press_kit/documents/art8.html [Accessed February 14, 2011].

Frontex (2008): Press Release, Frontext – UNHCR: reinforced cooperation, June 18, 2008. [online] Available at: frontex.europa.eu/newsroom/news_releases/art39.html [Accessed February 14, 2011].

Frontex (n.d.) What is Frontex? [online] Available at: frontex.europa.eu. [Accessed February 14, 2011].

German-Molz, J./Gibson, S., eds. (2007): Mobilizing hospitality. The ethics of social relations in a mobile world. London: Ashgate.

Global Commission on International Migration (2005): Migration in an interconnected world: New directions for action. Report of the Global Commission on International Migration. [online] Available at: gcim.org/attachements/gcim-complete-report-2005.pdf [Accessed February 14, 2011].

Gupta, A. (1992): The song of the nonaligned worlds: Transnational identities and the reinscription of space in late capitalism. In: Current Anthropology, 7, 1, pp. 6-23.

Honig, B. (2008): Another cosmolitanism? Law and politics in the New Europe. In: Benhabib, S. (ed.): Another cosmopolitanism: Hospitality, sovereignty and democratic iterations. Expanded Tanner Lectures with commentaries by Jeremy Waldron, Bonnie Honig and Will Kymlicka. Oxford: Oxford University Press, pp.102-127.

Honneth, A. (1994): Kampf um Anerkennung. Zur moralischen Grammatik sozialer Konflikte. Frankfurt am Main: Suhrkamp.

Jordan, B./Düvell, F. (2002): Irregular Migration. The Dilemmas of Transnational Mobility. Aldershot, Edward Elgar.

Jordan, B./Düvell, F. (2003): Migration. The boundaries of equality and justice. Cambridge: Polity Press.

Mangano, A. (2010): Gli africani salveranno l'Italia. Milano: BUR.

Mezzadra, S. (2001): Diritto di fuga. Migrazioni, cittadinanza, globalizzazione. Verona: Ombre Corte.

Ministero dell'Interno (Dec. 29, 2007) Comunicati Stampa, L'accordo Italia-Libia sul pattugliamento: i contenuti. [online] Available at: inteno.it/mininterno/export/sites/default/it/sezioni/sala_stampa/comunicati/0866_2007_12_29_I_contenuti_dellxaccordo_con_la_Libia.html [Accessed February 14, 2011].

Protezione Civile (Mar 30, 2009) Bando di gara. [online] Available at: protezionecivile.it/cms/attach/bando_di_gara.pdf [Accessed February 14, 2011].

Rosello, M. (2001): Postcolonial hospitality: The immigrant as guest. Stanford: Stanford University Press.

Schmitt, C. (1950): Der Nomos der Erde im Völkerrecht des Jus Publicum Europaeum. Berlin: Duncker & Humblot.

Senato della Repubblica, Legislatura 14° - Aula - Resoconto stenografico della seduta n. 686 del 02/11/2004, Interrogazioni. [online] Available at: parlamento.it/japp/bgt/showdoc/frame.jsp?tipodoc=Resaula&leg=14&id=00120892 &part=doc_dc-allegatob_ab-sezionetit_i:1&parse=no&stampa=si&toc=no [Accessed February 14, 2011].

Spindler, W. (2007): Between the devil and the deep blue sea: Mixed migration to Europe. [online] Available at: unhcr.org/news/NEWS/470658fe4.html [Accessed February 14, 2011].

Tangu Kwenzi-Mikala, J., ed. (2003): Tradition orale liée à la traite négrière et à l'esclavage en Afrique centrale. Paris: UNESCO. [online] Available at: unesdoc.unesco.org/images/0013/001324/132459f.pdf [Accessed February 14, 2011].

Urry, J. (2007): Mobilities. Cambridge: Polity.

Wright, J. (2007): The trans-Saharan slave trade. London: Routledge.

Unintended Effects of Immigration Policies for Governments and Migrants: Conclusions

Mechthild Baumann, Astrid Lorenz, Kerstin Rosenow

We started this book with the observation that the European and North American democracies fear the negative effects of their attraction to potential migrants from all over the world. They wish to channel and control migration and thereby shape the world according to their own policies and interests. To be able to do so, they have to engage in both national and international political bargaining processes that are tied to contemporary forms of migration management. Such negotiations usually fail to focus on the subjects of the policy choices—the migrants themselves. The aim of this book project is to shed light upon the interrelations between immigration policies and migrants' choices of moving across and around borders. As stated in the introduction, we want to understand how immigration policies affect migrant's journeys and vice versa.

In this chapter, we draw empirical and theoretical conclusions based on the various analyses contained in this volume that focus on the European and U.S. migration regimes. We conclude that immigration policies have a multitude of unintended effects which affect both migrants and governments in the countries of origin, transit, and arrival.

This chapter begins with an overview of the interest policies inside and outside the 'defended' territories. In the U.S. a lucrative internal market of border control has emerged, whereas the EU's externalized border control includes the neighboring countries. The second part describes the unintended effects arising due to inconsistent general policies of the countries of arrival and origin, which often contradict the official immigration policies. Following this, the limited effect of border control measures on immigrants and their journeys are discussed. In the fourth section we explore in more detail the unintended effects in the form of new areas of cooperation, including new forms of self-organization, local interest groups, and sanctuary movements. The final section summarizes the various unintended effects and offers recommendations for decision makers in the field of migration policy.

Interest Policies Inside and Outside 'Defended' Territories

The articles reveal that all of the actors involved in the migration control process—countries of arrival, origin, and transit, as well as the immigrants themselves—pursue their own interests. Both of the two receiving regions under examination, the EU and the U.S., employ a defensive approach to immigration control. One could say that the aim of their policies is to build a castle with a moat around it. However, while the U.S. focuses on domestic solutions to defend its borders, the EU has increasingly externalized its border control, creating unintended effects concerning the necessary political negotiations with its neighboring countries, as discussed below.

The U.S. chooses a rather militaristic defense strategy to protect its territory from unwanted 'intruders' who come mainly from and via its southern neighbor Mexico. In 2006, the U.S. government decided to erect a 700-mile border fence along the U.S.–Mexican frontier (US 2006)[1]. This is the latest in a series of restrictive policies aimed at preventing undocumented immigrants from crossing the border to the U.S. by controlling und monitoring the border. Similar to the EU, the U.S. border control and surveillance measures are extremely technology-driven. Border surveillance has become a highly lucrative business. Private corporations involved in this market pay big money to support their allies in the U.S. Congress and to lobby for a continuation of the walling-off of the country (see Staudt/Garcia-Rios in this volume). Immigration control thus follows its own economic dynamics, which is also stimulated by anti-immigrant reporting in the media. The U.S. control and surveillance efforts are supported by certain segments of the population. As Staudt/Garcia-Rios and Bloch/Rocha Silva point out, civil society actors have also been involved in reporting illegal border crossings and supporting national border guards.

The EU is also attempting to protect itself from unwanted migrants by strengthening the control of its borders around its territory (EU 2006; 2008a). It has established various protective/defensive circles around its territory that are reminiscent of the moats around medieval castles, the castle wall being its external borders and the moat the EU's neighboring countries and the more distant third countries. This form of externalization is one key characteristic of the EU's migration control policy which Gil Araújo analyzes in her article. This means that migration control has been complemented by control measures outside EU territory. These politics of "concentric circles" were

1 The government of Greece, the main entrance to the EU for undocumented migrants from Turkey, recently planned to copy the U.S.-American fence. Although the EU Commission disapproved of this plan, it became clear that some actors within the EU favor a U.S.-like militaristic defense strategy to deal with undocumented migration.

introduced by the Austrian EU presidency in 1998. A major general objective of the European Neighbourhood Policy (ENP) and the EU's global approach to migration (EU 2008b) is to involve the neighboring countries in the control of migration to the EU in order to "strengthen prosperity, stability and security of all" (European Comission: European Neighbourhood Policy). The EU even goes one step further, by trying to persuade transit countries and migrants' countries of origin to assist the EU in controlling migration. A major economic and political player, the EU does not hesitate to use its power. It negotiates on the basis of a reward system, with the main reward being EU accession.

However, countries of origin and transit pursue their own interests as well. Like any other country, they are interested in increasing and promoting prosperity. They rarely have a genuine interest in preventing (transit) migration to the EU or U.S. and only assume the role of 'deputy sheriff' if they are under political pressure or if there is a genuine economic or political incentive. Several articles in this volume suggest that such states act as economic entrepreneurs and therefore may have a rational interest in preventing more of its citizens from emigrating in order to enhance their bargaining power and to increase rewards for their efforts to curb emigration.

Morocco, a transit country, even benefits from irregular migration. Heck has found that many sub-Saharan migrants find themselves stranded in Morocco while trying to reach Europe. The EU pays Morocco €70 million per year to protect its borders and prohibit undocumented migration to Europe. This deal has led to a strange system of gratification. Morocco justifies these generous payments by the large number of apprehensions at its borders. There is but one problem: According to Heck, the Moroccan border guards systematically defraud the European authorities of large amounts of money by playing a cat-and-mouse game. They catch the same migrants over and over again, take them a few kilometers behind the border, and wait for them to pass through Morocco again, thus altering the statistics in favor of Morocco every time the Moroccan guards catch them, which justifies additional payments from the EU.

In her investigation of political incentives Bilecen-Süoglu shows that the prospect of EU accession was one of the key motivating factors for Turkey to change and restrict its migration regime, highlighting Turkey's difficulties in defining a genuine national interest in migration matters. Turkey actively sought to comply with the EU's demands, notably the implementation of the Schengen acquis, until it became evident that the EU member states are divided over whether Turkey should become a full EU member. Since then, Turkey has significantly reduced its efforts to implement EU standards. Indeed, if it turned out in a few years that Turkey's accession to the EU is all but certain, the country may actually lose all motivation to further strengthen and restrict migration to the EU. For transit migrants, Turkey's position in the European migration regime is of utmost importance. Turkey is the bridge between Asia and Europe and is still an important route for regular and irregular migration to the EU.

Haase has made similar observations. Ukraine, formerly a transit country, has become a reluctant country of arrival since it started implementing the migration control measures demanded by the EU. As a result, it has become an 'immigration country of second choice', for migrants who are on their way to the EU and who often find themselves stranded in Ukraine. However, the country lacks the infrastructure and experience to deal with immigrants, and the existing xenophobic trends in Ukraine have become worse as a result of this situation. Although Ukraine hopes for EU accession and is therefore willing to deal with this situation, it would be wrong to interpret its efforts to implement EU standards as docile eagerness to please the EU. After all, Ukraine was quite able to pursue its own interests in the negotiations of EU visa facilitation for Ukrainian nationals in exchange for the readmission agreement demanded by the EU.

Obviously, the carrot-and-stick strategy of the EU may prove rather costly, including the possible unintended effects described above. The economic approach of rewarding its neighbors and other transit countries for complying with its political objectives often works out only on paper. Moreover, the EU risks getting blackmailed. It expects the major transit countries such as Morocco, Turkey, and Ukraine to do the 'dirty work' of keeping migrants out. But transit states are rational actors. The willingness of these countries to comply with the EU's demands depends on the (perceived) benefits and costs in each transit state. If these countries were to find that their costs exceed their benefits, they might ask the EU for greater financial compensation. They may also cooperate with each other to put the EU under severe pressure. Countries with limited prospects of EU accession such as Turkey and Ukraine would have little to lose. Hess's article in this volume also highlights the unintended outcome of the EU transit policies since "the newly labeled 'transit countries' learn to use this categorization for their own power games." Future policy planning should take these observations into consideration.

Unintended Effects of Inconsistent Policies and Economic Interests: The Encouragement of Ongoing Emigration

Migration policies of the U.S. and the EU member states are influenced primarily by economic interests which very often contradict the zero-tolerance approach to undocumented migration. As the following overview shows, economic interests prevail both in the countries of origin and arrival, which also highlights the inconsistent nature of existing anti-migration policies.

Kreienbrink describes the interest of the Spanish government in regularizing migrants. In his analysis he identifies Spain's labor market as the strongest pull factor to produce unintended effects on EU migration policy. State authorities generally fail to maintain effective internal control, particularly in the agricultural and construction industries, both of which have a constant demand for new labor. This tolerance towards irregular labor gives Spain certain competitive advantages on the macroeconomic level, with possible regularization providing an additional incentive for undocumented migrants to come to Spain. Regularization attempts in Spain and a number of other European countries aimed at furthering national economic interests therefore contradict the EU's immigration policies

In Mexico, the enactment of the North American Free Trade Agreement with the U.S. (NAFTA) in 1994 only yielded marginal improvements. In fact, it even prevented the intended effects of the anti-migration measures. According to Staudt and Garcia-Rios, it led to increased foreign direct investments and overall productivity, and reduced inflation. However, NAFTA was not able to create sustainable jobs at living-wage levels, which would have made emigration to the U.S. less attractive. Mexicans living in the U.S. transfer large portions of their income home to their families. Unsurprisingly, these remittances are the second most important source of income in Mexico, just after oil exports and before foreign direct investments (Randall 2006). Mexican remittances figures grew to US$27 billion in 2007 and decreased to US$22 billion in 2009 and 2010 (World Bank 2011). Emigration to the U.S. is supported by the Mexican State because migrants remain one of the most important sources of revenue for the Mexican economy.

The case of Senegal reveals another paradox of inconsistent policies. Tsagué shows in this volume that several measures implemented by the EU and European enterprises have aggravated the living conditions in Senegal and have thus proved to be a push factor for emigration to Europe. A good example of this is the overexploitation of the sea along the Senegalese coast by European enterprises, which has been partially tolerated and compensated financially by EU member states[2]. A very poor country, Senegal is in a relatively weaker negotiation position. When the EU cynically asks Senegal to implement measures to prevent irregular emigration – which, after all, was at least partially triggered by European intervention – the Senegalese government is very cooperative because it hopes for better access to the internal EU market and for stronger relations with the EU. Senegal even boasts about its

2 See Agreement between the European Economic Community and the Government of the Republic of Senegal on fishing off the coast of Senegal, for the period from 1 July 2002 to 30 June 2006, OJ L 349/45.

excellent exit control, despite the fact that this contradicts Senegal's national interests. Similar to the situation in Mexico, remittances from Senegalese emigrants are of utmost importance for the country's national economy, but are jeopardized due to tougher controls. As in other countries of transit and origin, this political dilemma has several consequences for the society of Senegal. In the Senegalese culture, the decision to send the member of the family who is most likely to succeed in Europe is made by the family collective, who consider their support as an investment. Pressure on the migrants is very high and many of them do not dare return to Senegal because they fear they will be unable to meet the high expectations. If the Senegalese government wants to bring them back and prevents others from leaving, it has to set up a return policy which can be accepted by the local population and create jobs for those who were designated to leave and must now stay at home.

One can conclude that inconsistent EU and U.S. policies are policies which aggravate the living conditions in potential emigration regions rather than improving them. Negative externalities of such policies as well as national and individual economic interests can significantly reduce the efficiency of anti-migration measures.

Unintended Effects on Migrants' Behavior: The Limited Effects of Border Control

According to the World Migration Report 2010, the number of international migrants has more than doubled in the last four decades, from 82 million in 1970 to about 214 million in 2010 and a projected 405 million in 2050 (IOM 2010: xix). With the growth of international migration occurring at a time of increasingly restrictive admission policies, unauthorized migration has picked up dramatically in recent years. Nevertheless, it is estimated that only between 10 and 15% of today's international migrants live in an irregular situation (Ibid: 29).

The articles in this volume confirmed empirically that physical barriers do not discourage people from crossing borders. This finding is supported by statements of migrants who succeeded in crossing the border. Naturally, the deterrence capacity of border control and surveillance is difficult to assess, but the interviews with the would-be migrants suggest that the deterrence capacity of border security is limited. Obviously, border control measures are unlikely to deter migrants from migrating if they perceive that they have nothing to lose at home and much to gain in the country of destination. Border fences can do little to keep them from emigrating.

In fact, the articles show that migrants are led by reason and use every means at their disposal to pursue their objectives. The concept of agency—in the sense of the migrant acting as a *Homo economicus*—thus makes sense for migrants, too. Most migrants show a high degree of initiative and the will to actively shape their lives. In most cases, they are self-determined subjects. Or, to put it conversely: Migrants are not objects that can be controlled by political actors at will. As Friese and Hess point out in their contributions, migrants make their own decisions; they trade off different options and implement their objectives. This requires survival skills, personal resources, and capabilities. For these reasons, a description of migrants should not portray them as victims or as a threat to the security and welfare of Western industrial nations, but as active agents.

The argument that border control has a limited effect on migrants' behavior is also supported by Staudt and Garcia-Rios, albeit from a different perspective. They identify economic factors as the main explanatory variable for immigration rates from Mexico to the U.S. According to their study, border or immigration policies, as far as they exist, are only an intervening variable. Border control and surveillance do influence the way migrants move, but they hardly have any influence on the decision of whether to emigrate or not. As in the Spanish case, economic and immigration policies in the U.S. are not only non-convergent, they are contradictive. While immigration policies try to prevent or even 'fight' irregular migration, the constantly high demand for low-wage labor in the U.S. is a strong incentive for Mexicans to migrate despite legal obstacles.

This estimation is complemented by Cornelius, who notes that "immigration law and policy are huge experiments in behavior modification". He points out the helplessness of governments and their inability to intervene in international migration flows, stressing that it is easier for governments to initiate migration flows than to stop them. The budget for the virtual fence between the U.S. and Mexico is tremendous. However, Cornelius' interviews with 4,000 Mexicans in Mexico show that fewer than half of them have been caught crossing the border irregularly. Moreover, border control does not make potential migrants reconsider their decision to emigrate. The economic incentives provided in the U.S. are too attractive and the living conditions in Mexico and further south are too harsh.

The decrease in illegal migration from Mexico to the U.S. in recent years is due mainly to the economic crisis in the U.S. and the lack of employment. Neither interior enforcements such as workplace raids nor a hostile environment affect migrants' decisions to go to the U.S. as strongly. Even many green card holders have left the U.S. But this is not a permanent situation. Cornelius makes it clear that "many stay-at-homes are only postponing migration until the U.S. economy improves." Again, it is the economic interests of some employers that conflict with the government's or society's intention to control and deter undocumented Mexican immigrants.

The same is true for Spain where, according to Kreienbrink, the phenomenon of irregular labor is widely accepted in small enterprises. The possibility of finding employment and being regularized is a strong incentive for migrants to cross borders illegally. Even if regularization is only temporary, it is often a step toward obtaining legal status and noticeably improving their economic and social situation.

In order to avoid the tightened border control, migrants usually take alternative routes, which are becoming increasingly difficult and dangerous. While border control and surveillance may not prevent immigration altogether, they do have an influence on *which* people migrate, and *how* they do so. Many migrants are unable to make their journey on their own and have to seek the 'professional support' of people smugglers. This has led to the emergence of a new smuggling market in Europe and at the U.S.–Mexican border over the last two decades. Smuggling profits are even increasing, because the product offered by these entrepreneurs, the chance to cross the border, has become increasingly difficult to obtain.

At the same time, the number of deaths attributed to unauthorized border crossings—i.e., crossings excluding entries with forged passports or crossings with unlawfully obtained visas—is on the increase worldwide. Several thousand people drown or die of thirst on both sides of the Atlantic each year. According to the NGO UNITED for Intercultural Action, there were 13,824 fatal border crossing attempts into the EU between 1993 and 2010 (www.unitedagainstracism.org). Figures for the U.S. are equally dramatic with an average of more than one migrant dying every day along the southwestern border, resulting in over 5,600 officially casualties so far (see Cornelius).

On the whole, one can conclude that the decision to migrate is accompanied by serious unintended effects, such as the emergence of people smuggling and other related crimes, increasing casualty rates, and people being stripped of their individual rights due to their irregular status. With regard to the controversial establishment of EU "transit zones", which are "designated places where rejected migrants are physically detained until they are returned" (Tóth 2006), it has been critically remarked that irregular migrants are kept from "the full panoply of procedural rights which apply to immigration and asylum" despite the fact that they are subject to the jurisdiction of the territorial state, which remains bound by its international obligations on human rights (Ibid.). Similarly, in this volume Hess criticizes the manifestation of precarious transit zones, which "keep people caught in mobility and transforms border regions into zones of increased circulation […] [that] restrict the social, economic, and political rights of migrants".

Unintended Effects on Alliance Building and the Pending Issue of Legal Rights

Another unintended consequence of migration policies are the new forms of alliance building among the migrants themselves which have developed in recent years but have not yet been adequately described in the academic literature. In addition, the establishment of legal rights for undocumented migrants still remains a contentious issue both in the U.S. and the EU.

Concerning the new forms of alliance building, the articles in this volume observe that migrants on both sides of the Atlantic find new forms of self-organization and micro-politics to deal with their situation of being in transit. In Morocco, for example, irregular migrants live together in the 'underground' in small groups of approximately 10 people. In the desert and in the outskirts of the cities migrants set up makeshift camps. This shows that a completely new form of residence has emerged in Morocco, a fact the Moroccan government refuses to acknowledge. Similar forms of makeshift residences can be observed in Turkey and Ukraine. Ukraine in particular, with its extremely strict border control and surveillance, has become a country where many former transit migrants find themselves stranded and now have to learn to manage their lives there. These cases confirm the observation made in the preliminary studies to this book that migrants organize their lives 'around' border control measures.

Friese describes another form of alliance building that has emerged on the island of Lampedusa. In 2009, something extraordinary happened on the tiny island in the Mediterranean Sea off the Italian coast. Tourism is one of the most important sources of revenue for Lampedusa, but the industry is severely hampered by border surveillance measures on and around the island. In addition, Lampedusa experienced increasing numbers of migrants arriving on its coast. Reception camps were soon overcrowded, and the Lampedusani felt abandoned by the Italian government. When the Lampedusani and the migrants realized they could no longer tolerate this situation, they joined forces and took to the streets of the tiny island together to demonstrate against the policy of the Berlusconi government.

The sanctuary movement in the U.S., though having a different motivation, has had a similar outcome in that it, too, has led to joint demonstrations against stricter immigration policies. In 2006, for example, both documented and undocumented Mexican-born residents demonstrated against stricter immigration policies. According to the article by Bloch and Rocha Silva, the sanctuary movement was initiated by various churches in Los Angeles in the early 1980s. Its aim was to offer asylum for Central American immigrants in churches and synagogues as places for worship and refuge. U.S. citizens who join this movement protect immigrants from detention and deportation[3].

It should be noted that the examples of Lampedusa and the U.S. sanctuary movement are the exceptions that prove the rule. Xenophobic attitudes prevail and the preservation of distinct national identities in EU member states and the U.S. usually prevent the liberalization of immigration policies. However, even where undocumented migrants are not welcome, the regional population and the governments of the countries of arrival have to deal with them. In the long run, they have to consider fundamental issues such as individual rights, health care, and education for undocumented immigrants and their children, as well as for potential migrants who are still waiting for their chance.

At least to some degree, the rights of undocumented migrants are protected under international human rights law (Council of Europe 2007), but the translation into specific EU measures is still lagging behind. Cholewinski notes that, so far, "no specific EU measures have been adopted to protect the rights of irregular migrants, despite statements that fundamental rights, such as access to education for children or basic health care, need to be protected" (Cholewinski 2010: 7f.). In the U.S., alien rights of undocumented immigrants have been a matter of controversy as well. While Joppke (2001: 343ff.) points out that in the 1970s and 1980s American courts generally used to rule in favor of equal protection rights for illegal aliens, Bloch and Rocha Silva (in this volume) focus on ballot initiatives at the state level that were aimed at banning "undocumented aliens from using health care, welfare, and other public social services", the most prominent example being Proposition 187 in California in 1994. Although this proposition was eventually found unconstitutional, the debate on the issue of alien rights between federal, state, and local legislation still continues today (Thomas 2010). An interesting question for future research would be to examine the role migrants and their alliances can play in this process (Hing/Johnson 2006; Laubenthal 2007).

Summary and Outlook

The analyses presented in this book indicate that the objective of the U.S. and the EU to only allow friends, acquaintances, traders, and business partners to enter their territory has not been achieved. This observation confirms the reports cited in the introduction, of about 1.9 to 3.8 million undocument-

3 For a parallel analysis of the European case and its pro-regularization movement see Laubenthal 2007.

ed migrants living in the EU, and over 10 million in the U.S. However, border control and surveillance have become increasingly sophisticated on both sides of the Atlantic. Many enterprises have a great interest in serving decision makers who have a strong enthusiasm for technology. Border management has become a business factor and, at least from a technical point of view, an impermeable border seems to be feasible.

However, the analyses collected in this volume also raise serious doubts as to the efficiency of such a strategy. The existing migration management strategies and inconsistent general policies are already creating various unintended effects. The castle and moat structure described in this chapter is risky and very costly. Inconsistent policies encourage ongoing emigration, but tightened border control does not prevent people from migrating. Rather, the supposedly 'impermeable borders' often give rise to new forms of crime such as people smuggling, which can increase the de facto punishment for undocumented migration to the death penalty, as can be seen from the deaths of thousands of migrants who have attempted to cross the borders in recent years. At the same time, changing policies also stimulate the emergence of new forms of alliances and self-organization which can strengthen the migrants' resources and challenge traditional path-dependent institutions on the regional level. Alliances between migrants are formed throughout their entire journey and continue when dealing with civil society or local residents who support their claims.

Increased technical control measures would only partly prevent these unintended effects because migration policies are complex, cross-sectoral phenomena. Even small adjustments in one policy area can have an immediate effect on others. The approach of today's migration policy, which tends to ignore migrants' interests, the status quo in the countries of origin and transit, and the national interests of all of the countries involved, is often too simplistic and one-dimensional and should therefore be readjusted.

The reasonableness of increasingly strict border regimes becomes even more doubtful when we take into account that migration management is the result of political decisions based on many other aspects not covered in this book. Most Western societies fear that increased migration may result in cultural and religious *Überfremdung*, the collapse of social security systems, an influx of low-wage foreign laborers, and a xenophobic backlash, among other things. Politicians take these attitudes into account when making policy decisions. There are various examples of the "negative framing of migration" (Guiraudon/Joppke 2001). Casanova (2006) discusses the fear of terrorism and sleepers, liberal feminist discourses against imported patriarchal fundamentalism, the preservation of a secular tradition in Europe, and a xenophobic nativism. Huysmans (2000) talks about the fear of welfare fraud and the use of immigrants as scapegoats to explain the struggling welfare systems (cf. Beck 2008). Similarly, Weiner (1995) cites sources which portray migrants as a social or economic burden and a possible threat to cultural identity.

We argue that instead of approaching migration in traditional national categories, a global approach taking into account the inherent global and interconnected facts of migration might create a win-win situation. Receiving societies could benefit from the migrants' knowledge and experience. Particularly in times of demographic change, these societies can benefit from economic migrants while simultaneously increasing the safety of migrants. History clearly shows that multicultural and multiethnic societies are the most advanced. However, the possible consequences of a brain drain for the countries of origin have to be taken into account as well, particularly for labor-sending countries that are situated close to labor-receiving countries (Adams 2003).

Finally, this volume also confirms the institutionalist assumption that even systems with a negative or doubtful performance can be stable and decision makers may not be aware of better alternatives. There are several reasons for this phenomenon: The longer a system exists the higher the costs of changing it, because all actors and contexts have adapted to the situation (David 1985; North 1990). For example, in repeated interaction situations the actors' ideas tend to converge. Even where many actors are dissatisfied with the status quo and would like to change it, failure to compromise on alternatives can make it impossible to effect any changes at all. Path dependency is substantiated with the theoretical argument that short-term cycles of issues covered by the media, medium-term cycles of issues at the political agenda, and long-term cycles of values of the society are often incompatible. This leads to the unintended effect that decision makers avoid adjusting political institutions (Wiesenthal 2002).

So even if the EU and the U.S. were to realize that their migration policies and inconsistent general policies have various unintended effects, it is likely that they will not readjust their policies because the sequence of past events and decisions pre-structures the options for change. Changes to the 'path' are possible, but they should not be expected to come about easily. Such changes are more likely to occur as a result of 'exogenous shocks' (Beyer 2005), such as if transit countries which have adopted EU-style migration control measures started to blackmail the EU.

The nation-based design of this policy is another factor impeding change in migration control policies. It usually takes a long time for (collective) ideas and core beliefs to change (Scott/Meyer 1994: 234). Migration control is still adjusted along the concept of the Westphalian state, a nation state whose territory needs to be protected from external enemies. However, more so than any other movement, migration is a cross-border or even a transnational phenomenon (Basch et al. 1997). The various aspects of transnational networks, which can have cultural, economic, political, or religious dimensions extending between and beyond two or more geographical spaces (Pries 2001; 2008), must therefore be considered comprehensively, without the limitation of 'methodological nationalism'.

In view of the more than 1,000 official deaths at EU and U.S. borders every year, it remains a delicate and very important task to reach a consensus on the question of whether liberal countries or state unions which are dedicated and committed to protecting human rights, such as the U.S. and the EU, respectively, can bend their liberal ideal to the point of saying that it was the migrants' choice to accept the potential 'death penalty' for crossing the border illegally. Countries of arrival are fully responsible for their border control and surveillance measures and indeed even offer incentives for migrants to come, whether they have proper documents or not.

We hope that this book will provide new empirical material that can serve as a basis for an open and empirically based discussion of the interrelations between immigration policies and migrants' journeys. The articles contained in this volume explore this issue from the joint perspective of political science and ethnography, an approach that has proved extremely fruitful.

The resulting conclusions for policy making are clear: Governments need to take into consideration that negotiation partners may undermine the carrot-and-stick strategy and increase their demands concerning the EU's externalization strategy. Rather than focusing on anti-immigration control alone, countries of arrival should act consistently across all policy sectors which affect countries of origin and transit. Governments would be wise to accept and communicate to their electorate the fact that hermetic borders will never prevent migrants from attempting to immigrate, but only make their journeys more dangerous. Policy makers should therefore reevaluate whether the immense costs and risks of their migration policies are acceptable. Researchers and politicians should endeavor to develop and discuss alternative solutions for a more humane immigration policy that takes into account the active agency of migrants as well as the multilayered interests of their social and political environments.

References

Adams, R. H. Jr. (2003): International Migration, Remittances, and the Brain Drain. A Study of 24 Labor-Exporting Countries. Policy Research Working Paper 3 069. The World Bank. Poverty Reduction and Economic Management Network. Poverty Reduction Group.

Basch, L./Glick Schiller, N./Szanton B., C. (1997): Nations unbound. Transnational projects, postcolonial predicaments, and deterritorialized nation-states. Amsterdam: Gordon and Breach.

Beck, U. (2007): Weltrisikogesellschaft. Auf der Suche nach der verlorenen Sicherheit. Frankfurt am Main: Suhrkamp Verlag.

Beyer, J. (2005): Pfadabhängigkeit ist nicht gleich Pfadabhängigkeit! Wider den impliziten Konservatismus eines gängigen Konzepts. In: Zeitschrift für Soziologie 34, 1, pp. 5-21.

Casanova, J. (2006): Einwanderung und der neue religiöse Pluralismus: Ein Vergleich zwischen der EU und den USA. In: Leviathan, June, pp. 182-207.

Cholewinski, R. (2010): Irregular Migration and Mixed Flows. Background Paper WMR 2010. Geneva: IOM.

Council of Europe (2007): The Human Rights of Irregular Migrants in Europe. CommDH/ Issue Paper (2007) 1.

David, P.A. (1986): Understanding the Economics of QWERTY: The Necessity of History. In: Parker, W.N. (ed.): Economic History and the Modern Economist. London: Basil Blackwell, pp. 30-49.

European Commission: European Neighbourhood Policy. [online] Available at: http://ec.europa.eu/world/enp/index_en.htm [Accessed January 12, 2011]

EU (2006): Policy priorities in the fight against illegal immigration of third-country nationals. European Commission, COM (2006) 402, final of 19 July.

EU (2008a): A common immigration policy for Europe: principles, actions and tools. European Commission, COM (2008) 359, final of 17 June.

EU (2008b): Strengthening the global approach to migration: increasing coordination, coherence, synergies. European Commission, COM (2008), final of 8 October.

Guiraudon, V./Joppke, Ch. (Hg.) (2001): Controlling a new migration world. London: Routledge.

Hing, B. O./Johnson, K. R. (2007): The Immigrant Rights Marches of 2006 and the Prospects for a New Civil Rights Movement. In Harvard Civil Rights-Civil Liberties Law Review 42.

Huysmans, J. (2000): The European Union and the Securitization of Migration. In: Journal of Common Market Studies 38, 5, pp. 751-777.

International Organization for Migration (IOM) (2010): World Migration Report 2010. The Future of Migration:
Building Capacities for Change. Geneva: IOM. [online] Available at: http://publications.iom.int/bookstore/free/WMR_2010_ENG LISH.pdf [Accessed January 12, 2010].

Joppke, Ch. (2001): The Legal-domestic Sources of Immigrant Rights: The United States, Germany, and the European Union. In: Comparative Political Studies 34, pp. 339-366.

Joppke, Ch. (2001): The Legal-domestic Sources of Immigrant Rights: The United States, Germany, and the European Union. In: Comparative Political Studies 34, pp. 339-366.

Laubenthal, B. (2007): The emergence of pro-regularisation movements in Western Europe. In: International Migration 45, 3, pp. 101-133. Special issue on irregular migration, edited by Sarah S. Willen.

North, D. C. (1990): Institutions, Institutional Change and Economic Performance. Cambridge: Cambridge University Press.

Pries, L. (Hg.) (2001): New transnational social spaces. International migration and transnational companies in the early twenty-first century. London: Routledge.
Pries, L. (2008): Die Transnationalisierung der sozialen Welt. Sozialräume jenseits von Nationalgesellschaften. Frankfurt a.M.: Suhrkamp.
Randall, L. (2006): México se reinventa. In L. Randal (ed.): Reinventar México: Estructuras en proceso de cambio. Perspectiva política, social y económica. Mexico City: Siglo XXI.
Scott, W.R./Meyer, J.W. (1994): The Rise of Training Programs in Firms and Agencies. In: Scott. W.R./Meyer, J.W. (ed.): Institutional Environments and Organizations: Structural Complexity and Individualism. Thousand Oaks: Sage, pp. 228–254.
Thomas, S. (2010): Mi Casa No Es su Casa: How Far is Too Far when States and Localities Take Immigration Matters into their Own Hands Comment. In: Chicana/o—Latina/o Law Review 29, pp. 103-121.
Tóth, J. (2006): A Typology of «Transit Zones». European Parliament: Directorate-General Internal Policies: Policy Department C: Citizens Rights and Constitutional Affairs. Briefing Paper. ,
[online] Available at: http://www.libertysecurity.org/article1187.html#nh29 [Accessed January 12, 2011].
United States Government (2006): An act to establish operational control over the international land and maritime borders of the United States, Bill Number H.R. 6061, Public Law 109-367, published 26 October 2006.
Weiner, M. (1995): The global migration crisis. Challenge to states and to human rights. New York: HarperCollins College Publ.
Wiesenthal, H. (2002): Reformakteure in der Konjunkturfalle—Zur gegenläufigen Entwicklung von theoretischem „Wissen" und praktischem Wollen. In: Nullmeier, Frank/Saretzki, Thomas (eds.): Jenseits des Regierungsalltags. Strategiefähigkeit politischer Parteien. Frankfurt/New York: Campus Verlag, pp. 57-83.
World Bank Remittances Factbook 2011.

List of Authors

Mechthild Baumann, Dr., director of the Institute for Migration and Security Studies, Berlin (Germany).

Basak Bilecen-Süoglu, Ph.D. candidate and lecturer at the Bielefeld University (Germany), Bielefeld Graduate School in History and Sociology.

Avital Bloch, Prof. Ph.D., University of Colima (Mexico), senior research professor and director of the University Center for Social Research.

Wayne Cornelius, Prof. Ph.D., co-director of the Center of Expertise on Migration and Health, Division of Global Public Health, University of California-San Diego (USA), Theodore E. Gildred Distinguished Professor of Political Science and U.S.-Mexican Relations, Emeritus.

Heidrun Friese, PD Dr., Ruhr University Bochum (Germany), Chair of Social and Cultural Anthropology and member of the Mediterranean Research Center.

Sergio I Garcia-Rios, Ph.D. student at the University of Washington, Seattle (USA), Department of Political Science.

Sandra Gil Araújo, Dr., researcher at the University of Granada (Spain), Faculty of Educational Sciences, Department of Social Antropology, Laboratory of Intercultural Studies.

Marianne Haase, researcher at the Federal Office for Migration and Refugees, Nuremberg (Germany).

Gerda Heck, Dr., researcher at the University of Cologne (Germany), Research Institute for Intercultural Studies and post-doctoral fellow at the Viadrina University Frankfurt/Oder (Germany).

Sabine Hess, Prof. Dr., Georg-August University of Göttingen (Germany), Institute for Cultural and Social Anthropology, Chair Cultural Anthropology/European Ethnology

Axel Kreienbrink, Dr., Federal Office for Migration and Refugees, Nuremberg (Germany), Chair of Research Division I: Worldwide and Irregular Migration, Islam, Demography, Research Transfer, academic director of the Ph.D. program.

Astrid Lorenz, Prof. Dr., University of Leipzig (Germany), Institute of Political Science, Chair The Governmental System of the Federal Republic of Germany/Governance in Europe.

Ma. Alejandra Rocha Silva, Prof. Dr., University of Colima (Mexico), professor and researcher at the Faculty of Literature and Communication.

Kerstin Rosenow, Dr. des., researcher at the Ruhr University Bochum (Germany), Institute for International Law of Peace and Armed Conflict.

Kathleen Staudt, Prof. Ph.D., University of Texas at El Paso (USA), Department of Political Science.

Florence Tsagué Assopgoum, Dr. des., lecturer at the University of Siegen (Germany), Department of Political Science.

Books you need to read

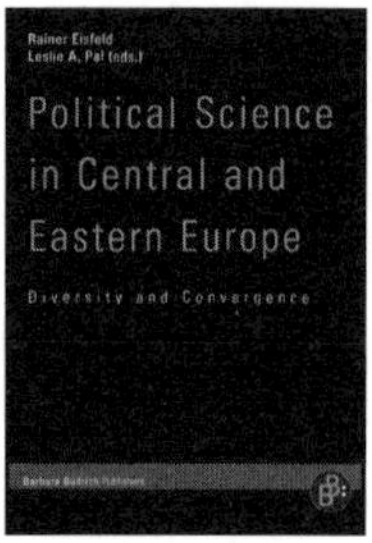

RAINER EISFELD & LESLIE A. PAL (EDS.)
Political Science in Central and Eastern Europe
Diversity and Convergence
2010. Ca. 500 pp. Hc. 79,00 €, US$119,00, GBP 69,95
ISBN 978-3-86649-293-6

GUNDA WERNER INSTITUTE (ED.): Roadmap to 1325
Resolution for gender-sensitive
peace and security policies
2010. 226 pp. Pb. 22,00 €, 22,70 € (A), 39,00 SFr
ISBN 978-3-86649-311-7

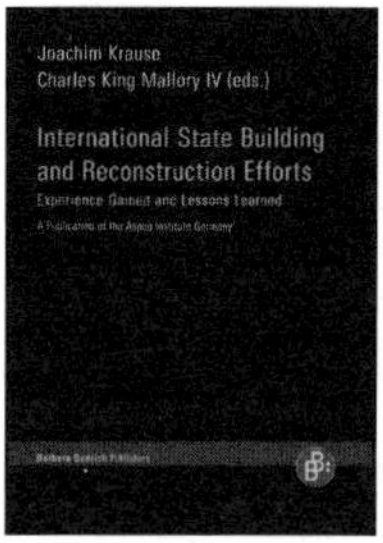

JOACHIM KRAUSE & CHARLES KING MALLORY IV (EDS.)
International State Building and Reconstruction Efforts
Experience Gained and Lessons Learned. A Publication of the Aspen Institute Germany
2010. 177 pp. Hc. 29,90 €, US$45.95, GBP 26.95
ISBN 978-3-86649-271-4

SUBRATA K. MITRA & MALTE PEHL & CLEMENS SPIESS (EDS.)
Political Sociology – The State of the Art
The World of Political Science – The state
of the discipline.
2010. 156 pp. Pb. 19,90 € , US$29.95, GBP 17.95
ISBN 978-3-86649-143-4

Verlag Barbara Budrich • Barbara Budrich Publishers
Stauffenbergstr. 7. D-51379 Leverkusen Opladen
Tel +49 (0)2171.344.594 • Fax +49 (0)2171.344.693 •
info@budrich-verlag.de
US-office: Uschi Golden • 28347 Ridgebrook • Farmington Hills, MI 48334 • USA •
www.barbara-budrich.net

www.barbara-budrich.net